## Politics and International Relations of Southeast Asia

GENERAL EDITOR

*George McT. Kahin*

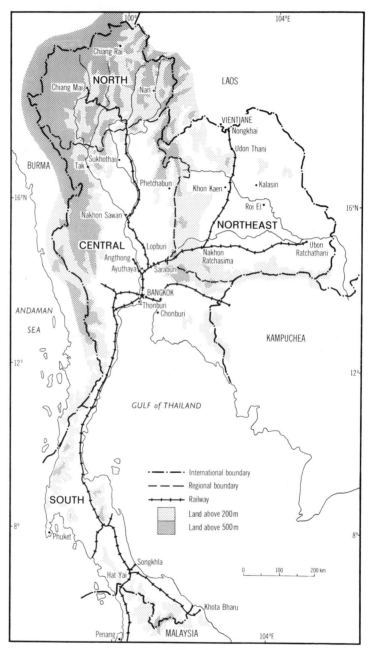

Thailand

# THAILAND

*Society and Politics*

JOHN L. S. GIRLING

*Cornell University Press* | ITHACA AND LONDON

First published 1981 by Cornell University Press.
Published in the United Kingdom by Cornell University Press Ltd.,
Ely House, 37 Dover Street, London W1X 4HQ.


International Standard Book Number 0-8014-1130-0
Library of Congress Catalog Card Number 80-69822
Printed in the United States of America
*Librarians: Library of Congress cataloging information appears on the last page of the book.*

# Contents

# Foreword

That broad area lying between China and India which since World War II has generally been known as Southeast Asia is one of the most heterogeneous in the world. Though it is generally referred to as a region, the principal basis for this designation is simply the geographic propinquity of its component states, and the fact that collectively they occupy the territory between China and the Indian subcontinent. The fundamental strata of the traditional cultures of nearly all the numerous peoples of Southeast Asia do set them apart from those of India and China. Beyond that, however, there are few common denominators among the states that currently make up the area except for roughly similar climatic conditions and, until recently at least, broadly similar economies and economic problems.

The political systems presently governing the lives of Southeast Asia's 350 million inhabitants have been built on considerably different cultures; the religious component alone embraces Buddhism, Confucianism, Christianity, Hinduism, and Islam. Except in the case of Thailand, the politics of all these countries have been conditioned by periods of colonial rule—ranging from little more than half a century to approximately four—each of which has had a distinctive character and political legacy. Even the nature of the Japanese wartime occupation, which covered the entire area, varied considerably among the several countries and had different political consequences. And after Japan's defeat, the courses to independence followed by these states diverged widely. Only through revolutionary anticolonial wars were two of the most populous, Indonesia and Vietnam, able to assert their independence. Although the others followed routes that were peaceful, they were not all necessarily smooth, and the time involved varied by as much as a decade.

Moreover, subsequent to independence the political character of these states has continued to be significantly affected by a wide range of relationships with outside powers. In a few cases these have been largely harmonious, attended by only relatively minor external efforts to influence the course of local political developments. However, most of these countries have been the objects of interventions, covert and overt, by outside powers—particularly the United States—which have been calculated to shape their political life in accordance with external interests. Thus the range of contemporary political systems in Southeast Asia is strikingly varied, encompassing a spectrum quite as broad as the differing cultures and divergent historical conditionings that have so profoundly influenced their character.

This series, "Politics and International Relations of Southeast Asia," stems from an earlier effort to treat the nature of government and politics in the states of Southeast Asia in a single volume. Since the second, revised edition of that book, *Governments and Politics of Southeast Asia,* was published in 1964, interest in these countries has grown, for understandable reasons, especially in the United States. This wider public concern, together with a greater disposition of academics to draw on the political experience of these countries in their teaching, has suggested the need for a more substantial treatment of their politics and governments than could be subsumed within the covers of a single book. The series therefore aims to devote separate volumes to each of the larger Southeast Asian states.

Presumably one no longer needs to observe, as was the case in 1964, that the countries treated "are likely to be strange to many of our readers." But even though the increased American interaction with most of the countries has clearly obviated that proposition, many readers are still likely to be unacquainted with their earlier histories and the extent to which their pasts have affected the development of their recent and contemporary political character. Thus all these volumes include substantial historical sections as well as descriptions of the salient features of the present social and economic setting. In order to provide as much similarity of treatment as is compatible with the range of cultures and political systems presented by these states, the authors follow a broadly similar pattern of organization and analysis of their political history, dynamics, and processes. This effort to achieve some basis of comparability may appear rather modest, but to have attempted any greater degree of uniformity would have militated against the latitude and flexibility required to do justice to the differing characteristics of the political systems described. All the books are written by political scientists who have lived and carried out research in one or more of the countries for a considerable period and who have previously published scholarly studies on their internal politics.

Although each of these volumes includes a section on the foreign policy of the country concerned, the increased importance of Southeast Asia in international relations that transcend this area has suggested the need for the series to include a few books focused on the foreign relations of its major states. As is true elsewhere, the foreign policies of these countries are heavily influenced by their own domestic politics; hence all contributors to the volumes that are concerned primarily with international relations are also specialists on the internal politics of the country, or countries, about whose foreign policy they write.

In addition, the series includes some in-depth treatments of particular aspects of the politics of the major states of the area. In these cases the focus is on an element of central importance in the political life of the country concerned, the understanding of which helps illuminate its government and politics as a whole.

The present volume on the society and politics of Thailand is written by a scholar who knows that country and its international context well. In it John L. S. Girling brings to bear extensive professional as well as scholarly experience. During fourteen years in the British Foreign Office he dealt extensively with Thailand and its Asian neighbors and spent five years in Bangkok. When in 1966 he turned to an academic career at the Australian National University, where he is senior fellow in international relations, he maintained his interest in and research on Thailand, visiting the country numerous times, most recently in 1980. As his previous book and many scholarly articles on Thailand testify, John Girling had already developed an impressive foundation of knowledge about Thailand before his most recent research there in connection with this book. Two other books by him—*People's War: Conditions and Consequences in China and Southeast Asia* (1969) and *America and the Third World* (1980)—show the breadth of scholarly interest that underlies his ability to assess Thailand's politics in perspective as well as in depth.

GEORGE McT. KAHIN

*Ithaca, New York*

# Preface

I have long been interested in, have lived in, and have regularly returned to this fascinating and disturbing country. It was as a result of an analysis I wrote after one such visit made in 1975, at perhaps the most hopeful time during the brief democratic period, that I was asked to undertake this study. Significantly, the analysis was entitled "Conflict or Consensus?"

Most of modern Thai history has been fashioned around consensus, based on traditional Thai values, patterns of behavior, and institutions—in some aspects adapting to, and in others resisting, the impact of change. Such a consensus does not mean simply mutual cooperation; on the contrary, rivalry among cliques of leaders and followers—carried on and usually resolved by force, or more often the threat of force—is part of the rules of the game: those rules, or rather understandings, of the limits of cooperation and conflict are the basis of the traditional Thai consensus.

This consensus is expressed through personality, patronage, customary values, and—the embodiment of all three—the bureaucracy. Policy is habitually decided not by constitutions, elections, or parliaments (when permitted to exist), but within the bureaucracy, in which the armed forces, particularly the army, play the key security role. The values sustaining the "bureaucratic polity" are those of a status society: essentially this means "knowing one's place" in a hierarchy in which individuals are ranked according to their power, prestige, and, increasingly, wealth. Relations between superior and subordinate, "patron and client," are the natural form of interaction in this hierarchical society. Clients (followers) provide loyalty and services in return for protection and advancement by patrons.

Such intensely personal, voluntary, reciprocal relationships cut across the formal "legal-rational" chains of command functioning in the modern centralized bureaucracy. Both are contrary to the egalitarian demands of parliamentary democracy or popular sovereignty. The intersecting of patronage and bureaucratic modes results in shifting, unstable, impermanent patterns of political behavior within bounds set by the dominant leader at a given period, and clique rivalries, reflecting the absence of unchallenged authority, at another. This political system is buttressed by a mutually advantageous partnership between leading bureaucrats and big business, including the multinationals; and it receives the symbolic support of the monarchy and the Buddhist hierarchy.

This is the political order that only in recent years has been substantially affected by the forces of change. Such forces, the product of modernization, are: the impact of the international market economy, the development of industry, the rise of a service sector, the growth of urban middle and lower "strata," the expansion of education, critical changes in the countryside, and the influx of rural migrants into the towns. These forces create new, or at least newly "aware," groups, movements, and classes that no longer fit the "orderly" traditional system.

The new era was inaugurated by the dramatic ousting of the top military leaders in 1973 by "extrabureaucratic" individuals and organizations—an unprecedented event for the country. And although the forces of order reasserted themselves in 1976, bringing down the fragile structure of democracy in the process, the struggle is not over.

Thailand cannot return to the old "accepted" system because the consensus on which it was based has been lost. It is to be hoped that a new consensus can still be created, bringing in the previously neglected and repressed elements of Thai society; otherwise a harsher conflict than has yet appeared will surely take its place.

## Acknowledgments

Above all, I am grateful to Tula and Chancham Bunnag, Tej and Jane, and Tew Bunnag, for their kindness, hospitality, insight, and understanding: may they stand for other good friends made over the years.

I am deeply indebted, as this book will show, to colleagues and friends in Thailand and overseas. I am grateful to Somsakdi Xuto, who has so ably imparted his knowledge of people and events, to Khien Theeravit for all his help and concern, and to Chaianan Samudavanija for generously providing me with the draft chapters of his excellent work (in collaboration with David Morell). I also thank many others, including Puey Ungphakorn, Amphon Namatra, Kramol Thongdhamachart, Kamol Somwichien, Wiwat Mungandi; Boonchit Santikarn, Prasat Panyarachun, Akin Rabibhadana, Chirayu Issarangkul, Likhit Diravegin, Issara Suwanabol, Suthep Sunthornphesat, Paijong Laisagoon; T. H. Silcock, Pierre Fistié, Francis Cripps, Astri Suhrke, E. C. Chapman, Jeffrey Race, B. J. Terwiel, and John and Kornvalai Funston.

I have benefited greatly from the penetrating comments by Benedict Anderson on the first draft of this study, from the encouraging assessment by David Chandler and the illuminating comments by Prudhisan Jumbala on the second draft, and from the constructive judgment of George Kahin on both.

I gladly acknowledge the fine research facilities of the Australian National University and its provision of fieldwork funds, which have assisted me so much in my task.

None of these people or institutions is responsible for what I have written, but this book could not have appeared without them.

JOHN L. S. GIRLING

*Canberra*

# Note on Spelling

Thai words may be rendered into English in two ways: as they are written or as they are pronounced. My own version, like Thai usage, is not altogether consistent. I have generally respected the way Thai authors write their own names in English, even if this is usually a literal rendering rather than according to pronunciation. But for Thai words other than personal names, and for names of individuals well known in their spoken form, I have followed the pronunciation method. Even this choice is not very satisfactory, unless the phonetic alphabet with tone marks is used, but at least the results are recognizable.

# THAILAND

*Society and Politics*

# 1 | Past and Present

Thai chiefs and their warrior bands, migrating from southwest China, founded the first Thai capital, Sukhothai, in the thirteenth century. But the land they entered had been the scene of flourishing civilizations many hundreds of years before.

The area that is now Thailand had been part of the Funan Empire, centered on the lower Mekong valley and with a culture derived from India, which flourished from the first to sixth centuries A.D. The Mon people, who were settled in the Chaophaya valley, the heart of present Thailand, then founded the independent kingdom of Dvaravati, which became subject in the eleventh century to the Khmer Empire, with its capital at Angkor. The Thai people, however, were originally one of the minorities in the kingdom of Nanchao, in Yunnan, southwest China. Groups of Thais gradually "infiltrated" south, overcoming and settling amidst the Indianized Khmers (Cambodians), Mons, and Burmans. From the foundation of the Thai kingdom of Ayuthaya (1350), the Thais "borrowed from Cambodia their political organization, material civilization, writing and a considerable number of words." From the Mons and Burmans, on the other hand, "the Siamese [Thais] received their juridical traditions, which were of Indian origin, and above all Sinhalese Buddhism and its artistic traditions."[1]

There are two main branches of Buddhism: Theravada ("the doctrine of the elders") and Mahayana ("the greater vehicle"). Theravada Buddhism, which adheres to the earliest texts, is prac-

---

1. George Coedès, *Les états hindouisés d'Indochine et d'Indonésie* [Paris: Editions Boccard, 1964], pp. 346–349, 402–403; Eng. trans. *The Indianised States of Southeast Asia* (Honolulu: East-West Center Press, 1968). See also Charnvit Kasetsiri, *The Rise of Ayudhaya: A History of Siam in the Fourteenth Century* (Kuala Lumpur: Oxford University Press, 1976), pp. 31–36.

ticed in Sri Lanka (by the Sinhalese), Burma, Thailand, Laos, and Cambodia. Mahayana Buddhism, which is more varied, metaphysical, and speculative, is observed in one form or another in Tibet, China, Korea, Japan, and Vietnam: Zen Buddhism is one of its most famous variants. In "Indianized" Southeast Asia, Mahayana Buddhism, as well as Hinduism, was associated with the royal cult of the god-king (deva-raja) and had little or no popular appeal. By the eleventh and twelfth centuries, however, ordinary people in Thailand, Cambodia, Laos, and Burma had become deeply influenced by Theravada Buddhism with its simplicity, equality, and universality, and they had previously absorbed the doctrines of *karma* and rebirth.[2]

The Thais absorbed this cultural heritage, creating in turn their own distinctive civilization: a product of Indianized concepts of king and state, Theravada Buddhism, and indigenous beliefs, customs, and social organization. This remarkable synthesis of externally derived and indigenous spiritual, political, and social ideas and activities was characteristic of the Ayuthaya dynasties that followed (mid-fourteenth to mid-eighteenth centuries)—and it still is, with the assimilation of two new elements: the impact of the West and the influx of Chinese.

In this chapter, I will discuss three aspects of Thai history: (1) the state system, particularly the division of labor in a hierarchical society, from the king, princes, and nobles at the top down to the "common man" at the base; (2) the fusion, according to traditional concepts, of state and society, civil and military, the religious and the secular; and (3) the impact of the West, the transformation of the economy, and the modernization of the "bureaucratic polity."

Important *changes* have taken place in Thai society, particularly in the role of the king, the functions and powers of the administration, the personnel of the bureaucracy, and the transformation from subsistence agriculture to an export-oriented economy. But the elements of *continuity* are no less important. Indeed features of "traditional" Thai culture are extraordinarily significant in the present political situation. Among the most noteworthy are these:

(a) The aura of sacredness surrounding the monarchy, whether "absolute" or constitutional, after 1932.

2. See "Thai Buddhism" below.

(*b*) The distinctive role of the "leader" and his followers in the administration: again, this is evident under absolute monarchy, and under the rare civilian but predominantly military regimes that follow.

(*c*) An elitist society: the importance of hierarchy (ranking superior and subordinate) with reciprocal, but unequal, relations between patron and client.

(*d*) The critical impact of the regional environment, including the dynastic rivalries of the past and the national or people's wars of the present.

(*e*) The pervasive influence of the Buddhist outlook: the conjunction of merit and power.

(*f*) The role of Thai values: tolerance for individual variations in behavior on the one hand; dependence on power and respect for authority on the other.

Far more than in most societies, the past in Thailand is reflected in the present. To understand the nature of modern Thai society and politics, therefore, a knowledge of Thai history is indispensable.

## The State System

"A society which makes its tradition sacred," according to Bronislaw Malinowski, "has gained by it inestimable advantages of power and permanence." Such beliefs and practices, he added, will have a "survival value" for the type of civilization in which these ideas have evolved.[3] The Thai scholar who quoted this passage was referring to the sacred tradition of the monarchy, but Malinowski's observation applies equally and more widely to the "power and permanence" of the bureaucratic state, its officials, its sustaining beliefs, and its material foundations, all of which form the subject matter of this chapter.

Thai history, then as now, reflects the interplay of personality—the importance of a leader and his following—within a hierarchical structure of authority. In the past this was the authority of king, princes, and nobles. (The king in theory was an absolute monarch;

3. Bronislaw Malinowski, *Science, Religion and Reality*, quoted by Prince Dhani Nivat, "The Old Siamese Concept of the Monarchy," *Journal of the Siam Society*, December 1947, reprinted in Clark D. Neher, ed., *Modern Thai Politics: From Village to Nation* (Cambridge, Mass.: Schenkman, 1976).

in practice there was more often a "balance of power" among the three elements.) The power of these men derived from their control of labor—the "common man"—both as a levy in war and for the production of wealth. Traditional society was elaborately stratified in the *sakdina* system (explained later in this chapter), which ranked every individual according to his status; status correlated in principle, with power and wealth.

Thai society, as a unified system, may in this respect be seen as the equivalent of the European feudal system: a society made up of those who fight (king, princes, nobles), those who pray (men of religion), and those who work.[4] Traditional values, expressed partly in religious beliefs and practices, and partly in ideas, attitudes, and behavior considered proper to a hierarchical society, sanctioned and sustained this "preordained" division of labor.

The general acceptance of this division of labor, perhaps as much by force of habit as by habituation to force, should not be taken to imply that deference to authority, respect for status, age, and experience, and avoidance of controversy or conflict, which are still widely regarded as norms of Thai society, indicate an idyllic harmony of interests between rich and poor, between superior and subordinate, and between metropolitan and provincial. Such norms indeed "put a halo of sanctity round tradition" (Malinowski), justifying inequality as "natural" to society, but the great differences in status, power, and wealth that existed and still exist cannot be ignored. It is a thesis of this book that should these differences become acute, and the values of society thus diverge markedly from social reality, then a conflict between the need for order and the demand for justice will ensue.

### The Power of Authority

The Thai monarchy, at the apex of society, has been characterized throughout history by contrasts. For example, the early informal, patriarchal style, which was based on personal relations, is different from the later bureaucratic-legalistic concept of an exalted head of state ruling through an elaborate administrative

4. But note that although *sakdina* is often translated as "feudal," this term is misleading. Thai society lacked the attributes of European feudalism: a military caste, population tied to the land, and the manorial system. See Walter F. Vella's review of H. G. Quaritch Wales, *Ancient Siamese Government and Administration* (New York: Paragon Book Reprint, 1965), in *Journal of Asian Studies* 25, no. 3 (May 1966):555.

hierarchy. And the absolutist theory of an all-powerful god-king (*chao chivit*, "lord of life") contrasts with the reality of a balance of power among king, princes, and nobility.

The life of the thirteenth century ruler of Sukhothai, Ramkhamhaeng, illustrates the kingly ideal of the brave, wise, and compassionate "father of his people." According to the famous inscription made during his reign: "... this city of Sukhothai is prosperous. In the water there are fish, in the fields there is rice. The lord of the country levies no taxes on his subjects. Whoever wishes to trade in elephants or horses does so; whoever wishes to trade in silver or gold does so.... If the people, nobles or chiefs disagree, the king makes a true inquiry, and then decides the matter for his subjects with full impartiality; he does not connive with the thief and the dishonest man; if he sees the rice of another he does not covet it; if he sees the riches of others he is not jealous...." Petitioners with grievances or other troubles have only to strike a bell at the entrance to the palace and the king will appear to "judge the matter impartially."[5]

The power and personality of this warrior chief maintained the kingdom of Sukhothai; when he died, much of the area under his control was lost.[6] Sukhothai, after a precarious struggle for survival, succumbed to the new, centralizing, hierarchic, "Indianized" dynasty of Ayuthaya.[7] Its founder, King Ramadhipati I, codified Thai laws and customs. With the subsequent assimilation of the classical Indian "laws of Manu," this system "provided the basic principles of Siamese law for centuries... and has not been entirely superseded by modern legislation."[8] In the fifteenth century King Trailok reorganized the bureaucratic structure of the king-

5. Inscription of 1292. Coedès, *Recueil des inscriptions du Siam*, quoted in *Les états hindouisés*, p. 376.

6. Charnvit, *Rise of Ayudhaya*, pp. 14, 19, 87. There was a revival under the scholarly Lu Tai, known for his treatise on Buddhism in 1345, the *Trai Phum* or "Three Worlds," which for centuries was a basis of popular Buddhist beliefs: Barbara Andaya, "Statecraft in the Reign of Lu Tai of Sukhodaya [Sukhothai]," *Cornell Journal of Social Relations*, Spring 1971, pp. 62–64.

7. The king of Sukhothai, defeated in 1378, was forced to take the oath of allegiance to Ayuthaya; by the mid-fifteenth century Sukhothai lost its vassal status and was integrated into the kingdom of Ayuthaya: Charnvit, *Rise of Ayuthaya*, pp. 128–131.

8. D. G. E. Hall, *A History of South-East Asia* (London: Macmillan, 1952), p. 152. See also M. B. Hooker, "The Indian-Derived Law Texts of Southeast Asia," *Journal of Asian Studies* 37, no. 2 (February 1978):201–219.

dom, grading in minute detail the ranks, duties, and privileges of every official.

According to ancient Indian concepts—taken over by the Khmer Empire and transmitted to Ayuthaya—the function of the ruler was to harmonize activities on earth with the cosmic forces of the universe. This was achieved by organizing the kingdom as a universe in miniature: the king's palace represented the sacred Mount Meru, city of the gods, while his four chief ministers corresponded to the guardian deities of the four cardinal points of the universe. The capital itself stood for the whole country: "It was more than the nation's political and cultural center: it was the magic center of the universe."[9] Thus, in striking contrast to the unpretentious *pho-khun* (father-ruler) of the kings of Sukhothai, the elaborate ceremonial titles adopted by the kings of Ayuthaya, and still used today, provide an aura of the sacred mingled with majesty.[10] "Only the king is highest in the land, because he is god-like," stated a royal decree of the eighteenth century. "When the king gives an order it is like the axe of heaven."[11] The king is "feared and respected almost like a god," confirmed a French observer in the mid-nineteenth century. "No-one dares look at him in the face."[12] Yet, although in theory the kings of Ayuthaya and of nineteenth-century Bangkok were divine and absolute monarchs—"lord of the land" and "lord of life"—with total power over every subject and every possession, they were motivated not only by the ambition to become a "universal emperor" but also by the ideal of the "Righ-

9. Robert Heine-Geldern, *Conception of State and Kingship in Southeast Asia* (Ithaca, N.Y.: Cornell University Southeast Asia Program, Data paper no. 18, 1956), pp. 1–7.

10. *Phrabat somdech phra chao ... borom chakraphad rachathiraj ... bophid phraphuthachao yu hua* [excellent, divine lord ... supreme emperor ... august Buddha seated over the heads of the people]: These are some of the titles of King Ramadhipati, quoted by Somsamai Srisuthonphan, *Chom na sakdina thai* [The face of Thai feudalism] (Bangkok, 1974), p. 146. Somsamai was the pseudonym of Chit Phumisak, an outstanding young Marxist scholar, who was imprisoned during the Sarit era (1958–63), went underground, and was killed in 1966.

11. Quoted by Akin Rabibhadana, *The Organisation of Thai Society in the Early Bangkok Period, 1782–1873* (Ithaca, N.Y.: Cornell University Southeast Asia Program, Data paper no. 74, 1969), p. 44.

12. Mgr. Pallegoix, *Description du royaume Thai ou Siam*, adapted by M. Dassé (Bangkok: D. K. Books, 1976), p. 90. Bishop Pallegoix lived in Siam from 1830–1862 and was a close friend of King Mongkut (Rama IV). He wrote his *Description* in 1852.

teous Monarch," inspired by Buddhist virtues.[13] Thai kings fervently expressed the wish to protect the Buddhist religion, and it was not uncommon that edicts were promulgated "for the welfare and happiness of the people."[14]

Yet the power of the monarch was arbitrary rather than absolute: it depended on the personal qualities of the king and the strength or weakness of princes and nobles. "The nobles were the real element of continuity in the system, single families continuing for as many as seven generations with a member in a ministerial position. The nobles put and kept kings on the throne, and kings maintained the semblance of royal power only by carefully manipulating public appointments so as to balance the noble families against each other by bringing in others to compete with them."[15]

Powerful factions in the capital and in the provinces could effectively check the absolutist pretension of monarchs. This is evident from the difficulty faced even by strong kings in ensuring an approved succession to the throne. The "ancient laws," according to a European visitor at the end of the seventeenth century, were that the crown devolves on the king's brother or the king's eldest son. "But this rule hath been so often broken through and the Right of Succession brought into such a confusion, that at present upon the death of the King he puts up for the Crown who is the most powerful in the Royal Family...."[16]

13. The ancient legal treatise, the Thammasat, prescribed four principles of justice to be upheld by a righteous monarch: to assess whether all services rendered him were right or wrong; to uphold the truth; to acquire riches through none but just means; and to maintain the prosperity of the state through none but just means: Prince Dhani Nivat, "The Old Siamese Concept of the Monarchy," in Neher, ed., *Modern Thai Politics.* See also Hooker, "The Indian-Derived Law Texts of Southeast Asia."

14. Wales, *Ancient Siamese Government,* pp. 245–246.

15. David J. Steinberg, David K. Wyatt, John R. W. Smail, Alexander Woodside, William R. Roff, and David P. Chandler, *In Search of Southeast Asia: A Modern History* (London: Pall Mall, 1971), p. 64. This is a cooperative work, but the sections on Thailand are chiefly by David K. Wyatt, who is cited hereafter.

16. Kaempfer's account of a visit to Siam in 1690, quoted by Jeremy Kemp, *Aspects of Siamese Kingship in the Seventeenth Century* (Bangkok: Social Science Association Press of Thailand, 1969), p. 41. From the record of the royal chronicle of Ayuthaya, however, it is evident that the king's *son* customarily succeeded to the throne; but as often as not he was deposed and usually executed after only a few months: David K. Wyatt, trans. and ed., "The Abridged Royal Chronicle of Ayudhya of Prince Paramanuchitchinorot," *Journal of the Siam Society* 61, pt. 1 (January 1973):25–50.

The frenetic and bloody intrigues surrounding disputed succession, however, must be seen in the context of long periods of royal stability. The founder of Ayuthaya, Ramadhipati, and his brother-in-law reigned, with an interval of one year between them, for nearly four decades. In the next (fifteenth) century, the latter's great grandson, followed by his son (Trailok), who "gave titles to the nobles and assigned them ranks of paddy land," in the words of the chronicle describing the *sakdina* system, reigned 25 years and 40 years respectively. After the fall of Ayuthaya to the Burmese in 1569, the prince who was to become King Naresuan, descendant of the rulers of Sukhothai, drove off the invading Khmers and defeated the Burmese. (It was during his fifteen-year reign that, in a famous battle, he slew the Burmese crown prince in singlehanded combat). During the seventeenth century, two usurpers—a former "ecclesiastical dignitary" (Song Tham) and a high court official and kingmaker (Prasat Thong)—ruled for 18 and 27 years, respectively.[17] One of Prasat Thong's sons, after disposing of two kings in one year, ascended to the throne as King Narai. It was towards the end of his 30-year reign that the French, in rivalry with English and Dutch traders, formed a close alliance with the king of Siam; but it collapsed with the death of Narai, and because of the opposition of high officials, in 1688. One further long reign—a quarter of a century—was to ensue before the final destruction of Ayuthaya in 1767.

The significance of the great kings of Ayuthaya, in history and in legend, and of their successors in the present Chakri dynasty has endured. For in this century they have become a major source of cultural inspiration and patriotic fervor, sedulously promoted by the state authorities, enshrined in ceremonies, and inculcated in the schools.[18]

17. "However vicious the struggle for power, success in attaining the crown was an indication of the accumulation of merit . . . which befitted one for high office": Kemp, *Aspects of Siamese Kingship,* p. 44.

18. "[Particularly in remote rural areas] the local elementary school is overwhelmingly the main source of national consciousness and loyalty. Lessons in the national language [Central Thai], in Thai history, religion, and geography—however superficial and imperfectly remembered—have a profound effect on village life": Michael H. Moerman, *A Memorandum: A Northern Thai Village* (Bangkok, 1961), quoted by Charles F. Keyes, *Isan: Regionalism in Northeastern Thailand* (Ithaca, N.Y.: Cornell University Southeast Asia Program, Data paper no. 65, 1967), p. 20.

The Authority of Power

From these extensive periods of rule, as from the turbulent intrigues during crises, we see the interplay of three factors: the majesty of office, the personal qualities of powerful men, and the institutional arrangements of government. From the first two flow absolute power and absolute insecurity: all titles and offices, the sources of power and wealth, are at the discretion of the sovereign. Yet the king in turn suspects and fears the vaulting ambition of his own sons and relatives, the plotting of powerful nobles, and the hostile designs of foreign kings. Such, the French envoy de la Loubère noted, is the "extreme distrust in which the Kings of Siam do always live. . . ."[19]

Traditional administrative arrangements, reflecting the aura of office and the inconstancy of personality, were an attempt to regularize these shifting relationships. Such was the case with the system of *sakdina* (literally "power of the land") or "dignity marks,"[20] which endured for more than four centuries until the end of absolute monarchy, in 1932. The number of marks accorded every individual in the kingdom ranked his status, from royalty down to beggars and slaves. Thus the king's brother by a royal queen (*chao fa*) in charge of an official department (*krom*) received 50,000 marks, but—and this indicates the importance of holding office—only 20,000 if without *krom* rank. Similarly, high officials (*chao phraya*) in charge of important ministries had the *sakdina* grade of 10,000, and so on down to the lowest noble officials (*khunnang*) with only 400.[21] Each dignity mark represented one *rai* of land (two-fifths of an acre). In effect, a noble with *sakdina* grade 400 controlled sixteen men, each of whom was estimated to cultivate up to twenty-five *rai*, or ten acres.[22] These controllers of men were the leaders in Thai society.

19. Simon de la Loubère, *A New Historical Relation of the Kingdom of Siam*, from the Eng. trans. in 1693 (Kuala Lumpur: Oxford University Press Historical Reprint, 1969), p. 105. The author was French envoy at the Court of King Narai.

20. Wales, *Ancient Siamese Government*, p. 35.

21. Akin, *Organization of Thai Society*, p. 98, table 2 (p. 101), table 3 (p. 103).

22. Wales, *Ancient Siamese Government*, pp. 34–38. Chaianan Samudavanija, *Sakdina kab phathanakan khong sangkom thai* [*Sakdina* and the development of Thai society] (Bangkok: Nam Aksorn Press, 1976) lists the *sakdina* grades in the appendixes. Chit Phumisak disputes this assessment. According to the hierarchy law, he points out, only a small proportion of commoners had the right to cultivate twenty-five *rai*:

Control of manpower, rather than territory, was essential for the land was abundant and the population small. (Even as late as the mid-nineteenth century, a country the size of France was inhabited by only 5 million to 6 million people, compared with more than 40 million today.) People were necessary both to cultivate the land and to defend it. Control of manpower was vital to maintain or expand power in peace and war; to extract wealth, by means of the obligatory labor service (*ken raeng ngan*, often translated as *corvée*), taxation, and slavery; and to assure prestige and status for the ruling class.

Exploitation of manpower provided the means for the upkeep of an elaborately organized royal court; for the construction of palaces, monasteries, roads, canals; for meeting the expenses of nonsalaried and semihereditary officials (princes and nobles); and for supplying weapons for war. These goals were achieved mainly in the form of labor service, but also by obligatory delivery of produce (later often commuted into money payments), by judicial fines and confiscations, by the formation of royal trading monopolies, by various kinds of taxation,[23] and, by the nineteenth century, by tax monopolies (taxes farmed out to individuals, often Chinese, for a price).[24]

The great mass of the population—the common people (*phrai*) and slaves—provided the manpower to serve the king, princes, and nobles. Slaves at all periods formed a substantial part of the population. In the mid-nineteenth century they were estimated to number at least one in three. Most of them were actually debtors,

---

the average was fifteen *rai* for "middle level" *phrai* (common people), and only five (the lowest on the *sakdina* scale) for poor men, beggars, and slaves: *Chom na sakdina thai*, p. 173.

23. Chit Phumisak gives a detailed account of the various forms of taxation: delivery in kind; customary payments; excise duties on trade, transit, and vegetable and fruit gardens; and taxes on the produce of rice fields. There were also taxes on gambling and prostitution. The land tax, which amounted to 2 million *baht* under Rama IV, increased to 7 million under Rama VI: *Chom na sakdina thai*, pp. 246, 252, 257, 277–300.

24. Tax farms went to the highest bidder; therefore it was in the interest of the monopolist to recoup his expenses, and more, by all kind of extortionate practices. "One cannot imagine how much misfortune and oppression the people suffered, given the unlimited powers granted to monopolists by the king," observed Bishop Pallegoix in his *Description du Royaume Thai* (p. 124). Tax farming brought in nearly half the government revenues up to 1903: Walter F. Vella, *The Impact of the West on Government in Thailand* (Berkeley: University of California Press, 1955), p. 346.

rather than slaves in the literal sense, being bonded to a patron until they paid off the debt. Ironically, the condition of "slaves," apart from war captives or true slaves, was often better than that of "free men," especially those subjected to the royal *corvée*. According to Bishop Pallegoix's observation, "in general . . . the Thais behaved with humanity toward their slaves, did not work them too hard, and treated them often much better than servants are treated in France."[25]

Everyone among the *phrai*, from the fourteenth century onward, had to be registered under a leader, for the *phrai* as such had no legal status, and therefore no legal protection, except through their leaders.[26] The more *phrai* a leader possessed, the more wealthy and powerful he would be: "By assigning *phrai* under the princes and nobles, the population of the whole kingdom was organised into groups, very much like an army in which the princes and the nobles were the officers."[27]

Yet the hierarchical grading of the *sakdina* system, in principle correlating status with power and wealth, became distorted through the inherent weaknesses in society. Among the most important of these were the fissiparous tendencies resulting from rivalry among king, princes, and nobles; the harsh conditions of the *corvée*, which led to continual attempts by the *phrai* to evade their obligations; and finally the effect of economic changes introducing new forms of wealth (discussed in the last section of this chapter).

From the foundation of Ayuthaya, the system of government reflected tension between the centralizing efforts of the monarch and the striving for autonomy among princes and nobles. In the early period, royal authority successively diminished as it radiated outward from the capital (the "magic center" of the kingdom) in three concentric circles. Within the first circle of nearby cities the king maintained control chiefly through close family alliances. In

25. *Description du Royaume Thai,* pp. 119–120. See also Akin, *Organisation of Thai Society,* pp. 109–112, 117; and Wales, *Ancient Siamese Government,* pp. 58–63.

26. Kajorn Sukpanich, "The Free Man Status: The Free Man-Patron Relationship in Siam, with Economic and Cultural Implications, from 1341 to 1905," *History and Politics* (Thammasat University, 1974); Eng. trans. in Likhit Dhiravegin, ed., *Social Science Review* (Bangkok: Social Science Association of Thailand), no. 1, 1976, p. 102.

27. Akin, *Organisation of Thai Society,* p. 174.

the second circle were petty states, governed by their own local ruling families, but which (like Sukhothai) had come to accept Ayuthaya's sovereignty. Finally the outer circle contained supposedly vassal states (like Chiangmai) with their own rulers, who at times asserted their independence (or came under foreign sway) and at other times paid tribute to Ayuthaya.[28]

As a result of the first fall of Ayuthaya in 1569, however, a centralizing policy was imposed, and royal princes were no longer sent out to rule provincial cities; instead they were kept in the capital, where they had their own forces of men, registered under the *sakdina* system. Power struggles then occurred within Ayuthaya instead of between the capital and tributary states. Even the territorial division of the kingdom, under two high officials governing the northern and southern provinces (cosmologically oriented to the left and right of the king, facing east on his throne), represented not so much a geographical division of labor for purposes of efficiency, Akin suggests, but a royal policy of divide and rule.[29]

The checks and balances of the traditional system operated right down through the nineteenth century. Thus royal preference in the choice of provincial governors went to resident noble families, with succession from father to son, while in return sons of governors came to the royal court as pages. This was not only in preparation for their official careers but also as a means of security to the king with regard to the loyalty of the governors.[30] Like the king in his realm, so the head of a province was "absolute master of all executive power and jurisdiction" in his area. None of these officials received salaries; under the traditional practice of *kin muang*, "eating the realm," "they were allowed to pocket all the fees which they could take in performing their duties."[31]

Control of manpower played a most important part in power struggles. The *phrai* were divided into two categories: (1) the *phrai luang*, who were subject to six months' *corvée* every year for the king, who assigned them to noble officials, and (2) the *phrai som*, who directly belonged to, and served, princes or nobles.[32]

28. Charnvit, *Rise of Ayudhya*, pp. 98–99.
29. Akin, *Organisation of Thai Society*, pp. 25, 172.
30. Klaus Wenk, *The Restoration of Thailand under Rama I 1782–1809* (Tucson: University of Arizona Press for Association of Asian Studies, 1968), p. 27.
31. Akin, *Organisation of Thai Society*, p. 73.
32. Both kinds were allowed to clear and cultivate five to twenty-five *rai* (two to ten acres) of land, while part of their produce went to the lord they were "reg-

*Phrai luang* detested the hard, unrewarding, and time-consuming work of the *corvée* (which left little opportunity to provide for themselves from their own plots), and they often tried to escape. There were several possibilities: to run away to the jungle and clear land for cultivation; to join surreptitiously the retinues of the nobles (who were always ready to increase the manpower at their disposal); to become a monk; or to run up debts and become a slave.[33] The oppressive, if sporadic, character of this system, resulting in constant attempts to evade the hated royal *corvée*, became a source of conflict between king, princes, and nobility which had fateful consequences. Since the pool of labor was relatively constant, the more the princes and nobles accumulated manpower, the less the king had at his disposal. The rise of overmighty subjects thus weakened power at the center, contributing to the disastrous fall of Ayuthaya to the Burmese in 1767 and the destruction of the dynasty.[34]

But although Ayuthaya had fallen—the capital was moved to Thonburi and in 1782 to Bangkok—the values sanctioning the hierarchical order of society remained.

## Values in Society

The values of a society reflect the power and permanence of the established order, but they also prescribe ethical standards by which actual behavior can be judged. Thus in an analytical sense, Thai Buddhism, emphasizing meritorious action and individual responsibility, can be placed at the inspirational end of a spectrum

istered" with. But *phrai luang* were obliged to work on alternate months, without food or payment, building royal palaces, city fortifications, monasteries, irrigation canals, and other public works, while *phrai som* had an easier life, providing "gifts" to their noble patrons and serving under the latter's command in times of war or civil disturbance: Akin, *Organisation of Thai Society*, p. 30; Pallegoix, *Description du Royaume Thai*, p. 117. *Corvée* was reduced in the Bangkok period to three months; it was finally abolished by King Chulalongkorn.

33. Wales, *Ancient Siamese Government*, p. 132; Kajorn, "Free-Man Status," p. 111; Akin, *Organisation of Thai Society*, pp. 33–35, 86–87.

34. Akin, *Organisation of Thai Society*, esp. pp. 172–178. Phya Tak, a half-Chinese general, rallied the shattered forces of the kingdom and drove back the invaders. He was made king and set up his capital at Thonburi, across the river from the present Bangkok. King Tak Sin later developed religious obsessions. In 1782 he was deposed by his foremost general, the founder of the present Chakri dynasty. (By decision of the sixth king, these monarchs are also entitled *Rama*: thus King Mongkut is also known as Rama IV, King Chulalongkorn as Rama V, and so on.)

of values, while "lay" values, which serve to maintain the social hierarchy, are at the expedient or pragmatic end. In practice, however, there is no sharp dichotomy between secular and religious beliefs, but a continual shifting from one to the other as time and circumstances suggest, or an undifferentiated, all-embracing, acceptance of both.

In the traditional outlook, as a scholar of Thai Buddhism points out, the "cosmological design" of authority and administration does not distinguish conceptually between territorial and functional organization, or civil and military, or religious and secular. The result, rather, is a "totalization": a fusing together of "all those considerations that we moderns might disaggregate as religious, political, administrative, and economic conceptions." Thus the *dharma*—the moral law, according to Hindu and Buddhist concepts—of kingship "should ideally encompass and order society morally, politically and economically, that is, multifariously"; the political organization of society is not distinguished from its civil aspect, nor state marked off from society.[35]

Much of this traditional, unified, cosmological way of thinking has persisted up to the present. Consider these recent statements: "The Buddhist way of life is an integral part of Thai national life."[36] "The traditional and most viable collective representations of the Thai are the monarchy and Buddhism. Buddhism therefore can serve as a means of political integration. It is the unifying ideology of all classes within Thai society...."[37] "The government expects the Monastic Order to keep out of politics, yet to operate within the administrative system as a moral and religious force."[38]

These traditionalist attitudes inevitably sanction the type of authority that promotes and sustains such values. In the past this authority was held by the king, patron and protector of Buddhism,

35. S. J. Tambiah, *World Conqueror and World Renouncer: A Study of Buddhism and Polity in Thailand against a Historical Background* (Cambridge: Cambridge University Press, 1976), pp. 140, 148–149.

36. *Thailand Official Yearbook 1964*, quoted by Yoneo Ishii, "Church and State in Thailand," *Asian Survey*, October 1968, p. 865.

37. J. A. Niels Mulder, *Monks, Merit and Motivation* (Dekalb, Ill.: Northern Illinois University, Center for Southeast Asian Studies, 1969), p. 14. Mulder is indicating the official attitude.

38. K. E. Well, *Thai Buddhism: Its Rites and Activities* (Bangkok, 1960), quoted in Mulder, p. 13.

governing with the princes and nobility. In the present it is the authority of the bureaucratic state. In the past, as in the present, the essential congruity or harmony of state and religion, ruler and subject, center and provinces, is taken for granted: it is self-evident. Even now it is customary for government leaders to explain that "officials and people are intimately related like the members of one family."[39]

But the traditional consensus based on paternalism—with the underlying assumption that the leader is head of the family, the officials are elder brothers, and the people like young children, respectful and obedient[40]—has been disrupted by the magnitude of contemporary social and economic change. The resulting expansion of bureaucratic tasks and the demand for professional expertise have introduced new attitudes within the bureaucracy. Above all, the development and growth of manufacturing and commercial and service sectors have created "extrabureaucratic" forces in Thai society which no longer accept without question their subordinate role. The evident tension is a result of traditional values that still persist, and pervade the attitudes and activities of government, although the conditions that gave rise to them have long since passed.

A further consequence of the decline in the traditional consensus is the breaking down of the apparent unity of the value system so that different kinds of values can now be distinguished more readily. Some values, related closely to a particular situation, are ephemeral; others may be seen to form part of a distinctive "way of life" that provides a sense of satisfaction, of belonging, to its adherents; while a third kind has a timeless quality that goes to the heart of the human condition.

39. From the policy of the "government party" headed by Field Mashal Thanom Kittikachorn in 1968. Montri Chenvidyakan et al., *Phak kan muang thai yuk mai* [Thai political parties of the new era] (Bangkok: Krung Thai, 1968), p. 7. See also Chapter 4.

40. The threefold division of labor, among authoritative leader, executive officials, and obedient masses, is even more clearly brought out in a recent study by a well-known army general, who is not considered to be a conservative. "The government should function like the brain, the various institutions of government should function like the body, and the organisations of the people like the limbs": General Saiyud Kerdphon andSomchai Rakwijit, *Anakhot khong thai* [Future of Thailand] (Bangkok: Krung Sayam, 1975), p. 401.

Since these values are the link, reflecting the old order and carrying over into the new, it is appropriate to discuss them here before considering the modern society resulting from the impact of the West. First I shall consider Thai Buddhism, both in its transcendent and its social implications.

### Thai Buddhism

The Buddhist conception of the universe is one of impermanence, of ceaseless change, in an unending cycle for all living things of birth, adolescence, maturity, decay, death, and rebirth. The individual's situation, at any one time and at all times, is determined by the law of *karma:* that good or meritorious actions will produce good results; sinful actions will produce bad results. The consequences are inescapable, but they will not necessarily appear in the span of one lifetime. This unending cycle of existences, according to the teaching of the Buddha ("the enlightened one"), is characterized by suffering. Man's attachment to the material world is suffering. Because nothing lasts, all that man most desires will fade and disappear. Greed (desire for wealth, power, even happiness) leads to suffering; anger (envy, hatred, lack of self-control) is suffering; illusion (unawareness of the nature of the world) is suffering. Only detachment from the world—the selfless renunciation of greed, anger, and illusion—can free man from the cycle of birth and rebirth, which is his fate and his sorrow.

Such are the classic tenets of Theravada Buddhism, the "pure" Buddhism of the early texts, whose influence spread from Sri Lanka and Burma to the kingdom of Sukhothai. Theravada or Pali Buddhism (the language of its scriptures) underlies the great tradition of Buddhist art, literature, drama, and philosophy. It provides ethical standards or concepts which Southeast Asian Buddhists recognize as *ideal* forms of thought and action, but which are tempered in practice (as in all religions) by what is attainable. The ideal of total renunciation, leading to Nirvana (extinction), is impossible for ordinary men. Instead, they are given rules of conduct, informed by the ideal, and indeed difficult to live up to, but falling short of the absolute. These, for laymen, are the "five precepts": abstain from taking life of any kind; give freely, but take nothing that is not given; abstain from wrong sensual pleasure; abstain from speaking what is false; and abstain from intoxicating drinks or drugs.

Even these principles of behavior, strictly interpreted, are practically impossible to achieve—not to kill insects, even inadvertently, for example, or to abstain from exaggeration or gossip. So a more tolerant construction is admitted: eating meat and fish is permissible; killing mosquitos and poisonous snakes cannot be avoided. And if the remaining precepts are also breached in moderation, this is the "way of the world" (*thang lok*) as distinct from the "way of the monk" (*thang phra*).[41]

The Buddhist outlook, for the layman, is in fact reoriented around the twin themes of "making merit" (*tham bun*) and avoiding sin (*bap*). It is the overall or *karmic* balance between merit and demerit which decides the individual's existence in this and future lives. The aim, therefore, is to behave in a way that ensures a happy state of mind and maybe physical contentment, now or in the near future, and a more fortunate rebirth. The best and most natural way to do this is by supporting the monks (by giving food, alms) and by maintaining the monkhood (by giving sons for ordination, repairing monastery buildings, constructing new ones). The monks reciprocate by blessing the hosts and participants at religious ceremonies and on important occasions in the life cycle—birth, marriage, departures, sixtieth anniversary, and death.

The various rituals performed at these ceremonies—chanting the sacred Pali texts, pouring or sprinkling consecrated water, tying a "sacred thread" around people or buildings, worshiping at images of the Buddha, and so on—are designed both to acquire merit in general *and* to bring the "power" in the sacred words, water, and other ritual objects to bear on specific problems.[42] Thus two conceptions are involved: the Buddhist concept of "right conduct" determining one's place in the "hierarchy of merit" leading (ultimately) to Nirvana and, in practice, to a better rebirth;[43] and the "magico-animistic" complex of beliefs and practices on which Buddhism, historically at least, has been superimposed.[44] In the

41. The monk, for example, observes 227 rules of discipline, compared with the layman's five precepts.
42. James B. Pruess, "Merit-Seeking in Public: Buddhist Pilgrimage in Northeastern Thailand," *Journal of the Siam Society* 64, pt. 1 (January 1976):169-206.
43. Lucien M. Hanks, "Merit and Power in the Thai Social Order," *American Anthropologist* 64, no. 6 (1962), reprinted in Neher, ed., *Modern Thai Politics*.
44. B. J. Terwiel, "A Model for the Study of Thai Buddhism," *Journal of Asian Studies* 35, no. 3 (May 1976):395-399; "The Five Precepts and Ritual in Rural Thailand," *Journal of the Siam Society* 60, pt. 1 (January 1972):339-342.

minds of ordinary people, however, these concepts do not represent two distinct levels of consciousness: one's own *karmic* destiny
on the one hand, and the power of magic (or spirits) on the other.
Instead, magic has its uses for particular, especially critical, occasions to provide protection from dangers on a journey, to ward off
ill-health, to win a prize, and so on, while making merit generally
improves one's chances in this life and the next. The two conceptions are complementary; and thus they are often combined,
whether in Buddhist, Brahministic, or animistic ceremonies,[45] as
well as in personal conduct.

Now, although Theravada Buddhism is strictly concerned with
*individual* salvation (which cannot be achieved either by divine intervention or by the use of ritual), in practice the individual layman
acts (making merit, avoiding demerit) in a *social* context, that is, in
the help he gives others, in support for the monks, and by par-
ticipating in ceremonies. Indeed the social organization required
for religious activities plays a prominent part in Thai behavior,[46]
even though attendance at sermons and other religious practices is
now diminishing, especially in the towns.[47]

As for the monasteries, for centuries they have had three important functions: ordination, merit-making, and education. It was,
and still is, customary for every male to become a monk for a
certain period (from a few weeks to three months for most people,
up to a lifetime for a few). This gave men the opportunity to perfect themselves and to preach the *dharma* (religion or righteous-
ness), that is, the teachings of the Buddha. Serving the monkhood
(with food, religious offerings, or a son for ordination) also provided an outlet for the community, especially the women, to per-

---

45. Brahministic rituals include the use of lustral water, the sacred thread, and
"calling the *khwan* [spirit essence]." See S. J. Tambiah, *Buddhism and the Spirit Cults in
North-East Thailand* (Cambridge: Cambridge University Press, 1970), pp. 223–237,
and Donald K. Swearer, "The Role of the Layman Extraordinaire in Northern Thai
Buddhism," *Journal of the Siam Society* 64 pt. 1 (January 1976):151–168.

46. Jane Bunnag, *Buddhist Monk, Buddhist Layman: A Study of Urban Monastic
Organisation in Central Thailand* (Cambridge: Cambridge University Press, 1973), pp.
2, 30, 59–62, 145, 185.

47. Mulder notes the secularization of belief in Thailand: a seeming general
decline in the vitality of Buddhism; merit-making becoming less personal and more
businesslike (to give lavishly is to enhance one's status). Even in the villages religion
is no longer the dominant force, which has become, instead, concern for market
prices, educational opportunities, and access to provincial capitals: *Monks, Merit and
Motivation,* pp. 7–8, 27.

form meritorious deeds. Finally, the most important historical function of monasteries in towns and villages was to provide at least a rudimentary education in reading, writing, and the principles of the faith. And to the talented, even among the poor, monasteries offered an advanced education in the religions, arts, and sciences of Indian civilizations.[48] Village abbots, because of their wisdom and piety, were often the most respected leaders in their communities, as they still are.[49]

What then are the implications of the Buddhist outlook for Thai society? First, Buddhism in its rites, ceremonies, and precepts is a socially integrating and stabilizing force. The practice and the shared belief bring people together in a cheerful or peaceful frame of mind. Monastery fairs, for example, arranged for purposes of social cooperation, also provide an opportunity for entertainment, buying and selling, and making merit—all combined. Similarly, Buddhism, Brahminism, and the cult of guardian spirits (or protection from malevolent spirits) are not considered to be divisive or even mutually exclusive: each has its place in the Thai world-order.[50]

Second, the monkhood as an institution encourages social mobility. It provides an assurance of status (the most revered in all Thai society), a means of education (up to and including university level in Bangkok), and an opportunity to travel to monasteries throughout the country, which are available even for the poor and underprivileged.

Third, the belief in *karma* is an essential element in the Thai conception of social hierarchy. For those who are superior—in

48. Wyatt, in Steinberg et al., *In Search of Southeast Asia*, p. 40. Education in the *wat* (monastery) was a stepping stone to employment in the king's service—as royal scribes, physicians, astrologers, or in legal or religious affairs: David Wyatt, "The Buddhist Monkhood as an Avenue of Social Mobility in Traditional Thai Society," *Sinlapakon*, 1966, quoted by Tambiah, *World Conqueror and World Renouncer*, p. 288.

49. In 1976 there were some 213,000 monks and 115,000 novices in more than 25,000 temples. Of these, just over 30,000 had been monks for ten years or more; some 70,000 were temporary monks during the Buddhist Lent; while the rest, monks for about three to five years, came from poor to very poor rural families, seeking a chance for education or to fulfill traditional values: Niels Mulder, *Everyday Life in Thailand: An Interpretation* (Bangkok: D. K. Books, 1979), pp. 132-133.

50. Tambiah, *Buddhism and the Spirit Cults*, esp. diagram p. 338, pp. 263-264, 312-324, 340-342. "Village religion is dominated by Buddhism, *khwan* ritual and the cult of the guardian *phii* spirits; the malevolent spirits figure as breaches in this ordered world" (p. 332). Monks, however, take part only in Buddhist and, to a lesser extent, Brahministic ceremonies—not in the spirit cults.

status, wealth, or power—are deemed to have "earned" their position as a result of the merit they have acquired in present or previous lives. Similarly, those who are now subordinate may, by their meritorious acts, become respected, powerful, or prosperous in the future.

Fourth, the Buddhist view of the impermanence of all living things and all human creations is reflected, socially, not only in the fluidity of patron-client (superior-subordinate) relations, which are perpetually subject to dissolution and change according to the fluctuating fortunes of the persons involved, but more generally in the uncertainty characterizing Thai expectations of society, nature, and the individual. This attitude is conducive to a desire for dependence on (protection of) superiors (or superior forces) and, at the same time, to a sense of wariness, or even distrust,[51] because of the fleeting and arbitrary nature of any such arrangement or expectation.

However, the practice of Buddhism, too, is subject to change. In marked contrast to the continuing engagement of villagers and other provincials in religious matters, involving considerable, even lavish, expenditure on ceremonies,[52] there is the growing disinterest or unconcern among many urban dwellers, especially in Bangkok. As one observer points out: "The householders from higher income groups tend to spend more money on the acquisition of luxury goods such as cars, refrigerators and television sets, and at the same time to use a comparatively insignificant amount of money for religious expenditures."[53] Urban professional people sponsor relatively small-scale "life crisis" rituals (cremation, ordination, marriage blessing) and neglect altogether those optional activities, such as visiting Buddhist shrines and attending *wat* (monastery) fairs, that are a major source of entertainment for

51. Steven Piker, "The Relationship of Belief Systems to Behavior in Rural Thai Society," *Asian Survey*, May 1968, reprinted in Neher, ed., *Modern Thai Politics.*

52. Most merit-making is in public, and some forms are very conspicuous; substantial donations are always given substantial publicity. A family life cycle celebration may cost more than one year's income of an average villager, though the cost is spread among relatives, friends, and neighbors: David E. Pfanner and Jasper Ingersoll, "Theravada Buddhism and Village Economic Behavior: A Burmese and Thai Comparison," *Journal of Asian Studies* 21, no. 3 (May 1962):341-362. See also Jane Bunnag, *Buddhist Monk, Buddhist Layman*, on the traditional model of spending on a lavish scale, pp. 127-128; also detailed case histories, pp. 149-164.

53. Bunnag, pp. 127-128.

their humbler fellows.[54] The impact of socioeconomic change with growing numbers of educated, higher-paid, urban professionals, business people and officials evidently affects the practice of, and to some extent the belief in, religion.[55] Yet the fundamental *assumptions* of the Buddhist world-view remain, even if they are increasingly combined with, or adapted to, a modern way of life.

### Individuality and Power

Two historic models, different and yet complementary, are central to an understanding of Thai attitudes and behavior: the Sukhothai and Ayuthaya kingdoms. The kingdom of Sukhothai was founded on personal loyalty to a paternalistic ruler who protected his people, promoted their welfare, and settled disputes in accordance with his sense of justice. The kingdom of Ayuthaya, on the other hand, combined personal rule with an elaborate civil law and a large and increasingly complex bureaucracy.[56] Throughout Thai history there has been this continuing dialectic between bureaucratized, formal hierarchy and personalized, informal clientship.[57] This dialectic reflects both the contrasts and the interaction in Thai society between the individuality that is customarily permitted (particularly at the family and village level) and the severe limitations on individualism imposed by status differences, obedience toward those in authority, and dependence on power.

For Thai society is very much a status society: even the monasteries are divided into grades of importance, just as prov-

54. Ibid. The example is of professional people in Ayuthaya, many of whom commute to work in Bangkok.
55. According to the assistant secretary-general of Mahachulalongkorn (Buddhist) University, secular schools, hospitals, courts of law, recreational facilities all took away the previous functions of the *wat* (monastery). One result was the alienation of lay society from the monks, who were considered intellectually old-fashioned and wanting in relation to the new prestigious knowledge: Quoted in Tambiah, *World Conqueror and World Renouncer*, p. 415. Tambiah's own view, however, is that the substantial turnout for ordination processions, *kathin* ceremonies, Buddhist holidays, and visits to shrines indicate that "Buddhism is a flourishing religio-social activity," even in Bangkok; much gift giving to monks and temples still continues, as does the "compulsive" consultation of astrologers, many of whom are monks: Ibid., pp. 509–510.
56. A. B. Griswold and Prasert na Nagara, "Kingship and Society at Sukhodaya," in G. William Skinner and A. Thomas Kirsch, eds., *Change and Persistence in Thai Society: Essays in Honor of Lauriston Sharp* (Ithaca, N.Y.: Cornell University Press, 1975).
57. Skinner and Kirsch, "Introduction," in ibid.

inces or cities were ranked in the past, and as political parties are today—that is, according to whether they are "government" or opposition parties and according to the status of party members.[58] Yet power effectively underlies status: "Those with most power are likely to have the highest status."[59] It is power that is most sought after: "Power, from the smallest degree to absolute power, can change a man's life. . . . Those without power, such as poor people or villagers, praise and respect persons according to their power."[60]

Patriarchy and bureaucracy; the informal and formal; individualism and belief in authority; freedom and obedience; merit and power: each is logically incompatible with the other. And yet in the Thai context they are as much complementary as contradictory. Thus the characteristic mode of patron-client relations mediates the individual and society, superior and subordinate, householder and administration. Similarly, in spite of the Buddhist emphasis on individual salvation, the Thai practice of religion—making merit—requires a social framework. For a meritorious act depends both on motivation (purity of intention) and effectiveness (a large donation from a wealthy man is deemed more meritorious than the pittance which may be all the poor man can spare); power is supremely effective; therefore power is also associated with merit.[61]

In secular terms, the key to this "fused" traditional outlook is the concept of patron and client; for it underlines the importance of *personal* relations in a *stratified* society.[62] The patron is the *phu yai* or "big man" and the client is the *phu noi* or "small man," considered in terms of status, power or wealth: for example, a senior official and a young entrant to the civil service, respectively; or a member

58. Kamol Somwichien, *Prachathipatai kab sangkom thai* [Democracy and Thai society] (Bangkok: Thai Wathana, 1973), p. 58. Kamol, a political scientist at Chulalongkorn University, became a leading official of the Democrat party in 1976.

59. Ibid., p. 59. See also Mulder, *Everyday Life*, pp. 39–40, 49–53, 111–112.

60. Phaitoon Khruekaew, *Laksana sangkom thai lae lakkan phathana chumchon* [Character of Thai society and the principles of community development] (Bangkok, 1963), quoted by Kamol, p. 59.

61. However, "effectiveness of action stems from enduring moral principles that govern the cosmos; [therefore] gains made on this basis outlast gains from amoral power": Hanks, "Merit and Power."

62. As Akin notes of the early Bangkok period: "How personal the conduct of the government was. In all appointments, or duties given to any important officials, consideration was taken of the personal lives, connections, and kinship ties of the various officials. The king governed his officials as a father would his children. Their quarrels, likes and dislikes, were all taken into account": *Organisation of Thai*

of a wealthy family and a poor relative from the provinces. Theirs is essentially an exchange relationship: each party benefits, but to an unequal degree (reflecting their superior or subordinate status) and in different forms. The patron, displaying generosity and providing protection, assures himself of a loyal following, which he uses to enhance his influence and power.[63] The client is at the beck and call of his patron, and in return for these "services" benefits from the advancement of his patron's interests: he will rise in the social hierarchy (and receive incremental rewards) as his patron rises. Indeed, patron-client relationships provided (and still provide) the main channel of social mobility in Thailand. A poor relative or acquaintance, taken into the service of a prosperous or powerful patron, receives in this way the education, training, personal contacts, and "sponsorship" required to launch him on his own career.[64]

Patron-client relations thus reflect two deep-seated, and complementary, values in Thai society: (1) *personal freedom*[65] (it is a voluntary decision to join, or leave, a patron's clientele) and (2) *social order*—that is, the ranking of every individual according to

---

*Society*, p. 128. Even today, personal ties are considered more important than formal administrative ties in accomplishing important tasks, according to 84 percent of 50 top provincial leaders in a recent survey: Clark D. Neher, "A Critical Analysis of Research on Thai Politics," in Neher, ed., *Modern Thai Politics*, rev. ed. (Cambridge, Mass.: Schenkman, 1979).

63. The *phu yai*, as a morally superior person, should behave in such a way as to gain the respect of his inferiors, by being calm, kind, generous, and protective. The *phu noi*, reciprocates by deferring to the *phu yai*, complying with his wishes, and by "fearing to displease" (*krengchai*): Akin Rabibhadana, "Clientship and Class Structure in the Early Bangkok Period," in Skinner and Kirsch, eds., *Change and Persistence in Thai Society*. See also note 66.

64. Thai society, according to Phaitoon, approves of patrons with a generous mentality, who are not mean with money, but spend lavishly, act like a "man," and make a big show; they are also expected to be kind-hearted, benevolent, and charitable: Phaitoon Khruekaew, *Laksana sangkom thai* [Nature of Thai society] (Bangkok: Thong Thai, 1970), pp. 97, 100. Phaitoon, an experienced official in the newly organized Community Development Department, resigned to found the Democratic Front party, which won several seats in 1969. During the last democratic period, in 1976, he was head of the foreign affairs committee of the House of Representatives.

65. "Act according to your own will" (*tamchai*); look after your own affairs and do not be concerned with others: this is what Kamol calls the "freedom-loving" (*isaraniyom*) component of Thai behavior, as opposed to dependence on power, (*amnatniyom*): Kamol, *Prachathipatai*, pp. 52–53.

wealth, power, birth, and status; "knowing one's place" in the hierarchy; and behaving accordingly.[66] It is a "whole" relationship that unites politics and economics: on the part of the patron, political influence or power ensures access to wealth, while wealth is an essential ingredient of power; as for the client, he provides the services that contribute to the patron's wealth (and power) while he shares, in proportion to his "degree," in the proceeds.

It is a symbiotic relationship—each needs the other to derive the benefits they both receive. It is an ever-changing, incalculable relationship for it depends on personality, personal interest, and personal expectations, which in turn depend on the activities and attitudes of other individuals, and so on throughout society. Thus patrons rise and fall, they grow old and die, and their clients are dispersed and then seek new patrons, or shift from one to another as advantage or opportunity offers.

The very ambiguity of the relationship between shifting personal choice and the enduring restraints of power has caused much controversy about the "loose structure" of Thai society.[67] The implications of this controversy are important, for those scholars who focus on the lack of rigid obligations and the voluntary qualities of Thai behavior tend to derive both of these from, or associate them with, the Buddhist ethic of personal responsibility.[68] It is more than likely, too, that such advocates are influenced, consciously or unconsciously, by the laissez-faire ideals of classical liberalism in politics, social affairs, and economics. Those, on the other hand, who

66. Each should "know his place," whether as a member of the younger or older generation in the family, or as the superior (*phu yai*) or subordinate (*phu noi*) in society. The *phu yai* is distinguished either by his position and status in society or his high rank in the administration, his age, and his experience. The *phu noi* should behave respectfully and considerately toward his superior and should ask for the latter's opinion and not offer his own in case it differs from that of the *phu yai* or disturbs him: Phaitoon, *Laksana sangkom thai* (1970), pp. 94–96.

67. The concept first appeared in the article by John F. Embree, "Thailand—A Loosely Structured Social System" (1950) reprinted in Hans-Dieter Evers, ed., *Loosely Structured Social Systems: Thailand in Comparative Perspective* (New Haven: Yale University, Southeast Asia Studies, 1969). "Loose structure," in Embree's view, signifies "a culture in which considerable variation of individual behavior is sanctioned"; he contrasts "individualistic" Thai culture with the cultures of Vietnam or Japan, which emphasize to a greater degree "the importance of observing reciprocal rights and duties" (p. 4).

68. For example, Adul Wichiencharoen, "Social Values in Thailand," in *Journal of Social Science Review* (Eng. Ed., Likhit Dhiravegin, ed.), vol. 1, no. 1, March 1976.

stress the importance in Thailand of structures of power and authority do so because they are aware of what these have meant for the majority of Thai people: the harsh reality of the *corvée* in the past and, in the present, the authoritarian practices and elitist attitudes of a bureaucracy that ordinary people are powerless to influence, let alone control.

My own view is that both sides are right: both "looseness" and "structure" can be found in Thai culture; these categories are not mutually exclusive. Rather, the scope for individuality and the constraints of power (and wealth) operate along a continuum.

From the family level to the level of administration, we see a progression from more individualistic to more structured behavior. At the family level, as one anthropologist points out, the key relationships are parents/daughter, woman/husband, and father-in-law/son-in-law. A young married couple tends to live, initially at least, with the wife's parents, and the husband starts to work for his father-in-law until the couple earn enough to live on their own.[69] But, as another anthropologist notes, these observed rules of behavior stem more from a feeling of what is proper than from the exercise of parental (or other) authority. "Authority within the domestic group is restricted to a minimum, and the members seem to enjoy relative equality.... The children select spouses of their own choice. They decide on their own initiative whether they will help in the farming or not.... The husband represents his household to the outside, but in almost all cases he consults with his wife in deciding important household affairs...."[70]

At the village level, too, both structural and autonomous features can be found. Potter contends that there are eleven "structural elements" common to all Thai villages, whatever the variations in

69. Jack M. Potter, *Thai Peasant Social Structure* (Chicago: University of Chicago Press, 1976), p. 124.

70. Koichi Mizuno, "Thai Pattern of Social Organisation: Notes on a Comparative Study," in Shinichi Ichimura, ed., *Southeast Asia: Nature, Society and Development* (Honolulu: University Press of Hawaii for Center for Southeast Asian Studies, Kyoto University, 1977), p. 17. Mizuno was studying a village near Khon Kaen, in the Northeast, but his findings have been widely confirmed. On marriages, for example, Gehan Wijeyewardene notes that they are nearly always related to personal choice, except for the few (elite) marriages arranged to cement political alliances or consolidate property holdings. See his "Some Aspects of Rural Life in Thailand," in T. H. Silcock, ed., *Thailand: Social and Economic Studies in Development* (Canberra: Australian National University Press, 1967), p. 67.

other ways. These are the family relationships (discussed above), bilateral kindred, neighborliness, cooperative labor exchange groups, the junior-senior relationship, class and status divisions, (patron-client) entourages, political factions, administrative hamlets, the village community, and the *wat*.[71] However, a number of these structural elements seem to dissolve under scrutiny. Anthropologists working in the Central Plain, for example, indicate that the majority of kin are usually considered no more than neighbors or casual acquaintances.[72] "Neighborliness" is itself a vague concept; and while labor exchange groups are indeed a characteristic feature of village life, they are often arranged on an ad hoc basis—usually for help with harvesting or building a house—and have no enduring organization.[73] Compared with structured village life in India (the caste system), traditional Vietnam (communal property), China (the collective responsibility system), and notably Japan (authoritarian family and strong personal obligations), Thai "social groups lack a strict norm and coercive force," according to Mizuno. Where there is conformity, Mizuno adds, it depends partly on respect for males, relatives, and elders, on "sympathetic" commitment to a group, and partly on the value placed on interdependence and reciprocity.[74] Finally, there is a voluntary quality about (continuing) participation, as Piker points out, even in those functionally important groups that do exist, namely, the monkhood, family, and kindred: "disengagement is an always present, always legitimate option."[75]

As for the Thai ranking system of status differentiation and its embodiment in the bureaucracy, it is "one of the most clearly and tightly structured phenomena of Thai life," as Phillips acknowledges.[76] But even in these more formalized sectors there is considerable latitude for the play of personality. Civil servants may be granted extensive paid leave, sick leave with pay can be obtained

71. Potter, *Thai Peasant Social Structure,* ch. 8, "Form and Variation in Thai Peasant Social Structure."

72. Steven Piker, "Loose Structure and the Analysis of Thai Social Organisation," in Evers, ed., *Loosely Structured Social Systems,* p. 64.

73. Herbert P. Phillips, "The Scope and Limits of the Loose Structure Concept," in ibid., pp. 36–37; see also Phillips, *Thai Peasant Personality: The Patterning of Interpersonal Behavior in the Village of Bang Chan* (Berkeley, Calif.: University of California, 1965), p. 17.

74. Mizuno, "Thai Pattern of Social Organisation," pp. 18–19.

75. Piker, "Loose Structure and Analysis," p. 63.

76. Philips, "Scope and Limits," p. 30.

with little trouble, and "moonlighting" in one form or another is widespread. Moreover, "the often tolerant or forgiving nature of the patron-superior . . . often affords the lowly civil servant a degree of freedom that is unknown in many Western formal organisations. . . ."[77]

Here, then, we can see three characteristic features of Thai behavior: the value attached to individual autonomy even within a highly structured organization; related to this, the ability to sustain such diverse social postures as loyalty to superiors along with independence in pursuit of one's own interests;[78] and, perhaps a prerequisite of the above, maintenance of outward harmony and public avoidance of controversy through polite forms of social expression, which may conceal internal feelings of anger or resentment.[79] The function of these cultural norms is evidently to reconcile the individual to, for the most part, an unequal status, with unequal rewards, in a stratified society and thus preserve the social equilibrium from discord and disruption.

But the maintenance of social equilibrium is achieved at a cost. The need to subdue one's own feelings for the sake of conformity, or deference to authority, or obedience to the powerful results in tensions that, though hidden, are never far from the surface. When too long or severely repressed, or when touched off by circumstances, such tensions may erupt in violence. This usually takes a personal form (bullying, assault, revenge killing, etc.), but group violence is not infrequent (for example, among rival bands of students) and mass violence, when it occurs, may be cataclysmic (student power in October 1973; the military coup of October 1976).

77. Piker, "Loose Structure and Analysis," pp. 68-69. This "degree of freedom" may also have its antisocial aspects: for example, when a patron in the civil service tolerates his "clients'" incompetence, laziness, arrogance toward the public, or even wrong doing.

78. Ibid., p. 72.

79. Titaya Suvanajata, "Is Thai Social System Loosely Structured?," *Journal of Development Administration* (October 1973); Eng. trans. in *Journal of Social Science Review*, no. 1, 1976, p. 176. Mulder has some extremely interesting observations in *Everyday Life*. He distinguishes between two basic attitudes: (1) being friendly and kind toward third persons, recognizing those in power and behaving accordingly, and (2) being friendly and kind with intimates, which expresses good humor and trust and is pleasant and rewarding. The first type of behavior—in relations with the outside world—is pragmatically inspired by gain or utility; it is quite superficial compared to the deeper relationship of care and community feeling shown in the second type (pp. 95-96).

The ever-present tension between the individual and authority, among individuals in their struggle for power, and even within the individual psyche is reflected to an extraordinary degree in the contrast between outwardly cooperative values and strong internal distrust. Potter himself, while emphasizing cooperation among villagers as a basic theme of social relations ("We all help one another; we are all kinsmen") was astonished by the simultaneous existence of "abiding hates, jealousies and fears that pass from one generation to another." The result, in the case of the village he studied, was intense factional rivalry between patron-client and kinship groups. The village was split into two halves, "which oppose each other on almost all issues and which channel most of the tensions and hatreds in the village." As Potter comments: "It is extraordinary that such an important dual division can be maintained within a natural village community that is bound together by the unifying sentiments and associations."[80] What goes for the village goes for the nation too.

The final cost of the normative acceptance of the status quo, implicit in values sanctioning severe social inequality, is the exploitation of subordinates. These social inferiors, in a hierarchical system based on the labor of the masses, are, of course, the majority of the Thai people. Up to a point, the disfavored majority may accept this situation as the effect of personal merit or demerit (the law of *karma*).[81] Moreover, the harshness of objective conditions may be tempered by the reciprocal exchange relationship between patron and client—the former is expected to help the latter in hard times—and by the "sympathy" for others generated within the family and the group. Sympathy within the family is related to the important concept of *bun khun,* indicating a long-term moral obligation to those who have protected, helped, and nurtured the child. As he has been cared for when young, so as an adult he will care for his aging parents. This sense of moral obligation is extended to teachers, who are respected for imparting knowledge and culture, and ultimately, according to traditional values, to the

80. Potter, *Thai Peasant Social Structure,* pp. 23, 42, 50. Note also Neher's insistence on the need to take conflict into account in "A Critical Analysis."

81. Phaitoon draws attention to the effect of religion, especially the belief in *karma (kam* in Thai), on passivity in politics; people tend to attribute their misfortune not so much to the inefficiency or injustice of the state or government, as to their personal misdeeds in present or previous lives: *Laksana sangkom thai* (1970), pp. 170–171.

king himself. An individual may be under a similar sense of obligation to return a favor done him.[82]

But if deprivation increases as a result of demographic, political, or economic changes, then the assurance conveyed by traditional values loses its force. In rural society, a farmer who has lost his land can no longer play his part in cooperative labor exchange and so loses an association he values. Similarly in the cities, poorly paid workers realize that traditional attitudes of deference to superiors and respect for authority do little to improve their conditions. It is when the contrast between value and social reality can no longer be reconciled that conflicting valuations occur, as in the contemporary era among farmers, workers, students, professionals, and even among members of the bureaucracy. And these, if unresolved, lead to conflict in action.

The economic and political changes that have brought about the new contending forces in modern Thailand, transcending the bounds of the old society, will be described next.

## Impact of the West and the New Bureaucracy

The intervention of the West, in overwhelming military, political, economic, and scientific strength, transformed the region of "Further India," now known as Southeast Asia, and with it Siam (now Thailand).[83] It did so mainly in two ways. First, in each country of the region, a largely self-sufficient economy was converted into a dual economy, one part traditional and the other increasingly commercialized. The latter produced agricultural raw materials and minerals for a world market, receiving in exchange Western manufactured goods.[84] The second change was the replacement (in

82. Titaya, "Is Thai Social System Loosely Structured?" pp. 181–182.

83. "Thailand," the English translation of the popular *Muang Thai* or formal *Prathet Thai*, became the country's official name in English in 1939. And so, after a brief reversion to "Siam" after the Second World War, it has remained.

84. The Bowring treaty of 1855, described by its author as a "total revolution" in the financial machinery of the state, replaced the old royal trading monopolies and cumbersome internal dues by low, fixed import and export duties. The treaty (and its successors) opened up the country to Western enterprise and to the Chinese merchants who traded in their goods: James C. Ingram, *Economic Change in Thailand 1850–1970* (Stanford, Calif.: Stanford University Press, 1971), pp. 34–35. (The Chinese were able to trade freely because, unlike Thai commoners, they were exempt from residence regulations and "registration" under the nobility.) The influx of cheap Western textiles in particular had the effect over much of the country as elsewhere in Asia, of ruining the indigenous village handicraft industry. The

Siam the transformation) of an arbitrary, "self-sustaining," diffuse political authority (typically, absolute monarchs ruling through, with, and at times against a semihereditary elite, each combining military, administrative, judicial, and financial roles) by a colonial, or in the case of Siam, colonial-style, centralized, functionally differentiated bureaucratic state.

Although Siam escaped colonial rule, foreign experts were employed at the highest levels of the administration for two or more decades beginning in the 1890s. Europeans, especially British, directed or advised ministries or departments of finance, customs, internal revenue, survey, forests and mines, police, education, irrigation, railways, military, judiciary, and foreign affairs.[85] It was by use of foreign advisers and other means that King Chulalongkorn, whose reign (1868 to 1910) spanned the most intensive period of transformation, set up a government organized in the Western manner, exerting for the first time fairly effective and continuing control over both central and outlying areas.[86] His chosen model for the latter task was the British colonial administration in Burma and Malaya.[87]

The Thai polity was thereby reorganized according to the pattern of colonial administration—the monarch taking the place of the colonial governor—while the economy, or an important part of it, was integrated into the international capitalist system. This worldwide system, though far from being internally harmonious, was of course dominated by the same colonial powers, including America, whose representatives (the foreign advisers) were working so thoroughly to "modernize" Siam.[88]

---

ensuing "great alterations in the whole social fabric of the country" are described by an observer at the turn of the century. See Peter F. Bell, *The Historical Determinants of Under-Development in Thailand* (Yale University, Economic Growth Discussion Center, 1969), pp. 12–13.

85. Vella, *The Impact of the West*, pp. 342–344. There was however a certain division of labor, according to the principle of divide and rule, in the appointment of foreigners: the British were prominent in financial and economic affairs, Belgians and French in judicial, American in external, Danes and Germans in police and military affairs, and so on.

86. Ibid., p. 336.

87. Michael Vickery, "Thai Regional Elites and the Reform of King Chulalongkorn," *Journal of Asian Studies* 29, no. 4 (August 1970):873, 875.

88. There was intense rivalry among the leading European powers, and this was projected in their colonizing ambitions abroad. An echo of this rivalry appears in the rather derogatory comments of a former British adviser in Siam on his "Teutonic"

This historic process has given rise to the theory that "indirect colonization" of Siam is largely responsible for the subsequent stunted or distorted political growth of present-day Thailand. Thus Siam's success or failure, from Chulalongkorn onward, is to be understood primarily as a result of "European imperalist pacification of Southeast Asia." The centralizing policy of the dynasty in Siam, as everywhere else, according to Benedict Anderson, "was accelerating as a result of the demands by, and the opportunities derived from, the expanding global capitalist system." But because the construction of a centralizing colonial-style state was effected by the monarchy, the growth of an authentic, popular Siamese nationalism was stunted, which in turn was a central reason for the failure to achieve modern national political integration of minorities, and to create a stable legitimate political order.[89]

In effect, so it is argued, the country's leaders during the period of semicolonial tutelage came to perform the function of a dependent elite: they were able to maintain their authority and privileges in the domestic sphere in return for their service as agents (or intermediaries) of the imperialist powers dominating the international sphere. Both sides had a common interest in "stability": to preserve the local power structure on the one hand and, with it, the security of foreign concessions, trade, and investment, on the other. (This view of late nineteenth and early twentieth century Siam is similar to the current neocolonialist theory of the Third World, whose members are considered to be formally, that is, politically, independent, but structurally and economically dependent on the advanced, industrialized powers.)

This thesis is a plausible one; however, the ambiguous or contradictory nature of much of the evidence permits different interpretations. My own conclusion is that the Thai elite associated with Chulalongkorn adopted certain practices of colonialism

---

colleagues: W. A. Graham, *Siam*, 2 vols. (London: De La More Press, 1924).

89. Benedict Anderson, "Studies of the Thai State," for the conference on "The State of Thai Studies" (Association for Asian Studies, Chicago, Mar. 30, 1978), pp. 26–27. I disagree with some of Anderson's interpretations and inferences, but his challenging presentation and detailed research are immensely stimulating. Anderson's "Studies of the Thai State" is published in Eliezer B. Ayal, ed., *The Study of Thailand: Analyses of Knowledge, Approaches and Prospects in Anthropology, Art History, Economics, History and Political Science* (Athens, Ohio: Ohio University papers in international studies, Southeast Asia series no. 54, 1978). See also comments on Anderson's paper by Sulak Sivarak and Clark D. Neher.

primarily in order to *escape* colonialism. By this I mean that economic or administrative benefits of colonialism were outweighed by its demonstrable political disadvantages: that is, the very real danger of foreign domination. Foreign intervention, they realized, could readily result from domestic political schism or other internal disorders (with one faction, as so often happens, seeking external support against the other), or from serious economic weaknesses, such as failures to repay foreign loans, or from debilitating rivalry over concessions. Most of these factors were present in nineteenth-century Siam, and all of them were either cause or pretext for foreign intervention in one country after another throughout the world, from Egypt to China and, among Thailand's neighbors, from Burma to Vietnam. Siam itself had narrowly avoided such a fate during the first crisis of Chulalongkorn's reign.

The young king's first attempt at reforms—affecting slavery, the judiciary, finance, and the political process—was seen as a calculated attack upon the old order, including the vested interests that thrived on traditional ways of administration and judicial corruption. The opposition to reform centered on the "second king," a protege of the hitherto dominant regent, who began to mobilize troops and sought the support of the British. During the ensuing crisis, early in 1875, the foreign consuls proposed the partition of the country into three parcels, ruled by the king, the second king, and the ex-regent. The episode, which was finally resolved by compromise, set back the king's project for reforms by a decade.[90]

As Chulalongkorn was to assess the situation, there were three ways to protect the kingdom against internal and external dangers: "Firstly, we can maintain peaceful relations [with foreign powers]; secondly, we can possess sufficient power to defend the peace within our country, and thirdly, we can make our administration as good as theirs."[91]

The first way of assuring independence, by diplomacy, was consistently pursued at the cost of extensive territorial concessions after the French ultimatum of 1893.[92] However, the desirability of

90. David K. Wyatt, *The Politics of Reform in Thailand* (New Haven: Yale University Press, 1969) pp. 50–61.

91. Quoted by Tej Bunnag, *The Provincial Administration of Siam, 1892–1915* (Kuala Lumpur: Oxford University Press, 1978), p. 92.

92. The king "collapsed in remorse" at the extent of the territorial losses along the east bank of the Mekong and the failure of his new cabinet system to resolve the

maintaining Siam as a buffer state between the two rival imperialist powers led to the Anglo-French agreement of 1896 guaranteeing the country's autonomy. This assurance "released for local investment much wealth which had been withheld owing to the uncertainty of the situation." Trade more than doubled between 1894 and 1904.[93]

The effect of contact with Western powers, as Tambiah points out, was paradoxical. By expanding Siam's economic capacity, the Western powers provided King Chulalongkorn with the economic and power resources he needed to strengthen his authority *against* external pressures. Moreover, by attaining the second and third of his objectives—the assertion of internal control through a reorganized administration—the king made the decisive move to a more centralized system of domination by a "patrimonial" bureaucracy.[94]

To improve and extend royal authority, to maintain kingly power in a changing, uncertain, even hostile environment: these, of course, were dynastic rather than "national" aims, at least in the modern or democratic sense.[95] Chulalongkorn, like Louis XIV, might well have declared, "*L'Etat, c'est moi*" ("I am the state"). Unlike Louis XIV, however, Chulalongkorn did *not* lead his country into ruinous wars for the sake of dynastic ambitions. On the con-

---

crisis. For the next twelve months, "the wheels of government almost completely ceased to turn": Wyatt, *Politics of Reform,* pp. 95–96. Siam had to renounce the western provinces of Cambodia to the French in 1907, and the four southernmost Malay states to the British in 1909.

93. Graham, *Siam,* vol. 2, p. 102.

94. Tambiah, *World Conqueror and World Renouncer,* p. 526. "Patrimonial" authority, in Max Weber's characterization, develops from patriarchal authority when the prince no longer rules by purely personal qualities, but through a "process of routinisation" so that "the organisation of authority becomes permanent." The ruler's disciples and followers become priests, vassals, "and, above all, officials": H. H. Gerth and C. Wright Mills, trans. and eds., *From Max Weber: Essays in Sociology* (London: Routledge & Kegan Paul, 1970), pp. 296–297. Norman Jacobs follows Weber in his important study of Thai patrimonial bureaucracy: Jacobs, *Modernization without Development: Thailand as an Asian Case Study* (New York: Praeger, 1971).

95. Benedict Anderson rejects what he calls "Western scholarly axioms" that the Chakri dynasty's historical role was "modernising" and "national." He is "tempted to argue" that identification of the monarchy with the modern Siamese nation on the scholarly level has "systematically distorted understanding of twentieth century Thai politics" and, on the political level, has retarded the development of the Siamese nation. As he puts it, the evidence points to a semicolonial, indirectly ruled condition wholly incompatible with the "national" terminology of most Western scholarship: "Studies of the Thai State," conference paper, pp. 10, 13, 25.

trary, he was spared the possibility of warfare with Siam's traditional enemies or rivals, Burma and Vietnam, because their rulers had been overthrown or rendered harmless by colonial occupation; and, as we have seen, he successfully sought to avoid conflict with either Britain or France. As a result of these and other factors, conditions were favorable for economic development, the extent of which is indicated by the enormous expansion of rice cultivation and the tenfold increase in exports in half a century.[96]

Thus in contrast to prerevolutionary France, the situation in Siam signified a better livelihood for the new class of independent farmers—the *phrai* who were in the process of emancipation from slavery and feudal obligation—as well as increased revenues for the government. Under such circumstances, it would not seem unreasonable for the monarch to equate, in the paternalist style, "the progress in the development of the country" with "the prosperity of the people which I have so much at heart."[97]

It is important to make this point precisely because paternalism, and the sense of obligation that goes with it, have been characteristic of Thai ruling attitudes from the days of Sukhothai, through the centuries of absolute monarchy, to the dictatorship of Marshal Sarit, and beyond. According to the materialist interpretation, the values prevailing in society are essentially a means of legitimizing elite privileges and possessions or mystifying the masses. But I would argue that a sense of obligation, which has social consequences, also plays a role in the conduct of "benevolent despots." This is not to deny the importance of material interests, but merely to point out that *gratification of power*—which is inherent in responsibility for, or manipulation of, others "for their own good"—may be no less strong a motivation than materialism. (Indeed the "Sarit era" is a good example of both.)

It is through the gratification of power that a patron's sense of responsibility for his client, a ruler's concern for his subjects, tempers the inequities of a hierarchical society. Indeed this view is implicit in the Thai conception of the moral and the realistic aspects of state power, expressed in the terms *phra khun,* which may be translated "meritorious power," and *phra dej,* "objective power."

96. Ingram, *Economic Change in Thailand,* pp. 37–38, 43–44.
97. From a speech in 1907, quoted by Graham, *Siam,* vol. 2, p. 145.

Of course, such values are often, and perhaps largely, disregarded. But even the rhetorical expression of paternalist sentiments does create certain expectations of a leader which, like values everywhere, are more or less fulfilled according to personal proclivities and time and circumstance.

The reform period in Siam was one of those rare periods that time and circumstance permit. It was made possible by the convergence of a number of favorable factors:

(a) An enterprising and far-sighted king.

(b) A gifted circle of brothers and close relatives.

(c) The stimulus of external danger, as we have seen, without the disruption caused by war.[98]

(d) The diffusion of a spirit of rational inquiry, challenging old ways and traditional ideas.[99]

(e) The removal, in gradual stages, of inefficient "feudal" survivals like slavery and the corvée.

(f) The consequent release of peasant free-men with an incentive to exploit new economic opportunities provided by the increase in world demand for rice, new means of transportation (steamships replacing sail), and shorter voyages (through the Suez canal).

(g) The growth of business made possible by the spread of financial institutions.

(h) The large-scale employment of Chinese immigrant labor (re-

98.  Wars resulted not only in the defeat of the enemy, but in the destruction and looting of enemy cities and, most importantly, the seizure and transportation of captives to reinforce the supply of manpower for the victorious side. Whole populations were transferred from one kingdom to another without regard for suffering: H. G. Quaritch Wales, *Ancient South-East Asian Warfare* (London: Bernard Quaritch, 1952), pp. 127, 184–185; Wales, *Ancient Siamese Government*, pp. 64, 157–158. Only a century before Chulalongkorn's accession, the fall of Ayuthaya had resulted in the decimation of the royal family and nobility, and breakup of families, and the deportation of thousands into captivity. "The kingdom, so heavily dependent on personal relationahips and upon an ordered patron-client structure, came apart": Wyatt, in Steinberg et al., *In Search of Southeast Asia*, p. 107.

99.  Study of Western science and use of Western techniques became increasingly evident, especially from the reign of the scholarly King Mongkut (1851–1868). Steam engines, the printing press, astronomy, mathematics, gunnery, use of clocks and sextants, and articles on physics, physiology, chemistry and medicine all made their appearance. Skepticism with regard to traditional superstitions and empiricism (from the use of techniques and gadgets) reinforced each other. Religion came to be seen as social ethics, realizable through Siamese institutions: Craig Reynolds, "Buddhist Cosmography in Thai History, with Special Reference to Nineteenth Century Culture Change," *Journal of Asian Studies*, February 1976.

placing the Thai *corvée*) for the construction of roads, canals, bridges, ports, buildings.[100]

(*i*) The extension of a railway network linking in a matter of hours (instead of days or weeks) the outer regions with the capital.[101]

(*j*) As already noted, the availability of foreign experts, themselves the product not so many decades before of modern education, "careers open to the talents," and the expansion and specialization of government roles.

The thrust of the reformed Thai bureaucracy, resulting from this interplay of factors, was felt in three main directions, each of which was to have momentous consequences for the present day: (1) the functional reorganization of ministries and departments based in the capital; (2) penetration of the provinces through the direct replacement of the local ruling aristocracy, carrying on traditional forms of administration, by paid officials responsible to the capital, although a more gradual, indirect approach was followed in the North and South; and (3) the buildup of the military, from an archaic and inefficient feudal levy in war[102] and a mercenary rank-and-file in peace[103] to a professionally trained force. The strengthening of the armed forces and the extension of central authority into the provinces went hand in hand. Thus universal military conscription was introduced in 1904[104] in response to rebellions in the north and northeast which, in turn, were "reactions

100. The dominant economic role of the Chinese is discussed toward the end of this chapter and in Chapter 2.

101. As Chulalongkorn explained in 1907: "By bringing the different parts of the country within close communication the railway renders possible that close and beneficial supervision which is necessary to effective administration. By furnishing rapid and easy means of transportation, it adds materially to the value of the land and its products. . . . The railway wherever it goes carries with it enlightenment and encourages the growth of that national feeling which is so important an element in the welfare of a country": quoted by Graham, *Siam,* vol. 2, p. 145.

102. Wales, *Ancient South-East Asian Warfare,* p. 127.

103. Most of the nineteenth century military units were manned by Vietnamese, Khmers, Mon, and Lao, who were either descendants of war captives or immigrant adventurers offering their services to the king: Noel A. Battye, "The Military Government and Society in Siam, 1868-1910," Ph.D. thesis, Cornell University, 1974, pp. 20-21, quoted by Anderson, "Studies of the Thai State." p. 15.

104. Men over twenty-one years old were liable to two years of service in their nearest military district, but those who paid rates and taxes above a certain sum were exempt: Graham, *Siam,* vol. 1, p. 315.

to the extension and intensification of Siamese government into former tributary states."[105]

Tighter central control was imposed through the division of the country into a small number of administrative units (*monthon*), each coordinating several provinces, under the supervision of a royal commissioner. The latter, who was responsible directly to the minister of the interior, was chosen for his loyalty to the government and was given broad powers of enforcement. Each commissioner was assisted by a legal official, who sought to bring order into the tangle of arbitrary and corrupt judicial methods, and by a treasurer, who was responsible for collecting taxes—hitherto the preserve of the local aristocracy—and for paying out salaries to officials. At first all these activities came under the Ministry of the Interior, but in time separate branches of the Ministries of Justice and Finance were established. Thus the Ministry of the Interior paved the way for the eventual extension of all ministries into the countryside.[106]

The expansion of central control and replacement (or bypassing) of the provincial nobility was carried out most rapidly and drastically in the Central region and the Northeast. However, the largely autonomous Malay-Muslim states of the South and the historic principalities of the North, which for nearly three centuries had been either independent of Ayuthaya or vassals of the Burmese, were permitted for the time being to retain their ruling families, local customs, and traditional powers.[107] In the Northeast, by con-

---

105. Battye, "The Military, Government and Society," pp. 429–430, quoted by Anderson, p. 17. On the "Holy Man" rebellions in the Northeast, see Tej Bunnag, "Millenarian Revolt in Northeast Thailand, 1902" (in Thai), *Sangkomsat Porithat* [Social science review], 1967), who points out that the uneasiness and agitation that helped create the preconditions for the emergence of *phu mi bun* (holy men) were related to socioeconomic problems. In 1902 agricultural failure, lack of alternative sources of income nearby, and hardship caused by exploitative local officials had made life in the region intolerable: quoted by Yoneo Ishii, "A Note on Buddhistic Millenarian Revolts in Northeastern Siam," in Ichimura, ed., *Southeast Asia* pp. 71, 74.

106. Vickery, "Thai Regional Elites," p. 876.

107. The ancient sultanate of Pattani remains an inspiration to many of the Malay Muslims in present-day Thailand. Pattani declared its independence after the fall of Ayuthaya, and was only subdued with the establishment of the Chakri dynasty. As Klaus Wenk points out: "Thai pretensions to control over the regions were not based on legal title voluntarily accepted by the Malayan states but simply on the claims of the stronger to extend its boundaries at the expense of the weaker,

trast, the elites were almost totally excluded from high office under the new system. The decision not to make allowances for local particularism in this region, Vickery suggests, was partly due to the strong prejudice of the minister of the interior (prince Damrong) with regard to "Lao" nationalism—he even forbade the use of the word *Lao* in official census reports—and partly to residual resentment of their uncertain loyalty to Bangkok, which was aggravated by the presence of the French in Laos, just across the river Mekong.[108]

Thus the extension of central authority into the provinces was achieved; but at the cost of subordinating local political interests to central Thai objectives. The career prospects of the newly appointed civil servants depended on conforming to the demands and pressures of the central rather than the local system. "Northeasterners began to feel that political power was the prerogative of the 'Thai' rather than of themselves."[109] And even the more relaxed attitude toward local particularism in the far North and South only postponed the problem of the assimilation of ethnic minorities, which was later to arise when authoritarian governments in Bangkok tried to extend their centralizing control.[110]

The structure and personnel of the bureaucracy were reformed: functional ministries in the Western style replaced the old territorial division between the ministries of the North (*Mahadthai*: the name is still retained in Thai for the Ministry of the Interior), the South (*Kalahom,* Defense) and Center (*Khlang* or Finance), while

---

together, perhaps, with declarations of loyalty made under compulsion at the time of earlier conquests": *Restoration of Thailand under Rama I,* p. 100.

108. Ibid.; see also n. 109.

109. Keyes, *Isan,* pp. 17–18. The area of the Khorat plateau (now the Northeast region) had been fought over since the sixteenth century by the Lao and Siamese kings. By the early nineteenth century, rulers of the three Lao kingdoms of Vientiane, Luang Prabang, and Champassak had become vassals of Bangkok. The final attempt at independence was made by Chao Anu of Vientiane in 1827. For a time he occupied most of the Khorat plateau, but on his defeat both Vientiane and Champassak were reduced to the status of provinces within the Thai administration. The formal structure of unification was imposed by Chulalongkorn, and by 1932 the incorporation of all provincial and district officials in the area west of the Mekong was virtually complete: *Isan,* pp. 7, 10, 11, 17.

110. Resentment of Muslim-Malays at the imposition of the Thai-Buddhist system and the clash of cultures, combined with the problems of opium growing and lana hunger, among hill tribes in the North, have been important factors in the outbreak of insurgencies from the mid-1960s (see Chapter 7).

salaried civil servants, subject to periodic transfer throughout the country (to prevent the formation of local ties) replaced the old semihereditary ruling families. But the authoritarian attitudes stemming from a hierarchical society persisted. For government officials (*kha luang*, king's men) saw their status enhanced as the power and scope of the bureaucracy expanded.

Thus the two most vital areas of "modernization,"—what are now known as "nation-building," that is, the integration of outlying regions under centralized authority, and "state-formation," through the creation of a salaried, professional bureaucracy—revealed both favorable and unfavorable aspects. In the two decades that followed the death of Chulalongkorn (in 1910) these negative aspects or consequences came to overshadow the positive.

The two changes of major political significance were the remarkable decline in royal authority, undermining the traditional conception of the absolute monarchy as the dominant force in the official hierarchy, and, intimately related to this, the rise of "new men," educated, recruited, and trained to manage the powerful bureaucratic machine that king and court had set in motion.

The extraordinary contrast between the adulation of King Chulalongkorn, particularly after his death (an annual ceremony is still devoted to his memory) and the mounting elite criticism of his successor, Vajiravudh (1910-1925), followed by open lack of confidence in Prajadhipok (abdicated 1935), signified the end of the mystique of royal absolutism. Vajiravudh was a talented literary and artistic figure and an important purveyor of cultural nationalism, but his excessive royal expenditure—amounting to more than 10 percent of the national budget, compared to between 0.13 and 0.33 percent for European and Japanese monarchies—aroused great criticism.[111] Further, his attempt to build up a private army (the "Wild Tiger Corps" and a special Guards Brigade) was bitterly resented by the regular military forces. It provoked an officers' plot in 1912, although this was foiled.[112]

Prince Damrong, minister of the interior from 1892 until 1915 (when he was dismissed by Vajiravudh), complained in 1925 of the

---

111. Benjamin A. Batson, *Siam's Political Future: Documents from the End of Absolute Monarchy* (Ithaca, N.Y.: Cornell University Southeast Asia Program, Data Paper no. 96, 1974), p. 3.

112. Vella, *Impact of the West*, pp. 354–355.

"deplorable inheritance" that was transferred to Prajadhipok: "The authority of the sovereign had fallen much in respect and confidence, the treasury was on the verge of bankruptcy, and the government was corrupted and the services more or less in confusion."[113] A few years later, Prajadhipok, modest and well intentioned, confessed that the burden of governing during the crisis of the great depression was beyond him. To admit publicly to "mistakes and doubts," commented the British envoy, was a "somewhat risky experiment for an absolute monarch."[114]

King Prajadhipok, moreover, added to the weight of criticism by permitting the virtual monopolization of high office by royal princes, in contrast to Vajiravudh's preference for lesser royalty or commoners,[115] at a time when an increasing number of members of the nobility and wealthy families had been educated and professionally qualified for the highest grades of the bureaucracy. (Already by 1910 the Ministry of the Interior alone, with 15,000 salaried officials, exceeded in numbers the total salaried staff of the bureaucracy before the 1892 reforms).[116] Prince Damrong himself, as minister of the interior, had been actively engaged in seeking out talented people to train as officials. In 1905 he had urged "governors and district officers, on their tours of inspection throughout the countryside" to "consciously look for polite, quick-witted, clever men" in the government schools and the monasteries. (Temple schools, the traditional source of education, had been pressed into service under Chulalongkorn, with the collaboration of the Prince Patriarch, to provide modern education in the provinces.)[117] As many as possible from these schools, Prince Damrong advised, should be persuaded to join the administration and trained as clerks. From among them district officers would be selected, and even higher officials.[118]

113. Prince Damrong's memorandum to King Prajadhipok, Aug. 1, 1926. Text in Batson, *Siam's Political Future*, p. 38.

114. In the royal address of Feb. 5, 1932, the king admitted that "the present situation is beyond me": ibid., pp. 74, 77.

115. Charnvit Kasetsiri, "Each Generation of Elites in Thai History," *Thammasat University Journal*, May 1974, trans. in *Journal of Social Science Review*, no. 1, 1976, pp. 197–198.

116. William J. Siffin, *The Thai Bureaucracy: Institutional Change and Development* (Honolulu: East-West Center Press, 1966), pp. 80, 94.

117. Wyatt, *Politics of Reform*, pp. 234–254.

118. Tej Bunnag, *Provincial Administration of Siam*, p. 194.

In Bangkok, the establishment of new schools, such as Suan Kulab, the Rama V (Chulalongkorn) military academy, and the Civil Service School, produced a generation of officials who, for the first time, were not members of the royal family or high-ranking aristocrats.[119] In 1916, the Civil Service School and the medical school were amalgamated to form Chulalongkorn University. Education abroad, at first available only to sons of high princes or great nobles, was also gradually opened up to other wealthy or powerful families, generally through government scholarships. By 1930 there were some 200 people studying in England, 50 in the United States, and 40 in France.[120] Although few in number, these Western-educated students exercised a disproportionately great influence. "Upon their return to Siam they would expect to attain relatively high official positions at an early age. Their technical and professional skills were a source of power, and the prestige attaching to things Western gave additional weight to their ideas."[121] It was from among these returned students that a secret association known as the "People's Party" was organized late in 1931 with the aim of overthrowing the absolute monarchy.[122]

Corresponding to the advance of the "new men," blocked only at the highest levels, came a change in Thai perceptions of the Chinese. Hitherto treated as a favored instrument of the Chakri dynasty, whether as wage laborers, traders, or tax farmers, the Chinese showed growing economic strength that increasingly came to be regarded with suspicion. The traditional view, as expressed by Chulalongkorn as late as 1907, was that the Chinese should have equal opportunities in Siam "for labor and for profit." "I regard them not as foreigners but as one of the component parts of the kingdom and sharing in its prosperity and advancement."[123] The extent of the change can be seen not only in Vajiravudh's notorious denunciation of the Chinese as "the Jews of the East,"[124] but even in the more measured doubts of his successor.

119. Charnvit, "Each Generation of Elites," p. 205.
120. Vella, *Impact of the West*, pp. 362–363.
121. Batson, *Siam's Political Future*, p. 55.
122. Toru Yano, "The Political Elite Cycle in Thailand in the Pre-1973 Period," in Ichimura, ed., *Southeast Asia*, p. 195.
123. Quoted in Batson, *Siam's Political Future*, p. 22.
124. G. William Skinner, *Chinese Society in Thailand: An Analytical History* (Ithaca, N.Y.: Cornell University Press, 1957), pp. 163–164.

"The Chinese," Prajadhipok wrote in 1926, "are very useful in Siam." Formerly they married Siamese women "and became very good Siamese citizens." But "since the Chinese revolution [the overthrow of the Manchu dynasty in 1911] there has been quite a change. Now the Chinese bring their wives from China, and are determined to remain Chinese." They were setting up their own Chinese-language schools. "This is a rather disturbing state of affairs, as we lose a source of good and laborious citizens, and with the new ideas filtering through, it becomes a latent danger.[125]

The danger of republicanism; the trend from assimilation toward ethnic separatism among the Chinese, matching the growing nationalism of the new Thai elite; and the Chinese "stranglehold" over the economy, brought home dramatically by the great Chinese strike of 1910 which paralyzed Bangkok for three days, made Thais aware of the extent of their dependence on Chinese trade and business.[126] All these tendencies were to play their part, not only in the short term, but, more important, in the long evolving balance between Thai political and Chinese economic power.[127] However, at least one of the king's fears did not materialize. This was that in the event of moves toward parliamentary government, "the parliament would be entirely dominated by the Chinese," since "they hold the *hard cash*."[128]

The danger that Prajadhipok faced came from a different quarter: the great crisis of international capitalism in the early 1930s, whose repercussions in Siam were sufficient to bring down a flawed monarchical regime. The price of rice, the country's principal export, fell by more than half during the depression years; this reduced the incomes of farmers, especially in the Central Plain, worsened the burden of taxation, and increased the pressure by moneylenders to repay debts.[129] The value of tin exports was halved; rubber prices fell even more drastically. Government reve-

125. King Prajadhipok's memorandum on "The Problems of Siam," July 23, 1926: text in Batson, *Siam's Political Future*, p. 21.
126. Skinner, *Chinese Society in Thailand*, pp. 155–163.
127. See Chapter 2.
128. From "Democracy in Siam," a discussion of possible constitutional changes, probably written by the king: Batson, *Siam's Political Future*, p. 48, emphasis by Prajadhipok. This is not to say that money plays no part (see Chapter 4).
129. Ingram, *Economic Change in Thailand*, p. 162.

nues, dependent on trade, fell far below expectations. In an effort to reduce the budget deficit, many officials were dismissed, both civilian and military.[130] "The present situation is beyond me," the king publicly confessed, "and I am forced to make the cuts."[131]

It was characteristic of the regime that among the new taxes it imposed was a salary tax that "affected mainly middle class government officials and employees of Western-style firms. In particular, it left practically untouched royalty and the higher nobility, a major part of whose income was derived from sources other than salaries." The Chinese merchant class was excluded for similar reasons.[132]

The economic depression brought great misery to the poorer classes, both in Bangkok and the countryside. As many as a third of Thai farmers in the Central Plain were unable to pay their debts and forced to sell their land; they became tenants or laborers.[133] But as a contemporary report points out: "There is no evidence that the masses took any part in the recent Demonstration [the June 1932 coup ending absolute monarchy]. The discontent of the salaried classes, and especially the officers of the Army and Navy, clearly accounted for most in the movement. . . . An educated class of officials, administrators and officers, having once been formed, it was only a question of time and opportunity before they demanded a share in the government of the country."[134]

The "promoters" of the coup, who called themselves the "People's Party," consisted of not more than 70 people in four different groups: senior army officers, junior army officers, navy officers, and civilian officials. All the senior officers had studied in Germany, while the younger army officers and civilians had been students in the early 1920s in France. The actual organization and control of the party were initially in the hands of fewer than twenty

130. Thawatt Mokorapong, *History of the Thai Revolution* (Bangkok: Chalermnit, 1972); excerpts in Neher, ed., *Modern Thai Politics,* p. 92.
131. Batson, *Siam's Political Future,* p. 77.
132. Ibid., p. 75, note 14. All through the depression, the scale of Chinese remittances to China had not diminished, according to an eminent Chinese banker in 1932: quoted by K. P. Landon, *Thailand in Transition* (University of Chicago Press, 1939), p. 80.
133. Ingram, *Economic Change in Thailand,* pp. 66, 162.
134. *Bangkok Times,* July 8, 1932: quoted in Landon, *Thailand in Transition,* p. 26.

men; the remainder were recruited immediately before the coup from among those who worked for, or studied under, their leaders.[135]

The 1932 "revolution"—and this was to be the pattern of subsequent coups—far from being a democratic or mass movement, was not even the work of officials or professionals as a whole. It was rather the replacement of one oligarchy by another.

135. Yano, "The Political Elite Cycle," in Ichimura, ed., *Southeast Asia,* p. 195. See also Thak Chaloemtiarana, ed., *Thai Politics: Extracts and Documents 1932-1957* (Bangkok: Social Science Association of Thailand, 1978), Ch. 1.

# 2 | Economic Change—Political and Social Implications

Thailand's political and economic transformation, during the latter half of the nineteenth and the early twentieth century marks a watershed in its history, dividing the traditional from the modern era. This transformation, as we have seen, took two main forms: (1) the development of a colonial-style modern sector with the diffusion of a money economy into the traditional sector and (2) the creation of a colonial-style, centralized, bureaucratic state. These twin developments resulted from the fusion of Western political-economic forms of expansion with indigenous attitudes and institutions.

The resulting synthesis in Thailand differed from that in other countries in Southeast Asia because the impact of the West differed in each country. It varied, for example, from French indirect rule with minor economic change in Laos to outright colonization with extensive commercialization in Cochinchina (southern Vietnam). In addition, the geography, politics, history, and social structure of each country—or what was left of each country after colonization or semicolonization—also differed. Thus each country's relationship with the imperialist powers varied from extreme economic and political dependence, as in Cochinchina, to a substantial degree of autonomy, as in Thailand. Indeed the very magnitude of the changes effected by Thailand's entry into the international capitalist system and by its rulers' emulation of a colonial-type administration provided the Thai elite with the economic and political resources it needed to strengthen indigenous authority. Modern Thai history is therefore as much a product of the interplay of forces released by the impact of the West as it is of the constraints imposed by that Western impact.

The colonial-style economy was willingly accepted by forward-looking elements in society, who anticipated enhanced power and wealth, but was resisted by conservatives and by those with vested interests in the old system. These three elements in the early period of Chulalongkorn's reign were known as "Young Siam," "Conservative Siam," and "Old Siam." "Young Siam," the king's party, was composed of many younger members of the royal family and officials who identified themselves with the king either because of their favorable attitudes toward Western civilization and ideas or out of long-standing political rivalries with the predominant cliques. Their common denominator, David Wyatt states, was youth and reforming zeal. "Conservative Siam" was represented by the regent and other members of the Bunnag family, whose bureaucratic ability and experience, power, and wealth gave them a secure political position. This faction had taken risks in working for the accommodation with the West embodied in the treaties of the 1850s and 1860s and was now in a position to consolidate its gains. Finally, "Old Siam" comprised especially the older and lesser officials of the capital bureaucracy, whose families had created small niches for themselves in the ministries and departments of government, and who feared any change.[1]

The "imposition" of a colonial-style economy had three major consequences. First was the transformation of "feudally" encumbered peasants into independent owner-cultivators, producing rice (especially in the Central Plain) and other raw materials for export. Second was the spread of Chinese enterprise: at the lowest economic level as urban laborers and artisans; at the next level as "middlemen" in the staple export trade—buying, storing, and transporting rice—and in retail throughout the country: and at the highest level as competitors of Western firms or collaborators ("compradores") in banking, insurance, and large-scale export-import business. The third consequence of a colonial-style economy was that the increased revenues deriving from improved administrative methods (as well as from the opium and gambling monopolies affecting chiefly the Chinese) made possible the strengthening of the Thai state and a vast increase in its personnel.

1.  David K. Wyatt, *Politics of Reform in Thailand* (New Haven, Conn.: Yale University Press, 1969), pp. 44–48.

From 1892 to 1902 government revenues increased from 15 million to 40 million *baht* (without imposition of new taxes) chiefly through improved administration. Two direct taxes (land and capitation) provided only 8 to 12 percent of total revenues in the early 1890s, while the opium and gambling monopolies produced 40 percent. Profits from opium were still the largest source of revenue (about 20 percent) up to 1926. After the new tariff code of 1927, import duties steadily increased, bringing in 27 percent of total revenue by 1950.[2]

In this chapter I will discuss three aspects of the Thai economy: (1) the implications for the present day of the economic transformation outlined above, that is, the division of labor between Thai agricultural producers, Chinese middlemen, and Thai (elite) officials, and the ensuing interplay of Thai political and Chinese economic power; (2) the inequality in society resulting from uneven economic and political development; and (3) the effect over the past three decades of the 'new wave' of foreign involvement—that of the United States and Japan. (See the chart, "Chronology of Economic and Political Events.")

*Implications of Economic Change*
Uneven Rural Development

The period of massive rural changes over the last hundred years can be divided into two overlapping phases, roughly equal in time. The first half of the period, up to the 1920s, was characterized by economic opportunities, government incentives, and availability of land. In the latter half of the period, however, the pressure of population on resources grew, the end to the land frontier was approaching, and an oppressive tax burden, the so-called rice premium, was imposed.

This tax on the export of rice for the period 1955–1970 accounted for 25 to 35 percent of the total value of rice exports. The tax is paid by the exporter who in effect recoups the sum by paying the farmer less for his crop. James C. Ingram comments that nearly all economists who have studied the rice premium have ended up opposed to it. They argue that the tax is a heavy burden on a large

2. James C. Ingram, *Economic Change in Thailand* 1850–1970 (Stanford, Calif.: Stanford University Press, 1971), pp. 177–178, 186–187.

Chronology of Economic and Political Events

| | Economic Change | Military-Political Change* |
|---|---|---|
| 1930s | Great Depression | End of absolute monarchy (1932) |
| 1940s | Wartime: inflation | Phibun: militarism (1938–44) |
| | Peacetime: reconstruction | Pridi: party politics (1945–47) |
| | End massive Chinese inflow | Phin-Phibun coup (1947) |
| 1950s | Thai State enterprises | U.S.-Thai security treaty (1950) |
| | Harassment of Chinese | Phao (police)–Sarit (army) rivalry (1951–57) |
| | Formation of business-bureaucrat partnership | SEATO (1954) |
| | World Bank mission | Sarit ousts Phibun, Phao (1957); coup (1958) |
| 1960s | Economic Development Plan | U.S.-Thai security guarantee (1962) |
| | Manufacturing growth, rural technology, crop diversification | Thanom-Praphat era (1964–73) |
| | | U.S.-Thai contingency treaty (1965) |
| | | Beginning of insurgency (1965) |
| 1970s | Urban rice shortage (1973) | Massive demonstrations oust Thanom and Praphat (1973) |
| | Inflation | |
| | Recession, esp. textiles, strikes, lockouts, fall in investment | Democratic era (1974–76) |
| | | Peking recognized (1975) |
| | Ban on strikes | U.S. troops withdrawn (1975–76) |
| | | Military coup (1976) |
| 1980s | Rise in cost of living | Fall of Kriangsak (1980) |

*For an explanation of these events, see Chapter 3.

part of the population with relatively low incomes; that the tax is excessive, unfair, discourages productive effort, and hinders the improvement of farm technology.[3] Counterarguments that the tax encourages, or rather coerces, farmers to move out of rice into cultivating other crops, which is economically desirable, do not affect the point that it remains a burden to those who pay it—the rice growers in the Central Plain.

The *first* phase of rural change was the result, on the one hand, of foreign demand for rice, along with the invention of new ways of transporting it, chiefly steamship and rail, and, on the other hand, of rapidly expanding rice cultivation by Thai farmers in response to economic opportunities. Between 1870 and 1934 the volume of rice exports increased twenty-five times (while population doubled). The area under rice increased from nearly 6 million *rai*

3. Ibid., pp. 247, 255, note p. 256.

(about 2.4 million acres) in 1850 to more than 9 million *rai* in 1905 and up to 35 million *rai* (14 million acres) in 1950.[4] Almost half of the total area in 1950 was composed of the fertile flooded fields of the Central Plain, where crops could be transported readily for export through a network of canals, which had been continually added to since the days of Ayuthaya. Almost all rice exports came from the Central Plain—only 2 percent from the largely subsistence holdings of the North and the Northeast.[5]

This remarkable achievement, to repeat, was the result of individual initiative. It was the Thai peasants who undertook the arduous task of clearing the jungle, preparing the land for cultivation, buying draft animals, and risking their savings (or loans) until the first crop was sold. But capital requirements were low. The harvest from an average eight-acre holding could pay off costs in about one year.[6] Moreover, royal governments assisted in the expansion of rice farming, first by eliminating compulsory labor services and abolishing slavery, thus allowing free men to set up as farmers on their own, and, second, by granting exemption from land tax for newly cultivated holdings. (The land tax was increased after 1905, but virtually ended in the late 1930s.) It was, and in theory remains, government policy to encourage small-farm holding by the peasantry as the basis of Thai agriculture.[7]

Rice continued to provide about half the value of all Thai exports until well into the 1950s. For half a century, rice along with rubber (grown by Thai and Chinese small-farm holders in the South), tin (extracted chiefly by Western, but also by Chinese, firms in the South) and teak (from the northern forests) made up some 80 to 90 percent of all exports. But by 1968 the "big four" had declined to just over half of all merchandise exports.[8]

The 1960s wrought great changes. There was a remarkable expansion in cultivation of crops other than rice, including newly introduced crops,[9] along with large-scale introduction of new

4. Ibid., pp. 36–42.
5. Ibid., p. 44.
6. Ibid., pp. 56, 65.
7. Ibid., pp. 76–79.
8. Ibid., p. 265.
9. In fifteen years up to 1968, there was a fourfold increase in the area under crops other than rice. By 1968 these crops had surpassed rice in export value: ibid., p. 265. They included newly introduced crops such as corn, cassava, and kenaf, as well as

technology: expansion of irrigation, rapid spread of mechanization, use of fertilizers, pesticides, and improved seed, combined with better marketing facilities and more government extension services to farmers.[10] But the distribution of these crops is very uneven. For example, three-quarters of all corn, a major export

---

previously cultivated rubber, cotton, coconuts, sugar cane, fruit, and vegetables. Some of the fastest growth was in response to external demand. For example, all the cassava is exported, as well as most of the corn (for animal feed in Japan) and kenaf. This, too, is the result of initiative by peasant farmers. Such "rational economic behavior"—which, as Ingram points out, is contrary to the stereotype of "traditional" peasant inertia—is demonstrated by the "vigorous and impressive response" of farmers to the prospects of a far higher return from these crops than can be obtained from rice: ibid., p. 263. Since the 1960s, as a result of diversification, corn (maize) in certain years has rivaled rice and far surpassed rubber in export value, teak exports have dropped considerably, tin increased sharply in the 1970s, and sugar saw an even more dramatic rise in the early 1970s (and fell as far and as rapidly in 1976 and 1977). Kenaf, too has fluctuated wildly. Tapioca has become another major export, and since the 1970s, cement, fluorite, and garments have also become profitable. But Thai export commodities are subject to severe fluctuations in production because of floods and droughts and in price levels because of changing international demand. Rice exports, for example, reached an all-time high in 1977 (worth over 13 billion *baht*), but as a result of bad weather and declining world prices amounted to only 10.4 billion *baht* in 1978. The 1979 crop is estimated to be 48 percent up on 1978.

10. The irrigated area increased from less than 4 million *rai* in 1947 to 14 million in 1969, most of this in the Central Plain: ibid., p. 275. By 1976 it amounted to more than 15 million *rai* (still less than one-fifth of the total cultivated area of more than 82 million *rai*), but only half of this was reached by the canals and ducts needed to bring water to individual farmers: "Water for Thailand's Farms," *Business Review* (Bangkok), January 1978. Moreover, there are still serious problems of drainage and flood control: Yoshihiro Kaida, "Agro-Hydrologic Regions of the Chao Phraya Delta," in Shinichi Ichimura, ed., *Southeast Asia: Nature, Society and Development* (Honolulu: University Press of Hawaii for Center for Southeast Asian Studies, Kyoto University, 1977), pp. 179–180.

As for mechanization, there were practically no tractors in use in Thailand in 1950, compared with 25,000 operating in 1969; by 1970 more than half the area under crops was tilled by tractors, but the potential demand has been estimated at 80,000 to 120,000 tractors: Ingram, *Economic Change*, pp. 273–274. Fertilizer, too, was barely used in the 1950s, while in 1968 more than 250,000 tons were imported. However, only 4 kilograms were used per cultivated *rai* in Thailand, compared with 30 kilograms in Taiwan: ibid., p. 272. Fertilizer, 90 percent of which is imported, is more expensive than in India, Malaysia, Taiwan, or the Philippines—for some types up to twice the cost: Andrew Turton, "The Current Situation in the Thai Countryside," in Andrew Turton, Jonathan Fast, and Malcolm Caldwell, eds., *Thailand: Roots of Conflict* (Nottingham, U.K.: Spokesman, 1978), p. 114. See also comparative rice yields/fertilizer usage: Thailand (1962–73), 230–290 klg. rice per *rai* using 6 klg. chemical fertilizer per hectare: Taiwan (1968–71), 547–669 klg. rice per *rai* using 180 klg. fertilizer: ibid., p. 107, table. Demand for fertilizer in Thailand is estimated at around 1 million tons: Bruce Medford, *Business in Thailand* (Bangkok), August

crop, is grown in only four provinces out of the nation's seventy-two, cassava in another four, and sugar cane in five.[11] In many cases, rural growth can be attributed to good soils, transport facilities, availability of capital to open up new lands, and 'the active business enterprise of traders."[12] In fact, the benefits from new technology are unevenly distributed.

This uneven distribution highlights the problem of the *second* phase of development, which is largely the result of two basic factors: the virtual end of the land frontier and the inexorable increase in population.[13] There are now more than 30 million rural inhabitants, who make up some three-quarters of the Thai population (more than 45 million in 1979).[14] The result is that more and

---

1975. Nearly half a million tons were consumed in 1976: American Chamber of Commerce in Thailand, *Handbook Directory 1978*, p. 33. On problems of government extension services due to the "elite consciousness" of officials, see Takeshi Motooka, "The Conditions Governing Agricultural Development in Southeast Asia," in Ichimura, ed., *Southeast Asia*, pp. 287–288.

11. Rubber is produced exclusively in the South; three-quarters of all the corn is grown in only four provinces in the northern Central Plain; three-quarters of the kenaf in four provinces of the Northeast; and the same proportion of cassava in only four provinces (mostly Southeast); and sugar cane in five provinces of the Center and Northeast: Ingram, *Economic Change*, pp. 237, 260–263. For the concentration of crops in specific areas, see maps in Larry Sternstein, *Thailand: The Environment of Modernization* (Sydney: McGraw-Hill, 1976), pp. 145–148.

12. T. H. Silcock, *The Economic Development of Thai Agriculture* (Ithaca: Cornell University Press, 1970), pp. 125–129.

13. It is estimated that in the decade to 1985, the land available for cultivation will increase by only 0.5 percent, compared with a rate of 1.6 percent from 1962 to 1975 and 4 percent from 1950–1962. (The rate of population growth in the 1960s was 3.1 percent.) By 1985 all the resources of cultivable land will be exhausted: "The Land Squeeze," *Investor* (Bangkok), August 1975.

14. From 10 million in 1919, the population rose to nearly 15 million in 1937, 27 million in 1960, 34 million in 1970, and 45 million in 1978. The annual rate of population growth in the 1960s was 3.1 percent, a rate at which the population doubles every twenty-two years; according to population censuses, 1919 to 1970, the latter officially admitted to be an undercount: Prachoom Chomchai, "Thailand," in Shinichi Ichimura, ed., *The Economic Development of East and Southeast Asia* (Honolulu: East-West Center, Center for Southeast Asian Studies, Kyoto University, 1975), p. 144. January 1978 estimate of 45.2 million: *Bangkok Post*, Jan. 11, 1979. For a detailed earlier study, see Ralph Tomlinson, *Thailand's Population: Facts, Trends, Problems and Policies* (Bangkok: Thai Wathana, The Institute of Population Studies, Chulalongkorn University, 1971). Family planning was reluctantly approved by the military-dominated Thai government in 1970, and the target figure for 1976, down to a rate of 2.5 percent, was officially claimed to have been achieved: National Economic and Social Development Board statistics, quoted by *Business Review*, April 1977. However, the U.S. Central Intelligence Agency, *National Basic Intelligence Fact Book* (Washington, D.C., January 1978) indicates a rate of 2.8 percent in 1977.

more people are dependent for their livelihood on virtually the same amount of land. And even improved productivity cannot solve the problem of an ever-increasing rural population with a diminishing role in agriculture (since technological advances require less manpower) and with far from sufficient employment opportunities elsewhere.[15] Indeed, the introduction of technology, far from improving the rural situation, has made it worse. For it is the minority of better-off farmers with larger holdings who can afford the fertilizers, tractors, and insecticides that render their estates still more productive, thus widening the gap between the rural elite and the poor peasants who can no longer compete.[16]

The extent of rural inequality was revealed more than seventeen

15. To absorb surplus agricultural labor (due to the 1960s population increase of more than 3 percent per annum) it would be necessary to increase the rate of nonagricultural employment to 5 to 6 percent per annum. It is "very unlikely" that this can be achieved in Thailand, barring a drastic change in the structure of the economy: Chaiyong Chuchart and Manu Seetisarn, Division of Land Policy, Ministry of National Development, "National Seminar on Land Problems and Policies in Thailand" (Bangkok: U.N. Food and Agriculture Organisation, 1970). See also comments by the chief of the World Bank's regional mission in Bangkok on the serious consequences of "increasing pressure on land and stagnant yields" for the poor farmers in the North and Northeast and the problem of unemployment: *Bangkok Post,* Apr. 1, 1979.

16. According to the chief of the World Bank's regional mission in Bangkok, about half of the agricultural households in the *Central* region have shifted from growing rice to growing corn, cassava, or sugar, which has doubled (in some cases tripled) their income since 1960. The earnings of about half the farmers in the *North* and *Northeast*, especially those growing kenaf, corn, and cassava, have increased by about 70 percent since 1960. However, half of the farmers in the North and Northeast continue to grow rice under rainfed conditions and in small holdings, and have benefited least of all. "In fact, nearly three-fourths of all poverty households—about 8 million people—are in the rural North and Northeast." Of the 11 million living below the poverty level, 90 percent live in rural areas. By contrast, only 11 percent of urban households, mostly including unskilled workers, live in poverty: Address by Mission Chief Hendrik van der Heijden, reported in *Bangkok Post,* Apr. 1, 1979. See also analysis of the World Bank's in-house report in 1978 on the Thai economy by Ho Kwon Ping, "Thailand's broken rice bowl," *Far Eastern Economic Review,* Dec. 1, 1978. Referring to the rising aspirations for cash income and the progressive commercialization and mechanization of farming, an Australian specialist points out that "in contrast to earlier decades, much of the new land cleared for cultivation in the 1960s and early 1970s was retained in relatively large holdings, commonly exceeding 30 *rai.*" E. C. Chapman, "Agricultural Development in Thailand, in Retrospect and Prospect," paper delivered at Asian Studies Association of Australian Conference, Sydney, May 16, 1978, p. 3. Settlers can now own 100 to 200 *rai* or more, whereas the previous maximum permitted under the 1936 Land Act was 50 *rai,* or 20 acres: Ingram, *Economic Change,* p. 79.

years ago in the last nationwide agricultural census, and there is every reason to expect the gap between rich and poor to have widened since then. In 1963 the bottom ten percent of farms by size held only *one* percent of the total land area, while the top ten percent held 34 percent of the total.[17] In 1970, according to another rural survey, the bottom 20 percent of farmers shared only 5.5 percent of total farm incomes, and the bottom 40 percent shared only 14 percent.[18] In effect, three-quarters of a million well-off farmers and their family members (the "rural elite") culti- vated as much land as 10 million poor villagers—including land the latter did not own, but had to rent.

It is in the key Central Region, particularly in the provinces around Bangkok and Ayuthaya, that tenancy and landlessness are most acute.[19] Here, too, the largest number of absentee owners are to be found. While the average holding in the Center was nearly 27 *rai,* or just over ten acres (according to the 1963 census), the three landowners with the largest holdings owned more than 120,000 *rai* among them, while another 82 people owned between 1,000 and

17. Udom Kerdpibule, "Distribution of Wealth and Income in Thailand," in Prateep Sondysuwan, ed., *Finance, Trade and Economic Development in Thailand* (Bangkok: Sompong, 1975), p. 300.

18. 1970 survey of rural areas, i.e., outside the municipal areas of provinces: ibid., p. 295.

19. The "conventional wisdom" of increasing indebtedness, transfers of land, and social and economic inequality, especially in the Central Plain, has, however, been criticized by Laurence Stifel. In a detailed examination of land title deeds over the past sixty years in six sample villages (three in Ayuthaya and three in Nakorn Pathom provinces) he shows that the rate of "involuntary" transfers, i.e., of mort- gaged land, has actually decreased since the late 1940s. Yet his figures also show that the top 20 percent of landowners has regularly held between 50 and 70 percent of the total land area of the six villages during the period 1930 to 1970. Moreover, in 1970, 20 percent of the area in the Ayuthaya villages and 11 percent in Nakorn Pathom were owned by absentee landlords. See Laurence D. Stifel, "Patterns of Land Ownership in Central Thailand during the Twentieth Century," *Journal of the Siam Society* 64, pt. 1 (January 1976): 237–274. It must be pointed out, however, that Stifel is concerned only with land transfers and ownership. His findings are signifi- cant in that families as such have retained, by and large, much the same holdings as in the past. But he is not concerned with individual *members* of such families, num- bers of whom have either sold privately or otherwise disposed of *uneconomic* inher- itances in the family property. In order to live they must look for land elsewhere, work as tenants or laborers, or migrate to towns. This is the problem of "landless- ness and the growth of a large rural proletariat, dependent upon wage labor" referred to by Chapman and other specialists—a problem of *people,* if not of land, that is outside the scope of Stifel's study.

2,000 *rai* each.[20] From the data now becoming available it is estimated that in eleven of the twenty-six Central Region provinces full tenants and landless villagers comprise more than 30 percent of farm households.[21] Well over a quarter of the full tenants are renting from urban landlords.[22] The extent of landlessness and the growth of a large rural proletariat dependent on wage labor are new to Thailand.

Only the small northern region—with seven provinces and a population of some 8 million—has anything approaching the tenancy problem of the Center, whose population is twice as large. As a result of the hilly terrain of the North and a high rate of population growth, however, the average farm size is only 16 *rai,* compared with the national average of nearly 22 *rai:* A. N. Seth, "Report on Land Reforms in Thailand" (F. A. O. Regional Rural Institutional Office, Bangkok, 1970). Moreover, according to two specialists on agrarian reform, competition for scarce land in the North has "led to tension and violence between the [lowland] Thais and the hill-people". The South, with fifteen provinces and about 4 million people, is also a mountainous region. It is the area of tin mining and rubber estates and small-holdings, with a mixed population of Thais, Chinese, and Malays (the latter, numbering three-quarters of a million or more, form a majority in the four southernmost provinces). These specialists report that "land tenure is not yet an acute problem but increased population pressures, increasing Thai-Muslim hostility, and the apparent lack of Central Government concern, will exacerbate the situation." Finally, the Northeast, with 16 provinces and roughly a third of the Thai popu-

20. A list of thirty-nine landowners, more than half domiciled in Bangkok, owning more than 1,000 *rai* each in Chachoengsao province (in 1969) and forty-one landowners, nearly two-thirds residing in Bangkok, owning more than 1,000 *rai* each in Nakorn Nayok province (1978) is reprinted in a special report, "Land Reform," *Siam Rath* weekly review, June 5, 1978.

21. Division of Land Policy and Planning, Department of Land Development, Agricultural Land Tenure (province reports) 1977, quoted by Chapman, "Agricultural Development in Thailand."

22. Land Development Department, "Farm Land Tenure in 11 Central Plain Provinces in Thailand" (Bangkok, 1965). The average net income of a family that owns its land and does its own farming is 12,751 *baht* per harvest, while those renting land as tenant farmers have an average income of only 4,861 *baht* per harvest: 1976 survey in Saraburi province, considered representative of the Central area, reported by the Office of the National Research Committee: *Bangkok Post,* Oct. 28, 1976. (Not strictly in Center are several provinces in Southeast and Southwest.)

lation, is the poorest region: the average income in the Northeast is only half the national average. Poor soils, excessive floods and droughts, and lack of irrigation and water control all contribute to its impoverishment. It has the lowest tenancy rates in the country, but more than a quarter of its farmers own less than a subsistence-sized farm.[23]

Given the magnitude of the problem, involving some half a million to a million landless or near landless, the task of land reform is a daunting one. Concerned officials had for years been advocating a package of land reforms including such essential measures as: five-year contracts for tenants, with rents fixed at not more than one quarter of farm produce; subsidized fertilizers; land consolidation, especially of small farms under 20 *rai,* to prevent land fragmentation; minimum prices for rice, announced before the farming season begins, with proper storage facilities for rice stocks; improved coordination of government departments; an inheritance tax (none has so far existed); and a graduated land tax to yield revenue, break up large estates, and prevent land speculation.[24] It was only after the fall of the military-dominated government in 1973 that land reform legislation was seriously undertaken. An Agricultural Land Reform Office was set up in 1975. But note Sein Lin's and Esposito's comments: "Land reform to be successful needs the active and mass participation of the beneficiaries, namely the farmers. The Thai farmers have no effective organisation of their own.... The membership of the *changwat* (province) land reform committee includes far too many officials with too few farmers' representatives. These committees are the crucial links in the implementation of land reform.... Top level political support is a sine qua non for any successful land reform. Without it all the

23. Sein Lin and Bruce Esposito, "Agrarian Reform in Thailand: Problems and Prospects," *Pacific Affairs,* 49, no.3 (Fall 1976):425–442. See also Wolf Donner, *The Five Faces of Thailand: An Economic Geography* (New York: St. Martin's Press, 1978). One of the most critical problems is the drastic reduction in Thailand's forests from 51 percent of the total area in 1963 down to 25 percent in 1978. Destruction of forests is causing great ecological damage, including severe droughts and floods. The loss of forest cover is due partly to illegal logging, but even more substantially to land-hungry peasants occupying millions of *rai* of forest reserves: *Business in Thailand,* November 1979; *Bangkok Post,* May 14, 1980.

24. Chaiyong and Manu, "National Seminar on Land Problems"; Land Development Department, "Rice Production and Tenancy in the Central Plain, Thailand, 1965" (Bangkok, 1965). See also p. 221, n. 80.

land reform legislations, all the plans, and all the programs will be of little or no avail."[25]

### Business and Bureaucrats

Agriculture, employing four-fifths of the work force in 1950, provided more than half of the gross domestic product; by 1968 its share was down to less than one-third. This striking decline in the share of agriculture is due, most importantly, to the growth of industry—mining, manufacture, construction, power, and transportation. The industrial sector's share of the gross domestic product increased from one-fifth in 1950 to one-third (same as agriculture) by 1968. During this period, too, the service sector, including trade, finance, real estate, and public administration, rose from less than one-third to approaching two-fifths of the Thai product.[26] In these expanding sectors of the economy (which include the purchase, milling, storage, transportation, and export of rice and other crops), the Chinese minority, around ten percent of the population, have played a dominant role. What is the effect of their economic dominance on political power?

Contrary to the Marxist thesis, the Thai political "superstructure" is not merely a reflection of economic foundations. Nor are the factional struggles of the Thai elite simply the ideological forms (legal, political, or philosophic) in which men become conscious of the conflict between new productive forces and outmoded social relations and fight it out. Contrary to pluralist assumptions, too, the Thai state does not represent a bargaining coalition of interest groups—administrative, business, professional, labor, and peasantry—nor are the intricate maneuvers of the elite to be seen as fulfilling a process of interest aggregation, and articulation.

The Thai state (or rather, its bureaucratic managers) is the beneficiary of productive forces, both rural and urban, which it neither owns (except to a minor degree) nor controls. The material advantages that the state derives from the peasantry, for example, are made possible by the system of independent owner-cultivators

25. "Agrarian Reform in Thailand." See also Turton, "The Current Situation in the Thai Countryside," and Kriarkiat Pipatseritham, "Land Reform Program, 1977–1981: An Analysis," in Montri Chenvidyakan, ed., *Social Science Review* (Bangkok: Social Science Association of Thailand), no. 5, 1978.

26. Ingram, *Economic Change*, p. 235.

(only now coming to an end) which was introduced by the state and which provides benefits, admittedly unequal, to both the owner-cultivators and the state. Similarly, the advantages the state derives from the industrial and service sectors are the result largely of Chinese enterprise, which the state first encouraged and now, in a qualified way, permits. These advantages are derived as much on an informal, patron-client basis as they are through formal means of increased revenues from economic expansion.

The Thai state does not need to *possess* the material foundations—peasant agriculture, Chinese business—so long as it extracts from them sufficient resources to carry out its essential functions: paying for its personnel (and rewarding its leaders) and preserving or enhancing the conditions that sustain the economy through the provision of basic infrastructure and the maintenance of "law and order" internally and "security" externally. Leading Thai bureaucrats, whether military or civilian, have shown neither the will nor the ability to take over the economy, or even the direction of the economy, through agricultural cooperatives and nationalization of enterprises. They cannot simply rely on market forces or harmony of interests (private-public, rural-urban, Thai-Chinese), however, to provide them with the necessary sustenance; for they must use the power they have, political and coercive, to extract what they can.

Yet the leaders of the bureaucratic state are in something of a dilemma. As economic realists, they know they cannot squeeze too hard without destroying the sources of wealth. But as political realists—patrons requiring ever more funds to acquire still greater influence and a larger following in the ceaseless struggle with rivals—they cannot afford to seize too little. And since the struggle is never ending, their demands are insatiable.

It is this dilemma, posed by the requirements of economic growth on the one hand and the demands of political power on the other, which characterizes the ambiguous relationship between business and bureaucrats in Thailand. (It is ambiguous rather than contradictory, since it has been more often reconciled by compromise than divided by conflict). This relationship, over the last hundred years, has gone through three overlapping phases: the patron-client phase in a dynastic setting; the nationalist-competitive phase; and the current phase of pragmatic partnership. I shall analyze this relationship between business and bureaucrats in some detail because it is fundamental to an understanding of the Thai polity.

In the first phase, as we have seen, the Chinese immigrants provided "services" which the traditional *sakdina* levies could no longer adequately supply. Chinese immigration had been encouraged by Thai monarchs throughout the nineteenth century to develop trade, from which the kings benefited: to take charge of the various monopolies (opium, gambling, lottery, and spirits provided 40 to 50 percent of state revenues in the latter half of the century);[27] and finally to provide the skilled and unskilled labor force needed in an expanding economy. A threefold division among the Chinese—in finance, trade, and labor—persists today.

The second phase, competitive nationalism, emerged with the rise of "new men" from among the Thai nobility and the wealthier families who were less paternalistically disposed toward the Chinese than were the king and royal princes and more aware of the potential dangers of alien economic power. The Chinese had long dominated the retail trade—"penetrating every creek," as Bowring himself had noted in the 1850s, to buy up crops and sell imports of cheap Western manufactured goods in exchange.[28] During the economic boom between the First World War and the Great Depression, nearly 95,000 Chinese arrived in Thailand every year, producing a surplus (after departures) of about half a million.[29] By 1930 the Chinese population was around 2 million out of a total population in the country of more than 12 million.

Nearly all the Chinese were urban dwellers, which made their presence to the Thai elite still more conspicuous; about half of them lived within 50 miles of Bangkok. In the capital itself, as late as 1954, more than one-fifth of the inhabitants were Chinese nationals, nearly one quarter were local-born Chinese of Thai nation-

27. The Chinese themselves were motivated partly by the opportunities for economic advancement in peaceful Thailand, but also for negative reasons: to escape from unsettled, even anarchic, conditions, especially in southern China, and from natural disasters—floods and droughts—aggravated by overpopulation: G. William Skinner, *Chinese Society in Thailand: An Analytical History* (Cornell University Press, 1957), pp. 30–32, 120.

28. Ibid., p. 108.

29. Ibid., p. 172.

ality (ethnic Chinese), and just over half were ethnic Thais.[30] Even at the present time, as a Thai political scientist points out, "the majority of the directors and members of the trade associations in Bangkok-Thonburi have Thai nationality, but their patterns of life and occupations are largely those of the Chinese." However, certain of these members emphasize the "Thainess" of their association and the need for it to protect the interests of Thailand.[31]

Thai elite reaction to Chinese commercial enterprise and to the continuing influx of immigrants from a China torn by strife resulted in various forms of governmental restrictions on the Chinese. These chiefly affected immigration, occupations (a number being reserved exclusively for Thais), education (Chinese-language teaching was severely restricted, and many schools were closed), and political activities. The already reduced quota of 10,000 Chinese immigrants a year was cut to 200 by the military government in 1949.[32]

The government also established Thai "state enterprises," not only as an anticipated source of revenues for the government and to provide leading bureaucrats with an opportunity for private gain, but also as a way of developing Thai entrepreneurship. Hitherto this had been almost entirely lacking for a number of reasons: the Thai elite was historically and culturally predisposed toward bureaucratic, rather than business, careers; a Thai middle class, apart from the lower ranks of the civil service, was virtually absent; and the majority of the Thai people had either no wish or no opportunity (through lack of education and skill) to leave farming.

In a more ambiguous response to the Chinese challenge, the Thai bureaucratic elite developed free-wheeling, "semiofficial" Thai trading ventures, operating on patron-client lines and exploit-

---

30. Ibid., pp. 203–206. By 1978 it was estimated that 3 million or more of Thailand's 45 million population are ethnic Chinese, the largest concentrations by far being found in the Central Region and Bangkok. Of these, some 50 percent are Teochew, 15 percent Hakka, 12 percent Hainanese and the remainder Hokkien and Cantonese: Peter Fish, "Children the Key to Thai Integration," *Far Eastern Economic Review,* June 16, 1978.

31. Montri Chenvidyakan, "Economic Interest Groups in Thailand," in Montri, ed., *Social Science Review,* no. 5, 1978, pp. 236–237.

32. Skinner, *Chinese Society,* p. 177.

ing monopolistic privileges secured through political and bureaucratic influence. They also tapped Chinese financial resources and managerial expertise to provide funds for Thai political activities—chiefly to satisfy the demands of "government party" members—and to swell the ranks of a leader's clientele.

The *Saha Samakki* (an organization of war veterans) initiated a trading venture typical of the kind that flourished in the era of military-dominated governments following the 1947 coup. This organization, whose head in 1946 was General (later Field Marshal) Phin Chunhawan, was doing poorly in the soft drinks trade. To gain the benefit of Chinese expertise and to diversify their operations, the group worked in partnership with a Chinese rice merchant and mill owner from the Northeast. An association of rice millers, formed by this businessman, received powerful military backing—for Phin was on top as a result of the 1947 coup, which indeed he had promoted. This helped enormously in the struggle for markets and the control of transportation (the railway and trucking system). In return, Phin and his military and civilian bureaucratic colleagues were appointed members of the board of directors of the association, drawing handsome profits from the proceeds of a successful venture.[33]

This early experimentation in a mixed economy (Thai-style) led to the mature phase of pragmatic partnership beginning in the 1950s. This "collaboration of opposites" required the prior fulfillment of a number of conditions. The most important of these were the trend toward assimilation of Chinese into Thai society; the development of business-bureaucratic cooperation along clique, rather than institutional, lines; and, beginning in the late 1950s, the reversal of the state's role from competing with Chinese enterprise to underpinning the economy.

Events in China, as always, influenced the attitudes of the Chinese community in Thailand and the subsequent Thai reaction. Thus the communist victory in 1949 exacerbated Thai fears of its subversive effects on that community, which in turn contributed to the intensified official campaign of economic harassment and anticommunism in the 1950s. At the same time remittances by Chinese in Thailand to their relatives in China were drastically

33. Ibid., p. 347.

reduced. These remittances were estimated at under 100 million *baht* (about $5 million) per year in the decade after 1949, which is less than the Chinese contributed in taxation to Thai government revenues, and far below the 1946–48 rate of 25 million to 30 million *baht* a month.[34] Funds that were not remitted became available for investment in Thailand instead.[35]

Another reason for the trend to assimilation of Chinese in Thailand was that the century-long process of Chinese immigration had, as we have seen, come virtually to an end. There was no longer a perpetual renewal and reminder of "Chinese-ness" by the flow of incoming migrants. Also, increasing intermarriage,[36] education in Thai schools, and occupational change have all had a cumulative effect. More and more Chinese (cut off from the mainland) marry either local-born Chinese wives or Thai wives; more of their children are educated in Thai schools and universities:[37] and more use Thai names, take up "Thai" occupations—in the professions and, especially, in the bureaucracy—and consider themselves Thai. (The first prime minister of the constitutional period, after a royalist nominee, was of Chinese descent; so was the leading civilian intellectual and liberal politician, later prime minister, Pridi Phanomyong; and so were—and are—many other leading military and bureaucratic figures.) At present, 30 percent of special grade officials—the bureaucratic elite—come from Chinese trading families, and probably at least half have Chinese ancestry.[38]

The development of bureaucratic-business cooperation along clique lines, that is, according to traditional patron-client practices was not a result of institutional or functional collaboration, which is usually considered to be part of the process of modernization. Cooperation between wealthy Chinese "syndicates" and powerful

34. Ibid., p. 364.

35. Ammar Siamwalla, "Stability, Growth and Distribution in the Thai Economy," in Prateep, ed., *Finance, Trade, and Economic Development*, p. 34.

36. The Chakri dynasty itself is a notable product of intermarriage with Chinese or part-Chinese queens or concubines throughout the nineteenth century.

37. The great majority of third-generation Chinese are educated exclusively in Thai schools, and so are at least half of the second generation. In fact, the only ones in the third generation who identify in most social situations as Chinese are those with a Chinese education. Without such an education they become Thai: Skinner, *Chinese Society*, pp. 371, 381.

38. Research by Likhit Dhiravegin, quoted by Laurence D. Stifel, "Technocrats and Modernisation in Thailand," *Asian Survey*, December 1976.

That military officers and leading civilian bureaucrats, as in the case of the *Saha Samakki*, is merely a contemporary equivalent of the "informal" patron-client relationship between Thai kings and Chinese tax farmers more than a century before and between government officials and Chinese traders since then.

This is a partnership between elites. On the Chinese side, as Skinner has pointed out, a small elite controls business life to a remarkable degree: "Business and financial control is exercised largely through business associations and informal groupings of firms in the same line, through combines and syndicates of smaller, seemingly independent enterprises, by means of an elaborate system of interlocking directorates, and through kinship ties and intermarriage."[39]

Similarly, the Thai bureaucratic elite of high-ranking military officers, senior civilian officials, and their "representatives" in the cabinet dominates political life.[40] Yet serious obstacles to a mature

39. G. William Skinner, *Leadership and Power in the Chinese Community of Thailand* (Ithaca, N.Y.: Cornell University Press, 1958), p. 177. Currently, the five most influential Chinese banking families control or substantially influence more than 50 percent of Thailand's private sector, according to U.S. Embassy officials in Bangkok: Paul Wilson, "Bangkok's private banks make a counter-attack," *Far Eastern Economic Review*, Sept. 1, 1978. A directory of Thailand's 100 largest manufacturing companies compiled by the commerce faculty of Thammasat University shows that 63 of them are directly controlled by Chinese. Of the 25 men considered to be most influential in the business world, 23 are of Chinese descent. Among them are Chin Sophonpanich (Tang Pik Ching) of the Bangkok Bank, Chuan Ratanarak (Lee Bak Chuan) of the Bank of Ayudhaya, and Mongkol Kanjanapas (Ng Chue Meng) of the Hong Kong-based Stelux watch complex. "The Chinese 'big clans' regulate the money market and control the prices of land, medicine, construction materials, and even food. By intermarriage they have maintained a tight hold on the markets they carve up among themselves. They are also believed to have succeeded in influencing Thai politicians to protect their economic interests": Phijit Chong, *Far Eastern Economic Review*, June 16, 1978. See also Robert F. Zimmerman, *Reflections on the Collapse of Democracy in Thailand* (Singapore, Institute of Southeast Asian Studies, occasional paper no. 50, April 1978), diagrams 1-4. For details of the financial performance, ownership, and management of 1,200 top companies, each with more than 1 million *baht* capital (5 percent of the firms registered with the Ministry of Commerce in 1976-78) see *Million Baht Business, 1979-80* (Bangkok: Pan Siam Communications, 1979). Thirty-seven percent of the shares in Siam Cement, for example, one of the largest companies, are owned by the Crown Property Bureau: 1.6 percent by H.M. the King's Privy Purse (p. 799).

40. "Of 211 men who have held seats in the cabinet between 1932 and 1958, 84 had had previous careers in the civil service, 68 had previous careers in the military service, and only 13 could be clearly identified as nonbureaucratic": David A. Wil-

partnership between the two disparate elements had first to be overcome. These obstacles sprang from the pressures of Thai political and economic nationalism in the late 1940s and early 1950s, combining anti-Chinese regulations with anti-Communist campaigns. As a result, the two spheres of elite control (Thai politics and Chinese business), far from merging profitably, or even maintaining a balanced autonomy, perpetually grated on one another. Business confidence was badly affected. "No one knew when his particular line of business might be reserved for Thais or subjected to strict control, when the lease of his shop or title to his business property might be challenged, or when his business might be inspected by revenue officials, or raided by the police.[41]

Such a situation, bordering on anarchy, threatened the very foundations of the economy, and with it the material interests of both sides. To avert this disaster, a rapprochement took place. According to the classic account of this process, Thai political and economic pressures on Chinese businessmen forced the latter "to seek security among those able to offer protection—government officials, police and army officers. For their part, the Thai militarists and politicians who came to power with Phibun in 1948 [and especially after their coup in 1951]... lacked an economic base to bolster their political and military power and enable them to bid for higher prestige. Inexperienced in business, they could not simply appropriate the economic structure without its deteriorating in their hands."[42] Since they could not compete with the Chinese, and dared not destroy them, they decided to join them.

Three important developments took place. First, Chinese merchants reorganized their major commercial and financial corporations to include on the boards of directors top government officials

---

son, *Politics in Thailand* (Ithaca, N.Y.: Cornell University Press, 1966), p. 155. The pattern continues: from 1959 to 1974, 38 cabinet members were from the military, 10 from the police, while 93 were civilian bureaucrats. There were 4 nonbureaucrats. Only during the democratic period, 1975–76, did nonbureaucrats (35) outnumber officials (23). See Likhit Dhiravegin, *The Bureaucratic Elite of Thailand* (Bangkok: Thai Khadi Research Institute, Thammasat University, 1978), pp. 149–215.

41. Skinner, *Leadership and Power,* p. 191.
42. Skinner, *Chinese Society,* pp. 360–364.

and other members of the Thai elite with "good connections."[43] Second, most of the major corporations established after the 1951 coup became cooperative Sino-Thai ventures: the Chinese supplied the capital and entrepreneurial skills; Thai officials provided "protection" for the Chinese, as well as official privileges and, in some cases, government contracts. Third, semigovernmental business and financial organizations used the managerial skill and commercial acumen of local-born and naturalized Chinese by bringing them onto their boards and staffs.[44]

Thus a mutually profitable bargain was struck. Three features of this remarkable convergence of opposites—Thai and Chinese, businessmen and bureaucrats—are worth noting; indeed they are indispensable for an understanding of Thai politics. First, the rapprochement that took place was on an individual basis between leading Chinese businessmen and their Thai "connections" in the military, police, Ministry of the Interior, cabinet, and so forth. Second, this convergence did not involve any public reversal of official policy—that occurred later, as if to ratify a process that was virtually complete—but took place beneath the surface of politics, allowing the rhetoric to continue while the new arrangement was consummated. Finally, the partnership emerged in the context of clique rivalry: essentially between leading elements of the military, headed by the forceful Sarit, and the police under the control of Prime Minister Phibun's former right-hand man, Police General Phao. One group of Chinese businessmen came to be associated with Sarit's faction (which prevailed), another with that of Phao. Such factional rivalry, although muted, was evident during the ascendency of Sarit; it contributed to the downfall of the top military-political leaders in 1973; and it continues within the military, and between the military and police, involving civilian bureaucrats and Chinese businessmen, to the present day.[45]

43. The extremely important Bangkok Bank, originally entirely Chinese, was reorganized in 1953 with the minister of economic affairs as chairman, a former lord chamberlain as vice chairman, and two deputy ministers (both generals) and a police officer on the board of directors. The Asia Trust Company was reorganized in 1952 with the director-general of police (Phao) replacing a Chinese community leader as chairman. Similar reorganizations took place at the Siam Trading Company, the Thai Farmers Bank, insurance companies, shipping companies, and so on: Skinner, *Chinese Society*, pp. 142–196.

44. Ibid., pp. 360–361.

45. See the next two chapters.

It was with Sarit's victory over his rivals that the "ratification" of business-bureaucratic collaboration took place. This, on the advice of the World Bank, meant the reversal of state policy, from competition with Chinese enterprise to underpinning the entire economy. Teams of officials from the International Monetary Fund and the World Bank had previously visited Thailand in 1954, and there was a year-long visit by a World Bank mission in 1957-58. The mission's report[46] reinforced the views of modernizing officials in the Thai administration, and especially in the Bank of Thailand, that the government "should go further in building up the infrastructure for development—roads, power supply, irrigation—and improving the productivity of its existing economic activities—rice, rubber, tin, and other primary products—before it could profitably launch into industrial development."[47]

Thus during the Sarit era (1958-63), government economic functions were redefined. Rather than expanding state enterprises, which were wasteful and inefficient, government resources were concentrated on the task of developing *public* infrastructure for the use of *private* enterprise. This change of policy coincided, significantly, with a change in patronage methods—and patrons. As Silcock explains: "Sarit was well disposed toward the condemnation of government enterprises. Unlike Phibun [whom Sarit replaced] he did not base his power on patronage within the system of government enterprise, but had extensive private interests in which he used his political power to help his friends."[48]

Government intervention as a result became more circumscribed, but also better organized and defined. This was the achievement of largely Western-trained financial experts, managers, planners, and economists—the "technocrats." It was their responsibility both to allocate resources (including foreign aid) and to define national economic goals. The National Economic Development Board under key ministers was set up on the recommendation of the World Bank; and departmental expenditure came under the scrutiny of the new Budget Bureau, directed by the

46. International Bank for Reconstruction and Development, *A Public Development Program for Thailand* (Baltimore: Johns Hopkins Press, 1959).
47. T. H. Silcock, "Outline of Economic Development 1945-65," in Silcock, ed., *Thailand: Social and Economic Studies in Development* (Canberra: Australian National University Press, 1967), pp. 16-17.
48. Ibid., p. 20.

leading technocrat, Dr. Puey Ungphakorn, who was also governor of the Bank of Thailand. The first national economic plan, starting in 1961, gave priority to transport and communications, followed by agricultural improvements and community development.[49]

The rise of the technocrats, appropriately, was a matter of supply and demand. The supply came from the remarkable increase in the number of Thais educated abroad, particularly in the United States.[50] The demand for their services sprang both from Marshal Sarit's determination to make use of technocratic expertise to build up a more powerful, efficient, and integrated state (following in the footsteps of the nineteenth century absolute monarchs) and from the requirements for specialized staff of the newly established managerial and planning institutions. As a sympathetic observer notes: "The younger group of technocrats accepted the legitimacy of Sarit's commitment to development. They welcomed socialisation with the military elite in the National Defense College and they accepted the imperatives of national security. The rapid progress of the country strengthened their confidence in their own pragmatic judgements."[51]

The technocrats were given considerable authority within their spheres of competence (financial supervision, planning, engineering projects, even diplomacy), but they operated within the framework of the "bureaucratic polity."[52] The technocrats could improve the working of the system, but they could not change it, especially when powerful "traditional" elements of the polity restricted, undermined, or obstructed their modernizing aims. This is a universal dilemma: the experts have little say in deciding the *ends* of government policy, which inevitably shape the *means*, that is, the very spheres of competence in which the experts are employed.

Technocrats in Thailand have reacted in various ways to these circumstances. In some cases, liberal technocrats have identified themselves with more "open" democratic tendencies. They accept

49. T. H. Silcock, "Promotion of Industry and the Planning Process," in Silcock, ed., *Thailand: Social and Economic Studies,* pp. 280–283. The NEDB has since become the National Economic and Social Development Board.

50. There were about 50 Thais studying abroad at the end of last century, more than 500 in the late 1930s, and almost 6,000 in 1973 in the United States alone. The U.S. Operations Mission (USAID) to Thailand had trained more than 8,000 participants by March 1974: Stifel, "Technocrats and Modernisation."

51. Ibid.

52. See Fred Rigg's illuminating study, *Thailand: The Modernization of a Bureaucratic Polity* (Honolulu: East-West Center Press, 1966), esp. pp. 335–337.

the consequences of popularly elected governments—political fluctuation, pressure groups, public expression of grievances and demands—for the sake of the fundamental right of self-government, or at least government by the consent of the governed. In other cases, "middle of the road" technocrats are concerned about the anarchic potential of democracy, especially when mass demands for participation outrun the scope of political institutions set up for that purpose.[53] But they still *prefer* a polity that is "open" for themselves and for the "middle classes" in general: one in which technocratic values (economic growth, efficient administration, financial integrity, basic social welfare,) may be politically realized. Theirs is a middle course that seeks to avoid being overwhelmed by the pressure of mass demands *from below* (for fairer distribution, social justice, eradication of poverty) or by the power of vested interests *from above* (distorting the economy and impeding the free flow of information necessary for rational planning).

In most cases, however, technocrats have *collaborated* with authoritarian regimes, for two reasons. First, these regimes are capable of imposing the political stability they consider indispensable to economic growth, the foremost goal of the technocrats. Second, intelligent, "enlightened" experts believe in the use of reason to persuade, influence, or even convince the people in power that it is actually in their own interest to behave in a way that the technocrats approve. (This faith in the power of reason, an enduring characteristic of intellectuals, is, of course, frequently disabused).

I have discussed the role of the technocrats at some length because of their influence in shaping official economic policies, enlisting support for private enterprise, and encouraging foreign investment.[54] But their role is no less important in illustrating the different political attitudes (varying from criticism to compromise

---

53. For a classic study, see Samuel P. Huntington, *Political Order in Changing Societies* (New Haven, Conn.: Yale University Press, 1968), pp. 4–6. On the political effect of mass demands in Thailand, see Chapter 5 below.

54. Note, for example, Puey's support for the "wide open-door policy" in international economic relations. This is because "(1) We recognise the value of the international division of labor. We produce goods and services in which we have special skill, and trade them for capital goods which we cannot produce.... (2) We are short of capital, technical know-how, and managerial ability. Until we can remedy these shortages it is wiser to take advantage of the assistance made available to us by the various [foreign] governments, agencies and foundations." The advantages can

and collaboration) found among the newly modernized and modernizing elements in Thai society, particularly the younger, Western-educated administrators, independent professionals, and teachers and students.

## The Social Consequences

The priority given to economic growth, rather than concern for distribution, has had serious consequences. The former leading technocrat, Puey Ungphakorn, himself admitted that as an official he had concentrated too much on growth and not enough on the equitable distribution of the national product. In his time he had supported the conventional argument for, or rationalization of, official policies:

If we pay too much attention to social justice, overall growth would be slowed down, therefore we should put economic development first. Even though the rich will get richer, and the poor get poorer, soon growth will filter down to the poor automatically. . . . [But, Puey observed] we have used this method for 20–30 years now without success.[55]

These social consequences of "modernization without development"[56] are revealed in the unequal burdens imposed by successive Thai governments on the urban and rural poor (rather than on

---

be seen in the 7 to 10 percent a year growth in national income, which is comparable with that of South Korea, Taiwan, and Malaysia, even though "benefits from economic growth are not well distributed": Address to Thai Council of World Affairs, Bangkok, Oct. 20, 1969. Dr. Puey adds that "most of the credit [for progress in economic development] must belong to the private sector, with adequate savings, good capital formation and investments and increases in productivity": Address to Thailand Management Association, Bangkok, July 27, 1967: in Puey Ungphakorn, *Best Wishes for Asia*, (Bangkok: Klett Thai, 1975), pp. 44–46, 51.

55. Puey Ungphakorn, *Glancing Back, Looking Forward* (Melbourne: Shepparton Press, 1977), p. 25. "It is impossible to expect growth to filter down in societies where there is no equality of opportunity," writes an economist now with the World Bank. "If there are institutional rigidities, lack of mobility of labor, unequal levels of education, vastly unequal access to the means of production, and wide disparities in present income levels, it is inescapable that growth should get warped in favor of a privileged few, until fundamental institutional reforms are carried out": Mahbul Ul Haq, *The Poverty Curtain: Choices for the Third World* (New York: Columbia University Press, 1976), p. 61.

56. *Modernization without Development: Thailand as an Asian Case Study* is the title of Norman Jacobs' book (New York: Praeger, 1971). He defines modernization as the attempt, stimulated by novel, recently revealed ways of accomplishing tasks, to realize society's potential *within limits* set by the goals and fundamental structures of society. "Development," by contrast, requires an open-ended commitment to productive change, regardless of such limits: (pp. 4, 8–9).

those with proportionately more capacity to bear them) and in the creation and expansion of new social forces, as a result of the growth of industrial and service sectors, which have little or no participation in decisions affecting their livelihood. Also, symbolic of the widening gap between rich and poor, rural and urban society, and elite and masses, the ever-greater concentration of political and economic power in Bangkok is draining the resources of the rest of the country.

Government policies have contributed to the imbalance in two ways: first, by levying a heavy tax burden (the rice premium) on those least able to pay and, second, by failing to tax the rich effectively (against the advice of economists like Puey).[57]

The imposition of the rice premium in 1955, according to another noted Thai economist, had "harsh and abrupt" consequences for farmers who had previously enjoyed relatively favorable terms of trade.[58] The premium was imposed for two reasons: first, to provide revenue for the government, amounting at times to 10 percent or more of total revenue,[59] and, second, in effect to subsidize (because of the lower prices received by the farmer) the *urban* consumption of rice. This subsidy is to the advantage of civil servants, the most important "constituency" of any Thai government, and of industrial and construction workers, shop assistants, clerks, and other town dwellers. (The availability of cheap rice held down the cost of living, which reduced pressures for higher wages, and thus also facilitated industrial development.)[60] But the political motive is paramount: a materially satisfied urban population is

57. Puey Ungphakorn, *Sia chip ya sia sin* [Lose your life, don't lose all] (Bangkok: Klett Thai, 1974), advocating effective property taxes in particular: pp. 116–117.
58. Prachoom Chomchai, "Thailand's Industrial Development: Rationale, Strategy and Prospects": in Robert Ho and E. C. Chapman, eds., *Studies of Contemporary Thailand* (Canberra: Department of Human Geography, Australian National University, 1973), pp. 78–79. Ingram notes the relatively favored position of Thai farmers, exempt from paying taxes on newly cultivated land, from the 1850s to 1900. Land taxes were increased after 1905, but even up to the 1930s (when they were reduced) amounted to only about 10 percent of income, compared to 30 to 50 percent in other countries of the Far East: Ingram, *Economic Change*, pp. 76–79.
59. With the need to boost Thai rice exports in the early 1970s, the premium had been greatly reduced: but it was restored, in effect, by the military-backed government after October 1976. In 1977–78 it was increased to 24 percent of the export price: *Far Eastern Economic Review*, Feb. 10, 1978. Ob Vasuratna, outgoing president of the Board of Trade, urged the government gradually to remove the premium, which "is a form of tax" on farmers: *Bangkok Post*, Mar. 23, 1979.
60. Ammar Siamwalla, "Stability, Growth, and Distribution."

essential for the safety and survival of an elitist ruling system, which thus forms a protected enclave in the vast rural hinterland. (On the one occasion when the system broke down—after the Thanom-Praphat government had bungled its rice policy and there were food shortages in Bangkok—the government was overthrown. This was one of the contributing causes of the great demonstration of October 1973, a turning point in Thai history, which is discussed in the next two chapters.)

As for the lack of effective taxation of the rich, a similar self-serving political motivation prevails. In spite of the boom in real estate and construction, as a result of which a few people have made fortunes, no inheritance tax exists (legislation was proposed in 1976, during the democratic period, but was dropped after the October 1976 coup) and property taxes are low. Indirect taxation (especially import duties, excise taxes, and turnover tax), which proportionately has far greater impact on the incomes of the poor, provided more than 80 percent of revenues in 1969. Income taxes on individuals and corporations amounted to only 11 percent.[61] This situation still persists. In 1977 less than 19 percent of all taxes collected came from direct sources; income from property was estimated at only 0.5 percent of property value. The 1978 World Bank report on Thailand recommended more effective methods of tax collection, increased property taxes and excise on luxury items, a more progressive income tax, and the introduction of a capital gains tax.[62] But the historical record with regard to such recommendations is not encouraging.

As a result of official policies permitting relatively uncontrolled profits derived from economic growth, existing social disparities have widened among several groups:

(*a*) Between the outlying regions of the country, especially the Northeast, and the Central Plain.

(*b*) Between farmers and townsmen within the regions.

61. Ingram, *Economic Change*, p. 299.

62. "Taxation in Thailand," *Investor*, July 1978. On the World Bank report, see Ho Kwon Ping, *Far Eastern Economic Review*, Dec. 1, 1978. The chairman of the National Economic and Social Development Board, Sunthorn Hongladarom, in a 1980 report to the nation's chief economic planners, urged the government to consider lifting price controls on agricultural products and removing or reducing the rice premium. Rather than forcing down the prices received by farmers for their crops in order to keep food prices low for urban dwellers, the government should instead seek to raise the income of the poorer urban groups: *Bangkok Post*, July 17, 1980.

(c) Among villagers themselves—between the small number of better-off farmers, who possess sufficient capital or have access to credit to make use of modern technology, and the far larger and increasing numbers of "dwarfholders," tenant farmers, and landless laborers.

(d) Among the various strata of urban dwellers—between the educated, wealthy, bureaucratic, and business elites at the top of the social pyramid and the growing numbers of migrants from depressed rural areas, who live in slums, work as unskilled labor, or scratch a living from casual employment, at the bottom.[63] All these social and economic disparities, which are both reflected in and the result of the hierarchical order of the political system, are most apparent in the contrast between Bangkok and the countryside.

The people of Bangkok have more than two and a half times the average income for Thailand as a whole. Townspeople in the four main regions have about twice the average income (slightly less in the North). Although incomes of villagers in the Center are above the average for the nation, those in the South, North, and Northeast vary from only two-thirds to three-quarters of the average.[64] To put it another way, citizens of Bangkok earn nearly four times as much as villagers in the Northeast.[65]

63. The poorest 10 percent of urban dwellers share 2.5 percent of total income in contrast to the wealthiest 10 percent, who share 29.5 percent: from the 1970 household expenditure survey in urban areas, cited by Udom, "Distribution of Wealth and Income," in Prateep, ed., *Finance, Trade and Economic Development*, p. 287.

64. Socio-Economic Survey 1967-68, Table V: cited by Ammar Siamwalla in Prateep, ed., *Finance Trade, and Economic Development*, p. 46. A similar situation is depicted in the National Statistical Office survey, 1971-1973: the average annual household income in Bangkok-Thonburi is more than 24,000 *baht* [about $12,000] compared with the average for *rural* households of nearly 16,000 *baht* in the Center, 11,000 each in the North and South, and less than 7,000 in the Northeast: quoted in Turton, "Current Situation in the Thai Countryside," p. 108, table. The Central Region, with about one-third of the Thai population, receives 60 percent of the gross domestic product: the Northeast, with a slightly higher population, gets 15 percent: 1976 statistics quoted by Phisit Pakkasem, director of regional planning in the National Economic and Social Development Board, "Role of Local Governments in Regional Development," in Likhit Dhiravegin, ed., *Social Science Review*, 1977, pp. 46-70.

65. Forty-one percent of northeastern households had an annual income of below 6,000 *baht*, considered the poverty line, compared with the national average of 22 percent of households. In contrast, more than 44 percent of greater Bangkok households received an income of 30,000 *baht* or more: 1973 socioeconomic survey, quoted in *Business Review*, April 1977. Income per head, according to a 1975-76 survey of the Northeast, was 6,760 *baht* in urban areas; 2,855 *baht* in rural areas: Joyce Rainar, *Bangkok Post*, Mar. 29, 1979.

Juxtaposed to the rural world, therefore, is the capital city, Bangkok, which is in almost every sense a polar opposite. Eighty percent of the nation's telephones are in Bangkok and about half its motor vehicles. Bangkok consumes more than 80 percent of the nation's electricity, generates more than 80 percent of its business taxes, holds more than 70 percent of all commercial bank deposits, and absorbs slightly more than 60 percent of the total annual investment in construction.[66] Bangkok [and Thonburi] with nearly 5 million inhabitants—more than one-tenth of the entire population—is 40 times larger than the next biggest city, Chiangmai.

As a former adviser to the Thai government on municipal affairs points out:

Bangkok is the administrative seat not only of government but of industry. It is the financial capital and the distribution center. It is the one city in Thailand of a size sufficient to support a wide variety of services and to offer a full range of the world's goods. It is no surprise, then, that 70 percent of the city's labor force is engaged in tertiary activity, more than 35 percent being employed by service industries and another 30 percent by commercial industries. A quarter of all the employed are sales workers, a tenth are clerical workers and just under a tenth are administrators or professionals of one sort of another. Bangkok is also Thailand's most important processing center and a quarter of the labor force is made up of craftsmen and factory workers.[67]

To illustrate the hold that Bangkok exerts, more than half of all the doctors in Thailand practice in the capital; here there is one doctor for every 1,000 people; the ratio in the provinces, however, is about 1:30,000. "It is difficult to induce doctors to practice in the provinces although it is imperative that they be induced to practice there."[68]

This "primate city" is not only the vital center of government and administration and of industry and commerce; it also provides the educational facilities that are essential for the production and recruitment of businesspersons and bureaucrats alike. Of more than 1,300 private schools in the Central region, more than half (743) are in Bangkok and Thonburi—a number not far short of all the

66. Phisit Pakkasem, *Bangkok Bank monthly review*, August 1977.
67. Sternstein, *Thailand: The Environment of Modernisation*, p. 117.
68. Ibid., p. 57.

private schools (964) in the Northeast, North, and South regions combined. Half of all government secondary schools, too, are in the Center.[69] The majority of Thailand's universities, and the most prestigious, are in Bangkok. Nine out of the ten private degree colleges, authorized from 1970, are also located in the capital. (The other one is in Chiengmai.)[70]

The importance of Bangkok as the summit of achievement stands out in the context of educational opportunities open to Thais as a whole. Starting at the bottom of the educational ladder, there are some 6 million elementary school students in the country. More than 60 percent of the intake drop out after only two or three years; 19 percent go on to secondary schools; 2.3 percent enter universities.[71] Those who leave primary school, essentially from the rural eighty percent of the population, go on to become farmers and tenants or relatively unskilled and low-paid urban migrants. Only 6 percent of university students come from a peasant background.[72] Secondary school graduates qualify mainly for the skilled labor force or for white-collar employment and clerical rank in the civil service. They are in the middle-income bracket.[73] And the tiny fraction of students that graduate from a university either enter business management or join the higher ranks of the civil service. There is a close relationship, therefore, between level of education, occupation, and income. The daily minimum wage for a laborer, introduced in 1975, varied from 16 *baht* in the North and Northeast to 25 *baht* in Bangkok and in five nearby provinces; the latter was comparable to the minimum official wage, for a clerk, of 750 *baht* a month. A university graduate, however, entered the administration in 1975 with 1,750 *baht*, the holder of an M.A. degree with 2,230 *baht*, and a Ph.D. with 3,030 *baht*.[74]

---

69. M. Rajaretnam and Lim So Jean, eds., *Trends in Thailand* (Singapore: Institute of Southeast Asian Studies, 1973), pp. 39–40.

70. Amnuay Tapingkae, "Education and Development: A Thai Experience," *Asian Profile* (Hong Kong), December 1977.

71. Udom, "Distribution of Wealth and Income," p. 307. The school system has been changed, since May 1978, to six years at primary level (from seven years primary, and three and two years at secondary levels): Amnuay, "Education and Development."

72. World Bank 1978 report: Ho Kwon Ping, "Thailand's Broken Rice Bowl."

73. Udom, "Distribution of Wealth and Income," p. 307.

74. Veeraphol Suvannunt, *Business Review* (Bangkok), April 1975. According to NESDB statistics in 1975, the average annual earnings *per person* of more than 11 million members of farming families, making up two-thirds of the labor force, was

The educational advantages of Bangkok are illustrated by the following figures. According to the 1960 census, one-third of Bangkok males received more than four years of education, compared to only 5 percent of rural males. Only a tiny proportion of the latter proceeded beyond secondary school: yet nearly half the Bangkok males entering secondary schools continued on to pre-university levels. Six percent of Bangkok males had one year or more in a university, compared with 0.2 percent of rural males.[75] A survey of more than 150 well-known intellectuals reveals even more dramatically the magnetic attraction of Bangkok. All of these notable figures—apart from two each in the North and Northeast, and one in the South—lived in Bangkok. But well over half the total had actually been born and reared outside the capital.[76]

This extraordinary contrast between the concentration of wealth, power, and prestige in the hands of a small number of people in Bangkok and the dispersion of the poor, uneducated, and under-privileged throughout the countryside is both the strength and weakness of the social system. The glitter of Bangkok and the authority of its elite dazzle the multitudes outside. Many are drawn to it by the lure of a better life.[77] A fortunate few, through patronage networks, graduate to the inner sanctum, while the majority submit to a power and a destiny that they can neither attain nor resist.[78]

---

5,288 *baht:* the average for the (largely urban) wage earners, nearly 3.5 million people or one-fifth of the labor force, was 21,531 *baht;* and for less than 2.5 million "self-employed and property owners" it was 42,100: quoted by Peter Fish, "Thailand tries to plug the wage gap," *Far Eastern Economic Review,* Apr. 7, 1978. The minimum wage in Bangkok and five provinces was raised to 28 *baht* in 1977. and 35 *baht* in 1978, and 45 *baht* in October 1979.

75. Sidney Goldstein, "The Demography of Bangkok: A Case Study of Differentials between Big City and Rural Populations," Chulalongkorn University, August 1972, p. 31.

76. Herbert P. Phillips, "The Culture of Siamese Intellectuals," in G. William Skinner and A. Thomas Kirsch, eds., *Change and Persistence in Thai Society: Essays in Honor of Lauriston Sharp* (Ithaca, N.Y.: Cornell University Press, 1975), p. 327.

77. Reasons given for migration from the countryside to Bangkok, according to an International Labor Organisation report to the Thai government in 1965, are: shortage of land and lack of water, sterile soil, land tenure problems, and absence of industrial employment. The "pull" of Bangkok stems from seasonal opportunities for work, wage differentials, inducements of friends and relatives in the city, and desire for education: Visid Prachuabmoh and Penporn Tirasawat, "Internal Migration in Thailand, 1947–1972," Chulalongkorn University, 1974.

78. The middle and lower urban strata are particularly vulnerable to pollution, traffic congestion, housing shortages, uncontrolled land speculation (reflecting a

*Orbit of America and Japan*

To turn now to the international perspective, Thailand's strategic relationship with the United States has clearly been crucial for 25 out of the past 30 years (see Chapter 6). The present section is concerned primarily with the impact of the United States and Japan—chiefly military and economic in the first case, economic with political undertones in the second—on Thai *internal* developments. However, in analyzing the domestic sphere it is important first to establish the functions and the limits of the international power structure, whether American or Japanese, in order to assess the nature and the degree of the constraints and pressures on countries like Thailand, that is, on institutions and individuals within those countries. It is important, too, to point out that the international structure provides not only constraints but also *opportunities* to certain elements in society. These elements become the starting point for autonomous development, in contrast to others which remain dependent.

The American role, even during its heyday from 1950 to 1975, was not so much one of domination—that is, the subordination of the Thai domestic system to the global system—as of stabilization—that is, bolstering and maintaining the power, wealth, and influence of elite leaders in the midst of domestic upheavals and external threats. The two countries had common interests.

U.S. strategic policies, bolstering military regimes, were, of course, contrary to the interests of the majority of the Thai

lack of urban planning), and sharply increasing crime. There are estimated to be some 50,000 squatter families, over 5 percent of Bangkok's population, living in squalid and overcrowded slums. The continuing inflow of rural migrants from depressed areas, with natural increase, is expected to swell the capital's population to more than 7 million in 1985. Rising unemployment is estimated to affect a million people in the country as a whole, including, particularly in Bangkok, some 44,000 of the "highly and fairly highly educated." Sources: Chaktip Nitibhon, "Urban Development and Industrial Estates in Thailand," in Prateep, ed., *Finance, Trade and Economic Development;* Krit Sombatsiri, Secretary-General of the NESDB, on 1975 unemployment figures, reported in *Bangkok Bank monthly review,* January 1977; Sydney Goldstein, Visid Prachuabmoh, and Alice Goldstein, "Urban-Rural Migration Differentials in Thailand," Chulalongkorn University, February 1974: and Larry Sternstein, "Bangkok 2000," on Bangkok as a "primate city, not only in size but also in complexity, the fearful interrelatedness, the damnable immediacy, and the sheer number of problems wanting solution . . . ," in Ho and Chapman, eds., *Studies of Contemporary Thailand* (Canberra: Dept. of Human Geography, Australian National University, 1973).

*people*—including workers, farmers, students, small-shop keepers, minor officials, and professionals. This was belatedly recognized, by certain members of the elite, in the early 1970s. But the majority of the Thai people (apart from the 1973–76 period) had no influence on the Thai government.

A stable political situation in Thailand facilitated the economic interests of the Thai elite (as seen in the previous section) and of American corporate enterprise. And the Americans required political stability no less than the Thai elite to safeguard markets for their products, to acquire access to essential raw materials, and to ensure the long-term profitability of investments. Further, Thai political stability (and economic profitability) played its part in assuring *regional* stability. Thailand in effect was an important component of the American strategic network aimed at preserving Southeast Asia from communism (whether indigenous, pro-Chinese, or pro-Soviet), a goal that, again was in the interest of both parties.

The linkage between the international and the domestic hierarchy of power could also be considered as a form of patron-client relations. In the political field, for example, the United States with its military might and enormous wealth acted as the patron, while leading Thai generals and officials were clients. The imperial patron provided protection and some access to wealth: U.S. military and economic aid was furnished to Thai leaders who then distributed a part to their favored clients through their own domestic patronage networks. In return, the regime provided "services," notably support for U.S. strategic policies in the area. Economic penetration was also achieved, especially by Japanese and American multinationals, on a patron-client basis.

But even a strategy of stabilization has built-in limitations. The failure of this strategy with regard to Thailand's neighbors—South Vietnam, Cambodia, and Laos—despite massive U.S. military intervention on their behalf, makes this abundantly clear. Similarly in Thailand, when the U.S. military presence was at its peak (Thailand had replaced Vietnam in 1973 as headquarters for the U.S. air force in Southeast Asia), American backing for Prime Minister Field Marshal Thanom and his deputy Praphat could not prevent their being ousted as a result of the domestic upheavals of October 1973. Even the October 1976 coup, which put an end to the democratic interlude, was essentially the product of internal, and not international, forces. Thus the United States, rather than being involved in the 1976 restoration of Thai military rule, as the radical anti-imperialist thesis would have it, had withdrawn almost all its military personnel from Thai soil earlier in the year. Moreover, by then Washington itself had opted out of maintaining a strategic role in mainland Southeast Asia.

Thus although the *objective* of U.S. policy was to stabilize elitist regimes, its *capacity* to do so was limited by the very fact that it could not prevent domestic upheavals from undermining those regimes. This experience demonstrates the potential for autonomy of the domestic process. Nevertheless, the degree of autonomy of countries within the orbit of great powers differs considerably. This, too, is important in understanding the way in which international power and domestic structure are linked.

Consider, for example, the enormous difference between America's limited role in Thailand and its dominant role in the former South Vietnam. The latter role stemmed from the belief that a stable Vietnam was vital to U.S. security. But the more the internal upheavals in Vietnam appeared to jeopardize that security, the more the U.S. intervened to maintain stability, and thus the greater its impact on Vietnamese society. Washington, in particular, played a key role in maintaining "its men" in power in Saigon, particularly after the fall of Ngo Dinh Diem, when the country was falling apart. First Air Vice-Marshal Ky and then General Thieu were backed by all-out U.S. military, political, and economic means, while rival generals were warned that America would not tolerate another coup. This warning was reinforced by the threat of ending the U.S. military and economic aid on which the regime utterly depended.

Thailand's role in U.S. strategy, by contrast, was much more limited—hence the American impact was more limited—for two main reasons. First, Thailand served as a "backup" for U.S. intervention in Indochina, not as a direct theater of operations. Second, Thai stability was not in question, at least when judged by the standard of South Vietnam. In Thailand there was far less danger of disintegration, simply because there was no major *internal* threat: armed insurgency started only in certain areas in 1965 and has remained, in comparison with Vietnam, fairly localized and small-scale.[79] Therefore, because there was no significant threat of disruption, it did not matter very much to the United States which leaders were in command. A system favorable to the United States would continue, even if the personnel changed.

In the early and mid-1950s, for example, the major conduit for U.S. military aid was the police under Phao, who built up a paramilitary force with tanks, planes, and artillery. When he fell as a result of rivalry with the leading army clique, the United States had no hesitation in transferring its support to Marshal Sarit. The 1960s marked the zenith of U.S. backing for the Thai military, with Thailand functioning as a forward base for the war in Vietnam. Even when Thanom and Praphat were overthrown in 1973, U.S. airbases and intelligence centers in Thailand still operated. The advent of the parliamentary regime after 1973 did not substantially affect this situation, since military interests were well represented in the coalition government. What put an end to the alliance was not so much Thai internal politics, but, as we have seen, the failure of the United States to protect its clients. It was this above all that induced the Thai government under Kukrit Pramot to substitute accommodation of the communist powers for the outmoded policy of resistance.[80] In turn, the U.S. adapted to its failure in Indochina by reassessing—in effect, virtually abandoning—its former strategic interest in Thailand.

The historical record thus enables us to gauge the impact on indigenous societies of America's military-political-economic involvement as well as the *limits* to that impact (i.e., the strength of autonomous forces). Both impact and limitations were most apparent in the area of security. American power was most actively deployed—to the greatest benefit, directly or indirectly, of its Thai clients—during the decades up to 1975 when Washington perceived Southeast Asia as vital to its own security. Conversely, the

79. The insurgency is still serious, in Thai terms, because it is rooted in local conditions, especially in the Northeast, where it is a truly regional force. Much of the insurgency, however, stems from the struggle of ethnic minorities, such as the hill tribes in the North and Malay-Muslims in the South. This invests it with great appeal, but also tends to limit it to those communities. In this regard, the Thai insurgency is unlike the revolutionary struggle in Vietnam, which was based squarely on the Vietnamese peasantry, although it also drew support from among the ethnic minorities and the urban population. See Chapter 7.

80. See Chapter 6.

intensity of U.S. involvement diminished when U.S. strategic perceptions of the importance of Thailand diminished. America's interest in the Thai economy, however, has been much less affected by the vicissitudes of security.[81] Its limitations stem rather from the competitiveness of Japan.[82]

In this hierarchical world of military, political, and economic power, the changing balance sheet for Thailand can be drawn up as follows: The United States had a substantial military "stake" in Thailand in the 1950s and 1960s, which diminished sharply after the mid-1970s. In terms of foreign capital and trade, American influence on the economy was ascendent (replacing that of the British) in the immediate postwar years, giving way to Japanese economic superiority (but without a corresponding military capacity) beginning in the 1960s with Japan's role increasing in the early 1970s. However the political instability in Thailand during the mid-1970s, combined with the regional uncertainty after the communist victories in Indochina, have slowed the pace of American and especially Japanese economic penetration.

To conclude, even if U.S. involvement in Thailand never reached the intensity of the intervention in Vietnam, nevertheless it has had significant consequences for Thai society. The material effects (economic and military aid, logistical expenditure related to the Vietnam war), although substantial, are of limited duration. But the psychological effects, inculcating technocratic attitudes

---

81. According to the American Chamber of Commerce in Thailand, "American investments have gone to support a wide range of enterprises. These include manufacturing to local assembly, and distribution of pharmaceuticals, automobiles, chemicals, construction materials and equipment, electronic components . . . financial services and consultancy services. One industry in which there is a heavy American investment is mining. . . . Several American companies have been granted concessions by the Thai government to explore and develop petroleum resources in the Gulf of Thailand": American Chamber of Commerce in Thailand "Thai-American Trade Relations," *Handbook Directory 1978,* p. 42.

82. Thailand's most important trading partner is Japan, which for the past decade has provided more than a third of imports and has taken around a quarter of exports. Next in rank comes the United States, which provided an average of 15 percent of imports between 1965 and 1974 and purchased 12 percent of exports. The remaining trade partners have been mostly in the European Economic Community: Hazel Richter, "[Thai] Foreign Trade and the Balance of Payments" (Australian National University, seminar on aid to Thailand, Canberra, July 12–13, 1975), p. 6. Japan provides 40 percent of all foreign investment in Thailand, compared with America's 16 percent.

among the administrators and reinforcing cold-war attitudes among the military, remain important to the present day.

There are four main ways, then, in which Thailand has been affected by the United States:

1. By exposure to its technocratic attitudes and goals, particularly among the large numbers of students, teachers, and officials being trained or educated in the United States. The United States has provided foreign training experience to one in every four of more than 26,000 officials in the four highest classes of the civil service up to March 1974. In the top "special grade," two-thirds of officials under age 56 had foreign graduate degrees (mostly from the United States).[83]

2. By the *security* orientation of American aid efforts, even of ostensibly economic aid. "Except for a modest amount of technical assistance projects, most of which we are gradually phasing out, our assistance in Thailand is concentrated on counter insurgency activities: approximately 75 percent of our total effort is in this field," according to Robert H. Nooter, acting assistant to U.S. Agency for International Development for Asia.[84]

3. By the enormous sums expended by the American military machine in Thailand—on base construction, roads, supplies, rest and recreation facilities, hire of Thai labor, etc.—to promote the war in Indochina. From 1950 to 1975 the United States provided 13.5 billion *baht* in economic and technical cooperation aid, and 35.4 billion *baht* in defense and security aid to Thailand. The latter sum amounted to *more than half* of Thai government defense expenditures (63 billion *baht*) during the same period. U.S. base and logistic construction alone amounted to more than 9 billion *baht*.[85]

83. Stifel, "Technocrats and Modernization in Thailand"; and Likhit Dhiravegin, *Bureaucratic Elite*, pp. 110–111, 117, 123.

84. Quoted in "G.N.P.," *Bangkok Magazine*, Feb. 9, 1971. (See also Chapter 7.)

85. *Business in Thailand*, September 1975. Of the total official flow from the U.S. during the decade 1965–75—more than $2 billion—it is estimated that two-fifths went into consumption, three-fifths into investment in agriculture and industry: "Thailand's Balance of Payments," *Business in Thailand*, February 1976. The sum of $2 billion is equivalent to Thailand's total official foreign reserves: Richard Nations, *Far Eastern Economic Review*, Feb. 4, 1977. For details of U.S. military and economic aid to Thailand, see also W. Scott Thompson, *Unequal Partners: Philippines and Thai Relations with the United States, 1965–75* (Lexington, Mass.: Lexington Books, 1975), pp. 16–17, tables 1–3. (See also Chapter 6 below.)

4. As noted above, by the increasing integration (during two decades) of U.S. and Thai military attitudes, institutions, and personnel, both on a formal and informal (patron-client) basis. As many as 14,000 Thai military personnel were trained under the U.S. Military Assistance Program. As a Thai student of foreign policy points out, "association with a super military power like the United States had added prestige and security to the military regime, whose mode of existence was entirely modelled upon the American." Further, "the concepts of the Cold War—containment, confrontation, monolithic communism, etc.—are still very much in the thinking of military leaders committed to the defense of Thailand." As late as 1976 the then Thai Army commander-in-chief [later deputy prime minister] "openly stated that the Thai military would be helpless without continued American military assistance."[86]

However, looked at from the Thai rather than the international perspective, *indigenous* factors are at least as important in their impact on both economic development and security-politics. To take the latter first, the two decades of American military buildup in Southeast Asia had the effect of bolstering the power and privileges of the Thai military, thus rendering it less inclined to make any concessions to "extrabureaucratic" forces in Thailand or even to external pressures from an ally deemed contrary to its interests.

As for the major economic boom of the 1960s and early 1970s, this, as we have seen, was chiefly the result of peasant initiative, cultivation of upland crops, new marketing systems, the American-aided expansion of communications and transport, the spread of the commercial banking network, and Chinese enterprise and capital.[87] Certainly the development of manufacturing in Thai-

---

86. Sarasin Viraphol, *Directions in Thai Foreign Policy* (Singapore: Institute of Southeast Asian Studies, occasional paper no. 40, 1976), pp. 12, 51. See also *Business in Thailand,* September 1975. Thai military leaders had a strong material interest in a continuing American military presence in Thailand because of the hardware they received, as well as the contracts for transport and supply of equipment to companies on which they were represented: Denzil Peiris, *Far Eastern Economic Review,* Feb. 14, 1975.

87. See Silcock, *Economic Development of Thai Agriculture,* pp. 40, 122, 125, 127–130, 170-172, 196.

land has often been undertaken in conjunction with foreign capital: notably Japanese, also American, Taiwanese, West European, etc. But indigenous investment in Thai industry is far greater than all foreign investment combined. In officially promoted investment alone, Thai capital amounted to more than 70 percent of the total up to September 1976: Japan's, 11 percent; and the United States', 4.5 percent.[88] This is not intended to belittle the significance of "joint ventures" and the role of multinationals in stabilizing the system and in subsidizing Thai generals, bureaucrats, and politicians, but merely to put the role of U.S. capital into perspective.

The impact of Japan, by contrast, raises more specifically economic issues, notably Thailand's trading dependence on Japan, the problem of technology transfer to Thai industries,[89] and the multifarious—and nefarious—roles of the multinationals.

Dependence upon Japan provides constraints as well as opportunities. The constraints result chiefly from the enormous economic asymmetry of the two countries. "Thailand's dependence on Japan for its export market reached 25.5 percent and for imports, 31.2 percent, whereas Thai exports accounted for only 1.2 percent of Japan's total imports, and Thai imports for 1.7 percent of Japan's total exports."[90] Further, Japanese trading companies with branches in Thailand account for more than half of Thai exports and nearly two-thirds of Thai imports.[91]

Japan is now the largest foreign-aid donor to Thailand and has the largest foreign investment (nearly 40 percent of all foreign

---

88. Ito Teichi, *Ajia Keizai*, August 1977: quoted by Randy Stross, "The Junta Pursues Foreign Capital," *Southeast Asia Chronicle*, January–February 1978.

89. See Mingsarn Santikarn, "Technology Transfer: A Case Study" (about the Thai textile industry), Ph.D. thesis, Australian National University, October 1977, esp. pp. 20–30 and concluding chapter. On the larger problem of foreign investment, Ammar Siamwalla criticizes Thai government policy as being "mainly one of uncritical acceptance," without any clear criteria of Thai needs, foreign motivation, or costs and benefits. Very few of the promoted industries survive without tariff protection, apart from some major exceptions, such as textiles, hotels, cement, and glass: "Stability, Growth and Distribution," p. 38. See also n. 93, below.

90. Atsuko Chiba, *Far Eastern Economic Review*, Oct. 17, 1975.

91. Hikoji Katano and Phitaya Smutraklin, *The Role of Japanese Trading Companies in the External Trade of Thailand* (Bangkok: The Economic Cooperation Center for the Asian and Pacific Region, 1976), p. 34, quoted by Warin Wonghanchao and Carl A. Trocki, "Japanese Policy in Thailand: The Harmony of Business and Government," paper for Canadian Society for Asian Studies, Guelph, Ontario, May 1978, p. 7.

capital investment in Thailand compared to less than 16 percent for the United States).[92] Even the so-called joint ventures, in which Japanese firms own on average just under half the share capital, depend on Japan for their supply of raw materials, equipment, finance, and marketing. As one recent investigator points out:

The assignment to the Japanese side [of the joint venture] of key functions, such as the import of raw materials and sale of the product in export markets, is particularly important because many of the Japan-based MNCs [multinational corporations] find that it is these transactions, rather than the overall profitability of the joint venture, that provide the principal reward. Because the Japanese trading companies . . . are involved in such diverse activities, it is normal for these transactions to take place entirely within the parent company's empire.[93]

A Thai economist points out that Japanese investment in Thailand is in four main fields: vehicles and spare parts; textiles and fiber products; chemicals and products; and glassware (in that order). About half the textile machinery in Thailand is imported from Japan, as is about one-third of raw materials and intermediate outputs. In the 28 largest textile firms there are roughly equal numbers of Japanese and Thai directors, managers, and deputy managers. The author emphasizes the growing feeling among educated Thais, however, that foreign investment is not making a positive contribution to industrialization and to overall economic development. Foreign investment, over a decade, has had very little impact on overall productivity. Foreigners are reluctant to train Thais for important technical or managerial posts. Above all, the industries favored by foreign investors are, by and large, capital-intensive and urban-based and cater mainly to urban markets: the result is an increase in the disparities between rich and poor, rural and urban.[94]

92. Table in Ito Teichi, *Ajia Keizai*, reproduced by Stross in "The Junta Pursues." For the attempt by Sino-Thai trading companies to counter Japanese "hegemony," see Ho Kwon Ping, "Bangkok looks for export magic," *Far Eastern Economic Review*, Nov. 9, 1979.

93. Franklin B. Weinstein, "Multinational Corporations and the Third World: The Case of Japan and Southeast Asia," *International Organization*, Summer 1976, pp. 390–391.

94. Sura Sanittanont, "The Role of Japanese Investment in Thailand," in Vichitvong na Pombhejra, ed., *Readings in Thailand's Political Economy* (Bangkok: Bangkok Printing Enterprise, 1978), pp. 254–258.

Local partners, who are usually Chinese businessmen but also include Thai politicians and generals, fail to exercise a significant managerial role in joint ventures. As a leading representative of a major Japanese trading company in Bangkok candidly explained, joint ventures are so dependent on Japanese assistance in procuring raw materials, equipment, spare parts, financing, and marketing services that local owners are in no position to disregard Japanese advice, unless they are prepared to sabotage the entire venture.[95]

The constraints on Thailand in its economic relationship with Japan are *generalized* throughout the country. For instance, when prices are largely determined by Japanese interests—as in the sale of corn, sugar, and tapioca to Japan—both the Thai government (by receiving less in revenue) and Thai farmers stand to lose. Conversely, the opportunities of the relationship accrue to *individuals:* to directors of the local business monopolies associated with the Japanese (for example, eight Thai companies account for three-quarters of corn exports, while ten companies control two-thirds of tapioca exports);[96] to the owners of large corn and tapioca plantations (who at least have a ready market for their crops); and to the bureaucrats and politicians who receive payoffs for smoothing the path of business.[97]

Thus popular protests against Japanese economic "domination"—such as the student-led boycott of Japanese goods in 1972 and the demonstrations against the visit of Prime Minister Tanaka in 1974—indicate something more than *nationalistic* resentment of Japan's conspicuous economic presence and anger at the hard bargains driven by its powerful corporations.[98] They also

95. As Weinstein explains, "The top-level executives of most joint ventures on the local side are men who have numerous business interests—some of them occupy key positions in 10 or 20 companies.... Their chief interest is that the company run smoothly so as to maximise their profits" ("Multinational Corporations," p. 395).

96. Warin and Trocki, "Japanese Policy in Thailand," pp. 7–8.

97. "The Chinese business partners, in particular, are under great pressure to pay off those with power. [Thus they act as intermediaries between the domestic power elite and foreign interests.] These relationships [with the military] give them security and access to those officials whose approval is needed if business activities are to proceed; in exchange the Chinese help meet the financial needs of their military associates": Weinstein, "Multinational Corporations," pp. 398–399. Weinstein is referring to Indonesia, but his comments apply no less to Thailand.

98. All but two of the top ten general trading houses in Thailand are foreign-owned: three Japanese, two British, one Swiss, one German, and one Danish. Mitsubishi, with sales of $152 million, nearly twice that of its nearest rival, heads the list.

signify *populist* resentment of the "Japan business–Thai elite" connection, which permits this exploitation to take place (even if, for public consumption, spokesmen for the elite sometimes join in the criticism); it is members of the elite who benefit from this connection.[99]

## Conclusion

Modernization in Thailand has taken the form of uneven rural development, on the one hand, and business-bureaucratic partnership on the other, both within an international orbit of powerful strategic and market forces. The political consequences of this form of modernization, contrary to the democratic-pluralist conceptions of Western development theorists,[100] are:

(*a*) Increasing divergence (instead of integration) of the powerful, wealthy, educated Bangkok elite and the rural (and urban) masses.

(*b*) Prevention (and not promotion) of autonomous political parties because of the mutually advantageous association of Thai bureaucrats with Chinese businessmen which dominates the political process.

(*c*) Reinforcement (and not "neutralization") of the bureaucratic state and its business partnerships. Directly contributing to these consequences are more than two decades of American strategic interests in Thai stability and the continuing Japanese (and U.S.) economic interests in profitability.

---

The other two Japanese companies are Mitsui and C. Itoh. Teijin (textiles), Toyota, and Tripetch Isuzu are among the top ten industrial companies in Thailand: Orion Consultants, Ltd., *The Largest Companies in Thailand:* quoted by *Asiaweek* report, Dec. 9, 1977.

99. As Warin and Trocki point out: "The mobilisation of Japanese capital to bolster reactionary politicians was all too apparent during the brief period of parliamentary democracy in Thailand. This support derived from the extremely close links between Teijin and the Chart Thai (Thai National Party), which was led by Major-General Pramarn Adireksan. The largest Japanese investment is in textiles and the largest Thai-Japanese joint venture in this industry is the Teijin-Pramarn group. . . . Chart Thai was a major force in both the Kukrit and Seni Pramot coalition governments [1975–76]": "Japanese Policy in Thailand," pp. 14–15. (See also Chapter 5 below.)

100. For a classic statement of this point of view see James S. Coleman, "Conclusion: The Political Systems of the Developing Areas," and Gabriel A. Almond, "Introduction: A Functional Approach to Comparative Politics," in Almond and Coleman, eds., *The Politics of the Development Areas* (Princeton, N.J.: Princeton University Press, 1960).

The growing divergence between the concentrated power of a small urban elite, looking always to Bangkok for the promotion of careers and material advantages, and the large, dispersed, unorganized rural majority, has resulted in an ever-widening economic gap, as we have seen, and, no less important, a psychological distance between the two. For the urban elite, absorbed in the affairs of the metropolis, have lost contact with the villagers, fail to understand (or misconceive) their problems, and, while paying lip service to rural values—"the farmers are the backbone of the nation"—actually feel contempt for the poor, inferior, remote, "backward" peasants.[101]

These differences between urban elite and rural mass society could be reconciled, at an earlier period, by the assurance of some autonomy for the latter within a materially satisfactory environment. For the rural majority of the Thai people, such autonomy was in practice assured by the owner-cultivator system of land tenure, which emerged in the nineteenth century and still largely prevails, though it is coming to an end. During this period the Thai peasant, compared with his counterpart in countries like Indonesia or Vietnam, was relatively free both from severe material constraints and from intolerable official exactions.

The present situation is very different. Demographic, economic, and political-administrative pressures on Thai peasants (and the new urban strata) have greatly increased the gap between traditional values and social reality; the result is the breakup of the consensus that has hitherto obtained. Conflicting valuations, among more and more people, are no longer reconcilable: people are being forced to choose between justice and order. The result is growing rural unrest, armed struggle in certain areas, and urban discontent. The trend is from consensus to polarization—but the process is not complete, nor is it irreversible.

Another political consequence of modernization is the reinforcement of the bureaucratic state. This has been achieved partly through technocratic improvement and expansion of administrative capacities and partly through access of bureaucratic leaders to new sources of wealth (from business partnerships and from

101. Phaitoon Khruekaew, himself a former community development official, strongly makes this point: *Laksana sangkom thai* [Nature of Thai Society] (Bangkok: Thong Thai, 1970), p. 208.

abroad). The effect has been to cut out or diminish the need to raise funds by democratic means—for example, through progressive taxation, by the consent of the electorate, and so forth. Further, the lack (until recently) of a Thai business class has prevented the formation of an economically powerful force countervailing the bureaucracy. Indeed, the present generation of Thai business entrepreneurs, whether from semiofficial or state enterprises or from private industry (like General Pramarn), are closely associated with, and not independent of, the bureaucratic polity.

In the absence of an indigenous commercial and industrial bourgeoisie, as a French scholar points out, any impulse toward democracy could come about only through the efforts of civilian and military officials—"the only national bourgeoisie known to Thai society." But the aim of this small, politically conscious fraction of the population, rather than limiting state power (as in the classical economic liberalism of the West), was to take over state power altogether. As a result, "public life consists of clique struggles for official positions and the indirect advantages these offered."[102]

The fact that there is no countervailing indigenous bourgeoisie in Thailand, and that the Chinese, for all their economic power, cannot dominate the polity but have had to reach an accommodation with it, confirms Max Weber's view of the "patrimonial" state. The introduction of a money economy, he points out, rather than weakening bureaucratic traditionalism, in effect strengthened it. "This was because the money economy, associated with prebends [an office-holder's prerogative to receive yields from state property or other public income] created special profit opportunities for the dominant stratum." It "rendered paramount their own interest," Weber goes on, "in preserving those economic conditions so decisive for their own profit."[103]

Such is the socioeconomic context in which the Thai political process operates.

---

102. Pierre Fistié, *L'évolution de la Thailande contemporaine* (Paris: Armand Colin, 1967), pp. 256–257.

103. Max Weber, "The Feudal and Prebendal State," *The Religion of China* (New York: Macmillan, 1951), p. 61. Weber is discussing "patrimonial state organizations in the Orient" where with every advance of the money economy "we observe the concomitant and increasing prebendalization of state income": ibid.

# 3 | Course of Events

It is important at this stage to set out a chronological framework so that the political, social, and economic changes discussed in Chapters 1 and 2, starting with the assumption of power by the bureaucratic elite and followed by the formation of a bureacratic-business partnership, can be related to the successive phases of political change, beginning with the consolidation of military rule and ending with the checkered attempts to inaugurate democracy. The continuity of bureaucratic authority, in spite of the challenge of political parties, interest groups, and incipient mass movements, is evident from this survey of events. This chapter thus sets the scene for an analysis of the structure of the bureaucracy in its social context in Chapter 4, while Chapter 5 focuses on the role of the "new social forces" outside the bureaucracy, especially during and after the democratic period (1973 to 1976).

## Emergence of Military Dominance
### 1932–33

There were four main reasons for the 1932 coup that ended the system of absolute monarchy: the monopoly of power by the king and royal princes; the frustration of young, able, and ambitious commoners—especially those educated in England and France, and inspired with ideas of democracy and progress; the tolerant and indecisive character of King Prajadhipok (Rama VII); and the king's program of economizing on expenditure to balance the budget after the profligate reign of his predecessor, King Vajiravudh—by reducing salaries and dismissing military and civilian officials. The coup was "promoted" chiefly by Colonel Phahon, the highest ranking military commoner; Pridi Phanomyong, a brilliant French-educated student, lawyer, and intellectual; and the

subsequently important Major Phibun Songkram.[1] Their resentment at this program of austerity was aggravated by the great international slump of the early 1930s, which drastically lowered the
export price of rice and rubber, cutting down incomes and enlarg-
ing debts.[2]

The king, bowing to the promoters' ultimatum, accepted a restricted role. He abdicated in 1935. The coup leaders prepared a
constitution suggesting a three-stage approach to democracy: (1)
the coup group (known as the "People's Party") in control of government; (2) the People's Assembly, part-elected, part-appointed;
(3) direct election to the Assembly whenever more than half the
population had completed four years of primary education—but in
any case not later than ten years' time.[3] Pridi himself proposed an
"Economic Plan" inspired partly by the French and partly by the
Russian Revolution in reaction to the widespread distress caused by
the great slump. The plan envisioned nationalization of all farm
land, with farmers working for the government as paid employees
and receiving pensions. The government would also take over the
production and sale of rice, thus eliminating middlemen.[4] The
plan was condemned both by the royalist prime minister (Phya
Manopakorn) and by conservatives in the coup group as "com-

1. Each was also known by his "title" name: Phya Phahon; Luang Pradit Man-
udharm (Pridi); and Luang Phibun. Phahon and two other colonels (Phya Song and
Phya Riddhi) actually signed the ultimatum to the king. For details, see Thawatt
Mokorapong, "The Causes of the Revolution," in Clark D. Neher, ed., *Modern Thai
Politics: From Village to Nation* (Cambridge, Mass.: Schenkman, 1976), reprinted
from Thawatt, *History of the Thai Revolution* (Bangkok: Chalermnit, 1972); and Thak
Chaloemtiarana, ed., *Thai Politics: Extracts and Documents 1932 –1957* (Bangkok: Social
Science Association of Thailand, 1978), the first volume of a series.

2. A declaration by the coup promoters stated: "The king was above the law even
as his predecessors had been. His relatives and friends, even when without ability,
were given the highest government positions.... The king elevated the royal class
and permitted them to oppress the common people.... This country belongs to the
people. Where does the money come from that royalty uses? It comes from the
people.... Farmers must abandon their fields because they receive inadequate
profit. Students graduate from school and find no employment. Soldiers are dismissed from service and must starve. This is the work of a government above the
law": quoted in Kenneth P. Landon, *Thailand in Transition* (University of Chicago
Press, 1939), pp. 11–12.

3. Walter F. Vella, *The Impact of the West on Government in Thailand* (Berkeley:
University of California Press, 1955), p. 371.

4. Text of the plan is in Landon, *Thailand in Transition,* app.; see also the analysis
by Pierre Fistié, *Sous-développement et utopie au Siam* (Paris: Mouton, 1969).

munistic." Pridi went into voluntary exile; Phya Manopakorn sought to turn the dispute to his advantage by restoring royal authority, but failed; and Army Commander-in-Chief Phahon, balancing between reformers and conservatives, civilians and military, took over as prime minister. A royalist revolt was then decisively suppressed by forces under Phibun.

### 1934–38

This was a period of stabilization. Pridi, cleared of communism, became in succession minister of the interior, foreign minister (negotiating the end of foreign extraterritorial concessions imposed in the nineteenth century), and finance minister. Under Phahon, the ban on communism was reaffirmed, the Press Act (1934) legalized censorship, and the formation of political parties was disallowed.[5] However, expenditure on education quadrupled in four years. Despite the opposition of elected assemblymen claiming funds for economic improvements, the military budget doubled in the same period. (In 1937 twice as much was spent on the military as on education.) In 1937, 53 of the 78 appointed members of the Assembly were military, in contrast to only 8 of the 78 elected members.[6]

### 1938–44

Phibun, deputy commander-in-chief, succeeded Phahon both as prime minister and commander-in-chief. By 1939, Phibun had exiled or dispossessed the old guard military commanders of the 1932 revolution, leaving himself supreme.[7] As "leader" (a title borrowed in obvious imitation of authoritarian states) he fostered the military image: "New times have come to Thailand. The country has been placarded with the picture of a soldier shaking his fist in the air." The message read: the kingdom is home, and the military is the fence that protects the home.[8] Phibun especially admired

5. Vella, *Impact of the West*, p. 378; Landon, *Thailand in Transition*, pp. 58–60.
6. Landon, *Thailand in Transition*, pp. 65–67.
7. Vichai Suvannarat, "Revolution, Coup and Rebellion after the Change in Government of 1932" (in Thai), in Chaianan Samudavanija et al., *Sat kanmuang* [Political animal] (Bangkok: Thai Watana, 1971), p. 99.
8. Landon, *Thailand in Transition*, p. 66. Phibun, in addition to being prime minister and army commander-in-chief, held at various times the portfolios of defense, interior, foreign affairs, and education. He had complete control of mass

Japan, a formerly backward Asian country that defeated a European power (Russia in 1905), modernized itself by its own efforts, maintained its cultural traditions, exulted in nationalism, and followed the path of military expansionism. When the shadow of that expansionism fell across Southeast Asia in 1941, Phibun offered no resistance. Allied with Japan, he declared war against the West and seized "historically" Thai territory in Cambodia, Laos, Burma, and Malaya. Internally, he prolonged the status of government-appointed assemblymen for a further ten years. But while Phibun was accommodating to Japanese power, his great civilian rival Pridi (then regent) was organizing a secret "Free Thai" resistance movement. When the fortunes of war changed, and allied victory was inevitable, Phibun fell.

*Constitutional Interlude*
1945–47

Under Pridi's dominance came the emergence of party politics, a fully elected Assembly, the restitution of seized territories, and a liberal foreign policy (support for anticolonial independence movements). But Pridi paid for the economic deterioration caused by wartime inflation, shortage of goods, destruction of communications, and their postwar consequences—allied-enforced rice reparations, the growth of smuggling (owing to the difference between government and market prices), and the rise of corruption. The latter was the ominous result of economic difficulties (low official salaries were unable to keep pace with rising prices), the psychological shock of war upsetting traditional values, and the opportunities for gain in the unsettled postwar years. Against this disturbed background, political parties were promoted as vehicles for personal patronage, not as the institutionalized expression of social forces or political issues. The Free Thais, followers of Pridi, formed one major group. Royalists, now permitted to take part in politics,

---

communications: "Newspapers were also used to build up public admiration and faith in 'the leader.'" On his determination to build up the national character and inculcate "civilized" habits, see Thamsook Numnonda, "When Thailand followed the Leader," *Warasan Thammasat*, June–September 1976; on the influence of Luang Vichit Vadhakarn, an important cultural figure, see Kobkua Suwanthat-Pian, "Nationalist Historiography." Both are translated in Likhit Dhiravegin, ed., *Social Science Review*, 1977.

rallied to the aristocratic publicist Kukrit Pramot, who later joined the constitutionally oriented but politically conservative Khuang Aphaiwong's Democrat Party.[9] The military, humiliated by their association with the losing side, were for a time subdued. Their opportunity came with the violent death of Prajadhipok's successor, King Ananda—never satisfactorily explained—and with the bitter opposition to Pridi, dividing the civilian politicians, notably expressed by the Democrats.

*Military-Police Power and Rivalry*

1947–50

Malcontent officers, excluded by Pridi from political influence and thus from opportunities for enrichment, in November 1947 staged a successful coup.[10] Their leader was General Phin Chunhawan, with the support of the First (Bangkok) Army, the key strategic unit, acting on behalf of Field Marshal Phibun. The military, however, afraid of adverse international reaction (Phibun had barely escaped punishment as a war criminal), at first nominated Pridi's rival, Khuang, as prime minister. The latter formed an unusually well-qualified Thai government, because of its members' integrity, ability, education, and experience. Despite this, and the fact that the Democrats had won an electoral majority, Khuang's government succumbed to an army ultimatum by Phibun only a few months later.

According to Phibun's revealing statement, "public opinion [sic] wanted the change and as it could not be done by constitutional means, the former government having a majority in parliament, the army decided unanimously to get rid of it."[11] The traditionalist reliance on authority, concerned with the possession of power rather than the legality of the means to achieve it, was later set out

9. Vichai, "Revolution, Coup and Rebellion," pp. 102–103. There are interesting accounts of this period in the "political memoirs" of Thawee Bunyaket, an independent-minded follower of Pridi, and *Momrajwong* Seni Pramot, prime minister briefly in 1945 and later leader of the Democrats: see Jayanta Kumar Ray, *Portraits of Thai Politics* (New Delhi: Orient Longman, 1972); also John Coast, *Some Aspects of Siamese Politics* (New York: Institute of Pacific Relations, 1953). *Momrajwong* is the title of a descendant of royalty: see Chapter 4, note 44.

10. Pierre Fistié, *L'évolution de la Thailande contemporaine* (Paris: Armand Colin, 1967), p. 208.

11. Alexander MacDonald, *Bangkok Editor* (London: Macmillan, 1949), p. 175, quoted by Vella, *Impact of the West*, p. 390.

in a high court ruling: "The government in power and [in] lawful control of a country may be either a government de jure or de facto. In any case it is a principle of law that no country can be left without a government at any time. . . . To hold that [a country after a coup] could never be lawfully governed would be a dangerous legalism."[12]

Beside the general predisposition in favor of established authority there were important practical reasons, internal and external, for the Phibun government's success in consolidating its hold. First, this consolidation took place against a background of communist insurrections in Malaya, Burma, India, and Indonesia in 1948, the sharpening struggle in the Philippines and Indochina, and the final disintegration of the Kuomintang in 1949, resulting in the communist victory in China. These portentous events, closely following the rupture in 1947 between America and the Soviet Union, induced the Western allies to forget Phibun's past and welcome him to the anticommunist fold. Internally, Phibun benefited from the remarkable recovery of the Thai economy—by 1951 the *baht* was one of the strongest currencies in the world[13]—as well as from the disarray of his opponents. The failure of an attempted coup by Pridi in February 1949—Pridi himself went into exile in China—not only discredited Pridi's cause, but provided a further pretext for military and police repression.[14]

## 1951–57

A final spasm of revolt, by the Navy, was stamped out in March 1951. The victors, General Sarit Thanarat, commander of the First Army, and Police-General Phao Sriyanon, an aide to Phibun since

12. The Court of Criminal Causes, *Judgment in the Regicide Case,* September 1951, quoted by Vella, *Impact of the West,* pp. 392–393.

13. There was a favorable balance of trade by 1948–50, with continuing heavy world demand for Thai exports: James C. Ingram, *Economic Change in Thailand 1850–1970* (Stanford, Calif.: Stanford University Press, 1971), pp. 167–169.

14. The Free Thai movement was virtually eliminated as a power contender. Many of its members were arrested, and four former ministers were murdered. Phibun, Phin, and Phao also removed their rivals among the military, including Luang Kat, a leading participant in the 1947 coup: Vichai, "Revolution, Coup and Rebellion," pp. 105–111. See also Thak Chaloemtiarana, "The Sarit Regime, 1957–1963: The Formative Years of Modern Thai Politics," Ph.D. Thesis, Cornell University, 1974, pp. 39–65. On the role of the police, then and later, see Thomas Lobe, *United States National Security Policy and Aid to the Thailand Police* (University of Denver Monograph Series in World Affairs, 1977).

the 1930s, son-in-law of Field Marshal Phin, and director-general of police, represented the military-police power. The United States, which had signed a mutual security treaty with Thailand in 1950, stepped up aid to both services: the U.S. rationale was that Southeast Asia was "vital" to "free world" security. The army and police, frustrated by the largely verbal activities of the elected deputies, then staged a "silent coup" (November 1951): the 1949 constitution was abolished, parliament dissolved, and a half-nominated Assembly (as in 1932) restored.

The regime was marked by economic nationalism (the launching of "Thai enterprises," including the ill-fated National Economic Development Corporation); a campaign of harassment of Chinese combined with selective collusion (the pragmatic "partnership" between the Thai military-bureaucratic elite and wealthy Chinese businessmen described in the previous chapter); and an anticommunist drive which also involved crippling restrictions on Chinese schools and the virtual ending of Chinese immigration. The anticommunist law of 1952—directed in the broadest terms against "those who incite, advise, coerce others to act as communists or propagate communism, associate or rally, or are accomplices of communists, or prepare to do something communistic . . ."[15]— offered ample scope for police repression, exploitation, and extortion.

However, rivalry between Sarit's military clique and Phao's police clique, both armed to the teeth by Washington—Thailand had become a founding member of SEATO in 1954—became ever more acute. Sarit was now commander-in-chief of the army and deputy defense minister, his follower Thanom Kittikachorn was commander of the First Army, and Praphat Charusathien was the deputy commander. Sarit was profitably established on sixteen "major boards" of financial, commercial, or industrial enterprises (where three or more cabinet members are directors), Praphat on eleven, and Thanom on eight. Phao was on sixteen "major boards." The Bank of Asia and the Military Bank were dominated by Sarit men; the Farmers Bank and Bank of Ayuthaya by Phao; the important Bangkok Bank was shared between them.[16]

15. Quoted by G. William Skinner, *Chinese Society in Thailand: An Analytical History* (Cornell University Press, 1957), p. 335.
16. Fred Riggs, *Thailand: The Modernization of a Bureaucratic Polity* (Honolulu: East-West Center Press, 1966), p. 256 ff., 298–299.

At this stage Prime Minister Phibun, who had long lost direct control of the armed forces, tried to reassert himself. In the more relaxed international climate of the Bandung era (1955, peaceful coexistence) Phibun extended feelers toward Peking. Equally impressed by his experience during a world tour of public opinion in the Western democracies, he sought to strengthen his own internal position. Public meetings were permitted (in the Thai "Hyde Park"), political parties sanctioned, and elections promised. However, the "government party," benefiting from the resources, presence, and prestige of the state machine, was organized by none other than Police Director-General Phao. The Democrats reappeared in their customary opposition role. And various parties of the center-left rallied around the banner of a neutral foreign policy (opposing SEATO), a planned economy, and administrative decentralization.[17] This time the government's blatant rigging of the elections of February 1957—Phao, besides falsifying ballots and intimidating electors, spent ten times the amount spent by any other party[18]—went too far. Sarit capitalized on the disgust expressed by students and others, resigned with Thanom and Praphat from the government (followed by most of the appointed assemblymen), and then dispatched Phibun and Phao into exile.

*Sarit Era*
1958–63

After an uneasy interlude, at first under a caretaker prime minister, SEATO Secretary-General Pote Sarasin, and then under Thanom, Sarit staged his second coup: the 1952 constitution was abrogated, the assembly dissolved, parties banned, trade unions forbidden, the press controlled, "leftists" arrested, and the country ruled by decree (the notorious article 17) under martial law.[19] Sarit

17. Fistié, *L'évolution de la Thailande,* pp. 237–40.
18. J. L. S. Girling, "Parties of Thailand," in Haruhiro Fukui, ed., *Political Parties of Asia and the Pacific* (Westport, Conn.: Greenwood Press, forthcoming). See also David A. Wilson, *Politics in Thailand* (Ithaca, N.Y.: Cornell University Press, 1966), p. 31.
19. According to article 17 of the "interim" constitution, "whenever the Prime Minister deems appropriate for the purpose of repressing or suppressing actions whether of internal or external origin which jeopardise the national security of the Throne or subvert or threaten law and order, the Prime Minister, by resolution of the Council of Ministers [Cabinet], is empowered to issue orders to take steps accordingly. Such orders or steps shall be considered legal": quoted in D. Insor, *Thailand: A Political, Social and Economic Analysis* (London: Allen & Unwin, 1963),

claimed that "evils and corrupt practices had multiplied [during the more liberal "interlude"]. Subversion of the government was the order of the day. . . . The National Assembly, the press, and certain labor circles had also succumbed [to subversion]." The underlying rationale for Sarit's coup was, however, provided by Thanat Khoman, foreign minister for the next decade, in these words: "If we look back at our national history, we can see that this country works better and prospers under an authority around which all elements of the nation can rally. On the contrary, the dark pages of our history show that whenever such an authority is lacking and dispersal elements had their play, the nation was plunged into one disaster after another."[20]

The Sarit era was characterized by political authoritarianism, economic development, massive corruption (by the very man who led the drive against corruption), and external alarms. There was no letup in military-enforced controls: Sarit, prime minister, army commander-in-chief, supreme commander of the armed forces, minister of national development, also took charge of the police.[21] On the other hand, Sarit encouraged King Bhumibol Adulyadej, who had been restricted in his appearances by previous regimes, to tour the provinces, eliciting reverence and respect from up-country people.

Sarit epitomized the drive for national development, recruiting Western-educated technocrats, authorizing planning (Budget Bureau, Board of Investment, five-year economic plan), and enforcing decisions. He ruthlessly cut through red tape and bureaucratic compromise. He also cut corners in building up a vast empire of personal wealth: "Sarit dominated the Thai economy for five years. His character was a combination of the ruthless gangster, the traditional lavish oriental despot, and the shrewd judge of expertise. He built up immense private interests for himself in banking, real estate, construction contracting and other sectors. He placed

p. 99. For an excellent analysis of the Sarit regime, see Thak Chaloemtiarana, *Thailand: The Politics of Despotic Paternalism* (Bangkok: Thammasat University Press for Social Science Association of Thailand and Thai Khadi Institute, 1979).

20. Quoted in ibid., p. 110. For Sarit's philosophy, and the implementation of his system, see Thak, "The Sarit Regime," chs. 4-6.

21. David Wilson, *The United States and the Future of Thailand* (New York: Praeger, 1970), p. 117.

his trusted friends in key positions to make money for him and held people's loyalty by both gratitude and fear."[22]

Sarit's foreign policy was dominated by security relations with the United States, centering on the struggle for power in Laos. He actively supported right-wing Lao personalities (notably General Phoumi Nosavan) in opposition both to neutralists (Prince Souvanna Phouma) and the Left (Pathet Lao). He urged Western intervention on behalf of the rightists, then reluctantly accepted Kennedy's switch to neutrality (1961–62). In return Washington announced a unilateral guarantee of Thai security, which was also construed to cover support against insurgency (Rusk-Thanat agreement, 1962).

## Military Succession: Cliques, Constitution, and Coup
### 1964–68

Sarit died in December 1963. His multiple power was divided among his followers: the faithful Thanom became prime minister, supreme commander, and minister of defense; Praphat became deputy prime minister, army commander-in-chief, and remained (since 1957) minister of the interior. Direct command of the army and of a powerful centralized bureaucracy are key positions. The Interior Ministry controls not only the entire provincial administration, through governors and district officers, but also the police department, labor department, social welfare, and (from 1966 to 1980) rural elementary education. Nevertheless, Praphat, although accumulating power and wealth (in the manner of Sarit), was content to remain nominally second to Thanom. The latter came to rely on more liberal-minded advisers, and in fact a constitution was promulgated in 1968, after ten years' delay, with elections to be held the following year. Meanwhile a Senate was appointed with a membership of 105 military (including 80 from the army), 12 police, and 47 civilians, nearly all of whom were senior members of the bureaucracy.[23]

22. T. H. Silcock, "Outline of Economic Development 1945–65," in Silcock, ed., *Thailand: Social and Economic Studies in Development* (Canberra: Australian National University Press, 1967), p. 21.

23. For a perceptive and detailed analysis, see David L. Morell, "Power and Parliament in Thailand: The Futile Challenge, 1968–1971," Ph.D. thesis, Princeton University, 1974.

The Thanom-Praphat government undoubtedly benefited from the economic boom of the 1960s, which resulted in a more than 7 percent annual increase in GNP during the 1961–66 plan and the spread of industrialization, banking, highways, irrigation and electric power, and crop diversification. But it also faced a worsening external situation. Acting in accord with the Americans, the Thai government signed a contingency agreement with the U.S. military in 1965 and then became fully committed—through the use of Thai airbases, counterinsurgency training, and volunteers—to American intervention in Laos and Vietnam.

### 1969–71

These were years of uncertainty. Internally, the "government party" (United Thai People's Party) in association with Praphat-oriented independents gained a majority in the 1969 elections.[24] But the Democrats, victorious in Bangkok, had done well, and the deputies in general, restive after a decade of exclusion from politics, were fractious and difficult to control. (The usual offer of material rewards for loyalty only stimulated their appetite for more).[25] Externally, too, a decade or more of security within the American orbit was transformed into a period of anxiety. America's turning away from military involvement in mainland Southeast Asia, foreshadowed by Johnson's acceptance of negotiations on Vietnam, the 1969 Nixon Doctrine, and phased withdrawal of troops left Thai leaders uneasy and perplexed. Even the overthrow of Thailand's adversary Sihanouk in 1970 created more problems, because of the spread of revolution in Cambodia, than it seemed to have solved.

Thanat looked to regionalism as a potential substitute for the waning American presence. (The Association of Southeast Asian Nations, ASEAN, was founded in 1967.) He also sought reinsurance with China ("legitimized" by Nixon himself in 1971–72), despite the suspicion of the military. But the Thai government was

24. Thanom, leader of the UTPP, had written to director-generals of government departments and heads of divisions: "I hope for your cooperation . . . to persuade friends, relatives and colleagues to vote strongly for the [government] party candidates": quoted in *Siam Rath,* Feb. 6, 1969: see J. L. S. Girling, "Thailand's New Course," *Pacific Affairs,* Fall 1969.

25. For this period, see esp. Morell, "Power and Parliament in Thailand," pts. 3 and 4.

still deeply involved in the Vietnam war and sent "volunteers" to fight in Laos.

Amidst grave doubts as to the "reliability" of the United States, aggravated by China's entry into the United Nations, and faced with resurgence of domestic criticism of widespread corruption, military dominance in government, oppressive police powers in the provinces, emerging trade difficulties, and economic hardships, as well as the spread of insurgency (the Communist Party of Thailand had launched its armed struggle in 1965), the Thai military leaders resorted to the customary "solution" to problems—the coup. The army seized power in November 1971 because, Thanom said, "the current world situation and the increasing threat to the nation's security required prompt action, which is not possible through due process of law under the present constitution." Once again, as in 1951 and 1958 (and setting a precedent for 1976), the constitution was abrogated, the Assembly dispersed, political parties banned, and martial law reimposed.

*Demonstrations, Democracy, and Reaction*[26]
  1971–73

There was a ground swell of opposition to a regime whose leaders, after a decade of unchallenged power, had become ever more arbitrary, corrupt, incompetent, and complacent. The rising demand for genuine consitutional rule embraced all strata of urban society, from the king to the professionals, teachers, students, shopkeepers, and workers. Students forming a new nationwide network (National Student Center of Thailand) were the inspirational and organizing force. The authority of the regime was gravely compromised by leadership feuds and recurrent scandals, by its bungling of rice supplies for the cities, and by the onset of the world recession accompanied by steeply rising prices. In October 1973, when the Thanom-Praphat reaction to the widely supported demand for a constitution took the form not of conciliation but of repression, including firing on unarmed demonstrators, the king dissociated himself from the violence, and the army command (now under General Krit Sivara) refused to obey Praphat's

26. The 1970s are discussed in greater detail in Chapter 5. Only the salient points are noted here.

orders. The king named a new government, and Thanom and Praphat went into exile.

## 1974-76

There were important constitutional developments during this period. The Sanya caretaker government proposed labor and land reform legislation; elections in January 1975 resulted in Kukrit heading a coalition of parties, from the military-oriented extreme right to the business-professional center; and further elections in April 1976 saw the Democrats on top (led by Seni Pramot) who formed a similar coalition. Also during this time oil prices quadrupled at a time of domestic recession (especially affecting textiles, construction, investment). Although the minimum wage was doubled, there was severe labor unrest (with strikes and lockouts), continuing student activism (advising labor unions, "going to the countryside," staging urban demonstrations), and the start of peasant organizations.

Major external events influenced Thailand at this time. Following the communist triumph in Vietnam, Kampuchea (Cambodia), and Laos, the United States, unable to defend its clients, settled for a "Pacific rim" strategy. Kukrit shifted to a policy of nonalignment, involving the planned withdrawal of U.S. forces from Thailand, the recognition of Peking, and improved relations with Vietnam and Kampuchea.

There was mounting fear in military and official circles, among businessmen and the wealthy elite, of internal "subversion"— supposedly undertaken by "communist" students, workers, and farmers—as well as external threats. This rightist reaction took the form of building up the *Nawaphon* movement, rallying around the patriotic theme of "Nation, Religion, King," mobilizing the royally sponsored "village scouts," vocational student gangs, and dema gogic media personalities—all orchestrated against the "left" democratic parties, liberal academics, critical journalists, socialists, intellectuals, labor unions, student groups). The rightist strategy was to provoke disorder and unrest among the left, which could justify military intervention to restore "order." Thus the return of the exiles, Praphat in August and Thanom in September 1976, was calcutaed to unleash student protests, which resulted in the climax of October 6: the military-police attack on Thammasat University, accompanied by an unprecedented outpouring of mob hatred and brutality, incited by the extreme right, followed the armed forces' coup.

### 1976–The Present

The top military coup leaders formed a "National Administrative Reform Council" that appointed the Thanin government and named an assembly: the previous constitution was abrogated, political parties banned, martial law declared, and rule by decree enforced (article 21 of the provisional constitution). There was repression of the left and harassment of the center in an atmosphere of obsessive anticommunism, all in the name of "national security." The general public remained apathetic, however, apparently acquiescing in authority and approving stability. As for the opposition, hundreds fled abroad, went underground, or rallied to the communist revolution (the socialist and communist parties agreed to cooperate in a broad united front): this is the first stage in what is likely to prove a long, drawn-out struggle.

Meanwhile, after a year of maneuvering by rival military leaders and cliques (with an attempted coup in March 1977), amidst worsening relations with Prime Minister Thanin and Interior Minister Samak, the military's patience was exhausted. General Kriangsak, supreme commander of the armed forces, the mastermind of the October 1976 coup, became prime minister, promising more relaxed internal and external policies, to be followed by elections.

Kriangsak eased press censorship, established better relations with labor unions, and gave amnesty to the student leaders arrested in October 1976. He outmaneuvered his factional rivals, both in drafting a new illiberal constitution and in his military and governmental appointments. Kriangsak had no need to "win" the April 1979 elections since he could at that time rely on the appointed Senate and a minority of elected members. (The revived parties of the democratic period were in a majority.)

But external prospects have become more alarming, after Vietnamese troops in 1979 eliminated the buffer of an independent Kampuchea. This action, however, combined with China's attack on Vietnam, also caused serious problems for the Thai communists. As for internal politics, a looming economic crisis came to a head with drastic price increases imposed by the

Kriangsak government early in 1980. Kriangsak, facing mounting criticism from parliament and public, resigned because he could no longer count on military support. His successor, Defense Minister and Army Commander-in-Chief Prem, a professional soldier, was obliged to rely on the major opposition parties, especially Kukrit's technocrats, to cope with the serious economic situation. Prem's coalition offers some possibility of moving to a more open political system.

# 4 | Political Structure

Four related themes form the subject matter of this chapter: military leadership, bureaucratic structure, authoritative values, and socioeconomic change.

As is evident from the previous chapters, power and prestige in Thailand have, for half a century, been located in the "bureaucratic polity"—the armed forces, police, and civil administration—rather than in political parties operating under parliamentary rules. Riggs states the relative importance of the two elements clearly: "The failure of formal political institutions to achieve control over the bureaucracy has not meant the elimination of "politics" and the achievement of an "administrative state." Rather, it has meant that the arena of politics, the focus of rivalry, and the struggle for power, wealth or other public values have moved within the bureaucracy itself."[1]

The sanction of "traditional" values, those of a hierarchical society, sustains the bureaucratic polity and is in turn sustained by it. For training in "proper" behavior—respect for elders, the educated, and persons of status and power—starts at an early age within the family, continues through the educational system, and is confirmed by the adult's contacts with officialdom. In an "authority culture" like this, the assumption of superiority underlying the confidence of the ruling elite has its necessary counterpart in the *acceptance* of inferiority by those of lower status and those who lack organized power.

---

1. Fred Riggs, *Thailand: The Modernization of a Bureaucratic Polity* (Honolulu: East-West Center Press, 1966), p. 197. For a critique of Riggs' concept see John L. S. Girling, *The Bureaucratic Polity in Modernising Societies: Similarities, Differences, and Prospects in the ASEAN Region* (Singapore: Institute of Southeast Asian Studies, forthcoming), esp. ch. 2.

Lack of power, above all, is connected with the weakness or absence of countervailing *extrabureaucratic* forces. Ranging from the highest status to the lowest, neither a constitutional monarchy, nor an ecclesiastical hierarchy, (subordinate to the administrative hierarchy), nor an independent judiciary, (excluded from essential legal activity by the exigencies of "security" via martial law), nor business enterprises (coexisting with, but also dependent on, the bureaucracy), nor political parties (operating under crippling restrictions and for limited periods), nor professional associations, student groups, labor unions, and peasant organizations—none of these, except during the early to mid-1970s, has possessed the power, or, in the case of high-status institutions, made use of their authority, to challenge the bureaucracy.

Such is the static, institutional structure of Thai politics. The dynamics of the system, however, are provided by the incessant rivalry within the elite—the struggles for power and wealth by ambitious leaders and their followers—in the context of socioeconomic change. Economic development has put more wealth (and has introduced new forms of acquiring it) at the disposal of the elite. But industrialization and urbanization, the massive expansion of university education, and the training (often abroad) of managers and technocrats have also created substantial and growing new social forces in Thailand. These consist basically of an urban middle class, ranging from executives to clerks and shopkeepers; the beginnings of an organized working class along with a marginal subproletariat of migrants from the countryside and casual or unorganized workers, especially in the informal sector; and an incipient, dispossessed, rural proletariat.

These extrabureaucratic forces are still, for the most part, in an ambiguous state. On the one hand, a number of their members, particularly those organized in associations or unions, find themselves politically dependent on the existing power structure. Many, at all levels, are still affected by traditional values (sanctioning their subordinate status). And even those who are upwardly mobile remain, at best, junior partners in powerful patronage circles. On the other hand, members of the new social strata are growing in numbers and potential importance—through their acquisition of specialized skills—as a result of economic expansion and occupational differentiation. Indeed the democratic years of 1973–76 represented their struggle for autonomy as a basis for political participation—a challenge to the established power structure that could not be tolerated.

These new social forces originated and grew under conditions of dependence, but as their numbers increase, they are striving to develop their autonomy. In the process, not only is there a divergence of interests between the new forces as a whole and the old established order, but there are also deepening fissures among the various elements of the new forces: between labor and employers, poor peasants and well-off farmers, and urban and rural society.

Thus along with these new forces in society comes a new set of complementary, but also conflicting, interests and values. The old attitudes of superiority and subordination, proper to a hierarchical society, are no longer seen to be just, reasonable, or even economically effective from the viewpoint of the young and enterprising, the socially aware, and the poor and dispossessed.

This new situation has meant the *beginning* of structural changes in four important areas:

1. Transformation of *business* from the old-style Chinese family "partnership" with leading bureaucrats to interest-group politics increasingly expressed through parliament.

2. In the *bureaucracy*, especially in economic affairs, a shift from emphasis on paternalism and hierarchy to "progress" along technocratic, rather than liberal, lines.

3. Tendencies in the *military* toward a more professional and, among some younger officers, a more populist outlook. Despite the basic conservatism of the hierarchy, these moves to professionalism suggest coexistence between the military and (right-wing) politicians, like that which already exists between military and technocrats.

4. Growth of *popular* awareness: that is, recognition that social conditions are caused by people and institutions and are not simply the working out of karmic laws. From this awareness, change becomes possible. Popular consciousness was brought to fruition during the democratic period, when opportunities abounded for action and expression among students, workers, and (for a time) farmers; it cannot be dispelled by subsequent events. Such awareness may facilitate a reformist, evolutionary political process; but if this is thwarted by vested interests associated with the traditional

power-structure, it may take a contrary course. If so, growing social and economic problems both in town and countryside, which will be critical in the long term, create prospects for revolutionary change, as opposed to change within the system.

The organization of this chapter corresponds to the changing pattern of Thai society. It provides an analysis of military leadership, bureaucratic structure, political culture, and extrabureaucratic forces. Such a cross-section analysis of Thai society, as has already been pointed out, is static, abstract, and ahistorical. It represents at best an "ideal type" or model of the characteristic features of Thai society, and its prevalent values, over the major part of this century. But the way in which these factors operate—for example, the way values affect behavior and, above all, the relationship among leadership, bureaucracy, values, and new social forces—cannot be understood from a structural analysis alone. A chronological study of political *performance*, revealing the simultaneous, complex relationship among political, economic, external, and other factors is also needed. Chapter 5 presents such a study.

*Military Leadership*
Leaders, Rivals, and Followers

Formerly in Thailand, as we have seen, the king, princes, and nobility (the latter comprising a semihereditary "bureaucratic elite") made up the leadership structure. Within the *sakdina* system, struggles for power (and access to wealth) occurred either when a strong, centralizing monarch sought to establish his authority over the provincial nobility (and neighboring princes and kings) or, under a young or weak king or one beset with troubles, when the reverse occurred. Of course, there were also periods of stability when a rough balance between king and nobles obtained. Similar alternating cycles of dominance and rivalry have occurred under the leadership of the modern bureaucratic elite.

Just as in the old days, the contemporary struggle for power (and access to wealth) occurs in *either* of two ways. One ambitious leader may seek to extend his power and authority both formally, through political or bureaucratic institutions, and informally, through a network of patron-client relationships. Or when there is no single, unchallenged leader factional rivalry may develop between two or more powerful cliques. These cliques, in addition to competing within formal institutions and informal patronage arrangements, also compete for support among important nonbureaucratic groups (particularly the business community) and even among subordinate extrabureaucratic elements of Thai society such as political parties (when permitted to exist), members of the professions, the media, labor unions, and so on.

How can we account for both the crucial role of leadership and the prevalence of rivalry—and the alternating cycles they give rise to? The role of the leader in Thailand, as elsewhere, can be understood from the need people feel to make authority tangible, to incorporate it literally in a person or persons. This is the case at all levels of Thai society. The national leader is simply the "big man" of rural and later urban society—the dominant partner in patron-client relations—transposed to the political scene. However, the attributes of the big man, that is, his qualities of leadership, are precisely those that make rivalry with other leaders, or would-be leaders, unavoidable.

An essential clue to the state of rivalry is given in this example. It appears in an account of the social organization of a Bangkok slum: "The causes for the fights between [one] gang and other gangs are usually the protection of [a leader's] *liam* (edge), *khom* (sharpness) or *saksi* (pride). It seems to me that all these would really denote a kind of 'bigness' in the sense as in 'I am big here, and no one dares to do anything against my will.' . . . The clique [of friends and followers of the leader] admires a man who is fearless and clever, who would not allow anyone to blunt his *liam* (edge), or to [challenge] his *khom* (sharpness), or to make him lose his *saksi* (pride)."[2] This is the spirit of the *nakleng* (the tough, "the man") who is strong, generous, daring, and willing to take risks.[3]

Now, when a leader, tough and daring, meets another of the same stamp, it is not surprising that conflict ensues. There are occasions during a struggle for power, however, when one leader

2. Akin Rabibhadana, "Bangkok Slum: Organisation and Needs," paper presented at seminar, "Access to Basic Needs in Squatter Settlements," sponsored by Asian Council for Law and Development, Oct. 30–Nov. 3, 1977, p. 23.

3. Ibid., p. 24. Thak Chaloemtiarana characterizes Sarit in this way: the *nakleng* type of Thai folk hero, kind to friends, cruel to enemies, and renowned for gambling, drinking, and womanizing ("The Sarit Regime, 1957–1963: The Formative Years of Modern Thai Politics," Ph.D. thesis, Cornell University, 1974, pp. 432–434.)

surpasses all others in skill, cunning, courage, and decisiveness. After he defeats his rivals, his authority is unchallenged, which introduces the cycle of dominance. But in time this leader, too, suffers setbacks (or death), and new contenders appear on the scene. And so the cycle continues.

On the national scale, tough and daring commanders like Phibun and Sarit made their mark, the former by suppressing the royalist revolt of 1933, while the latter defeated the Pridi-backed attempted coup in 1949. Others, aspiring to status and authority, flocked to the banners of these rising men. This bandwagon effect provided the military and bureaucratic support both leaders needed to establish, and then consolidate, their ascendancy—hence the dominance of Phibun in the late 1930s and early 1940s and of Sarit from the 1958 coup until his death in 1963.

But Phibun's career also illustrates the way in which cycles of dominance and rivalry alternate. Phibun fell from power with the collapse of his pro-Japanese policy in 1944. Restored to office by the 1947 coup, he never regained the authority he had enjoyed as prewar and wartime leader. Increasingly dependent on ruthless and ambitious younger men, notably police chief Phao and army commander Sarit, Phibun tried to maintain a balance of power between them. But he eventually succumbed to the intense rivalry that was reflected throughout the nation's elite in military-police infighting, political maneuvers, business competition, and incessant personal intrigue. Similarly, after Sarit died, factions began to develop around the leadership of Prime Minister Thanom on the one hand, and his deputy Praphat on the other, and between Praphat and other powerful generals, culminating in the vicious internecine rivalry of 1972–73, which disrupted army solidarity in the face of the student upsurge. Even since the 1976 military coup there is still an uneasy balancing of factions rather than a stable dominance.

In such an environment of insecurity, the smaller men caught up in the struggle for power need a leader to protect them and to provide the opportunity for them to rise in the hierarchy as their leader rises. It is a symbiotic relationship. The leader supplies power and protection to his followers from the resources he commands (typically, from his bureaucratic and business connections); increased resources enable the followers to increase their "services," which further augment the leader's power; and so on. The resources are not unlimited, however, and are contested by rivals. The followers, uncertain of the outcome of this rivalry, may shift their allegiances as the fortunes of leaders appear to wax or wane.

If a clique does hold together, it is through the strength of *personal* ties. Conversely, if it dissolves, it does so because of the prior dissolution of the personal bond—that is, the follower no longer receives, or *believes* he will no longer receive, the protection or rewards to which his services entitle him. Moreover, because the relationship is a personal one, it is based on trust, just as rivalry (or dissolution of a clique) is based on distrust. Leader and followers, or one follower and another, cooperate accordingly. It is not an abstraction (loyalty) that they put their trust in, but a particular person whom they know well and with whom they have shared experiences, often from their youth.

Conversely, they distrust someone they do not know well. They do not know, or cannot be sure, what he is up to. All they know is that he is pursuing his own interests, as everyone does, and it is only prudent to assume that the two sets of interests do not coincide and may well conflict. Thus in close personal relations, as in expectations of the behavior of others, we find the juxtaposition of cooperation and conflict in Thai society.

This pervasive dualism characterizes the bureaucracy, which contains both leaders and followers and which provides both the resources for power and the means of security for leaders and followers alike. Within the bureaucracy, in crucial terms of power and security, it is the armed forces that are preeminent. Within the armed forces, the army dominates. And within the army, a very few men, usually not more than half a dozen at any one time, are the supreme contenders for, or sharers in, power.

## Bureaucratic Structure
### Armed Forces

The supremacy of the armed forces, especially the army, is clearly reflected in the composition of the Cabinet (*khana ratha-montri*, or Council of Ministers), which is the formal center of power. Nearly three-quarters of all Cabinet ministers between 1932 and 1958 had had previous careers in the military or civil service;

only 13 out of more than 200 "could be clearly identified as non-bureaucratic."[4] From 1959 to 1974, 141 bureaucrats (including 38 from the military) were cabinet members along with four non-bureaucrats. Only in the democratic period, 1975–76, did nonbureaucrats (35) outnumber officials (23). Still more significant is the virtual monoplization of key posts—prime minister, minister of defense, and minister of the interior—by army leaders. Such men have held the position of prime minister for some thirty-nine out of forty-eight years; civilians for under nine years. Army prime ministers have usually held the Defense portfolio: Phibum, for example, for some 15 years; Sarit during his entire five-year term; Thanom for the next eight years. Even under civilian prime ministers, the minister of defense has invariably been drawn from the armed forces.

The minister of the interior is customarily a retired senior official, but Praphat—first as a leading member of the Sarit coup group, then as deputy prime minister and army commander-in-chief—held the post, or its equivalent in 1971–72, for some fifteen years. The director-general of police, although under the overall authority of the minister of the interior, may also, if he is a substantial military figure, exert considerable independent political power. Such was the case especially with Phao, who was originally from the army, with Sarit who took over the job to control the police, and with his immediate successors.

But how did individuals like Sarit, Thanom, and Praphat come to power? And what did they do to defend, maintain, or enlarge their power? An analysis of the 1947 coup group, which put an end to civilian supremacy (under Pridi), thereby restoring the fortunes of the military leaders,[5] provides an answer to the first question, and the consequences of the coup suggest an answer to the second.

4. David A. Wilson, *Politics in Thailand* (Ithaca, N.Y.: Cornell University Press, 1966), p. 155. See also Suchit Bunbongkan, "Thai Military Intervention in Politics" (in Thai), *Warasan Sangkomsat*, April–June 1978. For the period from 1959 to 1974, see Likhit Dhiravegin, *The Bureaucratic Elite of Thailand* (Bangkok: Thai Khadi Research Institute, Thammasat University, 1978), pp. 199, 203.

5. The army's share of the total military budget averaged more than 43 percent from 1932 to 1956; the only exception was in the period from 1945 to 1947, when the army's share plummeted to less than 20 percent of a total military budget itself cut down by more than half: Chaianan Samudavanija, "The Politics and Administration of the Thai Budgetary Process," Ph.D. thesis, University of Wisconsin, 1971, quoted by David L. Morell, "Power and Parliament in Thailand: The Futile Chal-

Although the organizers of the 1947 coup were army leaders who had been retired by the civilian regime—notably Marshal Phibun, General Phin, and Colonels Kat and Phao—the effectiveness of the coup depended on the active service officers in key positions in the capital. Foremost among these was Colonel Sarit, commander of the first infantry regiment, his deputy, and the three battalion commanders (including Lieutenant-Colonel Praphat), the commanders of the armored regiment, the first cavalry squadron, the anti-aircraft regiment, and officers of the Royal Military Academy (including Lieutenant-Colonel Thanom) in charge of military cadets.[6]

After the 1947 coup and the displacement of the Khuang government a few months later, Phibun as prime minister and minister of defense, Phin, the army commander, and his deputy, General Kat, and Police Chief Phao, were the major actors on the military-political scene. In 1949, following the collapse of Pridi's attempted rebellion, the Free Thai movement as a potential source of obstruction was neutralized. In 1950 the ambitious and discontented Kat was removed. In 1951, after the suppression of a naval challenge, the "silent coup" organized by Phin, Sarit (now commander of the first army), and Phao eliminated the parliamentary opposition. In 1954 Sarit replaced Phin—by now completely absorbed in his business activities—as army commander. Three years later, Sarit, his deputy Thanom (concurrently commander of the first army), and Thanom's deputy, Praphat, commander of the first division, ousted Phibun and Phao. Praphat's deputy, Brigadier General Krit Sivara, along with Major-General Prasert Ruchirawong, commander of the antiaircraft division (a battalion commander during the 1947 coup) were the two other army members of the 1957 "military group." The air force was represented chiefly by Air Marshal Chalermkiat, a close friend of Sarit's, and the navy by its fleet commander, both of whom had participated in the 1947 coup.

---

lenge," Ph.D. thesis, Princeton University, 1974, pp. 473–478. This decrease in the army budget and the fact that Pridi's 1946 Constitution had forbidden serving military officers and civilian officials from concurrently being members of the Senate, lower House, and cabinet—the normal practice in Thailand—were reasons for the 1947 military coup. For the reasons professed by the military leaders, however, see Thak Chaloemtiarana, ed., *Thai Politics: Extracts and Documents 1932–1957* (Bangkok: Social Science Association of Thailand, 1978), pp. 541–549.

6. A list of coup members, with positions, is given ibid., pp. 558–562.

These few members of the 1957 coup group—apart from Sarit and Chalermkiat, who died, and one or two others—dominated the military-political scene for the next fifteen years. Indeed General Krit, promoted from second army commander to deputy commander-in-chief and then commander-in-chief in 1973, remained a power behind the scenes after the fall of Thanom and Praphat until his death in 1976. (Krit's protégés, Generals Bunchai and Serm, are still prominent today). However, the long years of power had fragmented the erstwhile solidarity of the group.

In the early 1970s, the bitter feud between the factions led by Krit and Prasert (director-general of police from 1963 to 1972) against their nominal superior Praphat, army commander (1963–73) and minister of the interior, who was associated with Thanom's son (and Praphat's son-in-law) Narong, had severe repercussions. These were felt throughout the bureaucratic hierarchy, disrupting the official chain of command, setting off one clique against another, intensifying the rivalry of business empires (allied with one or another strong man), and stimulating vicious attacks in the media, by elements that were openly bought or surreptitiously bribed. This pervasive rivalry, as we have seen, contributed in no small way to the fall of the military regime in 1973.

From this brief survey, four stages in the cycles of military dominance and rivalry can be discerned: the formation of the "group," the strategic deployment of force, the rewards of the coup, and division over the spoils.

The importance of group solidarity in the first three stages cannot be overemphasized: "Military cohesion is seen in the 'old boy ties' between graduates of the same class at the Military Academy or National War College, close links between men involved in a particular event (the 1932 coup promoters, the 1947 coup initiators, officers in the army unit which fought in Korea, and the 1957 inner military clique), intermarriage between leading families . . ." and membership on the same corporate boards.[7] Graduation from the same school, and especially membership of the same class, are particularly important. As Morell points out, *run diawkan* (literally,

7. David Morell, "Traditional Political Institutions and Modern Thai Politics: Bureaucracy, Military, and Monarchy," draft chapter, in David Morell and Chai-Anan Samudavanija, *Reform, Reaction, Revolution: Political Conflict in Thailand* (Cambridge, Mass: Oelgeschlager, Gunn and Hain, forthcoming).

"belonging to the same generation") creates moral obligations among members of peer groups, as well as the reciprocal exchange of material benefits, which may endure for years.[8] Thus it is said of General Serm, currently supreme commander of the armed forces and previously army commander-in-chief (1976–78) that he "went to the right schools and had the right classmates—a crucial factor in building up a power base in this country." Still more important, as an aide also explained, "General Serm happened to be on the right side in all crises in the past."[9]

Besides emphasizing personal attachments among top officials, civilian and military, the following observation points to the *institutional* backup that the bureaucracy, through its senior officials, extends to the leaders of a successful coup:

Most senior officials have known one another for many years. They have attended the same schools and have advanced up the promotion ladder together; their children have married their colleagues' children; their relationships in business transactions (e.g. while serving on the Board of Directors of the same company) influence the scope of later decisions concerning governmental matters.[10]

Shaped by a certain familiarity of outlook, and with a common overriding interest in "stability," institutions other than the bureaucracy have also placed their resources at the disposal of a successful military group. Foremost among these are Thai-Chinese and foreign business enterprises, agencies of the U.S. government, and, most conspicuously in recent years, the monarchy. The interlocking network of bureaucracy-business partnerships and the role of the United States in bolstering internal and external security, thereby favoring the leading military cliques at the expense of a more broad-based alternative, have been discussed in Chapter 2.

8. Morell and Chai-Anan, "Traditional Political Values and Political Culture," draft Chapter 2, ibid.

9. Report in the *Nation* (Bangkok), Sept. 30, 1978. Serm was president of cadets in the Chulachomklao Military Academy in 1940. Among his fellow graduates were General Saiyud, currently chief of staff, supreme command; Major-General Chartchai Chunhawan (son of Marshal Phin), foreign minister in the Kukrit government; Police General Suraphon Chulabrahm, recent head of the Border Patrol Police; and Thanom's younger brother, Police Major-General Sanga: Morell, "Traditional Political Institutions."

10. Morell, "Traditional Political Institutions."

Obviously there is a connection between powerful business empires, built up over a long period of time, and the political "stability" resulting from virtually unchallenged military rule. The fifteen-year period since Sarit's coup in 1958 was long enough for business executives to place their bets with some confidence on "strong men" like Praphat. The latter in turn benefited from the increased wealth accruing to business, a good part of which flowed on to leading military and civilian bureaucrats, to be used in founding their fortunes and for patronage purposes.

Besides material resources, the legitimizing authority of the monarchy (and of Buddhism, too, as we shall see) have been pressed into service by Sarit and his successors. (Phibun, a veteran of the 1932 coup, like his rival, Pridi, had always maintained an attitude of reserve with regard to the monarchy. Sarit, coming from a different generation and with a purely Thai upbringing, had no such inhibitions.) Although the king clearly favored the constitutional movement of the early 1970s, royal support for the "stabilizing" role of the military, which became more and more evident during the turbulent years after the fall of Thanom and Praphat, in effect sanctioned the 1976 coup, which put an end to the democratic era.[11]

Yet even if the military leaders and their supporters in and outside the bureaucracy are bent on stability, the armed forces are not immune to change. Younger officers, at the level of regimental and battalion commander in particular, have been repelled by the ingrained corruption, political repressiveness, and social insensitivity of the old-style generals. Some of these younger officers, motivated by ambition, simply wish to take the place of their superiors, who have been in power too long. Others, including a group of reformers known as the "Young Turks," although politically inexperienced, assert a more activist role. Still another group affirms its support for democracy. But while the factionalism is more issue-

---

11. Zimmerman quotes the king's address of Dec. 14, 1975, in which he warned against "a campaign of subversion" being systematically fomented by various means, and gaining in intensity every day. "All soldiers," the king urged, "should be fully aware and careful of the dangers which are creeping in nearer and nearer to us." Zimmerman comments: "This speech must certainly have encouraged the rightists to step up their activities against the leftists—even though the King himself condemned violence in all forms." Robert F. Zimmerman, *Reflections on the Collapse of Democracy in Thailand* (Singapore: Institute of Southeast Asian Studies, occasional paper no. 50, April 1978), p. 81.

oriented than before, it still takes on the traditional form of personal influence, bureaucratic politicking, and clique rivalry.

If real change in the military is to come about, it will be through the action either of the professionals (like the present army commander, General Prem, who in March 1980 became prime minister) or of the more socially aware field commanders. The latter, however, are in a dilemma. Unlike almost all the Bangkok elite, these younger officers, sent to fight the insurgents in the countryside, have personal experience with the hardships of ordinary people. They meet the villagers and, according to their own testimony, realize how the villagers are oppressed by officials. Sincere members of the Young Turks have little faith in the bureaucracy to carry out reforms; and they have not much respect for the "people's representatives," or members of parliament, either. They admit they have no answer to the problems they encounter. They just have a "burning belief" in the need to act.[12]

### Police

For the police, as for the armed forces, the demands of professionalism conflict with the "interests" of bureaucratic politics. But the problem is compounded for the police by their role within the polity—as an administrative organ with a security function. As an enforcement agency, the police have less coercive power than the army; but the power they have and the connections they can draw on—notably the king with his long-standing patronage of the Border Patrol Police—arouse military suspicion and rivalry.

A case in point, as we have seen, was the conflict in the 1950s between army and police, which still rankles.[13] As a result, from the fall of Phao in 1957 until well into the 1970s, three senior army

12. Private information (November 1978). On General Prem Tinsulanon's views, see the lengthy interview carried by *Motichon*, May 8, 1978. As deputy minister of the interior, Prem promised to improve its structure and wipe out its image as a "Mafia Ministry": *Athit*, May 16, 1978. See also *Siam Nikorn*, Sept. 3, 1979, which suggested support for Prem among the Young Turks, the Thai Nation and the Democrat parties, big business families, and the monarchy. This support contributed to the fall of Kriangsak in February 1980 and his replacement by Prem as prime minister. Prem has strengthened his position by the extension of his tenure as commander-in-chief until 1985.

13. Even after October 1976, with the return to authoritarian rule, only one senior police official was appointed member of the twenty-four-man ruling National Administrative Reform Council along with sixteen generals, four admirals, and three air marshals.

men—Sarit, Prasert, and Prachuab—took over direct control of the police, which they then used as an independent source of power. General Prachuab, director-general of police in 1973, also aligned himself with the anti-Praphat and anti-Narong factions. Prachuab remained director-general until early 1975; it was only then that professional police officers took the post.[14]

The police agency is a factional instrument in the struggle for power; a "prebendal" institution in its own right (extracting wealth and acquiring influence by virtue of police powers); and an agency of the civil administration responsible for preventing crime and enforcing regulations. There is no clear distinction in practice among these functions; indeed they usually overlap. This overlap of functions creates both internal and external repercussions. Thus the United States gave massive support to the police in the 1950s, for the sake of its anticommunist mission, without regard for the fact that its leader, Phao, was making use of American financial aid and military equipment to build up his power base against the army, to pursue his (often criminal) vendettas against civilian opponents, and to line his pockets through extortion, harassment, and protection rackets.

In spite of this experience, a decade later U.S. government agencies still aimed to develop the police force as a major instrument of counterinsurgency. "International security should have first priority" with regard to American aid, declared the Kennedy administration.[15] Kennedy himself sought to demonstrate that sophisticated counterinsurgency, especially through the expansion of police intelligence and village security, could defeat communist insurgency without requiring massive military intervention. Thailand provided the opportunity for American counterinsurgency specialists to put their theories into practice. As a result, nearly half of all U.S. economic aid to Thailand during the crucial four-year period beginning in 1965 went to the police.[16]

Yet one of the major U.S.-backed projects—the formation of a paramilitary, anticommunist indoctrinated "village security force"—

14. In succession, Police Generals Pote, Srisuk, and the present incumbent, Monchai.

15. National Security Agency Memorandum, Aug. 7, 1962, quoted by Thomas Lobe, *United States National Security Policy and Aid to the Thailand Police* (Denver, Colo.: University of Denver Monograph Series in World Affairs, 1977), p. 33.

16. Ibid., p. 49.

collapsed as a result of police opposition, or rather opposition by its factional leader. For both the Thai police chief, General Prasert, and the director of the Department of Local Administration— heads of the two most powerful agencies within the Ministry of The Interior—insisted on being in charge of the project. When the U.S. mission decided in favor of local administration, General Praphat, ordered him to do so. The project, which had been given "the highest priority," was canceled.[17]

Consider also the police record in preventing crime and enforcing regulations—the most "official" of its composite functions. What in formal terms appear to be broad legal powers of enforcement are in practice constrained (or nullified altogether) by the strength of vested interests within the police, the armed forces, and the bureaucracy. These interests cannot be "disturbed" by administrative measures, but only as a result of a power struggle. The narcotics suppression campaign, for example, vigorously supported by the post–October 1976 Prime Minister Thanin, ran up against powerful interests at high levels in the armed forces.[18] Under the circumstances, the most that could be done was to arrest—and execute—some of the middlemen in the drug trade, for the government's very survival would be at stake were it to investigate its patrons.

The same is true of the wider government drive against corruption. In the days of Sarit, for example, thieves, arsonists, and communists were liable to be put up against a wall and shot as a warning to the general public not to take up a life of crime. But for those who were corrupt on a grand scale (such opportunities for enrichment not, of course, being open to the populace), the very machinery of enforcement, in the hands of the enforcers, was transformed into an instrument of protection.[19]

17. Ibid., pp. 67–70.

18. Richard Nations, "Politics and the Poppy," *Far Eastern Economic Review*, Apr. 15, 1977. The antinarcotics squad operates within the Police Department.

19. Sarit, who was also director-general of police, was discovered by the official investigation committee set up after his death to have misappropriated some 740 million *baht* ($37 million), chiefly drawn from a secret fund in the Office of the Prime Minister and from the proceeds of the government lottery: Thak, "The Sarit Regime," p. 429. The present police chief, Monchai, points out that a number of police officers have lost interest in protesting against or suppressing crime, while some are criminals themselves: *Siam Nikorn*, Mar. 1, 1980. See also Mulder's comment on the dark side of Thai materialism; he states that when money and power dominate social intercourse, this seems "to explain the widespread *nakleng* [tough]

The point, to put it crudely, is the distinction between crime and corruption. Unlawful activities by ordinary people (crimes) are a source of disorder, and disorder leads to instability, which cannot be tolerated. Corruption, on the other hand—in the form of kickbacks, preferential contracts, use of inside information, diversion of funds, etc.—is not a crime in this sense because it poses no threat to the established order. Just the reverse is true: corruption "lubricates" the system. It is the means (along with other, more "proper," ways of making money) by which patronage operates in the modernizing world.

In an environment shaped by access to wealth that is derived from modern institutions but is still put to traditional uses— behavior which is condoned by many people, if not approved—the police role in enforcing the whole array of Western-oriented legal codes is clearly an uphill task. The problem is, of course, compounded by the fact that influential police officials are very much part of the system—with particularly favorable opportunities to benefit by it. The director-general of police, according to an official from the Ministry of the Interior, is in an "excellent position to dispense favours—or cause trouble. Such favours include visas, quotas, licenses, easy treatment on criminal cases, and special harassment of selected targets. This represents real, usable political power."[20]

There are decent and hardworking police officials. In fact, the present police chief, Police General Monchai, has a far better reputation than most of his predecessors. But in too many cases the "composite" pressures on police behavior create exactly the opposite effect of what is officially intended: the prevention of law and the enforcement of crimes. The police are both victims (of pressures from those higher up, especially in the military, to protect clients who have acted illegally) and oppressors—themselves carrying out prebendal roles, extorting protection money, and harassing suspects. The security police or "Special Branch" (*Santiban*) is just one example.[21] Such coercive prebendalism operates throughout

---

phenomenon, lawlessness and murders, excessive exploitation, profiteering, and the general practice of corruption": *Everyday Life in Thailand: An Interpretation* (Bangkok: D. K. Books, 1979), p. 81.

20. Quoted by Morell, "Power and Parliament," p. 559.

21. Puey Ungphakorn, *Sia chip ya sia sin* [Lose your life, don't lose all] (Bangkok: Klett Thai, 1974), p. 10.

Thai society, but its impact is far harsher on the poor than on the rich, for the poor have no assets to spare and no socially acceptable way (influence, connections) to resist.

Union organizers have been jailed and peasant activists assassinated in order to eliminate popular leaders and to intimidate their followers into accepting low wages, poor conditions, or exorbitant land rents. Student demonstrators have been attacked by hired thugs, and opposition party rallies have been bombed. Even though a number of people have been killed and many wounded in these attacks, as a result of influence or pressures "from above," police investigations have failed to reach a conclusion or have been called off. Such activities were particularly evident during the democratic period; indeed their purpose was to bring it to an end.

Civil Administration

The administrative civil service is organized into such important ministries as Interior, Finance, Agriculture, Communications, Education, and the Office of the Prime Minister.[22] It underpins the entire system by providing basic functions of government: economic planning, allocation of resources, agricultural services, development of infrastructure, education and health promotion, etc.

The administration as such poses no threat to the security functions of the military. On the contrary, it is an ally in the joint concern for order as a basis for political stability and economic development. The administration and the military share the dominant value orientation of a bureaucracy which, as Siffin points out, is not directed to achievement goals (productivity, rationality, and efficiency) but to the maintenance of a "social system"—that is, a collection of basic and abiding rules and relationships that form the framework for the behavior of those within the system.[23]

Partnership between the military and civilian wings of the bureaucracy is made possible by a recognized division of labor. Broadly, the military does not interfere with administrative

22. The Office of the Prime Minister, described in the official Thai yearbook as "the vital center of the Government," includes the National Security Council, the National Educational Council, the universities bureau, the National Economic and Social Development Board, and other important agencies.

23. William J. Siffin, *The Thai Bureaucracy: Institutional Change and Development* (Honolulu: East-West Center Press, 1966), pp. 159-160.

functions;[24] nor do civilian officials (including those in the Ministry of Foreign Affairs) trespass on the field of security.[25]

This division of labor is acceptable precisely because it operates within a framework of assumptions and structural characteristics common to all components of the bureaucracy. They share common values: respect for authority, highly differentiated superior-subordinate relations, behavior defined by status, "knowing one's place," conformity rather than assertiveness, obedience rather than initiative. (But within this framework of common values, Western ideas may also find a place.)[26] The ministries, like the armed forces, function on the basis of centralized chains of command with little devolution of authority. The command structure of the Ministry of the Interior, at the district, provincial, and national level, is a case in point. As one specialist explains: "Bureaucratic domination of local self-government is inherent in the central government controls over policy, personnel, and finances of the local units and in the strength and influence of the territorial administrators. . . . It is clear that the central government possesses a dominance over local political action that is checked only within the bureaucracy itself by paternalism and inertia."[27]

24. In this, Thailand is unlike Indonesia, where thirty-one of the top ninety-six departmental positions are held by generals, rear admirals or air vice-marshals; two dozen of the country's twenty-seven provincial governors are generals; and almost every department under a civilian minister has a military man either as secretary-general or inspector-general: David Jenkins, *Far Eastern Economic Review*, Jan. 13, 1978. On Indonesian military penetration of the civil administration, see Girling, *The Bureaucratic Polity*, chs. 2 and 3.

25. It was Sarit's policy, however, to bring together highranking military and civilian officials in the National Defense College to participate in policy *planning*, but not decision making. By the end of 1963, 327 brigadiers, generals, and special grade civil servants graduated: Thak, "The Sarit Regime," pp. 362–370.

26. The ambiguity of this situation, in which an increasing number of individuals holding liberal views operate within a conservative institution (in terms of administrative decisions), is characteristic of the present stage of development in Thailand. The political implications are discussed later in this chapter. For a recent survey of liberal and conservative attitudes among bureaucrats, see Likhit Dhiravegin, *Political Attitudes of the Bureaucratic Elite and Modernization in Thailand* (Bangkok: Thai Watana, 1973). However, technocrats rather than liberals have become increasingly influential in the bureaucracy.

27. Frederick J. Horrigan, "Local Government and Administration in Thailand: A Study of Institutions and Their Cultural Setting," Ph.D. thesis, Indiana University, 1959, p. 294, quoted by Riggs, *Thailand: Bureaucratic Polity*, p. 196. This assessment of bureaucratic centralization in the 1950s is equally valid for the present day.

A further characteristic of the division of labor is the ambiguous relationship between autonomy and interdependence. The provincial setup, in formal terms, sanctions interdependence. Thus the district officer at the district level and the governor at the province level are responsible for the "lateral" activities of other ministries. But in practice the irrigation official, the rice or agricultural extension officer, the engineer, the forestry expert, or the physician report to their own respective departments and ministries in Bangkok. Autonomy at the province level, besides being a matter of professional solidarity, demonstrates the preeminence of Bangkok (and *not* the provinces or regions) as the "vital center" of decision making; it also reflects the importance for an official in the provinces of advancing his personal interests by attachment to the circle of powerful or influential patrons residing in the capital.[28]

Autonomy and interdependence, in sum, reflect the interplay between the individual and the organization. On the one hand, an impersonal, rational, established administrative structure; on the other, the prevalence of patron-client relationships—cuting across department or ministerial boundaries, disregarding the ordered hierarchy of established official positions, ignoring civilian-military or commercial-administrative distinctions—based on personal associations, which are flexible, voluntary, reciprocal, and impermanent. The bureaucratic polity is the product of this incessant interchange between structure and personality.

Finally, there is the eternal struggle among individuals (heading or staffing agencies, departments, and ministries) for greater allocations of scarce resources, for opportunities for advancement, for promotion of interests—and for the exercise of power.

---

28. As a scholar of Thai provincial administration observes, "the governor's influence in the political process depends essentially on his ability to attract effectively subordinates (who are his clients) and to develop advantageous relationships with his superiors in Bangkok. In the establishment of patron-client ties he has status, patronage, and access to funds. His ability to exploit these advantages will determine the degree of influence he is able to assert. By developing relationships with the Chinese business community and the wealthy landlords of his province, for example, the governor may have access to large amounts of money which he can allocate for development purposes or for the enrichment of his entourage": Clark D. Neher, *The Dynamics of Politics and Administration in Rural Thailand* (Ohio University, Center for International Studies, Southeast Asia Series, no. 30, 1974), p. 8.

The Thai bureaucracy, while acknowledging Western norms of public administration, functions in accordance with its own goals: to maintain the system at a certain level of equilibrium and to provide material advantages to its members, roughly according to their place in the hierarchy. Thus, as Riggs points out, criticism by Western administrators, economists, and political scientists of Thai bureaucratic rigidity, inefficiency, overstaffing, lack of initiative, conformity, and overlapping jurisdiction largely misses the point. These strictures are based on achievement-oriented "administrative criteria," whereas the "inefficiency," etc., of the Thai bureaucracy actually reflects the establishment-oriented goals of the bureaucracy and the play of political interests. Thai bureaucratic behavior, in Riggs's view, can be reduced to four basic rules of an implicit "operational code." These are:

1. Reduce the work load for officials; avoid the necessity of making hard decisions, especially those which could antagonize other (higher) officials.

2. Reduce tensions between the bureaucracy and the public, since measures incurring popular wrath or resistance only make life more difficult for officials. Thus is it better to provide "services" to the public than impose regulations on them.

3. However, means of subsistence for officials have to be extracted from the public, by taxation and other means of increasing official incomes: "one should squeeze the hardest where the victims are least able to make trouble."

4. A satisfactory situation in the bureaucracy requires promotions, transfers, and improved job assignments, with rewards for seniority and status. "If the essential rewards of the system are to be accorded to those within its hierarchy, then the rule of deference to superiors follows as an inflexible norm." In terms of the play of political interests, intrabureaucratic rivalry is "conducted according to a set of operating rules designed to eliminate major points of friction and to maintain the system at a low level of tension."[29] However, rivalries, as we have seen, may become too powerful and too vicious to be "eliminated" in this way, while social and economic issues have become far too serious and deep-rooted to be dealt with effectively by the interplay of bureaucratic politics.

29. Riggs, *Thailand: The Modernization of a Bureaucratic Polity*, pp. 237, 335–337, 358.

To sum up thus far, the *static* or institutional structure of Thai politics consists of the dominant armed forces—notably the army—and the civilian administration, relying on two main sources of nonbureaucratic support: the largely Chinese business community (providing wealth in return for protection and enhanced economic opportunity) and the Thai landowning peasantry (economic producers, but not political participants). The bureaucracy also receives the *symbolic* support of religion and the monarchy, while the inculcation of traditional values through the educational system completes the picture. Nonbureaucratic institutions, typical of pluralist societies, either lack political influence or are only recently emerging. In the absence of countervailing forces, apart from parliamentary interludes, whose brief effects have usually been quickly reversed, the bureaucratic polity remains unaltered. If its leaders have changed, either coming into or going out of power by means of a coup, the polity goes on.

The *dynamics* of the system, however, are provided by the "traditional" rivalries of powerful or influential officers and officials, supported by their followers, in the context of economic and external change. Economic change creates new forms of wealth, greater social differentiation, the growth of class consciousness, and, increasingly, disruption of established ways of living (urban and rural). Changes in the external environment have given the elite new opportunities (under the safeguard until 1975 of the American alliance) as well as new threats to its existence (from the emergence or revival of national and ideological rivals).

*Political Culture*

"Nation, Religion, King"

"Nation, Religion, King" [*Chat, satsana, phramahakasat*] is the patriotic slogan coined by King Vajiravudh, shortly after his accession, to inculcate "devotion to Fatherland, Nation, and our Holy Religion" as a focus for Thai unity.[30] The slogan was revived by the 1947 military coup leaders, strongly emphasized under the Sarit regime, and it has since become the watchword of the post-1976 coup regimes.

30. See Walter F. Vella, *Chaiyo: King Vajiravudh and the Development of Thai Nationalism* (Honolulu: University Press of Hawaii, 1978), p. 33.

This patriotic slogan, extolling the "three fundamental institutions," aptly summarizes the political culture that sanctions and sustains the bureaucratic polity. The veneer of an idealized past covers up or transforms (depending on one's point of view) the reality of rule by military-bureaucratic cliques, maintained by the periodic use of force. Yet despite its appeal to the Thai past, the slogan also encapsulates attitudes and ideas imported from the West. Even from a conservative standpoint, the words "Nation", "Religion" and "King" are open to a range of interpretations spanning the old and the new. "Nation" symbolizes the unity of leader (with bureaucracy) and people, according to the paternalist conception of Vajiravudh himself, of Sarit, and of the current military chiefs. Yet it also represents the democratic concept of the will of the people, fitfully expressed during parliamentary interludes, and paid lip service to, at least, by the official description of the era as "constitutional" since the downfall of absolute monarchy in 1932.

"Religion," too, cannot but mean different things to different people. In the strict sense, the Buddhist tradition is one of detachment from the material sphere, including, of course, politics. But the Buddhist hierarchy has itself been integrated into the secular administration in the course of nineteenth and twentieth century measures of political centralization. And Buddhism as a religion (in opposition to "atheistic materialism") and a number of Buddhist monks, trained in a quasi-secular role, have been co-opted in the service of state objectives. However, unauthorized political expressions among Buddhist laymen and monks, particularly those of a democratic nature or voicing sympathy for action by the poor, have been rigorously suppressed.[31]

Even the awe and reverence evoked by the "King" among Thai people, especially in the countryside, is only dimly reflected in the actual experience of the dynasty in this century. The last of the absolute monarchs abdicated not long after the 1932 coup; he was succeeded by a minor who died in mysterious circumstances in 1946; and the present king, Bhumibol, was kept under certain restraints by government leaders until Sarit's takeover in 1958.

31. Examples are given by Ben Anderson, "Withdrawal Symptoms: Social and Cultural Aspects of the October 6 Coup," *Bulletin of Concerned Asian Scholars,* July–September 1977.

King Bhumibol approved the twin themes of the Sarit era: development (national and regional) and security (internal and external). In time, however, the king became uneasy about the regime's failure to adopt a constitution and its penchant for corruption, which were evident under Sarit and became blatant under his successors. The king therefore supported the 1973 constitutional movement, but, alarmed by the ensuing spread of turmoil and (he believed) subversion, came out in favor of military-enforced stability.

Thus the ostensibly unifying traditionalism of "Nation, Religion, King" actually reveals in each one of its components a mixture of symbol and reality, ideal and interest, old and new. The same amalgam characterizes social and political attitudes, especially among the educated and urbanized, beyond the confines of the ruling group.

Contemporary Thai political culture continues to accept the role of the supernatural—the importance of luck, auspicious days, being born under the right stars—to an extent that seems unusual in the West.[32] This belief in the supernatural may also be taken to symbolize the insignificant, precarious, and uncertain position of man before powerful forces he can propitiate but cannot control—forces within the psyche, in society, and in nature itself. Tradition also manifests itself in pragmatic, customary attitudes of respect of elders, dependence on influential or powerful individuals (*phu yai*), and thus an emphasis on personal relations rather than principles—all of which have obvious political relevance.[33] And yet, as a Thai political scientist (and former practicing politician) points out, Thai citizens, particularly in Bangkok and the larger towns, are increasingly exposed to political campaigns, a more competitive career outlook (especially in the search for "acceptable" jobs), the

32. Prime Minister Thanin, a doctrinaire ideologue and former judge, believed he could retain power by "swallowing" the rays of the sun.

33. The importance of personal ties and advancement by patronage are emphasized by Kovit Buraphathanin, "Civil Servants and the Development of the Administration" (in Thai) in Likhit Dhiravegin, ed., *Kan phathanakan muang thai* [Development of Thailand] (Bangkok, Phrae Phithaya, 1976). Respect for seniority and experience, feelings of loyalty and gratitude toward patrons (esteemed as meritorious persons), and the inferior's desire not to disturb or upset (*krengchai*) his superior, are age-old values affecting bureaucratic behavior. They are not conducive to efficiency or modernisation: pp. 41-42.

influence of Western concepts in higher education, and new forms of economic behavior.[34]

One important consequence of the spread of modernization is that wealth (access to wealth rather than the actual production of wealth) has greatly increased in the scale of values: "The Thai people perceive money and all other forms of wealth or property . . . as the most important and desirable aspect of life. Money is the most crucial factor determining the behavior of the Thai people."[35] Wealth can now procure status; in the past it was the other way around. Increasingly, businessmen donating to royally sponsored charities or police department projects receive decorations and awards. But for the Thai elite, as Chaianan points out, it is not the achievement of making money that is respected (contrary to the Chinese business ethic), but having money and using it: this is essential for patronage.

Materialism, denoting affluence and conspicuous consumption, is now widespread (or aspired to) among the elite and the urbanized "middle strata." But if Thai behavior can be judged increasingly by material standards this behavior is still far from—even contrary to—the rational calculation of long-term costs and benefits considered necessary for a Western type of economic development. This is because the "patrimonial" outlook of the Thai elite and would-be elite, characteristic of the bureaucratic polity, still dominates the way in which wealth is considered and made use of.

This patrimonial outlook, according to Norman Jacobs, is a major deterrent to nation-building, particularly in the rational use of economic resources. The nub of his critique of modernization in form (without substantive development) is that "property in the general economic sense of control over economic resources in and of itself is insecure, because it is ever subject to arbitrary and capricious patrimonial political control, supervision or competition."[36] While there is less evidence now of "political harassment and sei-

34. Kamol Somwichien *Prachathipatai kab sangkom thai* [Democracy and Thai society] (Bangkok: Thai Wathana, 1973), pp. 36-37.
35. Sawai Simekarat and Somsak Sivaluk, "Personalism in Thai Public Administration" (in Thai) in the Thai *Journal of Social Sciences,* January 1971, quoted by Morell, "Power and Parliament," pp. 55-56.
36. Norman Jacobs, *Modernization without Development: Thailand as an Asian Case Study* (New York, Praeger, 1971), p. 153.

zure" of assets than during the time when Jacobs was writing, the continuing political instability and uncertainty inherent in factional rivalry at the top, combined with the severe economic distortions produced by monopolistic practices (a "material" feature of the bureaucratic-business partnership), are certainly not conducive to the long-range economic security which, as Jacobs put it, encourages calculable control of the market, whether the market is public, private, or mixed.

Nor is the "patrimonial" society conducive to political development in the Western style, that is, through the formation of an autonomous industrial and commercial bourgeoisie, which, as in eighteenth and nineteenth century Western Europe and America, came to act politically in defense of its interests.[37] For the formation of political parties directly expressing the interests of the business community, as in the West, is still inhibited in Thailand by the prevalence of patron-client relationships and by the variety of interests among businessmen themselves. Of course, this does not prevent individual businessmen or technocrats from being co-opted into the system either as politicians heading economic ministries during the democratic period, such as Boonchu Rojanasathien of the Bangkok Bank (now once more in the ascendant), or as ministers in bureaucratic governments.

Businesspersons, whether of Thai or Chinese origin, have differing interests and groups and have not yet emerged as a collective force. They are, however, affected by the climate of official thinking, which is developing along technocratic lines, cutting across the traditional paternalism. The aim of the technocrats, who are increasingly influential in the bureaucracy, is to encourage "free market" forces and discourage state intervention in the economy, especially on welfare grounds. (The technocrats emphasize economic growth and accordingly favor the "productive" members of society, meaning the wealthy—actually known more for conspicuous consumption than investment—and the entrepreneurs, for the sake of capital accumulation. They believe taxation of the rich will only inhibit enterprise; that substantial profits should be guaranteed to provide funds for investment; that efficiency is paramount;

---

37. Pierre Fistié, *L'évolution de la Thailande contemporaine* (Paris: Armand Colin, 1967), p. 252.

and that welfare measures, subsidizing the poor, only divert resources into "unproductive" channels.)

This competitive free-market policy assists some groups of businesspersons and hinders others. Moreover "special interests," fostered by patronage rather than economic rationality, are still rife. Further, the state apparatus itself stifles enterprise in a maze of bureaucratic regulations.

Official economic policy is still formulated by government and the bureaucracy, rather than by trade associations, which are hardly consulted. (Traders do, however, have an important negative role; they can effectively obstruct policies they do not like.) Thus the gap between business and bureaucracy remains wide. Officials still believe businesspersons to be motivated by their own "sectional" interests rather than the "public interest."[38] A prominent entrepreneur confirms the traditional distrust among bureaucrats for the private sector, which to them consists of exploiting middlemen who must be controlled.[39]

The pervasive impact of patrimonialism also limits the spread of liberal-democratic ideas among the "middle strata"—and, more

38. Montri Chenvidyakan, "Trade Associations and Public Policy-Making in Thailand: A Study of the Attitudes of Bureaucrats and Association Leaders," *Thai Journal of Development Administration,* October 1979. Montri's assessment is based on interviews with eighteen high-ranking bureaucrats and fifty-six trade association leaders in 1973. He also reports strong criticism by trade associations of government and bureaucracy for their inactivity and unresponsiveness, particularly the failure to help local industry.

39. Address by Paul Sitti-Amnuai, chairman of the PSA group of companies, reported in *Bangkok Post,* Mar. 3, 1980. He considers the bureaucracy to be the bottleneck impeding the growth of the Thai economy, and suggests a five-point policy to remove the obstacles to a more developed capitalist system: (1) Economic decisions should be left to businesspersons or technocrats. (2) There should be a "private-sector Czar" to run the economy and produce a higher growth rate, with the power to cut red tape and do away with the bureaucratic committee system. (3) The private sector should be encouraged to invest in the development of Thai mineral and other natural resources. Government should allocate land for plantations producing rubber, cocoa, palm oil, coconuts, and other crops. (4) Government should take a liberal attitude toward large local or foreign companies promoting big projects by guaranteeing a fixed return on investment for a specific number of years. Such projects could include mass transit for Bangkok, a deep sea port, a new airport for Bangkok, a new telephone system, even new roads. (5) Government and the private sector should cooperate in rural development, the government providing tax incentives, the companies providing voluntary aid and management skills to help villagers and generate employment. Paul Sitti-Amnuai's views have been strongly endorsed by Boonchu Rojanasathien, deputy prime minister in the 1980 Prem cabinet. See Chapter 5.

important, their conversion into political action. The ambivalence of these "new social forces"—chiefly outside the bureaucracy, but also including younger and Western-educated officials—is deeply marked. They are impressed by Western ideals of free choice and government by popular consent and by the institutional mechanisms of political parties, periodical elections, and parliamentary regimes intended to achieve these ideals. It is also in their interest to demand participation in political decisions (at present, of course, made by a small ruling group) by means of political parties and a parliamentary system, in which they could expect to be well represented.

But the Thai middle strata also fear the "turmoil" a more open society may lead to. And the experience of the democratic years, 1973 to 1976, reinforces this fear. Like the established members of the nineteenth century European middle classes, they believe the "masses" are not ready for democracy; that they are too ignorant, short-sighted, and too easily swayed by emotions to obey its rules and to make it work. Instead they are afraid that mass pressures and demands, encouraged or instigated by a "third hand" (*my thi sam*, referring to communist subversion), may get out of control and thus destroy not only the outmoded features of a narrow and repressive regime, which the middle strata also seek to remove, but also the moderate, practical, "responsible" institutions that the middle strata intend to establish in their place. (This is an unnecessarily alarmist attitude and one that has had dire consequences, notably the violent ending of the democratic process in 1976. But it is an understandable attitude, given the precarious situation of the middle strata, squeezed between a small and intensely conservative ruling group on the one hand and the pent-up pressures of popular demands and grievances on the other. The latter are the result of the social dislocation inherent in modernization and the great and growing gap between the haves and the have-nots). It is under such conditions that the middle strata accept the lesser evil of a return to military rule and firm authority, which, even if they do not approve, they can at least live with, rather than face the risk of drastic changes sweeping away all the familiar, comforting features of the world they know.

Only this ambivalence of the middle strata, who are neither strong enough nor unified enough to be considered a class, can explain the diversity of political opinions among their members, and the amalgam of attitudes that may be found within the individual. This is especially evident among students, the vanguard of the middle strata. For they are in a doubly ambiguous situation: they are "too young" and "inexperienced" to be taken seriously by people in authority,[40] yet at the same time they are potential recruits to those positions of authority.[41] This dual characteristic clearly emerges from a survey carried out in 1971. It showed a high degree of political awareness among students and a genuine desire for democracy, but also revealed the strong impress of authoritarian attitudes: the nation will make progress only if the people have discipline; Thailand needs able and strong leaders more than it needs laws and government programs; and the Thai people are not ready for democracy.[42] In a recent survey of northern villagers and province officials, Clark D. Neher makes the important point that, in the abstract, Thais favor democracy; but when queried specifically, the respondents prefer security, or development, deference, or economic stability.[43]

Of course, this survey does not reveal the swing to the democratic (and even radical) extreme of the "democracy-authoritarian" scale of ambivalence, which was so marked a feature of student attitudes after October 1973. Yet the return of many students to moderation and pragmatism after the military-bureaucratic "restoration" in 1976 reaffirms the ambivalent attitudes of the middle strata. The individual's desire for freedom and self-reliance, conducive to

40. These were the reasons given for the total exclusion of students and student leaders (who had done most to ensure the success of the constitutional movement) from the 2,436-member National Convention appointed by the king in December 1973.

41. In the late 1960s more than 43 percent of university students' parents were "proprietors and self-employed," and 25 percent were government officials: Richard Kraft, *Education in Thailand: Student Background and University Admission* (Bangkok: Ministry of Education, 1968), quoted by Ben Anderson, "Withdrawal Symptoms," n. 39.

42. Tinapan Nakata, "The Problems of Democracy in Thailand: A Study of Political Culture and Socialization of College Students," Ph.D. thesis, Vanderbilt University, 1972. The sample was a total of 946 male students from Chulalongkorn, Thammasat, and Chiengmai Universities, and from the military service academies in Bangkok: 467 were studying social sciences, 223 natural sciences, and 256 military science. Democratic attitudes (pp. 120–133) and authoritarian attitudes (pp. 135–141, 155) were tested.

43. "Research on Thai Politics," in Neher, ed., *Modern Thai Politics: From Village to Nation*, rev. ed. (Cambridge, Mass.: Schenkman, 1979).

liberal-democracy (as Kamol Somwichien puts it), clashes with the necessity of living under the control of superior bureaucratic power.

## Bureaucratic Values

Given the dominant role of the bureaucracy in Thai society and politics throughout the modern period (with the partial exception of the mid-1970s), bureaucratic values are exceedingly important. They are the values of a status society. Status is identified with the prestige and power of the official. This was derived directly from the king's authority (in the days of absolute monarchy), and it still retains the royal sanction in the very title of the civil service, *kharachakan*, or "royal servant." As *momrajwong* Kukrit points out, in the Ayuthaya period "a nobleman (*khunnang*) who left the king's service not only relinquished his official position but also lost his *sakdina* title, honors and royal-name . . . everything that was considered meritorious and bringing prosperity." Even today, Kukrit adds, 200 years after the fall of Ayuthaya, when both society and the system of administration have changed so much, the nobles' attitude of mind still persists.[44]

This is the attitude of the contemporary bureaucracy, that is, the "nation" represented by the administrative elite, according to traditional concepts, as opposed to the nation of the "common people" (in the democratic sense) whose role is considered later. The four "dominant social orientations," in the view of an expert on the bureaucracy, are these. First is hierarchical status: "The bureaucratic system is to a considerable degree organised and operated to give meaning and support to status." Second is personalism: membership in the bureaucracy is valued by the individual as a way of life too meaningful to be subjected to formal rules and regulations. Third is security, that is, the preservation of this way of life. And fourth is enjoyment of social pleasures (*sanuk*). Contrary to Western values, there is "no institutionalized general concept of individual rights against the system"; the rule of law does not play a

44. *Momrajwong* Kukrit, *Sangkom samai Ayuthaya* [Society at the time of Ayuthaya] (Thammasat University, 1967), quoted by Kamol, *Prachathipatai*, p. 60. (*Momrajwong* is the title given to children of princes, *Mom chao* or *Phra Ong Chao*, who are offspring of the king. Children of *Momrajwong* are *Mom Luang*; while the latter's children are commoners, in a declining scale of descent.)

central part; and although universalistic norms are fairly common, they are contingent and subject to "override," meaning that "a high-ranking official can often sweep aside rules which impede his immediate aims."[45] Jacobs, too, underlines the absence of a "perfectionist" orientation. Administrators, controlling and manipulating people, dominate the technicians, who seek to control and manipulate the environment.[46]

Family upbringing, education, peer values, and career expectations all contribute to the formation of these social orientations. The effect of schooling, for example, in inculcating "correct" behavior, has been widely acknowledged: "Youths grow up with the impression that they must know how to show great respect and deference to the elderly and their seniors; that they must know how to behave when among people of a different status or rank from their own; and that they must never argue when seniors or the elderly are in a foul humor."[47] And those who go on to university—particularly Chulalongkorn, originally set up in 1899 as the civil service training college and still the main source of recruitment for administrative officials—absorb the watchwords of "Seniority," "Order," "Tradition," "Unity," and "Spirit"—the values of the older generation.[48] Moreover, just as in the *sakdina* period, when nobles attracted able members of the "common people" into the administration, so nowadays village youths, provided they are fortunate enough to acquire higher education, may

45. Siffin, *The Thai Bureaucracy,* pp. 161–163. In Weber's terms, Thai bureaucracy is characterized by its patrimonial and prebendal heritage. It differs from Western legal-rational bureaucracy "with its principled separation of the private sphere of the official from that of the office": "Bureaucracy," in H. H. Gerth and C. Wright Mills, trans. and eds., *From Max Weber: Essays in Sociology* (London: Routledge & Kegan Paul, 1948), p. 208.

46. Jacobs also notes that use of the "cliental" system encourages vertical loyalty (of subordinates to superiors) but discourages horizontal cooperation. Vertical loyalty is associated with the scramble for prebends: *Modernization without Development,* pp. 76–85. Success in the civil service, as a Thai academic points out, is not achieved by using knowledge and ability (for the common good), but is the result of personal factors unrelated to the performance of duties. Most important among these factors are good family and connections with superior officials: Ekamol Saichan, "The Role of Intellectuals in Political Development" (in Thai), in Likhit, ed., *Kan phatanakan muang thai,* p. 253.

47. Tulyathep Suwanachinda, "As You Please, Sir . . . Political Culture in Thai Society" (in Thai), *Social Science Review,* March 1972, quoted by Morell, "Power and Parliament," p. 67.

48. Kamol, *Prachathipatai,* p. 42: the English words are used.

also be co-opted into the system: "Those who are of peasant stock, after joining the civil service become similar to the official class, with the same outlook, desires, beliefs and advantages to pursue."[49]

This inculcation of bureaucratic values in those of varied social origins is clearly important for the perpetuation of the system. But what is even more important for the formation of a bureaucratic caste is an apparent *decline* in social mobility—that is, less opportunity for poor people to enter the civil service—since the end of absolute monarchy.[50] One study concludes that "the bureaucratic elite has become more self-sufficient as new members have tended to be recruited from its own ranks." (According to a survey of two ministries, nearly half the senior civil servants entering after 1932 were sons of government officials; of those entering in 1932 or before, 40 percent had been sons of farmers; after 1932, only 10 percent.)[51] A recent, more detailed survey confirms the high proportion of senior bureaucrats coming from "official" families, but shows an equal number coming from business families in the next highest grade.[52]

49. Chaianan Samudavanija *Sakdina kap phathanakan khong sangkom thai* [Sakdina and the development of Thai society] (Bangkok: Nam Aksorn Press, 1976), app. 1, p. 7.

50. Declining social mobility runs contrary to the impression of various scholars, notably anthropologists, based on the assumption of a "loosely structured" society with an emphasis on status rather than person. This suggests Thai ability to move freely from occupation to occupation up and down the hierarchy of ranks. "A man rises because of merit and is accepted without regard for his humble origin," according to Lucien M. Hanks, "Merit and Power in the Thai Social Order," *American Anthropologist* 64, no. 6 (1962), reprinted in Neher, ed., *Modern Thai Politics*. However, as Akin Rabibhadana has pointed out, this description of social mobility, historically at least, fits well only in times of war, when rapid promotion was possible. But in peacetime upward mobility from slave and *phrae* to *khunnang* was almost nil: *Organization of Thai Society in the Early Bangkok Period, 1782–1873* (Ithaca, N.Y.: Cornell University Southeast Asia Program, Data paper no. 74, 1969), p. 119.

51. H. D. Evers and T. H. Silcock, "Elites and Selection," in Silcock, ed., *Thailand: Social and Economic Studies in Development* (Canberra: Australian National University Press, 1967), pp. 89–90.

52. Research by Likhit Dhiravegin over the period 1973–75 shows that more than 40 percent of some 2,000 officials in the top "Special Grade" had fathers who were also from the bureaucracy, while 31 percent had fathers in business. Less than 6 percent came from peasant families. Those whose fathers were workers represented less than 0.2 percent. More than one quarter of officials surveyed in the "First Grade" (a sample of 20 percent of the total of some 12,000 officials) had fathers who were officials, and about the same proportion had fathers in business; but the number from peasant families had nearly doubled to more than 10 percent. This indicates some degree of social mobility. But, as Likhit points out, there is no information on how many of "peasant" background are in fact sons of wealthy landlords

Foreign degrees, in particular, have become highly valued in the civil service. Of the approximately 2,200 special-grade officers "who hold the most prestigious and powerful positions in Thai society," 93 percent are college graduates, and one-third have graduate degrees, almost entirely from Western universities. More significantly, two-thirds of those under age 56 had foreign graduate degrees.[53] However, scholarships, the main means of acquiring foreign degrees, are mostly controlled by the Civil Service Commission. Those best placed to receive a scholarship are either government employees themselves (one-third of Thai students studying abroad in 1963 were officials taking leaves of absence) or sons and daughters of civil servants.[54] This is not necessarily a matter of nepotism or irregular administrative behavior. It simply reflects the importance of knowledge of English and a certain familiarity with Western behavior patterns in the competitive examination for scholarships and in recruitment to the civil service. These assets are more likely to be found among the Westernized bureaucratic elite.[55]

---

(or at least better-off farmers, who can afford a good education for their sons). Moreover, such mobility is largely restricted to families in the Central region. More than two-thirds of Special Grade officials and nearly the same proportion of the First Grade came from this region, while the remaining one-third were equally divided among the other regions. Likhit Dhiravegin, *The Bureaucratic Elite*, pp. 8–9, 52, 61, 70, 72, 79.

53. Likhit Dhiravegin, *Political Attitudes of the Bureaucratic Elite and Modernization in Thailand* (1973) and current research, quoted by Laurence D. Stifel, "Technocrats and Modernization in Thailand," *Asian Survey*, December 1976.

54. Evers and Silcock, "Elites and Selection," p. 91. Currently about 36,000 Thais go abroad to study every year (some 30,000 of them to the United States). "The inadequacy in education opportunities (in Thailand more than 200,000 students graduate from high schools every year, but universities can only absorb 40 percent of them), high salaries offered to foreign graduates, better chances of promotion, and social values honoring foreign degree-holders all contribute to the yearly exodus": *Hong Kong Standard*, quoting *Depthnews* report, Mar. 7, 1979. See also Likhit, *Bureaucratic Elite*, pp. 110–111, 117, 123, 125.

55. Siffin, *The Thai Bureaucracy*, pp. 172–173; Evers and Silcock, "Elites and Selection," pp. 90–91. But see also Likhit, *Bureaucratic Elite*, on the importance of favoritism and family connections, currying favor and a "good star" (*duang di*) as well as merit: pp. 135–148. See also the 1976 survey of 300 officials by Tinapan Nakata, *Bureaucratic Corruption in Thailand: Incongruities between Legal Codes and Social Norms* (Bangkok: National Institute of Development Administration, monograph no. 26, April 1977). Nearly all the officials believed Thai bureaucracy was dominated by patron-client relations (p. 31), including appointments and promotions (p. 35).

The formation and consolidation of the modern elite, heir to the immense historic role of the king's administration, combined with the weakness or absence of countervailing extrabureaucratic forces, gives rise, to an "authority-culture." The bureaucratic elite has the power and claims the right to govern;[56] and the governed defer (or are expected to defer) to the power and authority of those who govern.[57]

The military claim to rule because they provide leadership and security to the nation; the civilian officials, because they are convinced that only they—and not others—have the experience and knowledge of what the country needs.[58]

Fundamentally, however, bureaucratic rule is by "right of possession"—chiefly because of the absence, throughout most of this century, of a practical alternative—and therefore only dimly reflects the legitimacy attaching either to monarchy or to democracy. Military-dominated regimes since 1932 have neither the "sacred power" attributed to absolute monarchy nor the popular justification of government by consent of the governed—hence the repeated, but vain, attempts to find a solution in "constitutions," which reconcile democratic forms with bureaucratic substance. (The very word for constitution, *rat-thamma-nun*, incorporates the moral norm, *dharma* in Sanskrit, supposed to inspire conduct, as if to advertise the claim of modern regimes to be "rightful" successors to the ethical traditions of the monarchy and the *thammasat*.)

But in the absence of the legitimacy accorded by popular respect—for Thai constitutions, despite their connotations, have hardly proved inspiring models—the bureaucratic regime remains morally neutral: in itself it is neither good nor bad. This is in total contrast to the situation of the absolute monarch who, whatever his actual conduct, conceived his role, and it was so perceived by his subjects, as being essential to the congruence of the natural and supernatural order. Democracy, in turn, can also be seen as the

56. Tinapan Nakata, "Political Legitimacy in Thailand: Problems and Prospects," Eng. trans. in *Journal of Social Science Review* no. 1 (March 1976).

57. The fullest expression of modern paternalism is Sarit's version of benevolent despotism: government by strong leaders, through the bureaucracy, for the people's welfare: see Thak, "The Sarit Regime," pp. 207–208, 212–217.

58. Tinapan, "Political Legitimacy." Consider the bureaucratic attitude toward politicians, discussed in "Bureaucracy and Political Parties," below.

unity of the people and the leaders they have chosen: a less cosmic, but more reliable form of harmony. Yet if the bureaucratic polity is not itself morally charged, the actions of its members are still judged by moral (as well as practical) standards, according to whether they are "right" (*tham*) or not right (*mai pen tham*).

Lack of legitimacy of the bureaucracy as a ruling organ (it is not one of the three "fundamental" institutions: Nation, Religion, Monarchy) combined with moral judgment of the action of bureaucrats have had two important consequences: the continual striving to achieve institutional legitimacy through the (usually spurious) solicitation of the "people's will"; and the attempt to maintain *personal* bureaucratic behavior in line with traditionally accepted moral standards in order to offset the lack of institutional recognition.

Efforts to achieve legitimacy accordingly take three main forms:

1. The attempt to identify the bureaucracy with the "Nation" in the typical paternalist manner: the political leader is considered the head of the family, government officials are his younger brothers, and the people are like children: respectful, obedient, and looked after.

2. The attempt to "constitutionalize" the system but in a half-hearted way, modern in theory, but traditional in practice.

3. The emphasis on individual morality: officials are continually exhorted to act "properly" (*som khwan, chobtham*), in accordance with "principle" (*lak, laktham*), when they carry out their "duty" (*nathi*), as if a moral example is all that is needed to solve problems.

The traditionalist approach has been prevalent for much of this century. That is, it has provided a generally acceptable explanation of people and events. As we shall see, bureaucratic values have permeated the attitudes and behavior even of nonbureaucratic members of society to a remarkable degree. But during the last two decades in particular, the traditionalist values of a status society, allocating rewards in proportion to power and rank, have become less and less acceptable to the emerging new social forces. The ensuing conflict-and-compromise of attitudes in their relationship to the ruling elite is reflected in the political changes of the 1970s. (The actual course of events, needed to supplement the abstract character of the present discussion, is given in the following chapter.)

As a result of the bureaucratic polity's striving for legitimacy by traditional means, under conditions of rapid social change, two reinforcing tendencies are likely to continue into the 1980s, and to become intensified. First, the more internal pressures and external threats mount, the greater will be the polity's emphasis on "Nation, Religion, King." Second, the more these "institutions" are co-opted by the bureaucratic polity to cover up its own deficiencies, including its inability to cope with change, the more these institutions will lose their original, autonomous, "pure" force, derived from being regarded as "above the battle." They will increasingly become part of "politics" and will go the way of politics.

### Religion and Monarchy

The extrabureaucratic elements in Thai society—political parties, professional associations, the media, academics, labor unions, etc.—not only lack power, as was drastically revealed in October 1976; they also lack authority. In accepting (however reluctantly) a subordinate role, they conform, like Thai citizens and institutions in general, to Thai traditional values. These values, with some admixture of Western ideas and practices, shape their behavior in a manner considered socially "proper" and correct. "Order" (*rabiab riabroi*), knowing one's place in a hierarchical society, and "harmony" (*pen an nyng an diaw kan*) or "unity" (*samakii*)—reciprocal relations assuring mutual, if unequal, benefit—are the values appropriate to such a society. Since the fall of Ayuthaya these values have indeed permeated Thai society from top to bottom. And throughout this long period of more than 200 years, there has been no violent disturbance to indigenous structures of power and authority—a situation unique in Southeast Asia. (The 1932 promoters' coup removed the king as source of supreme power, but left the bureaucratic structure unchanged; even the 1973 "revolution" ousted the leading military figures without producing structural reforms.)

Of prime importance in this context are the *legitimizing* institutions of the monarchy and the Buddhist religion. Traditionally, both receive the very highest respect for their transcendent roles: the king as symbol of the nation, approached with an almost sacred awe by the mass of ordinary people, and the Buddhist monk, revered for his selfless quest for salvation (and his help in enabling others to gain merit). Both are, of course, essentially autonomous. Their purpose is an end in itself, beyond politics. But seen from a political perspective, they undoubtedly play an important part in Thai society, they have contributed greatly to shaping Thai values, and in this manner they have influenced Thai behavior, including political behavior. The Buddhist emphasis on *karma*, for example— the individual's responsibility for his own merit or demerit, his prosperity or misfortune—tends to preclude those suffering from poverty or injustice from blaming others for their misfortune and thus from criticizing (or attempting to change) the system of government, the state, or society itself.[59]

Further, whatever the otherworldly values of Buddhism, as an institution it falls within the purview of government. From the late nineteenth century, monks and monasteries have become part of an elaborate ecclesiastical hierarchy, parallel, and subordinate, to the administrative hierarchy. All the essentials of state control are provided for by requiring identification papers for all monks, registers kept by abbots of those residing in monasteries, the classification of abbots into four grades, the appointment of a supreme patriarch, and the creation of an official Ecclesiastical Department as part of the ministerial structure.[60] To carry the secular analogy further, whereas a parliament for the monkhood (*Sangha*) was set up in 1941 in an attempt to introduce some democratic procedures, this, like its civilian counterpart, was closed down by Sarit, who instead centralized and concentrated power in the hands of the supreme patriarch.[61]

As Tambiah points out, "the purification and regulation of the *Sangha* [especially in the acts of 1902, 1941, and 1962] are recurrent acts that are as much linked with political necessity as they are

59. Phaitoon Khruekaew, *Laksana sangkom thai* [Nature of Thai society], (Bangkok, 1970), p. 171.

60. The major changes in the ecclesiastical structure were produced by the *Sangha* Acts of 1902, 1941, and 1962. Each of the acts was directly related to the political system of the day: the "rational authority" of royal absolutism (1902), democratic forms under Phibun (1941), and Sarit's dictatorship (1962): S. J. Tambiah, *World Conqueror and World Renouncer: A Study of Buddhism and Polity in Thailand against a Historical Background* (Cambridge: Cambridge University Press, 1976), pp. 230–259; Yoneo Ishii, "Church and State in Thailand," *Asian Survey*, October 1968; and Charoenkiat Thanasukthaworn, "Religion and the Thai Political System," in Likhit Dhiravegin, ed., *Social Science Review*, 1977.

61. Tambiah, *World Conqueror and World Renouncer*, pp. 252–254.

with religious zeal."[62] The moves to set up a centralized religious hierarchy thus ran parallel to the secular drive for national integration—eliminating regional variants—pursued by absolute monarchs and military leaders alike.[63] So far from suggesting any incompatibility between Buddhism and the state, a sense of common purpose was evident in the prince patriarch's reminder in 1910 that although monks were subject to the monastic discipline, "they must also subject themselves to the authority which derives from the specific and general law of the state."[64]

However, with regard to religion as well as the monarchy, both integrating and autonomous tendencies are at work. Both result from the secularizing drive of the state. The intention of political leaders is obviously to draw "Nation, Religion, King" into the orbit of the regime. But one result of the attempt to politicize these institutions is to compel them to reexamine their objectives. Another is to provide them with opportunities for influence, which may be progressive or reactionary, but in either case go beyond the political bounds that integration presupposes.

The important symbolic role of the king, in the political context of the 1960s and 1970s, is discussed in the next chapter. Here it is sufficient to note the remarkable contrast between two kinds of legitimizing activity.

"Nation, Religion, King" played an important role in the progressive constitutional movement of the late 1960s and early 1970s. The paternalist "Nation" of Sarit had become discredited by the years of blatant corruption, vicious infighting, and repressive immobility, under his successors. Consequently it was to the *constitutional* "Nation" that students (the future bureaucratic elite), teachers, writers, lawyers, and finally the king himself turned,[65]

---

62. Ibid., p. 199. Buddhist monks, for example, were actively mobilized as agents for the promotion of primary education in the 1890s, leading one religious director to claim that "education and religious affairs are one and the same matter": ibid., pp. 220–221.

63. Ibid., p. 239.

64. Charles Keyes, "Buddhism and National Integration in Thailand," *Visakha Puja*, 1971; quoted ibid., p. 234. See also Chapter 1 above.

65. Morell emphasizes the king's concern for the future of Thai youth. The king regularly presides over university commencement exercises and periodically distributes diplomas to the graduates. Royal speeches at universities, especially up to the early 1970s, were particularly important. Morell, draft chapter, "Traditional Political Institutions." See also Charles F. Keyes, "The Power of Merit," *Visakha*

both as a means to improve the national image and to act as a check on military-bureaucratic excesses. Significantly, the prime minister appointed by the king after the fall of Thanom and Praphat in 1973, Sanya Thammasak, was a respected university rector, a member of the king's privy council, a former chief justice, and a prominent lay Buddhist—a perfect combination of the constitutional virtues.[66]

Three years later, the military coup of October 1976 saw a complete reversal of roles. The crisis of democracy revealed the darker side of the fundamental institutions.[67] It was now the "Nation" of *Nawaphon*, a far-Right nationalist movement,[68] the "Religion" of the militantly anticommunist monk Kittiwutto, and the "Monarchy" of the king who, in his fear of communism, sanctioned the return of the military.[69] Just as the conservative and conscientious Sanya was a key symbolic figure of the constitutional period, so Kittiwutto Bhikkhu represented the mob violence and hatred unleashed by the military and its supporters promoting the October coup. Kittiwutto, developing his own activitist strain of Buddhism,[70] became a militant spokesman for *Nawaphon* (partly in revulsion against the destruction of religion in Pol Pot's Cambodia).

---

*Puja*, May 1973, on the concept of the king having merit—in the popular Buddhist sense which serves to legitimize the contemporary sociopolitical order.

66. See Frank E. Reynolds, "Legitimation and Rebellion: Thailand's Civic Religion and the Student Uprising of October 1973," in Bardwell L. Smith, ed., *Religion and Legitimation of Power in Thailand, Laos, and Burma* (Chambersburg, Penn.: Anima Books, 1978), esp. pp. 140–145.

67. Charles F. Keyes, "Political Crisis and Militant Buddhism in Contemporary Thailand," in Smith, ed., *Religion and Legitimation*, pp. 148, 160.

68. *Nawaphon* was founded by a group of retired and serving generals, especially in the intelligence and countersubversion branches, with the aim of defending "Nation, Religion, King" against subversion and external aggression. For details see Chapter 5.

69. The king in effect approved the military coup of October 1976, which he saw as necessary to prevent the country from succumbing to political chaos, internal subversion, and external aggression: address of Dec. 3, 1976: text in *Siam Chodmaihet*, Dec. 2–8, 1976. See also Chapter 5.

70. According to Tambiah's survey of monk students at the Buddhist Mahachulalongkorn University in Bangkok, 1971, nearly half saw their concern with society primarily in religious terms (teaching religion and good behavior); 16 percent urged active engagement in social improvement (welfare work, relief of poverty); and nearly 30 percent supported a mixture of the two: *World Conqueror and World Renouncer*, p. 421. Among those who have stressed the social content of Buddhism is Phuthathat Bhikkhu (Buddha dasa), famous for his sermons, writings, and religious experiences: ibid., pp. 411–414.

He declared in June 1976 that "killing communists is no demerit." In his denunciation of communists and "leftists" (broadly defined), he argued that "whoever destroys nation, religion, or the monarchy" is not a complete person, but is doing the work of the devil (*mara*). "To kill the devil is the duty of all Thais."[71] Despite the furor aroused by this statement from the representative of a religion noted for its categorical rejection of killing, the high authorities of the *Sangha* took no action against him.[72]

In contrast to this inertia, the ecclesiastical hierarchy has given its assent to Thai government plans to harness the monkhood to official programs of community development; they regard Buddhism as a safeguard against the intrusion of "alien" (i.e., communist or radical) ideologies.[73] But for monks to act on their own initiative in support of "unauthorized" objectives is against the natural order of things. Thus when monks took part in a demonstration by poor farmers in November 1974, the army commander believed it was "the end of everything. There is nothing more serious than this"; and the Ecclesiastical Council hastened to condemn the errant monks.[74]

### Bureaucracy and Political Parties

In Thailand, political parties and politicians are seen by members of the bureaucracy as a disturbing element in the traditional scheme of things. They do not fit the ordered hierarchy of rank

71. *Kha kommunit mai bap*: "killing communists is not demeritorious" [*bap* is stronger than the word *demerit* suggests]; interview with *Chaturat*, June 29, 1976, quoted by Keyes, "Political Crisis and Militant Buddhism." Kittiwutto included among the enemies of "Nation, Religion, King" the liberal organization of the Young *Sangha*, founded after 1973, and above all the National Student Center of Thailand, as well as "leftist" journals and members of parliament: Keyes, "Political Crisis and Militant Buddhism," p. 157.

72. Ibid., p. 159. Only three months before, the supreme patriarch had denounced the political assasinations taking place in Thailand: "Lord Buddha's teachings specifically state that killing is forbidden. It is therefore tantamount to a sinful, shameful act for Buddhists, especially in a Buddhist country like Thailand": *Bangkok Post* report, quoted ibid., p. 158.

73. Charles F. Keyes, "Buddhism and National Integration in Thailand," *Journal of Asian Studies*, May 1971. Keyes considers that "the use of Buddhism to serve political ends" could have unfortunate consequences. See also Somboon Suksamran, *Political Buddhism in Southeast Asia: The Role of the Sangha in the Modernisation of Thailand* (London: Hurst, 1977).

74. General Krit Sivara, reported in *The Nation*, Dec. 3, 1974; quoted by Jeffrey Race, "Thailand in 1974," *Asian Survey*, February 1975.

and status. Both the theory and the practice of parliamentary democracy raise problems. In theory the elected deputies represent the sovereign power of the people—a concept that has no place in traditional Thai values. In practice, parliamentarians are predominantly members of the provincial elite—retired officials, lawyers, and local businessmen for the most part.[75] As a result, not only are they "distanced" from the mass of their village constituents, but they cannot stand up to the power, the prestige, and the authority of the more affluent, educated, sophisticated metropolitan bureaucrats they are supposed to control.

The derisive attitude of the Bangkok elite toward members of parliament comes out clearly in a speech in 1969 by the royalist commentator and historian Kukrit Pramot critizing their "unruly and corrupt ways." Although Kukrit himself was later to become an effective politician (and prime minister), his attitude is characteristic of the bureaucratic elite in its scorn for self-serving and parochial parliamentarians. He referred to:

These men who are obsessed by their political career with their eyes glued on the next elections. They will put local interests before national interests and will not pay any attention to or listen to the reason of national planning. They will make every effort . . . to divert the funds available to foster their local interests . . . at the expense of co-ordinated development planning and projects. . . . There will be men who are obsessed by money. They will regard every item in the budget with the constant thought: "What's in this for me and how much?" They will support measures which appear to them to have good contracts for themselves or their friends and relatives. . . . These men will be the core of obstruction and delay [of government measures]. . . . To them the success of national development is of secondary importance. They will not give to it the priority it deserves because they have been out of affairs so long and they do not know much about it anyway.[76]

75. See "Occupational Backgrounds of Elected Representatives, 1933–1969," from Vichai Tunsiri, "The Social Background and the Legislative Recruitment of the Thai Members of Parliament and their Political Consequences," Ph.D. thesis, Indiana University, 1971, p. 37, quoted by Morell, "Power and Parliament," Table VII-1, p. 310; Srethaporn Khusiphithak, "Background of Members of Thai House of Representatives, 1933–1969" (in Thai), in Chaianan Samudavanija et al., *Sat kanmuang* [Political animal] (Bangkok: Thai Watana, 1971); and Likhit Dhiravegin, "The Thai Legislators: A Study of their Sociological Attributes," in Likhit, ed., *Social Science Review*, 1977. See also below, "Social Origins of the New Forces."
76. "The Elections and Thailand's Development Future": excerpts from this speech in *Bangkok World,* text in *Siam Rath,* Feb. 11, 1969.

In fact, as one noted student of the period points out, the deputies' emphasis on money for local projects clearly corresponded to the wishes of their constituents[77] ("building local roads, bridges or schools" as Kukrit puts it).[78] Such wishes were often ignored by the central planners who were (and are) attracted by grandiose schemes, such as huge dams and superhighways, but who fail to carry out the small irrigation canals and feeder roads that directly benefit the farmers. Such small-scale projects, however, provide neither prestige nor material advantages to officials.

Admittedly, members of parliament laid themselves open to charges of corruption by their avid pursuit of profit—accepting bribes for switching votes, diverting funds, seeking kickbacks from development projects, and so forth. But this, as Morell points out, was petty corruption involving sums of 10,000 to 20,000 *baht* ($500 to $1,000), compared with the "truly enormous" bribes paid in the Ministry of National Development, Highway Department, Irrigation, Police, Communications, and National Lottery, with "millions of *baht* changing hands in a single transaction."[79] However, such large-scale corruption was usually carried on discreetly, while parliamentary bribery was more exposed to publicity.

77. Morell, "Legislative Impact on Articulation of Villager Grievances," ch. 8 in "Power and Parliament."

78. Kukrit, when he was prime minister during the democratic period (1975–76), introduced an important program of grants to village communes (*tambon*) for local projects.

79. Morell, "Power and Parliament," pp. 633–634. The chairman of the Committee for the Prevention and Suppression of Corruption, set up during the democratic period (1974), revealed that Thailand was still losing about 100 million *baht* ($5 million) every year through corruption on the part of government officials. (Officials in the Ministry of the Interior were by far the largest section of the bureaucracy involved in administrative irregularities; within the Ministry, the Police Department, the Office of the Under-Secretary of State for the Interior, and the Department of Local Administration had the largest number of cases): Chaianan Samudavanija, "Bureaucratic Corruption in Thailand" (mimeographed, 1977), pp. 27, 29–32. According to Tinapan's 1976 survey of 300 officials trained at NIDA, 62 percent believed that corruption was prevalent in the upper levels of the bureaucracy, while nearly three-quarters of the officials believed that superiors tended to conceal and protect offenses committed by their cliques: *Bureaucratic Corruption in Thailand*, pp. 39, 42, 72. A recent example of the tolerant attitude toward corruption is the case of an acting deputy rector of Chulalongkorn University who was found guilty of corruption charges by the Supreme Court (Dika). He had misappropriated more than 18 million *baht* from land sales in the 1960s, but his two-year jail sentence was suspended because, according to the court, the professor was old (retired), had been in the civil service a long time, and had never been convicted previously: *Bangkok Post*, Mar. 5, 1980.

Essentially, Kukrit's charges reflect the clash between two systems, one of which operated, both legally and illicitly, on a grand scale, the other according to the shabby and "trouble-making ways" that alone were available to "local" representatives of lower repute, status, power, and wealth. The parliamentarians, for all their cupidity, weakness, shortsightedness, and inexperience, however, posed a real challenge to the bureaucratic elite because they represented an alternative system based on local interests and popular needs. This was a challenge that the armed forces, claiming either that *they* represented public opinion[80] and/or that Thailand was "not ready for democracy,"[81] could never permit to develop.

Between the hammer of a military coup—which has cut short every parliamentary interlude in more than 45 years of "constitutionalism" after one, two, or at most three years—and the anvil of bureaucratic indifference or distaste, politicians and political parties have led a chequered, impoverished, and precarious existence. But even their struggle for autonomy, at least during the brief periods when parties were not banned, has been more apparent than real. This is because of the *projection* of the bureaucracy into the political arena, either by way of a government-appointed and usually military-dominated upper house,[82] countering the presumptions of the elected members, or by means of a "government party" (*phak rathaban*), or both.

The *Saha pracha thai* (United Thai People's) party, set up for the 1969 elections, is a perfect example of the way the bureaucratic polity works. The party head was Field Marshal Thanom, prime minister, minister of defense, and supreme commander of the armed forces. He had three deputies: General (later Field Marshal) Praphat, deputy prime minister, minister of the interior, and army commander-in-chief; Pote Sarasin, former prime minister, former

80. This was the claim of the 1947 coup group. The coup was necessary, it stated, because "the country is in a crisis; people are distressed because they lack food and clothing; prices are increasing; morality is declining"; Vichai Suvannarat, "Revolution, Coup and Rebellion after the Change in Government of 1932" (in Thai), in Chaianan Samudavanija et al., Sat kanmuang, pp. 1006101.

81. The assertion of the 1971 coup leaders: Morell, "Power and Parliament," pp. 633–634. This was also the rationale of Thanin's policy, after the 1976 coup, to attain full democracy in twelve years.

82. This is the case under the present (1978) constitution. For an informative discussion of the restrictive features of the constitution, see Kramol Thongdhamachart, "The April 1979 elections and post-election politics in Thailand," *Contemporary Southeast Asia* 1, no. 3 (1979).

SEATO secretary-general, minister of national development, who had thrown in his lot with the military leaders; and Police General Prasert, director-general of police. The party secretary-general was Air Chief Marshal Dawee Chunlasap, armed forces chief of staff; and his deputies were two army generals and a police general.[83] Besides these interlocking positions at the top, the party was closely connected with the bureaucratic structure. According to the party founders, its role was to "co-ordinate the party mechanism with the state mechanism" to achieve greater efficiency and uniformity, as well as to encourage "military, police and civilian officials to become party members."[84] The policy declaration of the party underlined loyalty to the "king as head of state," faith in religion, upholding of patriotism, application of "democracy in the Thai style," and security.[85] The party's electoral campaign, which was given the utmost publicity by visits of important government leaders in full official panoply to the provinces, emphasized that "people should know that the *Saha pracha thai* party is the party of the government that will help develop the localities, eradicate difficulties and meet the needs of the people."[86]

The establishment of the government party—headed by the military, to some extent integrated with the bureaucracy, staffed by professionals, and (hopefully) supported by the masses—was essentially a cautious attempt by government leaders to meet (or defuse) the increasing demands for some form of political participation by the growing "middle strata" of Thai society. These included professionals, small-business people, middle-level civil servants, academics, and others in Bangkok, as well as the "provincial elite," whose economic status had improved during the decade of national development promoted by Sarit, but at the expense of their exclusion from politics.

To meet such demands and "domesticate" their representatives by co-opting them into the system (in a subordinate role) was the purpose of the government party. It entailed some shift of responsibility for decision making, albeit at a relatively low level and under careful controls, from the bureaucracy to nonbureaucratic party

83. Montri Chenvidyakan and others, *Phak kan muang thai yuk mai* ["Thai political parties of the new era"] (Bangkok: Krung Thai, 1968), pp. 1–2.
84. Ibid., p. 9.
85. Ibid., pp. 3–4.
86. Ibid., p. 47.

members and deputies. This attempt to bring "responsible" middle elements into a kind of "limited partnership" with the bureaucratic elite—subordinate, but at least in higher standing than before— would also have the advantage of somewhat redressing the unbalanced character of Thai society, resulting from the overwhelming, virtually unchecked power of the military and civilian bureaucracy. These authoritarian tendencies were (and still are) aggravated by excessive centralization, causing inflexibility toward or disregard for local conditions, that is, the conditions of the majority of the Thai people.

However, even this circumscribed scheme to extend the range of political options foundered, only two and a half years after the elections, because of two basic features of the bureaucratic polity. First, the army (especially at this period, the Praphat clique) feared encroachment by elected members on the powers and privileges of the military.[87] Second, there were unstable factional rivalry and intrigue mainly between the "Government House" group, clustered around Prime Minister Thanom, who had launched the constitutional experiment but believed they could prevent it getting out of control by manipulation, and Praphat's followers, who were accustomed to a more traditional orchestration of threat and inducements (patronage, access to wealth). The climax came in 1971 as a result of mounting uncertainty about the vital "succession problem" (the question of when Praphat would take over from Thanom) involving a combination of both features. This tense situation was exacerbated by parliamentary "interference" with the bureaucracy (obstructing officials, delaying the budget), the embarrassing questions raised in the Assembly about police powers, press controls, and infringements of judicial independence, and finally the threat to Praphat's own power base posed by new elections (scheduled for 1973).[88] All this proved too much for the military, which proceeded to act in the usual way: by staging a coup.

*Extrabureaucratic Forces*

Weakness of Countervailing Power

The weakness of the Thai middle strata—their deficiency in power, wealth, and (with individual exceptions) status—reflects the overwhelming, virtually unchallenged (and hence unchecked)

87. Morell, "Power and Parliament," pp. 750–755.
88. Ibid., pp. 743–748, 759–765, 767.

presence of the bureaucracy and prevalence of bureaucratic values. It also reflects the absence in Thailand of colonial rule, which in the rest of Southeast Asia had provoked the rise of extrabureaucratic forces in the assertion of national interests and identity. Of no less importance, it was the revulsion against colonialism in the other countries of Southeast Asia that had weakened or displaced the hold of traditional ideas and indigenous administrative institutions, and thus permitted new social forces to develop.

Indeed the importance of the colonial factor (conversely, its absence in Thailand) can hardly be overstated. This is evident from even the most cursory comparison with the situation of Vietnam under the French. The consequences for modern Vietnam were decisive in a number of ways. First, the rapidity of the French conquest (in its various stages) was a shattering blow to the authority and prestige of the emperor, the Mandarin ruling class, and the Confucian ethic. Second, the new generation not only lost faith in the old order, but turned elsewhere in the search for an effective role and an alternative ideal. This ideal took the form of Western democracy, nationalism (inspired by the herioc past or by the current examples of China and Japan), or Marxism. Third, French colonial rule led to the disruption of an established way of life for the peasantry in the North (through the introduction of indentured labor) and especially the South (with the transformation of most of the peasant landowners into tenant farmers or landless laborers on large estates owned by Frenchmen or gallicized Vietnamese). The fourth consequence of an alien administration was that able and educated Vietnamese found themselves excluded from positions of power and influence in the armed forces and in the bureaucracy. Instead, the French formed the officer class and staffed the administration, even down to the level of clerks. Enterprising Vietnamese accordingly took the lead in the one sphere open to them, the professions. They became lawyers, engineers, doctors, publicists, teachers, and labor organizers. Finally, these Vietnamese, the product of French colonial rule, formed the vanguard in the national struggle against colonialism, using in turn constitutional methods, armed uprisings, mass agitation, and sustained revolution.

Much of Vietnam's experience (apart from the most recent phase) was similar to that of Indonesia, Malaya, Burma, and the Philippines. There was the same emergence of independent professionals (though in Burma and Malaya they were largely of Indian or Chinese origin), forming cultural associations or political movements, often on a mass basis, with the aim of ending colonial rule by peaceful means if possible or else by armed struggle. Thailand, by contrast, during these formative years experienced neither the key political role of the professionals, nor the emergence of nationalist movements, nor genuine mass organizations. In Thailand the bureaucracy *was* the "nation"; it claimed to embody the national ethos.

Precisely because of the assumed identity of interest of nation and bureaucracy in Thailand, resulting from the lack, after the end of absolute monarchy, of an alternative conception or practice, bureaucratic power has normally been expressed in a paternalistic fashion. The bureaucracy tolerates the activities of intellectuals, professionals, workers, and peasants *provided* they conform, but reacts sharply to any assertion of an independent, and hence "unauthorized" role, which is regarded as an unacceptable challenge to bureaucratic order. The other side of the coin, historically, has been the recognition by extrabureaucratic elements of the limits imposed by military-dominated regimes. Bureaucratic "tolerance" within those limits gave a sense of freedom (without the substance) which did more to sap the struggle for autonomy than severe repression would have done. For it was the unusually brutal last-minute resort to outright repression in 1973 by panic-stricken military leaders—who were in a state of panic simply because they had never before, in all their years of power, encountered massive opposition—that steeled the student movement to resist and to overcome.

In other words, the power and authority of the military-bureaucratic regime, which had been so long in existence, depended not so much on the physical means of coercion that it possessed (which, as in Iran in 1978, were ample for the purpose) as in the *acceptance* by extrabureaucratic elements of the inevitability of that power and their inability to challenge it. The attitudes of both sides were ingrained, because neither had experienced any genuine alternative. Consciousness of power on the part of the bureaucratic elite accompanied by consciousness of lack of power by the rest were the twin norms of Thai politics. It was the "abnormal" panic of 1973 that destroyed the self-confidence of the leadership, that brought about a new, and radically different, stage of development in Thailand. Even if the "restoration" of 1976 has physically checked the movement to autonomy of the new social forces, the state of conscious (or unconscious) submission, which more effectively held them in bondage, cannot be restored.

## "Acceptable" Institutions

From the viewpoint of the bureaucracy, momentarily eclipsed after 1973 but "restored" by the 1976 coup, there are three kinds of extrabureaucratic forces in Thai society. First are institutions and individuals that are "acceptable," either because of their acquiescence in their allotted (subordinate) place in the hierarchy or because of their utility as clients in patronage networks. The second kind consists of new-style interest groups (such as certain professional associations, the more responsible newspaper staffs, and moderate labor unions) and individual "reformers" (technocrats, academics, radio commentators, TV panelists, etc.).[89] These are institutions and individuals whose roles no longer quite fit the traditional criteria of hierarchy and patronage, but who do not openly oppose the old system. They have sought more active participation in shaping political decisions, in planning a more productive and yet more equitable allocation of national resources, in alleviating the hardships of the poorer members of society, and in countering or checking official abuses. Thus they are not acceptable (as the first group is acceptable) according to traditional bureaucratic ideas, because their desire for change upsets the natural order of things and threatens vested interests. But as moderates and "improvers," acting gradually and with circumspection, they are not (except in critical periods) regarded with deep suspicion.

In this regard they are unlike the third category of extrabureaucratic forces, the "antisystem" radicals and revolutionaries. "Radicals" refers to those who are (or were, before the October 1976 coup) prepared to operate by legal means, in the hope of changing the system by pressure from without (demonstrations, strikes, petitions) or by infiltration and influence from

89. Existing interest groups, such as trade associations and banking concerns, usually form part of the bureaucratic patronage networks; others (old student associations, religious or cultural groups) are nonpolitical and often traditionalist in orientation.

within. The revolutionaries in the Communist Party of Thailand, on the other hand, have been convinced since the 1950s that the system could never be changed, except by armed struggle.[90]

What characterizes "acceptable" institutions is either their right-wing or conservative orientation or their dependence on official sponsorship, subsidies, and control, or both. The first (but not the second) characteristic applies to the Democrat (*Prachathipat*) party, for example, throughout most of its three decades of "loyal opposition." Democrat leaders were people of wealth, standing, and integrity: they were royalists, supporters of a laissez-faire economy, longtime advocates of the American alliance, and proponents of constitutional government and honest administration. At the height of election campaigns (when permitted) Democrats sharply criticized martial law, corruption, and abuses of power, but their opposition has been largely verbal. They play according to the rules of the game.

The Democrats have been perhaps the single most important party in Thai politics in terms of longevity and vote-winning ability, especially in the capital.[91] Yet they never sought (at least until the 1974–76 period) to establish a permanent party organization with effective provincial branches, to acquire support at the grass roots, or to mobilize the masses—in short, to develop a genuinely democratic alternative to the bureaucratic system. Such an aim, until the 1970s, was literally foreign to the Democrats. Instead they relied, in the traditional way, on the prestige and following of Khuang Aphaiwong (one of the promoters of the 1932 coup) and his successor *momrajwong* Seni Pramot (descendant of royalty, distinguished lawyer, former prime minister). Electoral campaigns were extempore affairs, hampered by the vagaries of personality (factional rivalries and intrigues), lack of organization, and, especially, lack of funds. In every aspect, apart from factionalism, the Democrats, and still more the smaller parties, were at a grave dis-

90. On the origins of the Communist Party of Thailand see the following section and Chapter 7.
91. Until the disastrous 1979 elections, when the Democrats won only 1 seat in Bangkok (out of 32) and in Thailand altogether only 35, compared to 115 in 1976. See also in this chapter, "Social Origins of the New Forces," for an analysis of the role of the Democrats and other parties and movements during the democratic period.

advantage in confronting the authority, wealth, and administrative resources of the "government party."

The elections' over, such organization as existed was soon abandoned. The Democrats played their accustomed part in the parliamentary arena—promoting local interests in the provinces, representing the citizens of Bangkok, voicing interpellations, even moving votes of no confidence. There was little they could do but accept their fate when the inevitable coup closed them down.[92]

The military and civilian bureaucracy imposes limits on even the most acceptable institutions. Thus political parties acting more or less as an adjunct to the governmental machine operated from 1944 to 1947 (under Pridi's direction) and from 1948 to 1957 (under Phibun's and Phao's). But they were banned altogether by Sarit and his successor for the next decade. Democrats, socialists, and independents coexisted uneasily with the government party from 1969 to 1971, until the military's patience was exhausted.

Such bureaucratic limits on acceptability are imposed throughout Thai society—on professional associations, television, radio, the press, student organizations, and labor and peasant associations.

Even the judiciary, despite its high standing, is in an ambiguous situation. The judiciary rightly prides itself on its integrity and maintenance of the rule of law: "it is the only institution left where the people can find justice," claimed the leader of the Democrats, *momrajwong* Seni Pramot.[93] Yet at the same time it is a product of Thai society, like the bureaucracy itself. As one critic has observed, "although Thai courts of justice are free and worthy of respect, Thai judges, in general, have antiquated ideas and have not been

92. Much of the reason for the docility of political parties in the aftermath of coups (besides *force majeure*) stems from lack of public support. The elite tend to treat "politicians" with indifference or disrespect, the masses with unconcern. A columnist, writing after the October 1976 coup, put it this way: "Democracy does not respond to the needs of the people.... The people do not need elections, or political parties, or constitutions. They need peace, shelter, and a decent livelihood...." Kasem Sirisamphan, *Siam Rath,* Nov. 2, 1976. These sentiments did not prevent Dr. Kasem from joining Kukrit's Social Action Party and winning, with Kukrit, the only two SAP seats in Bangkok in the 1979 elections.

93. The statement refers to the 1970 proposal of the Thanom government to make the judiciary subject to the executive. This aroused strong opposition from deputies, students, the press, and others, and the government backed down: see Morell, "Power and Parliament," pp. 572-584. The regime tried the same move again in 1972, with the same result.

creative enough to bring about the reformation of Thai judicial procedures and to make them more relevant to the present needs of the society."[94]

Still more significant, there are times when the judiciary cannot operate: for example, when the executive rules by decree (under Sarit's article 17 or the similar article 21 of the October 1976 coup leaders) and during the lengthy periods when the country is under martial law. At such times, various cases may be subject to trial by military courts without right of appeal. Moreover, under martial law political meetings of five or more people are banned, which effectively puts an end to any organized activity, whether by academics, students, farmers, or workers, of which the government does not approve.

Under such circumstances, the very powerlessness of the extrabureaucratic forces has tended to frustrate or trivialize or silence their members. Their powerlessness tends to reinforce their habit of focusing on personalities (in terms of gossip, rivalry, intrigue) rather than issues and, in the absence of a constructive outlet, to deepen their dependence on patronage.

The situation of the intellectuals provides a good example. "The government is tolerant of the criticisms of the intellectuals," Sulak observes, "as long as it feels secure about its position. But when security is threatened or when there is a split among the political leadership, intellectuals who are outside of the establishment are either silenced or bought off." And the intense personal rivalries among intellectuals weaken their position in Thai society.[95]

94. Sulak Sivarak, "The Role of the Intellectuals," in M. Rajaretnam and Lim So Jean, eds., *Trends in Thailand* (Singapore University Press for Institute of Southeast Asian Studies, 1973), pp. 50–51.

95. Ibid. Sulak was the founding editor of *Sangkomsat porithat* [Social science review], which from 1963 on became widely read by students and intellectuals. The first student issue of the review in 1965 set the tone by its criticisms of Thai society and military domination. However, as Sulak himself points out, even after the events of 1973, when the country was supposed to have become more liberal and democratic, anyone who was critical of the Thai government or the free world could easily be branded as a communist. Alternatively, "it was claimed that those who wrote about the poverty and oppression within Siam . . . were not necessarily communists, but they paved the way for the communists to take over": Sulak Sivarak, *Nation Review*, Oct. 29, 1978. Sulak himself, although a champion of traditional Siamese culture, was accused in this way. For a recent selection of his articles, see S. Sivaraksa, *Siam in Crisis* (Bangkok: Suksit Siam, 1980).

The Thai educational system and its diffusion of traditional values, another scholar argues, produce literati rather than forward-looking or creative intellectuals. (The majority of intellectuals enter the civil service and find their intellectual status disregarded; they must simply respect and obey their superiors, according to regulations. If they do not conform in this way, they will not get far in the service; they will be appointed to unimportant posts, or sent off to serve in remote places). Intellectuals in Thailand, Ekamol concludes, are of three kinds: the old generation, such as the late Prince Wan, scholar and foreign policy adviser; the *phu yai*, such as M.R. Kukrit and Dr. Puey; and the present generation, including officials, teachers, merchants, and students.[96]

The experience of the third category is instructive. Sarit's ruthless anticommunist drive struck fear into the intellectuals, who did not dare voice opposition, even though students and lecturers had played an important part in protesting against the 1957 rigged elections—a protest that was to bring Sarit to power. During the relaxed period under Thanom the intellectuals revived, and they became more active and critical following the 1968 constitution and the 1969 elections. The concentration of power in the hands of the Thanom-Praphat-Narong "dynasty" after the 1971 coup, and their notoriety, stimulated further opposition. As a result, despite the conservatism of the Thai education system and Thai elite society, a number of students and intellectuals were able to free themselves from the restrictive way of thinking of the old order. Like Sulak, they expressed their concern with the development of contemporary Thailand, characterized by dictatorship, the spread of capitalism, and foreign military bases. In the vanguard were the independent groups of students that sprang up at this time but had to meet in secret: the *Sapha na Dome*, women's group, and economists' group of Thammasat, the Chulalongkorn "SOTUS" group, the *Sapha kafe* in Kasetsart, and so on. These groups pro-

---

96. Ekamol Saichan, "The Role of Thai Intellectuals for Development" (in Thai), in Likhit, ed., *Kan phathanakan muang thai*, pp. 253–254. Others of the old generation are the late Phaya Anuman Rajadhon, a senior official and renowned scholar of Thai customs and society, and former prime minister Pridi; among the *phu yai* are M. R. Seni, Phuthathat *Bikkhu*, and the archaeologist Prince Suphadradhit. (M. R. is the abbreviation of *momrajwong*.)

vided the critical analysis and intellectual stimulation to the student movement, which in 1973 brought down the military dictators.[97]

The removal of the "bad men" in power, Ekamol points out, denoted a change in leadership, but not in the system. Family behavior, values, customs, attitudes, the economic system, and the civil service itself continued in the old style. Indeed, the more the progressive minority of intellectuals demanded structural reforms, the greater the reaction from people in general, and from the conservative intellectual majority, which was afraid of change.[98]

Nor could Thai universities, whose main function has been to train students for official careers, escape the bureaucratic imprint. "The Thai university," as a lecturer described the situation in 1972, "is the Thai political system in miniature. The university puts an emphasis upon submissiveness and conformity to the authority-seniority system. The university system, as part of the bureaucracy, does not allow academic freedom. Its educational policy is to develop professionals rather than to encourage intellectual habits. The method of teaching does not contribute to initiative and creative thinking—it encourages good followers."[99]

Because of the low returns from academic research and the preoccupation with administration and routine, Tinapan points out, many academics look for advancement elsewhere. After a military coup, for example, some attempt to gain access to the ruling military elite by applying to serve as administrators, advisers, planning staff, and even as drafters of administrative orders. Others go so far as to try to "satisfy the power-holders by voluntarily spying on their colleagues on behalf of the chief of the revolutionary party in order to identify and report any act of dissent or opposition in the university." (This was most marked after October 1976, when rightists or careerists out of favor during the democratic period, sought revenge against independent or progressive colleagues.) Academics justified their attempts to seek power or influence through officials in three ways: (1) intellectuals had a direct responsibility to help formulate public policies; (2) those who wished to

97. Ibid., pp. 273–274. See also Chai-Anan, draft chapter, "The Student Movement," in Morell and Chai-Anan, *Reform, Reaction, Revolution*, and Chapter 5 below.
98. "Role of Thai Intellectuals," pp. 277–278.
99. Tinapan, "Political Legitimacy in Thailand."

translate their political ideas into action had to join those who are in power, for it is fruitless to spend long years in opposition; and (3) academics simply had to cooperate with the power elite because there was no other legitimate way to participate in government affairs.[100]

Similarly, students, up to the 1970s and during the Thanin regime after 1976, were not officially permitted to form unions. Students were widely regarded as politically passive, pragmatic, and career-oriented.[101] Two out of five students in the mid-1960s were children of government officials; half were from families of employers or the self-employed (professionals). Less than 7 percent of students at Thammasat University were from farming families; less than five percent from Chulalongkorn. Obedience, respect for teachers, and unwillingness to express ideas were seen as characteristic attitudes.[102]

Although the Marxist discussion groups of the late 1960s and early 1970s were already a training ground for student radicals, it was not until the ferment of mid-1973, culminating in the "October Revolution," that the majority of students developed an enthusiasm for change. Large numbers rallied to the constitutional movement, and although many dropped out of politics after 1973 (unwilling to follow the demands for structural change made by the radical leadership), they could still be mobilized on major economic or international issues.[103] The 1976 coup, however, was a traumatic blow to the student movement, driving hundreds of activists underground, and has resulted, temporarily at least, in a more pragmatic and politically reserved generation of students.[104]

100. Ibid.
101. A typical assessment of the time, not just of students, is by Donald Hindley, "Thailand: The Politics of Passivity," *Pacific Affairs,* Fall 1968.
102. Survey of 1966–67, quoted by Pricha Hongskrailers, "The Role of the Military in Thai Political Development," Ph.D. thesis, University of Queensland, 1974, pp. 290–292, 299.
103. On the change in student attitudes after October 1973 see, especially, Chaianan Samudavanija, *Prachatipatai sangkom niyom khomunit kab kan muang thai* [Democracy, socialism, communism and Thai politics] (Bangkok: Phikanet, 1975), pp. 276–278.
104. This is reflected in Mulder's assessment of the Thai middle strata, including students, many of whom admire fashions abroad, are apolitical, and self-centered: J. A. Niels Mulder, "Structure and Process: Ideas and Change," Chiangmai University, *Journal of Social Sciences* (in English and Thai), January 1978.

The media operate either directly under official (especially military) control in the case of radio and television,[105] or indirectly, as a mouthpiece for ambitious leaders, in the case of the press. Self-censorship rather than outright control normally keeps the press within accepted limits: newspaper editors and journalists learn by experience how far they can go without risking suppression. The press usually gets by on sensation and trivia. But with powerful protectors behind them, newspapers may also denounce or libel adversaries to a remarkable degree. However, attacks on the highest chiefs or criticism of the "fundamental institutions" are taboo. As a warning against transgression, editors have been murdered (by Phao), presses broken up by armed gangs (under Sarit), and newspapers and journals either suspended or closed down altogether (after the October 1976 coup).

Labor unions, in turn, far from being autonomous bodies promoting the interests of their members, tend to be manifestations of the patronage system. They also have been weakened by the personal and factional rivalries of their leaders (themselves clients of powerful politicians or officials) and by ethnic differences. Chinese provided the original labor force and formed the first labor federation under Pridi. Over the next two or three decades, however, Thai migrants from the countryside have flooded into Bangkok looking for jobs in the booming construction, manufacturing, and service industries. But attempts by workers—whether Thai or Chinese, organized or unorganized—to express their interests or assert their demands have met the same paternalistic reaction as in the case of academics, reporters, and students: they are either silenced or bought off. Sarit, as might be expected, chose the former alternative: unions were banned from 1958 to 1972. The civilian regimes that followed, with the support of moderates in the bureaucracy, tried in part to maintain a balance between labor and

105. For example, the national Thai TV station is under the administration and direction of the official Public Relations Department, while the army owns and administers Army TV: Kamol, *Prachathipatai*, pp. 100–101, and on problems of the press, pp. 96–97, 103. Similarly the national radio system is under the control of the Public Relations Department; there are numerous other radio stations, most of them operated commercially by government departments and the armed forces: Wilson, *Politics in Thailand*, pp. 184–185. One of these, the Armored Brigade Radio, broadcasting virulent propaganda, played a major part, whipping up mob feeling against students (branded as "communists"), in the events leading up to the 1976 coup.

capital; but they suffered the consequences of legitimate grievances being too long suppressed—an upsurge of strikes, demonstrations, and protests—in a deteriorating economic environment. This only confirmed the worst fears of the Right that under liberal democracy chaos or communism were bound to ensue—unless they acted first.[106]

Finally, peasants, unlike workers, have traditionally been "a world apart" from the urban ruling sector, and thus from many modernizing influences.[107] They are also separated from each other both by the nature of their work (on individual plots) and by the dispersal of villages throughout the countryside. These inherent obstacles to organization are aggravated by the fact that although Thai peasants cooperate at harvest time or in building houses for one another, their activities are generally on an ad hoc basis.[108]

Although villagers may be members of government-sponsored bodies, such as development committees and producer cooperatives, in most cases these groups do not function effectively (owing to nepotism or mismanagement), or they simply serve the interests of the rural elite: the headman, better-off peasants, traders, moneylenders and other "brokers" between the village and officialdom. Membership in these groups and associations accounts for about 10 percent of all people in rural areas. According to Phairat, "people who join groups are often heads of families with middle income, or with relatively high income positions in the villages or occupants of local administrative positions which their families have long occupied." A Thammasat University survey pub-

106. A recent assessment notes that "after years of military rule, Thailand's labor movement is weak and divided. Of the 167 registered unions, only 20 percent have more than 2,000 members and most of these are in the state enterprise sector with a stable, if stagnant, tradition of trade unionism. Jealousies among union leaders are easily manipulated among employers, police, the military, and outsiders": Richard Nations, "Laboring over a minimum wage," *Far Eastern Economic Review,* June 9, 1978.

107. "The stability of Thai society . . . is explained by its simple structure, consisting of an extremely large agrarian segment and a small ruling segment. These two groups interact in a tenuous manner so that the smaller does not irritate the larger . . . . The result is a gross two-class structure, in which the classes are physically as well as economically separate and differential status is satisfactorily justified": Wilson, *Politics in Thailand,* pp. 274–275.

108. See also the discussion of "loose structure" in Thai society under "Individuality and Power," in Chapter 1.

lished in 1974 indicated that only just over 10 percent of the villagers regularly visit their district office; almost half of those surveyed had never visited it. Instead certain people offer themselves as brokers or go-betweens for a return either in money or some kind of services.[109]

The aloofness of Thai villagers from collective activities is in marked contrast to the more structured behavior of villagers in Vietnam, Sri Lanka, India, and elsewhere. And it has important implications: for the virtual absence of permanent associations in most Thai villages—apart from Northern Thailand, where there is intensive cultivation and irrigation control, and the areas where communist networks have been formed—makes it difficult for the poorer peasants to organize effective opposition to the power of the rural elite, backed by the province officials.

A further obstacle to the development of militant action by the mass of the peasantry is the persistence of the cooperative values of the old society. A radical anthropologist like Turton, who convincingly documents the extent of peasant "indebtedness, landlessness, poverty, and growing inequality in wealth and control over means of production," has this to say: "While it might also be considered a weakness that poor and middle peasants may be tied to rich peasants by ties of kinship, locality, common social, religious and cultural activity, which can conceal relations of exploitation, at the same time members of the rich peasants may to a certain extent sympathise with, support and share common interests with poorer peasants, especially in opposition to the depredations of official strata and some urban elements."[110]

109. Types of local groups in rural Thailand are listed by Phairat Dejarintr, "Obstacles to the Development of Group Force in Rural Thailand," trans. in Likhit, ed., *Social Science Review*, 1976. Rural survey published by the Faculty of Political Science, Thammasat University, *The Attitudes of the Thai People toward Government Officials*, 1974, p. 79. See also Akin Rabibhadana, "Problems in the Work of Rural Development: Experiences of the Mekhlong Rural Development Project" (in Thai), *Warasan Thammasat*, July–September 1978. Well-off villagers make contact with important people from outside, including officials from Bangkok, while the poor do not; the former benefit from access to government services and technology, which only widens the income gap between them and the poor. He also notes the disruption caused by factional disputes within villages, even though the very existence of factions may be hidden from outsiders.

110. Andrew Turton, "The Current Situation in the Thai Countryside," in Andrew Turton, Jonathan Fast, and Malcolm Caldwell, eds., *Thailand: Roots of Conflict*

Like the "apathetic" students, however, who could be mobilized by an activist minority into a course of militant action, so under the leadership of a group of vigorous and enterprising peasants, many of the poor, downtrodden, and victimized villagers began in 1974 to petition the government and insist on their rights. But just as the progressive students aroused the reaction of conservatives and rightists, culminating in the October 1976 coup, so the peasants' challenge to authority was rapidly beaten down, their leaders assassinated, and their followers cowed into submission. At least 18 officials of the independently organized (hence officially "unauthorized") Farmers Federation of Thailand, founded in November 1974, were assassinated between February and August 1975. "Villagers were threatened with arrest as communists if they voted for candidates who supported the Federation's program. Government-controlled press and radio accused the Federation of 'mobilizing the massess,' which was made synonymous with subversion and treason."[111] (See table on page 176.)

### Social Origins of the New Forces

The new forces in Thailand emerge from this contrast between a narrowly elitist regime and the expanding groups and institutions emerging as a result of modernization. The country in its social and economic development was very different in the early 1970s from what it had been twenty years before; but during that time the political system had scarcely changed: in some respects it had regressed.

Bangkok-Thonburi, with a population of more than 4 million, had more than doubled; another 4 million people lived in provin-

---

(Nottingham, U.K.: Spokesman, 1978), p. 127. See also William J. Klausner, *Reflections in a Log Pond* (Bangkok: Suksit Siam, 1974), on the importance for Thai village society of maintaining harmony and avoiding overt acts of anger, displeasure, and criticism. Villagers living so close together in a subsistence economy require mutual aid and cooperation that would be put at risk if there were open antagonism: "The Cool Heart," pp. 45–49, 56–57.

111. Turton, "The Current Situation," p. 123. See also Chai-Anan, draft chapter, "Farmers and Modern Thai Politics," in Morell and Chai-Anan, *Reform, Reaction, Revolution,* giving details of the murders, which "seem to have been part of an organized plan of political intimidation." The campaign of assassinations struck a fatal blow at the Federation, which rapidly dwindled in importance; by 1976 it was seldom heard from any more.

Table 4.1. Military-bureaucratic view of institutions, 1973–1976.

| | *Acceptable* Reactionary to conservative | *Intermediate* New interest groups to reformist | *Antisystem* Radical to revolutionary |
|---|---|---|---|
| Political Parties (1974–1976) | Democrat (right) Social Action Thai Nation*† Social Nationalist*† Social Justice*† | Democrat (left) Social Action technocrats‡ Socialist | Socialist (after October 1976)§ Communist Party of Thailand |
| Media | Armored Brig. radio† Dusit-Thanin TV program† Siam Rath Thai Rath Dao Siam† Bangkok Post | Some television and radio commentators Prachachat Weekly (closed October 1976) Chaturat (closed 1976) Athipat (closed 1976) | CPT "Voice of People of Thailand" |
| Students | Pragmatic, career-oriented children of elite Red Gaurs (vocational)† | Middle strata‡ National Student Center of Thailand (1972–1973) | Activists§ Revolutionaries NSCT (after 1974) |
| Labor | [labor unions banned 1958–1972] | Labor Co-ordination Center of Thailand (1974) Federation of Labor Unions of Thailand (1976) | LCCT (after October 1976)§ |
| Peasants | Government-sponsored Community Development (Ministry of the Interior) Village Scouts (1971) (Royal patronage, Ministry of the Interior, Border Police)† | Farmers' Federation of Thailand (1974) (many of its leaders assassinated 1974–1975) | FFT members (after October 1976)§ |

*Three factions of former "government parties," each linked with military and civilian bureaucrats, and with important industrial and financial interests.

†= reactionary. ‡ = new interest groups § and ]

cial towns and cities. Regional centers had been set up in the North (Chiangmai), Northeast (Khonkaen), and South (Songkhla).[112] And there was substantial growth in other towns: for example, Ubon, Udorn, and Khorat, because of American military requirements, in the Northeast; Haadyai, a commercial center for rubber and tin, in the South; the river port of Nakorn Sawan in the Center; and important manufacturing towns near Bangkok.

There had been an enormous increase in people classified as "administrative, executive, and managerial": from 26,000 in 1960 to nearly a quarter of a million in 1970. In addition there were 284,000 professional and technical personnel (up from 174,000 in 1960): altogether around half a million people in the middle and upper strata of Thai society, chiefly in government but also in the private sector.[113]

University expansion in particular catered to the educational and occupational interests of the growing middle strata. In the 1960s, universities were set up in each regional center. The number of university students increased from 18,000 in 1961 to 100,000 in 1972.[114] Ramkhamhaeng, an open-admissions university, was founded in Bangkok in 1971 as a direct result of extrabureaucratic, parliamentary pressure. In its first year the same number of students were enrolled in Ramkhamhaeng as in all the other universities of Thailand. Most Thai graduates still tended to prefer bureaucratic careers,[115] but because of the gap between increasing student numbers and limited entry into the administration, more and more had to find jobs in the private sector. Two-thirds of the 1973 social science graduates (after education, the largest faculty)

112. On the development of Khonkaen, for example, see the extremely interesting account by Ronald L. Krannick, "The Construction Firm as Middleman," in *Urbanization in Thailand* (DeKalb: Northern Illinois University, occasional paper no. 2, 1974), particularly on the role of the construction firm and the use of government land for development.

113. Economic and Social Development Board, statistics on economically active population over eleven years, in Ivan Mudannayake, ed., *Thailand Yearbook, 1975–76*, p. E41 (Bangkok: Temple Publicity, 1975), quoted by Ben Anderson, "Withdrawal Symptoms."

114. Frank C. Darling, "Student Protest and Political Change in Thailand," *Pacific Affairs,* Spring 1974.

115. Nearly 53 percent of male students and 57 percent of females surveyed by the National Research Council in 1971 favored a career in the civil service, 22 percent wanted to work in private corporations, and nearly 14 percent wanted to set up their own private business: quoted by Tinapan, "Political Legitimacy," p. 87.

were employed in the private sector, as were more than half the much smaller number of scientists and engineers, and nearly half those in the humanities.[116]

With the increase in educational facilities at home and abroad, the number engaged in the professions grew considerably. By 1965 there were 165,000 teachers, more than twice the number in 1950. There were some 3,600 lecturers and professors in 1965, a sixfold increase; by that date, too, there were more than 4,000 physicians and 1,800 in the legal profession.[117]

As for the lower-middle strata, there were as many as 1 million clerical and sales staff in 1970,[118] while all those employed in the service sector had doubled in ten years to 1 million.[119]

The core of the working class, in manufacturing, rose from less than 200,000 in 1947 to nearly 700,000 in 1970, and around 1 million in 1976. About one-fifth were employed by firms with more than 50 workers; these "modern" enterprises were only a tiny fraction (0.03 percent) of the total number, but received nearly two-fifths of total earnings.[120] Besides workers in manufacturing, there were nearly a quarter of a million transport and communications workers in 1970 (about 400,000 in 1977) and more than 180,000 construction workers.[121] In contrast to other Asian countries Thailand has a very high proportion of women workers (surveys show

116. The total number of employed social scientists (in both public and private sectors) who graduated in 1973 was 1,542, compared to 285 scientists, 622 engineers, and 497 in the humanities. There were also 4,449 graduates in education (teachers), 85 percent of whom were in government service, 752 medical scientists (80 percent in government service), 315 lawyers (nearly 35 percent), 382 in agriculture (50 percent): "Employment of Students Graduating from Thai Universities in 1973," in State Universities Bureau, *Guides to University Education* (Bangkok, July 1976), quoted by Sansern Charoenphongse, "Social, Cultural and Vocational Aspects of Demand for University Education in Thailand," University of Tasmania, M.A. thesis, 1978, pp. 176, 194.

117. Derived from Hans-Dieter Evers and T. H. Silcock, "The Role of Professionals in the Development of Southeast Asia," in Silcock, ed., *Professional Structure in Southeast Asia* (Canberra: Australian National University, 1977), p. 31, table 2.1.

118. *Thailand Yearbook, 1975–76.*

119. World Bank, "Thailand: Current Economic Prospects and Selected Development Issues," November 1975, quoted by Ben Anderson "Withdrawal Symptoms."

120. Chirayu Issarangkul and Keji Taira, "Foreign Investment and Labor in Thailand," in Vichitvong na Pombhejra, ed., *Readings in Thailand's Political Economy* (Bangkok: Bangkok Printing Enterprise, 1978), p. 247.

121. *Thailand Yearbook, 1975–76.*

that women represent from 65 to 72 percent of the labor force): "They are traditionally pliant and easily intimidated and hold the least skilled jobs at the lowest wages."[122] For workers as a whole, wages were low and hours long. The emerging working class was "disciplined" under martial law, strikes normally being prohibited. During the entire period from 1958 to 1972 no labor unions or workers associations of any kind were permitted.[123]

At the bottom of the social pyramid, there were well over 11 million people working in agriculture, fishing, and other rural occupations in 1960, and more than 13 million in 1970. Average earnings in the agricultural sector in 1976 amounted to only *one-sixth* of wages in manufacturing and about one-tenth of the earnings of commercial employees.[124] These statistical aggregates, however, conceal great differences within the rural sector. Some 10 percent of farm families benefited substantially from crop diversification, increased mechanization, and use of fertilizer during the 1960s and 1970s, particularly in and near the Central Plain. But as many as one-third of the total were worse off, especially those dependent on rain-fed cultivation in the North and Northeast;[125] these were most vulnerable to population pressures, land fragmentation, unfavorable natural conditions (aridity, poor soils), and the end of the land frontier. In times of drought or flooding they faced

122. Richard Nations, "Laboring over a Minimum Wage," *Far Eastern Economic Review*, June 9, 1978.

123. From 1960 to 1964 there were virtually no strikes in Thailand. There were 17 strikes in 1965, rising to 34 in 1972, when limited associations of workers were permitted; in 1972 20,000 working days were lost in strikes. Labor unions were authorized during the democratic period after October 1973. There were 501 strikes in 1973 (297,000 workdays lost), 358 in 1974 (508,000 workdays), 241 in 1975 (723,000 workdays), and 133 in 1976 (496,000 workdays): Suvit Yingworaphan, "Labor Administration in Thailand" (mimeographed), Bangkok, Department of Labor, February 197, quoted by Chaianan, draft chapter, "Labor," in Morell and Chai-Anan, *Reform, Reaction, Revolution*. On the plight of the workers, revealed in a survey by Trairong Suwankiri and others in 1975 (the first of its kind), see Chaianan, *Prachathipatai sangkom niyom khomunit,* pp. 295–297.

124. National Social and Economic Development Board, income per head by major sectors: *Business Review* (Bangkok) April 1977.

125. Ho Kwon Ping, quoting 1978 World Bank report on Thailand, *Far Eastern Economic Review*, Dec. 1, 1978. According to Land Development Department figures, 48 percent of agricultural households (with less than 15 *rai,* or 6 acres, of land each) make up only 16 percent of total cultivated land. About half of this number own less than 6 *rai,* just over 2 acres, which indicates regular deficit: *Investor,* August 1975, quoted by Turton, "Current Situation in the Thai Countryside," p. 111.

severe hardship. Many were compelled to migrate to towns and cities, especially Bangkok, to look for work or seek land in other provinces, or squat illegally in forest preserves. As many as two-fifths of the farm families in the Northeast are estimated to live below the poverty line. (By comparison, only about one-tenth of urban dwellers live below the poverty line in the Center and in the Northeast.)[126]

Among the social and economic changes over the two decades up to 1973 were the expansion of business and professional sectors, the formation of an industrial working class (chiefly among the 200,000 workers concentrated in larger enterprises), the consolidation of a class of prosperous peasants (small in proportion to the total number living on the land, but with family members involving around a million people) and, at the opposite pole, the beginnings of a rural proletariat. Given the significance of these changes, the changes in the political system were small indeed. A "military group" of eight or nine powerful men ran the country in the early 1970s as it had done, with changes in personnel, in the early 1950s. The top military leaders required (and received) the cooperation of their subordinates in the military hierarchy and of the senior civil servants, notably the directors and deputy-directors of departments in the "special grade": let us say some 2,000 to 3,000 in the military and at most 2,500 civilian officials. In addition there was the network of formal and informal associations between bureaucrats and businessmen, involving not more than a few thousand mainly Sino-Thai business owners and managers.

If the composition and size of the ruling class had scarcely changed, neither had the character of its rule. Rivalry among top leaders, creating fissures deep in the bureaucracy, was a feature of the early 1950s as it was of the early 1970s. During practically the entire period there was no permanent constitution to restrain (if that is the word) the rulers; the 1971 coup had ended the last attempt at a constitution in 1968. Political parties were prohibited for all but six years of the two decades, labor unions were banned altogether after 1958; martial law was almost continuously in operation. There was virtually no check on arbitrary, corrupt, repressive military rule.

126. 1973 socioeconomic survey of rural and municipal households, quoted in *Business Review*, April 1977. See also Chapter 2 above.

The downfall of Thanom and Praphat in October 1973 broke the mold in which politics had become congealed for two decades. Apart from the hesitant attempt of 1968–71 to broaden the base of participation, which was obstructed by the bureaucracy and wrecked by military rivalry,[127] the political way forward lay open for the first time to the "new social forces." The entire spectrum of opinion, from extreme right to far left, was reflected in the formation of groups, parties, unions, and movements. But the fundamental division between politics and society, characteristic of the old order, reappeared in new guise. Although the new social forces were broadly united in their aspirations and interests by their constitutional demand, they were divided by the threat to some, and the need of others, posed by structural change.

Consider the range and content of political opinion during the democratic period. On the extreme right wing was the militant ideological movement *Nawaphon,* organized by disaffected members of the old order. The "political Right" was inspired by business interests in Bangkok and the provinces, exemplified by a former military clique leader, General Pramarn Adireksan, who was closely connected with Japanese joint ventures in the textile industry. Pramarn headed the "Thai Nation" (*Chat thai*) party and sought through patronage to influence the military and civil bureaucracy. On the moderate Right was Kukrit's Social Action (*Kit sangkom*) party, representing financiers, technocrats, and industrialists, which for the first time aimed to create a new constituency among the better-off farmers and to establish a *modus vivendi* with liberal bureaucrats.[128] Then there was the loose and unstable coalition of

127. Morell, "Power and Parliament," pp. 179–180.
128. The emergence of liberal bureaucrats is one of the most significant, but perplexing, phenomena in contemporary Thailand. Research by Likhit Dhiravegin (*Political Attitudes of the Bureaucratic Elite*) suggests the prevalence of liberal values among government officials. A detailed survey of 56 high-ranking officials from the Ministry of Interior, Ministry of Education, and Office of the Prime Minister, shows that almost all were college-educated and about half trained in the West, especially the United States. Almost two-fifths displayed liberal attitudes, about the same proportion had mixed liberal and conservative views, and one-fifth were conservative. (Classification into liberal and conservative is determined by their favorable or unfavorable attitudes toward change, egalitarianism, and tolerance of unconventional practices and ideas.) Since the younger officials—and those with higher education—were more liberal than conservative (and vice versa), "the implication . . . is that the future bureaucratic elite of Thailand should consist of an increasing number of liberal officials." As many observers acknowledge, however, the

"loyal opposition" conservatives, ambitious right-wingers, and enterprising lawyers and businessmen,[129] grouped in the Democrat party.[130] The "New Force" (*Palang mai*) was a party of professionals and intellectuals, voicing liberal and social democratic ideas.[131] There was also the "traditional" Left, long-established in the Northeast, and the "new Left" of student leaders, radical academics, and militant unionists, represented in parliament by the Socialist party (*Sangkom niyom*) and outside it by the National Student

---

liberalism of individuals has had little effect on the bureaucracy as an institution. Likhit's thesis is a variant on the theme of "tutelary democracy," which is usually expressed in the form of a one-party system, or rule by military "Young Turks," or by reforming bureaucrats, "guiding" the way to eventual democracy. Tutelary democracy can be considered the ideology of the financiers and technocrats associated with Kukrit's Social Action party.

129. Democrat ministers in the 1976 Seni Cabinet included: six with substantial business interests (Pichai, Krisorn, Samak, Lek, Siddek, and Damrong); five lawyers (Seni, Somboon, Sawet, Klai, and Chuan); one physician (Vira); one teacher (Khunthong); a former editor and municipal official (Surin); and one who came from a peasant family (Boonkerd). In addition, Lek and Siddek were leaders of the Muslim community; Samak was a newspaper columnist and TV personality; four were well-known southerners (Surin, Chuan, Klai and Siddek): Seni, Samak, Lek, Pichai, and Damrong were prominent in Bangkok: "Occupational Profiles of Members of the Seni Cabinet," *Business in Thailand*, May 1976.

130. Damrong Lathapipat, Democrat party Secretary-General, was prime mover in the expansion of the party organization to the provinces; 88 branches were set up in 1976. "Such an organisational attempt was quite new in Thai politics, since previously there had been no real attempt by political parties to build up strong mass support in the provinces and villages." In reaction to this move by the left-wing Democrats, the right wing, led by Samak and Thammanun (concurrently governor of Bangkok), mobilized conservative elements and anticommunist groups like the Village Scouts in an attempt to discredit Damrong's progressive faction: Chai-Anan, draft chapter, "Breakdown of the Coalition and Return to Military Government," in Morell and Chai-Anan, *Reform, Reaction, Revolution.*

131. The social democratic standpoint is well represented in a collection of articles by political scientists and economists from Chulalongkorn: *Nawa: wa duay lathi sangkom niyom* [Ship [of state]: about socialism] (Bangkok: Pikhanet, 1974). See for example, Chatthip Nathsupa, "Evolution of the Thai Economy," who points to three possible developments: continuance of a mixed *Sakdina*-capitalist system; communist revolution and restructuring of the economy; and peaceful economic change through social democracy—the most desirable course (pp. 287–291). See also Kramol Thongdhamachart, "Thoughts on Using the Socialist Economic System in Developing Countries." Kramol is aware of the social and political obstacles to the realization of democracy in the developing countries. He underlines the gap between rich and poor, and the way in which the rich make use of existing institutions to exploit the poor. On the other hand, the great majority of poor people, the farmers, are unable to unite effectively in order to gain political power and reform social institutions (pp. 266–268).

Center of Thailand[132] (*Sun klang nisit naksuksa haeng prathet thai*), the progressive press, and activist labor unions. Also outside parliament was the Farmers' Federation of Thailand (*Sahaphan chaona chaorai haeng prathet thai*), the organization of poor peasants which sought by direct action to win their rights under the government's land reform legislation. And finally, outside parliament and outside the law, even though the centrist parties had pledged themselves to repeal the 1952 anticommunist act, there was the Communist Party of Thailand[133] (*phak khomunit haeng prathet thai*).

But within the broad spectrum of political action opened up by the collapse of the military leaders and the emergence of the new social forces—action which varied all the way from the conspiratorial Right to the revolutionary Left—the parliamentary process itself played a limited role. Basically parliament represented the interests of the middle strata, extending the "Nation" of the bureaucratic elite to the "Nation" of the provincial elite. Businesspeople were the largest single group in the 1975 elected House of Representatives, with 35 percent of seats; next came members of the legal profession, 17 percent; government officials, mostly re-

132. The journal of the National Student Center of Thailand insisted that the only way to improve Thai society was through revolutionary means:
Put your purity and sincerity in the drawer,
Take up your ideology and weapons
And be ready to fire.
Obituary for an assassinated student: *Athipat*, Aug. 28–Sept. 3, 1974, quoted by Chai-Anan, draft chapter,"The Student Movement: Catalyst for the New Thai Politics," in Morell and Chai-Anan, *Reform, Reaction, Revolution.*
133. The first national congress of the CPT was on Dec. 1, 1942, when it put forward a ten-point program for the national-democratic revolution. The party readjusted to the postwar situation of "some democratic rights," which existed until the 1947 coup. By the close of 1949 the party realized the need to prepare for armed struggle. The second national congress took place in February 1952, calling for a "broad national-democratic united front" to struggle against "U.S. imperialism and its henchmen," by the worker-peasant alliance, with the rural areas as the base. Sarit's coup in 1958 "definitely convinced" the CPT that the only path to liberation was through armed struggle, using the countryside [in the Maoist formula] to encircle the towns. The third congress was in September 1961, after which leading cadres went to live and work in the jungle and mountainous areas. August 7, 1965, marked the date of the first armed clash with government forces in the Northeast. The People's Liberation Army Forces of Thailand were founded in 1969. After the October 1976 military coup, the party appealed for the "unification of the entire patriotic and democratic forces," against the military dictatorship. CPT statement, December 1977, printed in Turton, Fast, and Caldwell, eds., *Thailand: Roots of Conflict*, App. 1. See also Chapter 7 below.

tired, 12 percent; doctors, teachers, journalists, altogether 13 percent; and farmers, 9 percent.[134]

Parliament and the cabinet, dominated by business people and professionals, also linked the patrimonial society with the politics of interest groups. This was made possible by the interweaving for more than a decade of banking and business, trade and industry, with the interests of the bureaucracy, at virtually all levels and throughout the country.[135] The old-style patrimonialism operated through patronage networks formed by powerful officials and monopolistic entrepreneurs.[136] The new-style businessmen-politicians were not averse to using patronage, but they believed that their long-term interests were better served by the parliamentary system. The more parliament became established and accepted, the more favorable the "climate" would be for business confidence and expansion: business would be less subject to arbitrary, incalculable action by freewheeling leaders of the military and bureaucracy.[137] Rather than seeing parliament as a vehicle for

---

134. Chai-Anan, draft chapter, "Parliamentary and Electoral Process," in Morell and Chai-Anan, *Reform, Reaction, Revolution.* See also Saneh Chamarik, *Panha lae anakhot khong muang thai* [Problems and Future of Thailand] (Bangkok: Sangkomsat Porithat, 1976). Saneh Chamarik, political science professor at Thammasat University, points out that even after October 1973 the political parties were still not in a position to control the bureaucratic system. Moreover, there was a wide gap between parties and people, the parliamentary system did not express the problems and feelings of the people, and the parties had no real contact with labor unions or farmers' groups. The parties are only collections of individuals who, for the most part, are "old faces": interview with the political weekly *Chaturat*, pp. 419–420.

135. Mulder, "Structure and Process: Ideas and Change." At the present time, power begins to derive from direct control over economic resources (business) and from brain power (professionals, etc.). This power is primarily "social bargaining power" that seeks to influence the exercise of "power to rule" (the traditional power-structure). Thus, (*a*) business and banking have become respectable, accepted, and absorbed into the Thai system—they form powerful interest groups, both accommodating to and challenging the power to rule. (*b*) A capitalist class is emerging in the countryside with the tendency to concentration of land ownership with fewer full owners and larger holdings; but these people are still frustrated by Bangkok's paternalism and their own lack of effective political power. (*c*) the "intellectually mobile," students, academics, and others have become more influential; they express changing ideas and new views of society: Mulder, *Everyday Life in Thailand*, pp. 11–13. However, Mulder's conclusion (p. 196) is that there is "still an ethos of a highly autocratic society that breeds conformity more than initiative and avoidance more than involvement."

136. Clark Neher, *The Dynamics of Politics and Administration in Rural Thailand*, p. 74.

137. In terms of modernization, as Jacobs has emphasized, the drawbacks of the patronage system are severe. First, although patronage may well bring about indi-

the direct promotion of economic interests (although this was not excluded), they tended to consider that what is good for the nation (parliament) is good for business. This naturally combined a broader conception of the "national interest," hitherto narrowly defined by the bureaucratic polity, with a sense of what was "right and proper" for a modern society.

The parliamentary process also gave some expression to the demands of the submerged or repressed majority of the Thai people. In the 1975 parliament there was an unprecedented use of interpellations to draw attention to rural grievances and official activities. Forty-four percent of interpellations were concerned with local problems, 28 percent with the Ministry of the Interior, responsible for provincial administration and the police force.[138] Typical of peasant demands was a three-point petition to Prime Minister Sanya in June 1974. The government, it urged, should: oblige landlords to lease their land to landless farmers before the planting season begins; ensure that landlords conform to the land rents specified by law; and appoint as members of land arbitration committees only those officials who are genuninely sympathetic to farmers. In a further demonstration in August 1974, farmers argued that officials, having close relations with landowners, businesspeople, and moneylenders, were taking advantage of loopholes in the law to avoid carrying out its provisions.[139]

However, parliamentary exhortation is no substitute for bureaucratic *implementation*. Mass demands were not, and could not, be met by the patrimonial bureaucracy for two reasons. First, the bureaucracy had a strategic partnership with moneyed interests: in the towns and cities with banking, business, and real estate, and in the countryside with the rural elite of landowners,

---

vidual improvements, it is essentially an arbitrary process because everything depends on the personality of the patron rather than the importance of the underlying issues. Second, and following from the first, it is "capricious" in its impact on development. By favoring one enterprise rather than another for reasons of personal advantage (instead of for reasons of cost, quality, or efficiency) it distorts or impedes economic growth. Third, by diverting public resources to private gain, it leads to corruption. The more widespread and deep-rooted the patronage system, the greater the corruption.

138. Chai-Anan, "Parliamentary and Electoral Process."

139. The petition was by farmers from Nakorn Sawan, and the protest march by farmers from eight provinces in the Central Plain: Chaianan, "Farmers and Modern Thai Politics."

moneylenders, merchants, and often with *tambon* (subdistrict) and village heads. The second reason was the conservatism of the bureaucracy, which tended to regard workers' strikes and student demonstrations as a threat to national order and prosperity. Here again bureaucratic and economic interests are intertwined: for their mutual prosperity depends on a low-wage economy rein- forced by political stability, which can attract domestic and foreign investment.

Authoritarian attitudes are even more prevalent in the coun- tryside. Provincial governors and district officers, imbued with the values of hierarchy and order, cannot fail to regard any indepen- dent move by the peasants to defend their interests and seek justice as other than subversive, and therefore to be suppressed, either through arrests by the police or the use of armed force.

Of course there were (and are) liberal and concerned officials, who genuinely tried to improve the living conditions of the poor and sought to mediate impartially between capitalist and worker, landlord and tenant. But the bureaucracy as an institution (and as an instrument of the men in power) has a logic that overrides the convictions, however sincere, of individuals.

To conclude, the only way in which mass demands, middle strata interests, and bureaucratic authority could be reconciled was by evolutionary change, bringing the bureaucratic polity and the pat- rimonial economy into alignment with the new forces in society. But such an evolution had been held back for decades by the military-backed power of vested interests, unchecked by the bureaucratic hierarchy. By the time the political way was clear for evolutionary change, following the (temporary) withdrawal of the military in 1973, it was too late. With economic conditions aggra- vated by the recession, the established interests of businessmen- politicians (not to mention those of the old order) were too far removed from the pent-up, *immediate* demands of a substantial working class and the impoverished sections of the peasantry to be bridged by constitutional formulas or by political compromise.

# 5 | Political Performance

A period of turbulence, progress, and reaction was ushered in by the 1971 Thanom-Praphat coup, which put an end to three years of constitutional experiment. This in turn had followed a decade of autocracy inaugurated by Sarit's 1958 "revolution." The 1960s, however, despite the absence of political progress, had seen a considerable advance in economic growth. This was the result:

[The ruling] system was narrowly elitist, only gradually broadening its base by absorbing the newly-educated and the enterprising provincials. But it was remarkably stable so long as students could be recruited into the bureaucracy, as officials had reasonable salaries, or benefits, as population pressure on the land was not acute, as the economic boom of the 1960s proceeded and as the gap between living standards in the towns and countryside had not diverged alarmingly. These problems, slow but inexorably spreading fissures in Thai society, were contained by a combination of political passivity (why organise or struggle if the only result is repression?) and of economic growth. The growth took place both in the rural sector with new upland crops supplementing the staple export of rice, and in industry in joint ventures with Japanese, American and European enterprises, in finance (enlargement of the banking network) and commerce (trade expanding with improved communications).[1]

But by the 1970s the situation in every respect—external, economic, military-factional, and constitutional—had changed for the worse from the point of view of the autocratic regime.

In foreign affairs, the Thai government could no longer rely on the American commitment (sustained over two decades) once President Johnson started the process of U.S. military withdrawal from

1. J. L. S. Girling, "Thailand: Conflict or Consensus?," *The World Today*, February 1976.

Southeast Asia and his successor, Nixon, enunciated his doctrine of self-reliance for allies in 1969. Moreover, as Thanom put it, the gravity of the international situation created an urgent need for more revenue to pay for larger armed forces. This, at a time when the inflow of U.S. funds was decreasing, could come only from more taxes and tariffs (which the national assembly, seeking to put pressure on the government, obstructed in both 1970 and 1971).

Economically, too, for the first time in a decade, Thailand had a balance of payments deficit in 1969 and 1970. This had the depressing effect of undermining business confidence and reducing government expenditure. The balance of payments deficit was followed by a severe drought in the 1972 planting season and then by flooding, which cut the output of paddy rice by 10 percent and corn by 40 percent. Under these circumstances, continuing foreign demand for Thai products caused a rise in domestic prices.[2] The price of rice, the staple consumer item, sharply increased in 1973, and, as a result of government bungling, subsidized rice for townspeople virtually disappeared from the stores. For the first time in Thai history people had to line up to buy rice.[3]

Buffeted by strategic, political, and economic blows, the Thai leadership, which had ceased to be united after the death of Sarit in 1963, became increasingly disorganized, purposeless, and faction-ridden. Military leaders were faced with the problem of finding a successor to Thanom, whose military career had already been extended once beyond the retiring age (he was 60 in 1970), and with new parliamentary elections scheduled for 1973. They reacted to frustration in the usual way: the November 1971 coup, spearheaded by the Praphat group, abrogated the 1968 Constitution, closed down parliament, banned political parties, and placed the country under martial law.

### The October Revolution (1973)[4]

Student "rage," the king's supreme role at the critical moment, and the internal factionalism and outward repressiveness of the

2. Amnuay Viravan, "Trends in the Thai Economy," in *Trends in Thailand*, ed. M. Rajaretnam and Lim So Jean (Singapore: Institute of Southeast Asian Studies, 1973), pp. 70–72.

3. Saneh Chammarik, "Thai Politics and the October Revolution," trans. in *Social Science Review*, no. 1 (1976), p. 21. Inflation, well below 5 percent a year in the 1960s, rose to 11 percent in 1973 and 23 percent in 1974.

4. The October Revolution was a revolution in the sense, as Saneh puts it, that it

military were the triad of forces that produced the October Revolution.

Student attitudes and activities in the two main universities—training grounds for the future elite of the country—showed their frustration and idealism. Students felt frustrated personally because they were aware of the growing difficulty in getting jobs in the bureaucracy[5]—the traditional high-status career sought by Thai students—and, quite apart from their own ambitions, they were frustrated by the regime's regression from even the most limited political advance. The blatant and almost casual way in which the 1971 coup put an end to constitutional aspirations, in an atmosphere lacking either provocation or crisis, was an affront to the students' sense of what was "proper" in Thailand and an insult to their idealism.

In the enforced absence of parliament, it was the students who carried forward the constitutional ideal, and they did so effectively. Unlike the deputies, who were tainted with opportunism and self-interest, the mass of students following in the steps of the radical minority became increasingly zealous, idealistic, and well organized. It was the student body that reacted most keenly to, or bore the brunt of, every corrupt, scandalous, or repressive act of government.

Most important in the transformation of the student body into a national movement was the creation of new universities in the 1960s in the regions outside Bangkok. In Bangkok itself the pressure for access to higher education, abetted by the politicians, had resulted in the establishment of a new open-admissions university, Ramkhamhaeng, whose student enrollment increased from 10,000 in 1971 to more than 40,000 in 1973.[6]

Students, organized since 1970 in the revived National Student Center of Thailand (NSCT), became increasingly politicized by the

started as an intellectual movement, but came to deal with concrete problems and the real conditions of the masses. "The October Revolution was aimed at directly attacking the power structure of the privileged group"; it resulted in the release of economic and social forces which had been taking shape during the past two decades: ibid, p. 33.

5. As is common to most Third World countries, finding a job was difficult because of the huge growth in student numbers combined with a limited number of relevant jobs.

6. Ross Prizzia and Narong Sinsawadi, *Thailand: Student Activism and Political Change* (Bangkok: D. K. Books, 1974), pp. 10–18.

very nature of events. Student groups had informally supervised polling at the 1969 elections; that same year they successfully resisted government attempts to increase bus fares in Bangkok, which would have hit at the poorest sections of the city's population. And they turned out in force in 1970 against the dubious sale of university land by Chulalongkorn administrators to private interests, which was also an oblique attack on Praphat, then rector of the university.[7] Increasingly, students throughout the country were shifting from their initial elitist attitude—reflecting, for the most part, their origins as children of government officials and the well-to-do—to a populist stance. They realized the need to establish links with the public if they were to become an effective counterforce against the powers that be.[8]

Meanwhile the NSCT, inspired by a number of highly intelligent and radical student leaders, especially from Thammasat and Chulalongkorn (many of whom had taken part in the quasi-Marxist discussion groups of the 1960s), became the most vigorous and challenging extrabureaucratic force ever to have emerged in Thailand.[9] One of them, Thirayut Bunmee, a brilliant engineering student from Chulalongkorn who came from a poor family, was to play a key role in 1972–73 as secretary-general of NSCT. Thirayut started by organizing a popular boycott of Japanese goods in November 1972, which the government could hardly object to because of its patriotic overtones (Thailand's trade with Japan had been in deficit for ten years). At the same time the campaign subtly reminded the Thai people that Japan's economic dominance was actually being facilitated by the Thai ruling elite through their intimate connections with Japanese business.[10]

Hardly a month had gone by before the Thanom-Praphat "National Executive Council" (as the regime was known after the 1971

7. Prudhisan Jumbala, "The Emergence of the Thai Student Movement," *Southeast Asian Spectrum* (Bangkok), October 1975.

8. Prudhisan Jumbala, "The Democratic Experiment in Thailand; 1973–1976," *Dyason House Papers* (Melbourne), January 1977.

9. Chai-Anan Samudavanija, "The Student Movement: Catalyst for the New Thai Politics," draft chapter in David Morell and Chai-Anan, *Reform, Reaction, Revolution: Political Conflict in Thailand* (Cambridge, Mass.: Oelgeschlager, Gunn and Hain, forthcoming). Chaianan provides an excellent detailed account with profiles of the student leaders.

10. Prudhisan, "Emergence of the Thai Student Movement," and Prizzia and Narong, *Thailand: Student Activism*, pp. 26, 29–33.

coup) crudely attempted to subvert the last stronghold of integrity—the independent judiciary. It decreed that the minister of justice, a political appointee, had power to control the judiciary. This blatant move aroused such widespread opposition among professional people, the press, academics, and students that the government was forced to back down. Then in May 1973 a scandal over illegal hunting at a national park (Tung Yai) implicated officials close to Praphat. In June the rector of Ramkhamhaeng University dismissed nine students for daring to satirize the regime, which brought out large numbers in protest.[11] By now, social, political, and student issues were combined: the students were demanding a new constitution, an end to corruption, measures to deal with rising prices, and the withdrawal of American armed forces—a symbol of U.S. backing for the discredited military leadership.

Meanwhile the regime, which had succeeded in uniting so many diverse elements of society against it, was also tearing itself to pieces through the greed and ferocity of its internecine conflicts. The coup group of 1957, headed by the masterful Sarit, had long broken up into separate or rival cliques. Praphat's followers and the "Government House" group looking to Thanom were both colluding and contending during the parliamentary period (1968–71). But the situation changed dramatically after the 1971 coup, chiefly owing to the rise of Colonel Narong Kittikachorn, son of Thanom and son-in-law of Praphat and thus heir to the "godfathers"—a man whose ruthless character and driving ambition "struck fear into many people's hearts."[12]

Narong had been urging decisive action against parliament before the coup; after the coup he became the moving force in the so-called Board of Inspection and Follow-up of Government Operations (BIFGO). This innocuous-sounding body, with Thanom as

11. Students had written this poem, alluding to the attempt to justify the extension of service of Thanom and Praphat beyond retiring age:
   The jungle council of Tung Yai
   [nature reserve—scene of scandal]
   has passed the resolution to renew the official
   term of the jungle animal for another year
   Due to the fact that both internal and external situations
   are still not trustworthy.
Quoted in Saneh, "Thai Politics and the October Revolution," p. 28.
   12. Ibid., p. 21.

chairman and Praphat as his deputy, was ostensibly aimed at suppressing all forms of corruption. But in the hands of Narong it became an instrument for the systematic destruction of rival military factions.[13] The latter included factions headed by General Prasert Ruchirawong, who had established a powerful and profitable patronage network through his control of the police (he was director-general from 1963 to 1972), and by General Krit Sivara, an influential but enigmatic field commander, also with many business connections. Krit was deputy army commander at this time, but in September 1973 he took over from Praphat as army commander-in-chief.

Thanom, Praphat, Narong, and their supporters were all left alone by the BIFGO investigators to continue their lucrative pursuits,[14] while high-ranking bureaucrats, businessmen, and military officers belonging to the patronage networks of Prasert and Krit began to face charges of corruption and tax evasion. In response to Narong's aggressive thrust for power, Prasert and other threatened military figures urged Krit in mid-1973 to seize power.[15] Krit was reluctant to do so at that time, but the massive student demonstration in October and the near-complete public disillusionment with the rampant corruption of the regime provided the opportunity to intervene.

Thus the stage was set for the final confrontation.[16] On October 6, 1973, Thirayut and ten other activists from the "group demand-

13. Chai-Anan, "The Student Movement"; for the earlier period, see David L. Morell, "Power and Parliament in Thailand: The Futile Challenge, 1968–1971," Ph.D. thesis, Princeton University, 1974.

14. An official committee of investigation, appointed after the downfall of Thanom, Praphat, and Narong, assessed their wealth as follows: Praphat nearly 245 million *baht* (more than $12 million) and owing 160 million *baht* in unpaid income and property taxes; Narong nearly 23 million *baht* and owing 100 million; Thanom just over 9 million *baht*: *Bangkok Post*, Aug. 22, 1976, quoted by Chaianan, "Bureaucratic Corruption in Thailand" (mimeographed, 1977), p. 24. The question whether these "assets" are to be returned to these men or not became a major test for the Kriangsak government. To return corruptly acquired assets would be going back to the discredited ways of the old regime; not to return them would antagonize the Right. Kriangsak deferred the problem in 1978 by setting up a committee to "study" the matter.

15. Chai-Anan, "The Student Movement."

16. In addition to the sources already quoted, see "The Ten Days," published by the *Bangkok Post* in 1973; Stewart Meacham, "The Ten Days that Shook Thailand," *International Affairs Reports* (American Friends Service Committee), November 1973; J-C Pomonti, *Le Monde*, Oct. 17–25, 1973; *Far Eastern Economic Review*, Oct. 10, 22,

ing a constitution" were arrested for handing out leaflets. Praphat in his usual style announced they were "plotters" seeking to overthrow the government. The reaction was an enormous gathering of university students, vocational students, and high school pupils, joined by clerks, shopworkers, peddlers, and others, insisting on the unconditional release of those unjustly arrested. By October 13, faced with an ever-growing movement of opposition, amounting to some 400,000 people marching in protest along Rajadamnoen (the ceremonial avenue of Bangkok), the government backed down. But it was too late. Next morning, a band of dispersing students was fired on by the police. Immediately a peaceful demonstration turned into a riot and a riot into a revolt. Enraged students came under attack by riot police and troops equipped with tanks and helicopters. Praphat, denouncing the student leaders as "communist agents," ordered the army to move in to crush the demonstrators—but Krit refused. At this critical moment all parties turned to the king for a solution. The king persuaded Thanom and Praphat to resign and, with Narong, to leave the country. Then, in a solemn address to the nation, he announced on October 14 the appointment of Sanya Thammasak, rector of Thammasat and former Supreme Court judge, as prime minister. The military was in eclipse, the king was at the apogee of his reign, and the students had triumphed over tyranny.

## Conflict or Consensus? (1974-76)

The events of October 1973, as a result of which the two highest military leaders of Thailand were overthrown, represented more than a coup but less than a revolution; for if the leadership had changed, the social structure of the country remained unaltered.

This fact was crucial to subsequent developments. In fact, the nature of the social problem had already been apparent in the pamphlet issued by the constitutional movement, the arrest of whose leaders had triggered off the October crisis. According to the pamphlet, "The group demanding a constitution is a group of

---

Nov. 26, Dec. 3, 1973; and R-I Heinze, R. F. Zimmerman, and Prudhisan Jumbala, separate articles in *Asian Survey,* June 1974. For a detailed survey, with photographs, see Sa-at Chandi, *Wan Prawatsat* [Historic Day] (Bangkok: Thambanakhan, 1973).

the people formed to claim the rights of the people in ruling and administering the country for the true benefits of the people."[17] The supporters of the group represented a wide spectrum of opinion. Kukrit Pramot, in an interview, deplored the separation between the administration and the people and underlined the need for a constitution to restrain recourse to violence. Essays by an academic, Khien Theeravit, and a former official and party candidate, Praphansak Kamolphet, who were sympathetic to the students, discussed the constitutional issues. Sulak Sivarak wrote a memoir of the ill effects of coups; and one of the student leaders wrote a stirring exposure of the division in Thai society between the small number of rich, powerful, and privileged and the large number of the deprived.[18]

The sheer range of issues they faced demonstrated both the strength and weakness of the democratic movement. Insofar as the movement concentrated on constitutional objectives, it rallied the great majority of the elite (and much of the urban population), from the king downward. But insofar as it envisioned *social* change—to raise the living standards of the poor, to give equal rights to workers and peasants—the moderate majority took fright. They knew that to carry out these objectives meant a confrontation with the possessors of power and privilege, who would never yield without a struggle.

The enormous problem facing democrats, who genuinely desired a new and more broad-based consensus, was precisely the extent of the gap between rich and poor, between the powerful and the repressed, which had to be reduced if justice were to be done. Prime Minister Sanya, in office from October 1973 until the beginning of 1975, admitted that he "never thought the hardship of the people would be so much. . . . It is the duty of everyone to help the people have a better life."[19] Such hardship was to be confirmed by

17. *Klum riakrong ratthammanun* [Group demanding a constitution] (Bangkok: Bophit Press, Oct. 6–19, 1973).

18. Prasarn Maruekhaphitak, "The Rich and the Poor," in ibid., pp. 12–14. Prasarn had been president of the Chulalongkorn Students Union in 1970 and later was a member of the Central Committee of the Socialist Party; along with Thirayut, Seksan, and other former student leaders, he left Thailand early in 1976, just before the first wave of police arrests of leftists: see Michael Morrow, "Clampdown on the Left Begins," *Far Eastern Economic Review,* Apr. 23, 1976.

19. Message of March 1974, quoted by Saneh, "Thai Politics and the October Revolution," p. 32.

the National Economic and Social Development Board, which revealed that the agricultural sector, with three-quarters of the population, earned less than half the average income per head of those in the urban sector and that the people of the Northeast region received only a quarter of the income of those in the Center.[20]

This was the dilemma facing liberal reformers: to do little or nothing (beyond voicing good intentions) would preserve an immediate consensus, based on stability, while social problems would get worse; yet to attempt to push through effective reforms was bound to antagonize those whose power and authority were basic to Thai society. What made their dilemma acute was that the stability of the pre-1973 era was no longer possible. The downfall of the dictators had opened the floodgate of popular demands, which had previously been suppressed but could no longer be denied.

The impact of the October Revolution was felt in four main areas. First, the army, mainstay of the old system, had suffered a severe psychological shock, which inhibited it for a time from directly intervening in politics. The second effect flowed from the first. As a result of the "power vacuum" after October 1973, political parties, generally of conservative tendencies, began to play an important part in the political process. Third, new forms of economic power had emerged, reflecting the more complex and differentiated development of the Thai economy. Finally, there was both organized and spontaneous activity by formerly "submerged" groups: students, labor unions, and, for the first time, independent peasant associations.

The military, with General Krit at its head, kept a low profile. While the ousting of Thanom and Praphat had fractured the most important patronage networks, Krit stood to gain some of their leaderless followers. His aim as "caretaker" was to let time heal the trauma of October 1973. Accordingly, Krit, in spite of his own well-merited reputation as a "trading general," encouraged a more professional attitude among the military, and at the same time held

20. Average Thai per capita income in 1975: 5,718 *baht* (agricultural sector 3,115 *baht;* nonagricultural 6,341 *baht*). By regions: Center, 10,379 *baht;* South, 5,454 *baht;* North, 3,939 *baht;* Northeast, 2,587 *baht.* (The Northeast contains about one-third of the Thai population; the Center slightly over one-third.) NESDB report, quoted by Somporn Sangchai, "Democracy, Dictatorship or Domino?" *Trends in Thailand II* (Singapore University Press, for Institute of Southeast Asian Studies, 1976), p. 25.

the ring for an evolving conservative consensus, operating through parliament but without imposing "drastic" reforms.

The king, too, placed his great prestige behind constitutional developments. Prime Minister Sanya was his personal choice; he and his advisers selected the 2,436 members of the National Convention, which in turn chose an interim National Assembly. The latter included a substantial proportion of representatives from rural areas as well as active or retired civil servants (the largest single group), and a sprinkling of businessmen and professionals, with less than one-seventh of the members coming from the military or police. However, and this was ominously significant of the polarization that was to follow, students were totally excluded even from the Convention on the grounds that they were "too young" and "inexperienced."[21] Members of the Assembly "tended to be conservative and cautious" and refused to pass legislation detrimental to the wealthier and the entrenched elites.[22] All the same, the Assembly drew up a new constitution—the most liberal political charter, as one scholar noted, that Thailand had ever seen.[23]

Under the provisions of the constitution, elections took place in January 1975 and in April 1976. In each case the Democrats were the largest single party. But they were outnumbered in 1975 by four right-wing parties, representing various factions of former "government parties." These were: the Thai Nation, or "generals party," whose leaders belonged to the Phin-Phao clique of the 1950s, which had lost out to Sarit; the Social Justice (*Thamma*

---

21. Chai-Anan, draft chapter, "The Parliamentary and Electoral Process," in Morell and Chai-Anan, *Reform, Reaction, Revolution.* The most influential gathering in the Assembly was the "Group of 99," led by the technocrat Kasem Chatikavanij (later a minister in the Kriangsak government), which was closely connected with the king. Members of this traditionalist group included such high-ranking officials as the deputy director-general of police (Chamrat), the director of the Border Patrol Police (Suraphon), the secretary-general of the National Security Council (Sithi), and the army chief of staff (Charoen): Chai-Anan, ibid.

22. Somporn, "Democracy, Dictatorship or Domino?" p. 7. However, the Assembly members obliged Sanya to confiscate the property of the "tyrant trio," and land reform legislation was approved.

23. Under the provisions of the constitution, military or civilian officials had to resign if elected to the legislature. Ministers were prohibited from belonging to a board of directors or owning stock in a private corporation. Article 17, the mechanism for authoritarian control from the time of Sarit, was deleted. An administrative court, to adjudicate individual grievances against official actions, was to be set up. And there were sections in the constitution, for the first time, on land reform and local self-government: Chai-Anan, "The Parliamentary and Electoral Process."

*Sangkom*) party, headed by one of the "new rich," which was backed both by Krit and by Air Chief Marshal Dawee, survivors of the United Thai People's Party of 1969–71; the Social Nationalists (*Sangkom chatniyom*), managed by a Chinese-educated businessman and politician, a close associate of Praphat; and the lesser Social Agrarian (*Kaset Sangkom*) party.

The three major right-wing parties had extensive industrial, commercial, and financial interests, as well as intimate links with major military-bureaucratic factions. Thus they represented both the traditional order and its movement toward direct business involvement. These parties, either with the Democrats (in 1976) or Kukrit's Social Action Party (from 1975), formed the coalition governments of the democratic period. The opposition Center and Left were chiefly represented by a party of professionals and academics, the New Force (*Palang mai*), the Northeast-based Socialist United Front (veteran of earlier compaigns), and the Socialist Party backed by Thirayut and other student radicals.

A major weakness of the Kukrit coalition—and still more so that of Seni (prime minister from April to October 1976)—was that time and energy were spent either on political infighting or on tactical devices to keep the government alive at the expense of grappling with the really deep-rooted problems. Among the major political problems were the legacy of arbitrary and unjust authority and excessive centralization. Grave social and economic problems included population growth and migration to the cities, rural poverty, land tenure and indebtedness, unemployment and underemployment, labor relations, and the lack, especially in the countryside, of adequate health, education, and welfare. Both Kukrit and Seni were aware of the need to gain popular support (to provide them with some leverage against the bureaucracy), and they proposed a better deal for the poor (to undercut the threat of rural or urban instability). But the combination of political inexperience, personal rivalries for positions of power or status, and the diversity of interests represented in the coalitions did not make for efficiency, purposefulness, or solidarity.

A further significant change during the democratic period was the growing importance of business in politics, not just in the traditional informal, personal, patron-client relationship between leading generals and officials and selected Chinese businessmen, but in a more direct, formal, and specific manner. Bankers, industrialists in private or government-sponsored enterprises, and traders have always been called upon to provide "subsidies" for politicians and to finance party operations. But after 1973 businessmen both in Bangkok and the provinces were taking their place as of right in party politics. Given the traditional Thai disregard for business as an inferior or alien activity in contrast to service in the bureaucracy or owning land, participation by businessmen in politics denoted a clear change of attitude.

Economic interests were well represented in Kukrit's coalition. The prime minister himself, celebrated for his cultural activities, also had interests in publishing, banking, the hotel business, and commerce. His deputy, Major General Pramarn Adireksan, a leader of the Thai Nation party, was president of the Thai Industries Association and for years worked closely with Japanese enterprises. He had extensive banking, manufacturing (especially in the new growth industry, textiles), and media contacts. The agriculture minister, Thawit Klinpratum, of the Social Justice party, made his money by transporting supplies to American military bases. And Kukrit's party colleague, Finance Minister Boonchu Rojanasathien, had been executive vice-president (and later became president) of the extremely important Bangkok Bank.

The role of the "new men" in the 1976 Seni coalition was even more pronounced. Seni, prime minister and minister of the interior, and one of his deputies at Interior, were practicing lawyers. The other deputy ministers of interior were a retired official from the same ministry, a right-wing newspaper columnist and former company employee (Samak Sunthorawet), and a former village teacher. Besides the leaders of Thai Nation and Social Justice mentioned above, the coalition's foreign minister, Pichai Rattakun, was a businessman (he had also been one of the signatories of the "Group Demanding a Constitution" appeal), as were Prasit Kanchanawat, a wealthy rice trader and leader of the Social Nationalists, and five of the deputy ministers. Finally, on the left of the coalition were a former administrative official also with business connections (Damrong, the Democrat Party secretary-general), a young lawyer (Chuan), and a former newspaperman (Surin); all were members of the Democrat party.[24]

24. For profiles of members of the Seni cabinet, see *Business in Thailand*, May 1976. On the economic interests of the "Soi Rajakhru group" (Pramarn, Chartchai,

Finally, after 1973 there emerged new, hitherto latent or suppressed occupational groups—student movements, organized workers, farmers' associations. These groups were scarcely represented at all in the parties of the coalition, and not much better represented in the opposition parties of the Center and Left. But by mobilizing public opinion on certain issues, they were able to put pressure on, influence, or obstruct official policies. The range and intensity of their activities and their impact on the economic and hence on the political scene were among the major uncertainties facing the government.

Student unity, so memorably manifested against the autocratic regime, quickly fragmented in the wake of personal rivalries and ideological suspicions, the mutual distrust and even antagonism between "superior" university students and socially "inferior" technical and vocational students, and the withdrawal of the moderate majority from militant action after the overthrow of the "three tyrants."[25] But on issues arousing intense nationalistic emotions, such as Japanese economic domination, American military or intelligence activities, and "unfair" concessions granted to multinationals, students were readily mobilized. Further, student activists were in the vanguard of those seeking to help the workers unite and, above all, to politicize the peasants, making them aware of their rights, the possibilities of action, and the political power of organization.

A number of campaigns organized by students and others exposed corrupt business deals, abuses by bureaucrats, maladministration, and the general inequality of the social system. The campaign against the Northrop Company's proposed new airport, for

---

and Siri) leading the Thai Nation party, see "Money Power in Politics," *Athit,* May 16, 1975.

25. Seksan Prasertkul, a political science student from Thammasat, who played a major part in the October Revolution, resigned from the National Student Center of Thailand (NSCT) to form FIST (Federation of Independent Students) whose members were mostly Thammasat students and vocational students. However, groups of vocational students were also organized by the extreme Right into gangs disrupting left-wing activity. Sombat Thamrongthanyawong, a more moderate student from Kasetsart (agricultural) University, led the NSCT in 1974 and organized the "teaching democracy" program in rural areas in cooperation with the State Universities Bureau. Finally, Thirayut founded the smaller "People for Democracy" group, intended to be the nucleus of a national front of democrats. See Chai-Anan, "The Student Movement: Catalyst for the New Thai Politics."

example, revealed a high degree of collusion among bureaucratic, local business, and foreign interests, with much "lubricating" money changing hands during the Thanom-Praphat era. Similarly, the TEMCO issue, involving tin mining rights in the Gulf of Thailand, erupted after villagers, miners, the provincial governor (who paid for this later), and students joined forces to expose corruption by political-business interests, which allowed the country's mineral resources to fall into foreign hands. This greatly alarmed foreign investors and Thai big business, who saw the situation as detrimental to business confidence and the overall investment climate. Military atrocities against villagers during counterinsurgency operations also came under attack. Finally, the "Mayaguez affair," when U.S. forces used the Utapao air base, in collusion with the Thai military but without the Kukrit government's permission, aroused widespread anger against the United States.[26]

Most of the time, however, the majority of students, feeling that democracy had been achieved, were back at their studies. But the activist minority had become more intransigent and militant.[27] In 1974 Marxist activists gained control of the NSCT, and by 1975 every student union in Bangkok was under radical control. For active students it was a time of great excitement, with hundreds of books and pamphlets on Marxism and Maoism being published and widely read. Yet a distinction could still be drawn between radicals and revolutionaries, although it was perhaps more over tactics than fundamentals. Both believed the party system to be a sham, but radical students and workers were nevertheless prepared to take advantage of the freer political climate to pursue their aim

26. Prudhisan, "The Democratic Experiment."
27. Chai-Anan, "The Student Movement." Seksan himself criticized the "immature extremists" among the students. Their actions, he said, distracted public attention from practical issues of better working conditions or higher wages, while turning everything into a confrontation of students against government: speech in January 1975, quoted by Robert F. Zimmerman, *Reflections on the Collapse of Democracy in Thailand* (Singapore: Institute of Southeast Asian Studies, occasional paper no. 50, April 1978), p. 64. On the way in which student leaders sought to raise the level of struggle against the "old system," and to establish a common front (*sam prasarn* or "triple alliance") of students, workers, and peasants, see Chaianan Samudavanija, *Prachathipatai sangkom niyom khomunit kab kan muang thai* [Democracy, socialism, communism and Thai politics] (Bangkok, Pikhanet, 1975), pp. 273–278, 282–283, 295–298.

of building a mass movement of direct action. The attitude of revolutionaries (members of the Communist Party of Thailand), on the contrary, was governed by their experience of more than two decades of suppression of open political activities. They saw themselves more as an armed vanguard of professional revolutionaries, in the Leninist or Maoist style. Both types sought to rally the support of the mass of poor people in the cities and in the countryside. Yet the party cadres were only too aware of the likely reaction of the authorities to the "destabilizing" impact of an effective movement of workers and peasants.

The workers' situation, in turn, reflected the growth of the labor force,[28] especially in the Bangkok area, their freedom from restraint after more than a decade of bans on unions and on any forms of strike action, and the harsh effects of the economic recession, accompanied by inflation, into which Thailand had been plunged during and after 1973. Thus there was an enormous increase in sporadic protests and strikes, many caused by employers refusing to negotiate or retaliating to wage demands by unfair dismissals and cutbacks in hours employed. The worst hit were the women workers in the textile industry (most severely affected by the recession), whose hardships gave rise to a mass protest supported by all workers' associations in June 1975. As a result of the publicity that ensued, the workers gained considerable public support for their demands. These included an increase in wages, a law requiring disputing parties to negotiate, and authorization of systematic bargaining procedures. The passing of a labor relations law and the establishment of a labor relations committee were landmarks in Thai labor history.[29]

Although one of the associations that emerged, the Labor Coordination Center of Thailand, adopted a radical, anticapitalist standpoint, most unions, grouped in the Federation of Labor Unions of Thailand, were moderate. One of their leaders expressed their views: "I don't want to reject the present government.

28. The total nonagricultural labor force had increased from 2.2 million in 1960 to 3.2 million in 1970. By 1977, according to the Labor Department, there were 1 million handicraft workers; 1 million in commerce; 400,000 in transport and communications; 217,000 in the construction industry; and 1.4 million in the service sector: Chai-Anan, draft chapter, "Labor," in Morell and Chai-Anan, *Reform, Reaction, Revolution.*
29. Prudhisan, "The Democratic Experiment."

I just want to change its ways and to work more for the poor people."[30]

As for the government, its ambiguous attitude toward economic nationalism—publicly supported because it was a popular issue, and privately denied out of a desire to placate foreign firms and to encourage lagging foreign investment—also characterized its dealings with the labor movement.[31] On the one hand, unions were legalized, the seriously understaffed Labor Department valiantly sought to mediate in employer-employee disputes, and a minimum wage was fixed. This minimum wage doubled over the period 1973 to 1975 to 25 *baht* ($1.25) a day in and around Bangkok, less in the further provinces. On the other hand, the government was plainly alarmed at the increase in strikes and lockouts. There were some four times as many in the single years 1973 and 1974 as in the entire period from 1968 to 1972.[32] Understandably, given their very low standard of living, workers were insisting on increased pay, cost of living allowances, and welfare benefits. Employers' representatives, however, constantly inveighed against labor "disruption" and the role of students in supporting strikes, which they blamed for the current economic stagnation along with the international recession and the uncertainty caused by the collapse in 1975 of right-wing governments in Indochina.

Meanwhile in the countryside the situation was, and is, potentially the most serious of all. Rural problems are the result of a high annual rate of population growth (more than 3 percent during the 1960s) combined with limited cultivable land. The consequence is

30. Arom Pongpanon, president of the Labor Union of the Metropolitan Waterworks Authority, interviewed by *The Nation*, Jan. 11, 1976, quoted by Chai-Anan, "Labor." However, Arom's practical stance did not save him from arrest after October 1976. He was later released by the Kriangsak government. He died of cancer in 1980.

31. Direct foreign investment in the first five months of 1975 dropped by 51 percent over the corresponding period in 1974: *The Investor* (Bangkok), September 1975. Both foreign and domestic capitalists were reluctant to invest because of uncertainty about the political future, labor unrest, lack of clear-cut official policy on investment or industries, and the "maze of red tape" (these are still major problems). "Meanwhile, local money piles up in bank accounts or is funnelled abroad, often illegally. (For example, Thailand is one of the three largest sources of foreign investment for Hong Kong.)": Norman Peagam, *Far Eastern Economic Review*, July 30, 1976.

32. *Business in Thailand*, June 1975; also Labor Department statistics quoted by Chai-Anan "Labor."

fragmentation of holdings, indebtedness, lack of alternative employment, a striking increase in landlessness and tenancy, especially in the Central Plain, and extensive migration, particularly from the impoverished Northeast. The notable increases in production of rice and upland crops such as corn, tapioca, and kenaf had resulted largely from expansion of acreage, now coming to an end, while yields remained low. The "green revolution" has barely made its appearance in Thailand. But even if it does, in the absence of institutional reforms, it will benefit the richer and more enterprising farmers who have the capital or "credit-worthiness" to invest in seeds, tractors, water control, and fertilizers—at the expense of the growing number of landless laborers and mini-holders.[33]

The Kukrit government's intentions in 1975 were to reverse the notorious flow of wealth from the countryside to Bangkok, which has been brought about both by fiscal policies, such as the "premium" or export tax on rice, and by the banking network, which channels provincial investments into financing construction, joint ventures, or real estate speculation in and around Bangkok.[34] Its policies included land and tenancy reforms, inherited from the Sanya caretaker government, an imaginative agricultural price support scheme, the transfer of 5 percent of bank deposits as loans to farmers, and, most dramatically, the handout in 1975 of 2.5 billion *baht* ($125 million), increased in 1976 to 3.4 billion, to be shared equally among the 5,000 rural commune (*tambon*) councils.[35]

The reality, however, is that effective land redistribution depends not only on the composition of the committees set up to supervise the reforms and on preventing too many exemptions from the provisions, but on proper titles to land, which few Thai farmers possess. The poorest farmers, needing loans most, are the least credit-worthy; the price support scheme ran foul of urban interests and poor planning; and the government grants to the communes were dispersed among units too small to use the funds

33. See "Uneven Rural Development" in Chapter 2.

34. For example, the Northern region has only 5.7 percent of Board of Investment-promoted industries; the Center region has 82 percent: Henry Robbins, *Business Review,* May 1975.

35. For details, see Siriwan, "Money for the Grass Roots," *Business Review,* September 1975. Reviving the *tambon* fund was a major plank in Kukrit's and the SAP's campaign during the 1979 elections.

economically. Doubts were also cast on the reason for the grants (vote buying) and on the way in which they were spent. Dirt roads soon washed away by rain, administrative expenses, and over-priced construction material were three of the main charges.

Still more ominously from the standpoint of reforms, the one independent peasant organization, the Farmers' Federation of Thailand, which with student support had been championing the cause of tenant farmers (especially in the North) and urging the full implementation of land reforms and rent regulations, met bit-ter opposition from provincial officials (who regarded it as "il-legal") and from local landowners. During 1974 and up to mid-1975 many of its leaders were assassinated by unknown killers widely suspected to have been hired by elements of the extreme Right. The killings were a clear warning, as one observer points out, that the Federation's leaders should cease their activities if they wanted to stay alive. After the assassinations, the organization ceased growing and rapidly dwindled as an important element on the political scene. By 1976 it was seldom heard from any more.[36]

The political process in the three years of democracy, after the ousting of the former military leaders in October 1973, went through three distinct stages: preparing the electoral foundations (the royally appointed Sanya government), political construction (Kukrit's coalition, March 1975 to April 1976), and rapid and total disintegration (Seni's coalition). In each stage, two increasingly di-vergent tendencies became apparent. First was the political at-tempt, on the one hand, to build a new parliamentary consensus and thereby to establish a *modus vivendi* with the military and civil-ian bureaucracy, and, on the other, to carry out much-needed and long-delayed reforms. The second tendency was the reassertion of military power after the traumatic shock of October 1973. This was gradual at first, but gained increasing momentum, both in

36. Chai-Anan, draft chapter, "Farmers and Modern Thai Politics," in Morell and Chai-Anan, *Reform, Reaction, Revolution;* also Norman Peagam, *Far Eastern Economic Review,* Aug. 22, 1975; and "The Grave Issue of Rural Unrest," *Investor,* August 1975. See also the series in the weekly *Matuphum,* "From the Past to the Future: the Resistance and Suffering of Thai Farmers," especially Apr. 2, 1979, on the founda-tion of the Federation of Thai Farmers (*Sahaphan chaona chaorai haeng prathet Thai*), its struggle for implementation of land reform legislation, and the reaction of capitalists and landlords linked with government officials. Short biographies of the assassinated peasant leaders are given.

reaction to labor and student unrest and to the reformist aims noted above which were seen as a threat to military interests. (The military and right-wing reaction, culminating in the October 1976 coup, is analyzed in the next section.) The interplay of military factions has been extremely complex since the ousting of Marshals Thanom and Praphat in 1973. These factions are outlined in Appendix 5A.

The high point during the constitutional era in the move toward technocratic reform was the coalition of Right and Center parties under Kukrit Pramot. But at the same time the underlying divergence between military and politicians came into the open. This was partly the result of the power play of the deputy prime minister, Major-General Pramarn, leader of the Thai Nation party, who had been building himself up as the strong man needed for the salvation of his country. As defense minister he sought to promote his adherents to top military posts, at the expense both of the foremost military patron, General Krit, and of the increasingly active followers of the exiled Praphat.

Kukrit's rural strategy was intended to give a new deal to the countryside, and thus develop an important electoral base for his Social Action Party. An essential part of the strategy was the announcement in January 1976 of support prices for rice, which would benefit farmers, but would also mean higher prices for urban consumers. Trade unions and students, outraged by the jump in prices (and arguing that most farmers, having already sold their crop, would not gain), vehemently protested against this measure, and Kukrit capitulated. The opposition parties took advantage of his setback to propose a Center-Left coalition, whose leaders expected to come to power after a vote of no confidence in the Kukrit government.[37] To forestall this "unacceptable" alternative, military leaders made their intentions clear to Kukrit, who called for general elections instead. (The extreme-Right movement, *Nawaphon*, was already demanding the formation of a "national reform council" to replace parliament.)

37. The Democrats apparently agreed, with the New Force, Socialist Party, and Socialist United Front, on a policy of effective government control of the rice trade and state intervention in key sectors of the economy; abolition of the anticommunist act; and a shift toward a more nonaligned foreign policy: Chai-Anan, draft chapter, "The Breakdown of the Coalition and the Return to Military Government," in Morell and Chai-Anan, *Reform, Reaction, Revolution*.

Violence, intimidation, and harassment directed against the Center-Left and Socialist parties were notorious in the April 1976 election campaign. "Socialism of every kind is Communism" was a typical slogan used by the Right. As a result of these unremitting pressures and insinuations, combined with an emotional patriotic crusade, the left-wing parties were virtually wiped out. The Democrat Party, providing a safer alternative for voters, gained heavily, forming a new coalition government with the Right. But Prime Minister Seni (Kukrit's elder brother) was unable to assert his leadership over the disparate coalition or even over his own divided party. Left-wing Democrats, feuding with their right-wing colleagues, sought to replace the Thai Nation party with Kukrit's group and so revitalize the government's program.[38] Party factionalism, immobilizing the government, increased as military probes and pressures were stepped up.

It was General Krit, however, who stood in the way of all-out provocation. Krit's economic interests were best served by stability; he had a personal stake in the evolving conservative political process. And after retiring as army commander-in-chief he intended to pursue his own parliamentary aims. The death of Krit shortly after the elections not only removed the political "stabilizer," but let loose all the powerful, vengeful, and dissatisfied military and security elements hitherto held in check.

## Reaction (1976–1980)

The events of 1976 were the culmination of right-wing reaction to the student-led October Revolution three years before.

The traditional establishment, managers of the "bureaucratic polity" (the armed forces, police, and civil service), had been divided in their response to the "new dawn" of democracy. Some welcomed the greater exposure of the masses to modernization,

---

38. The Democrats were divided into factions, the "progressives," headed by party secretary-general Damrong Lathapipat, who favored economic and social reforms, and the "old guard," notably represented by Samak Sunthorawet, who had military backing and close connections with the Thai Nation Party. Samak was the only politician to join the postcoup Thanin government. As leader of the "Thai Citizens" party, he made a remarkable comeback in the 1979 elections. For a good political analysis, see Somporn Sangchai, "Some Observations on the Elections, and Coalition Formation in Thailand, 1976," reprinted in Clark D. Neher, ed., *Modern Thai Politics* (Cambridge, Mass: Schenkman, 1979).

which, it was believed, after the initial disorientation would provide an "integrating" stake in society for hitherto unpresented or repressed elements. Others were more skeptical about the alleged benefits of emancipating the masses; but they took comfort from the fact that the royally sponsored caretaker government (and its elected successors) were proceeding with caution and good sense, that the administration continued to perform, and that the post-1973 military leaders were behaving constructively (furthering their investments, keeping a low profile). Still others, however, notably among the army commanders and military intelligence, were appalled by the spread of student demonstrations, industrial action, and the stirrings of the peasantry. Steeped in counterinsurgency lore and tactics and obsessed with the problem of subversion—with the "lesson" of Vietnam, Laos, and Cambodia so close at hand[39]—they concluded that Thailand had become a prey to mass movements, guided by a "third hand" (communism) which the feeble institutions of democracy encouraged and could not control.[40]

This is not to suggest that the majority of the military-administrative establishment went along with the extreme rightists. On the contrary, the "mainstream" officers and officials would no doubt have preferred to stand aside and, as some of them stated at the time, to allow the parliamentary process to run its course.

39. See the interview with Colonel Han Phongsithanon, a former staff officer in the Internal Security Operations Command (ISOC), in *Chaturat,* Feb. 17, 1976, quoted by E. Thadeus Flood, "The United States and the Military Coup in Thailand," *Indochina Resource Center,* October 1976.

40. The view that the Left, especially the student activists, were more destructive of parliamentary "politics of balance and compromise" than were the Right, is the theme of an interesting analysis by Roger Kershaw, "The Denial of Pluralist Democracy in Thailand," *Art International,* January 1978. A similar argument, singling out student and academic "irresponsibility," underlies Zimmerman's *Reflections on the Failure of Democracy.* The short answer to Kershaw is that the "balance and compromise" shown in Western pluralist democracy depend on a basic consensus on values and goals: this consensus is missing in Thailand. Thus Kukrit's policy of compromise may have been desirable, as in a number of respects I think it was; but as a result of pressures from the powerfully placed Right and from the vociferous Left (these characterizations more accurately represent their respective strengths) the politics of compromise could not last. For a detailed refutation of Zimmerman's thesis see John Funston's review in the *Journal of the Siam Society* 68(1), 1980. And note especially Chaianan's commendation of political democracy combined with social democracy to bring about peaceful change: *Prachathipatai sangkom niyom khomunit,* pp. 283, 299–300, 304, 318.

Three factors, however, neutralized this apparent neutrality. First, even if the conservative mainstream did not work for a coup, its members did little or nothing to prevent the rightist offensive that led to the coup. (While moderates may have disapproved of the excesses of the right wing, they saw the latter as a necessary counterweight to the Left.)

The second factor was the rapid polarization of the country as a result of intensified rightist propaganda and of direct pressures by elements of the military. This brought about a corresponding reaction by left-wing students and workers, as the right intended. The ensuing paralysis of parliamentary government, deadlocked between parties of Right and Center, divided between irreconcilable factions and personalities, and therefore unable to agree on how to deal with an increasingly critical situation, in effect removed the "moderate" option from the scene, leaving a political void. The regular military hierarchy (itself a prey to faction and intrigue) and the conservative administrators could then no longer remain "above the battle," but were forced to act.

The crowning factor was the seal of approval by the king.[41] The king's fundamental political interests, one observer points out, are aligned with stability rather than change, with order rather than the disturbing "noise" of representative processes. Throughout 1975 and 1976, it would appear, the king became increasingly convinced that the results of an open political system threatened the very foundations of the monarchy; that student, labor, and farmer leaders were "communist agitators" or were influenced by them; and that even the demise of the Chakri dynasty, following the recent end of the monarchy in Laos, was a distinct possibility. That was the message the king was receiving from those whose advice he considered most valuable. What was needed, therefore, was a return to the earlier fusion of royal legitimacy and military power.[42]

41. See the informative article by Roger Kershaw, "Three Kings of Orient: King Bhumiphol Adulyadej of Thailand," *Contemporary Review,* May 1979. Kershaw points out that the king's behavior in 1976 destroyed his standing with Thai intellectuals and the student movement (which was previously very high). He notes that Kukrit had pleaded in vain for the monarchy not to take sides, but instead play a unifying, reconciling role. See also his assessment of the controversial position taken by the queen, preoccupied with the future of the dynasty, and the poor qualities of the crown prince.

42. David and Susan Morell, "Thailand: The Costs of Political Conflict," *Pacific Community,* January 1977. See also Zimmerman on the king's fear of communism

There is little reason to doubt the threefold strategy of the extreme Right: to provoke a confrontation with the Left, to isolate the Left (and liberals of the Center) by an aggressive propaganda campaign, and to create, in the public mind, fears of turbulence and insecurity. Under the resulting conditions of polarization, the Right would then be able either to proclaim martial law (as had been threatened more than once in 1975) or to use the "revolutionary-subversive" danger they had conjured up as a pretext for a takeover.[43]

This strategy had been developing in three main ways: (1) recruiting, training, and subsidizing counterrevolutionary gangs; (2) sponsoring mass organizations "with national ideology"; and (3) manipulating important means of communication (army-controlled radio stations, television, the press, leaflets, rumors) not only to disseminate patriotic themes extolling "Nation, Religion, King," but also to "expose" a wide range of opinion (from liberals and progressives to radicals and Marxists) as the voice of agents or dupes of communism.[44]

Thus the feeble structure of democracy began to break under the weight of steadily increasing military probes and pressures.

---

and the encouragement this gave to the Right: *Reflections on the Failure of Democracy*, p. 81. As another observer comments: " . . . in the minds of the conservative upper echelons, of which the king was the leading member, the distinction between Thai socialism and communism was at best one of semantics": Thomas A. Marks, "The Status of the Monarchy in Thailand," *Issues and Studies* (Taiwan), November 1977.

43. *Nawaphon's* spokesman, Wattana Khieowimon, openly declared in a speech at Khonkaen in October 1975 that his movement would polarize the domestic situation and create conditions of political unrest that would permit a coup: *Nawaphon* publication, *Kaen Prachachon*, quoted by Flood, "The United States and the Military Coup in Thailand."

44. Radical student leaders acknowledge the important role of the media in stirring up opinion against the Left before the October coup: "The military owns more than half of the radio stations in the country, and all but one of the TV stations in Bangkok. Except for a very few popular newspapers . . . all are either owned or connected with the ruling class groups. These controlled media were used to spread rumors against progressive groups, to distort information, . . . and make the people confused and bored by politics. To a large extent these efforts were effective" (statement by "National Anti-Fascist Front of Thailand," *Asian Student News* [special issue on Thailand], January–February 1977). Specific examples of right-wing propaganda denouncing students, teachers, and professors for stirring up antagonism in society in order to subvert national security are quoted in Chaianan, *Prachathipatai sangkom niyom khomunit:* see especially the letter from the "Free People of Thailand," pp. 287–288.

The right-wing campaign, which gathered force as the parliamentary governments lurched from crisis to crisis, received substantial support from two important sources: from the traditional
"establishment," fearful of where democracy could lead, and from
wealthy businessmen anxious to use their funds to "reinsure" with
the emerging power alternative.

The "shock troops" of the right-wing offensive were gangs of
disaffected vocational and technical students, dropouts, or other
unemployed youths, who were readily mobilized (for gain or envy)
against the socially "superior" university students. They were
armed and sent into action to disrupt university demonstrations
and political rallies, to break up strikes, and to be used as "guns for
hire."[45] Prominent among them were the Red Gaurs, or Wild Buf-
faloes (*Krating dang*) directed by officers of the Communist Suppression Operations Command (after recognition of China in 1975
renamed Internal Security Operations Command, or ISOC [*Kong
raksa khwam mankhong phai nai*]). A Red Gaur leader insisted that

45. Michael Richardson, "Thailand: How the Right Won," *National Times* (Sydney), Nov. 29–Dec. 4, 1976, includes an interview with Colonel Sudsai Hasdin, head
of ISOC's hill-tribe division, and a "key sponsor and adviser" to the Red Gaurs.
Members of the Red Gaurs are also said to have served among the CIA mercenaries
in Laos. See also Ben Anderson, "Withdrawal Symptoms: Social and Cultural Aspects of the October 6 Coup," *Bulletin of Concerned Asian Scholars*, July–September
1977. In Anderson's view, the new strata of middle and petty bourgeoisie, formed
by the great economic boom of the 1960s, provide the social base for quasi-popular
rightist movements like the Red Gaurs. The old ruling cliques still hold power, but
they have found new "popular" allies; this is the reason for the new level and style of
violence, symptomatic of the social, cultural, and political crisis in Thailand. For the
Red Gaurs are the children of a new and vulnerable petty bourgeoisie, who are
liable to a paranoiac response when economic conditions go wrong. (Anderson is
right about the petty-bourgeois anticommunism of the Red Gaurs, reflected in a
revealing interview with Somsak Khwanmongkon, head of their strong-arm unit, in
*Porithat*, Sept. 30, 1977. But Somsak also criticizes the failure of the postcoup government to listen to public opinion and to improve economic conditions. As he puts
it: "I was close to some of the present Ministers. Now they are big men, they may
forget me.") However, I think Anderson overstates the current systemic causes and
neglects the "traditional" way in which powerful or wealthy patrons make use of a
following, even among the rootless and insecure. The fact is that once the coup took
place, these extremist groups were discarded: they had played their part in creating
confusion and unrest (preconditions for the coup) and their usefulness was at an
end. In a period of (enforced) stability, their association with violence was an embar-
rassment. Note, however, Khien Theeravit's view that the reactionary groups still
survive, on the understanding that their services may be required by the government security agencies: "Thailand," in *Southeast Asian Affairs 1979* (Singapore:
Heinemann, for the Institute of Southeast Asian Studies, 1979), p. 304.

Thailand needed a strong government—to prevent communist subversion—and an obedient people: "Only calm will make the Red Gaurs disband: If the situation gets worse, we will be strengthened."[46] The ideologically oriented organizations include *Nawaphon* (new force, or ninth force, alluding to the king, ninth in the dynasty), set up by a group of "senior rightist army officers,"[47] the "village scout movement" (*luk sya chao ban*) under royal patronage; and intimately connected with all three, a well-known religious foundation run by the charismatic monk Kittiwutto. Such was the concrete manifestation of "Nation, Religion, King."[48]

The atmosphere of anger, prejudice, and fear animating the Right, and unleashed by the media among the masses, attained a degree of hysteria which one would hardly believe possible were it not for the example that other countries have shown, before and since.[49] Such hysteria was revealed in Kittiwutto Bhikkhu's notorious attempt to justify the killing of left-wing activists and com-

46. Interview with Colonel Sudsai reported by Norman Peagam, "Rumblings from the Right," *Far Eastern Economic Review,* July 25, 1975. The Red Gaurs at this time acted with impunity. Even though demonstrators and bystanders were being killed or wounded in repeated clashes and bomb attacks, the police made no move to arrest those responsible. (In 1980 Sudsai formed his "Mass Line" party.)

47. Ibid., for reports on leaders of the right-wing movement. The Morells point out that, just as the Red Gaurs are a product of counterinsurgency, so *Nawaphon,* too, clearly originated in the American-backed psychological warfare operations of ISOC and military intelligence: David and Susan Morell, "Thailand and the U.S.," *New York Times,* Nov. 22, 1976. *Nawaphon's* founder, Gen. Wallop Rojanawisut (formerly head of military intelligence), came to appreciate the importance of "the temple and the palace" in Thai society in 1953, "when I went abroad for the first time for further study in psychological warfare in the United States": Peagam, "Rumblings from the Right."

48. *Nawaphon* and the Red Gaurs made conspicuous use of the royal couple as a rallying symbol, often displaying their portraits during demonstrations against leftists. That no attempt was made to criticize or forbid such use was evidence for the Left of tacit royal support for the forces of the Right. The king's visit to a Red Gaur training site in 1976 was prominently publicized: Marks, "Status of the Monarchy."

49. Broadcasts by the Bangkok Armored Division radio were particularly important in whipping up mob feelings against "communists." If leftists do not change their line of thinking, according to one broadcast, "we will fight them . . . until the scum of the earth—these persons—are completely destroyed": quoted in Marks, "Status of the Monarchy." The defense minister of the Seni government, General Thawit, spoke up on the same radio in support of its operations, while hundreds from "Thai patriotic groups," including *Nawaphon,* and the village scouts, also demonstrated in support. (The Seni government had been considering whether to close down the station): Armored Division Radio, July 12, 1976.

munists, despite the fundamental Buddhist rule forbidding the taking of life.[50] And it was expressed even by moderate elements among the military. If protests against foreign interference go too far, declared General Saiyud, director of ISOC, and if they cause conflict between workers and employers, this enables "people from outside" to infiltrate and use workers' groups as a tool to destroy the stability of government.[51]

In this feverish atmosphere rightist groups flourished, and almost any act of violence (to destroy the subversive threat) was considered permissible. Thus the aim of *Nawaphon* was to rally householders, businesspersons, religious people, retired civil servants, provincial notables, and others who distrusted social change and feared for their possessions in a movement overtly opposed to "student power" and workers' associations.[52]

At this elemental level of mass emotion and fear the village scouts played a crucial role. Ostensibly nonpolitical and originating in the king's deepening concern with national security, the scouts were organized for village self-defense, trained to identify subversion, and imbued with a sense of patriotic mission. The village scouts were started in 1971 by an officer of the Border Patrol Police (BPP)

50. See Chapter 4, above, "Nation, Religion, King." In 1978 Kittiwutto figured in a scandal involving Sangad's brother (a major-general), smuggled Volvos, a woman friend, illegal timber operations, and arms traffic with right-wing Khmer and Lao dissidents: see story in *Athit*, Aug. 1, 1978; and Richard Nations, *Far Eastern Economic Review*, Aug. 11, 1978.

51. Similarly, violent or opposition movements of youth, students, workers, teachers, professors, democrats, socialists, and communists, who claim that the country is "not just" and that Thai values and institutions are "backward," are aiming to destroy the institutions and present system of government: General Saiyud Kerdphon and Somchai Rakwijit, *Anakhot khong thai* [Future of Thailand] (Bangkok, Krung Sayam, 1975), pp. 182, 301. Saiyud and Somchai (a research consultant to ISOC) are "cold war liberals," readily identifying most forms of unauthorized opposition, said to be creating "confusion" and "disunity," as communist-inspired; yet they also urge the reform of corrupt and oppressive organs of government in order to avert revolution.

52. Puey Ungphakorn, *Khwamrunraeng lae ratpraharn 6 tulakhom 2519* [Violence and the coup of October 6, 1976], Oct. 28, 1976 (roneo), p. 10. "*Nawaphon's* organisers used mass meetings to whip up support, combining the emotional appeals of nationalism and anti-communism. . . . The popular appeal of the nationalist message promulgated by *Nawaphon* was greatly strengthened by the public advocacy of Kittiwutto Bhikkhu": William Bradley, David Morell, David Szanton, and Stephen Young, *Thailand, Domino by Default: The 1976 Coup and Implications for U.S. Policy* (Athens, Ohio: Ohio University paper in international studies, 1978), p. 11.

and are quite distinct from the "Boy Scouts," who have long existed in Thailand. But the village scout movement did not take off until 1974, when the monarchy took the program under its direct patronage. Through the efforts of the BPP (also under royal patronage) the scout movement spread to all the provinces. Currently there are reported to be some 2 million village scouts, while the king hopes to bring this up to 5 million. Groups of 300 to 500, directed by the BPP, undergo training sessions in every province: they work and play together, listen to lectures, and sing patriotic songs. At the end of the course they take an oath to be collectively responsible for their country to defend it against communism.[53] The village scout movement, like *Nawaphon,* bears the hallmarks of American counterinsurgency work in Vietnam and elsewhere. Underpinned by the formidable power and resources of the Ministry of the Interior, the movement benefits from the lavish publicity given its royal visitors and from the donations of the wealthy elite.[54]

The increasingly strident propaganda of *Nawaphon* and similar organizations, the acts of intimidation by armed groups like the Red Gaurs, and the mobilizing of villagers in the scout movement provided the chief forms of support for the right-wing offensive.

It was in this atmosphere of crisis that the two exiled leaders, Praphat in August and Thanom in September 1976, deliberately returned to Bangkok, causing controversy among supporters and rivals in the military, protests among the students, and further confusion in the government. The king and queen, at this critical juncture, unmistakably showed their approval of the old order by personally visiting the royal monastery (Wat Boworniwet), where Thanom was ordained, to "pay their respects."[55]

53. "Chodmai chak muang thai," [Letter from Thailand], *Siam Times,* November 1976; and *Chaturat,* Aug. 19, and 31, 1976: quoted by E. Thadeus Flood, "Village Scouts: The King's Finest," *Indochina Chronicle,* January–February 1977.

54. Leadership of the village scouts is drawn heavily from the better-off farmers and the provincial elite: Natee Pisalchai, "Village Scouts," in *Thai Information Resource,* no. 1, May 1977, quoted by Ben Anderson, "Withdrawal Symptoms." Although the scouts flourished under the vehemently anticommunist Thanin regime, they became less conspicuous under Kriangsak. In March 1978, Kriangsak transferred the police major-general, who happened to be president of the village scouts, from his post as deputy commander of the Border Patrol Police, and in April 1978 he explicitly warned the scouts against interfering in state affairs.

55. David and Susan Morell, "Thailand: The Costs of Political Conflict."

Among the military, ambitious generals associated with Pramarn took advantage of the turmoil to prepare a coup, while Krit's men (Krit, appointed minister of defense by Seni, had died) tried to upstage followers of Praphat. In the protest against Thanom's return, two activists were killed and then hung (by local police) near Bangkok, further intensifying student rage. The murders were reenacted by two students in a demonstration at Thammasat University. In a press photograph, one of the "hanged" student actors appeared to resemble the Crown Prince, who had suddenly been summoned back to Bangkok by the royal family from military studies abroad. Whether this resemblance was intended or not, the incident was seized upon by the right-wing press and radio, which vehemently denounced the students for *lèse-majesté;* the militant National Student Center of Thailand was accused of being communist and of seeking to destroy the monarchy.

Early on the morning of October 6, while some 2,000 students were continuing a sit-in demonstration at Thammasat University, police (on the prime minister's orders to investigate) encircled the building. Gunfire broke out, but the police rejected the students' appeals for a cease-fire and their claim that they were holding peaceful and lawful assembly. The police commander then ordered his men to fire "in self-defense" against the students. This was followed by the arrival of the battle-trained Border Patrol Police, who launched a massive assault with grenades and high explosive shells. (It is not clear who ordered the assault.) Hundreds of extremist vigilantes (the Red Gaurs) were massed outside the university and bus-loads of village scouts were mustered from not far away where they were in reserve. The crowds had been worked up by incessant propaganda into a state of frenzy against "communist" students who deserved to die for attacking the "sacred institutions" of their country.

The bloody suppression of the student movement provided the coup conditions under which the military (whether the extreme Right, as was later alleged, or the "regulars" of the military hierarchy, who in fact displaced their rivals) decided to act. In the three days of news blackout, the supreme command headquarters patched together a "National Administrative Reform Council" of the top field commanders, staff generals, and naval and air force chiefs. Meanwhile, students, leftists, and Vietnamese migrants (to add color to the notion of a foreign plot) were rounded up, the provinces being much more drastically purged than Bangkok itself. Hundreds of students went underground or joined the communists in the jungle.[56] A government was then formed, with royal assent, headed by an honest, but vehemently anticommunist Supreme Court justice, Thanin Kraivichien, with Samak as minister of the interior, and three leading military representatives as deputy prime minister and minister and deputy minister of defense.[57]

The coup of October 1976, the king declared two months later, was necessary to prevent the country from succumbing to political chaos, internal subversion, and external aggression. "At a time when our country is being continually threatened with aggression by the enemy, our very freedom and existence as Thais may be destroyed if Thai people fail to realize their patriotism and their solidarity in resisting the enemy. . . . Accordingly, the Thai military has the most important role in defense of our country at all times, ready always to carry out its duty to protect the country."[58]

The fundamental assumption that unregulated democracy is too dangerous, because it allows communists to seize power by manipulating democrats, is shared by almost all the leaders of the armed forces.[59] From such extreme, but for the most part sincerely held, beliefs, the activities of military-backed regimes naturally flow. If military leaders believe that moderate and leftist elements in politics and society really are communist agents or dupes, then it

56. See Chapter 7.

57. General Bunchai, who had recently retired as army commander-in-chief, was appointed deputy prime minister; Admiral Sangad Chaloryu, ex–supreme commander of the armed forces, and General Lek Naewmali, former head of the National Security Council, were the minister and deputy minister of defense. The other deputy prime minister, a civil servant, was a personal friend of the prime minister. The deputy minister of the interior, and the ministers of foreign affairs, commerce, justice, education, public health, and the State Universities Bureau were all civil servants, and the minister of agriculture was a retired civil servant.

58. Address of Dec. 3, 1976: text in *Siam Chodmaihet*, Dec. 2–8, 1976.

59. Most clearly articulated by Prime Minister Thanin: "When you deal with politics, you've got to be wary of the middle ground because that is where the communists creep in, disguised as liberals. . . ." During the previous three years, "it was communist policy to persuade Thai politicians to take the middle ground by letting the communists participate in government. Their aim was a coalition government with some communist members and then replacing noncommunist members one by one": news conference for foreign correspondents, *Bangkok Post,* Nov. 19, 1976.

follows that they believe it is necessary to control or suppress leftist influence and opinions with the utmost rigor—hence the wide-ranging powers to detain "troublemakers" under military "Order No. 22,"[60] the reassertion of draconian provisions of the "Anti-Communist Law,"[61] the extreme bias in favor of the executive in the 1976 Constitution,[62] the stringent regulation of universities and schools,[63] the banning of strikes,[64] the purging of institutions in the

60. Order no. 22 was announced by Army Commander-in Chief General Serm na Nakorn on October 15, 1976. Nine categories of persons were described as being "potential dangers," including "persons who stir up trouble, persons who by one means or another urge the people to support any regime other than democratic rule with His Majesty the King as Head of State, and persons with occupations that offend good morals." Further regulations were made public on October 20, 1976. They provided that all those seized under martial law may be held for six months without trial, that all cases are to be decided by military tribunal with no right of appeal, and that wide areas may be designated "communist-infested areas." In these zones, civil liberties may be suspended, authorities may carry out searches without warrants "at any time," and all residents may be ordered out "within a set period": *New York Times*, Oct. 17 and 21, 1976.

61. The Anti-Communist Law, under which areas may be declared "communist-infested," was to have been repealed by the Kukrit government, but it failed to do so.

62. The Constitution of October 22, 1976, was decreed by the king and counter-signed by Admiral Sangad, head of the armed forces' National Administrative Reform Council (NARC). Article 18 states that the cabinet and the "Prime Minister's Advisory Council," comprising members of NARC, "shall jointly formulate policies for national stability." Article 21 states that "in cases where the Prime Minister deems it necessary to prevent, restrain or suppress any act subverting the stability of the Kingdom, the Throne, the national economy or the affairs of the State, or any act disturbing or threatening public order or the good morals of the people, or any act destroying national resources," the prime minister, with the consent of the cabinet and his Advisory Council, "shall be authorised to make any order or take any action," and the latter "shall be considered lawful." See also text in *Bangkok Post*, Oct. 23, 1976.

63. Thanin's minister of education, Dr. Pinyo, reported that the entire schools' curriculum would be "reconstructed"; most of the reform proposals of the Seni government had been rejected: *Bangkok Post*, Nov. 12, 1976. The State Universities Bureau (a government agency) announced the need for "greater supervision" of the universities. The bureau was empowered to restrain or stop the activities of educational institutions if they contravened regulations or "are a danger to stability, national security, peace and order, or the good morals of the people": Dr. Prasert na Nakorn, undersecretary of the bureau, in an interview with *Siam Rath*, Nov. 12, 1976.

64. The minister of the interior announced that, while martial law is in force, a strike by employees or a shutdown or lockout by employers is absolutely prohibited: *Bangkok Post*, Oct. 27, 1976. The supreme commander of the armed forces announced in January 1977 that strikes were harmful to national security, and violaters were threatened with imprisonment: Norman Peagam, *Far Eastern Economic Review*, Feb. 4, 1977.

provinces, and finally (and logically) the boosting of the enforcement machine.[65]

Although Thanin was not the military's first choice for prime minister after the October coup,[66] he had impeccable credentials: a justice of the Supreme Court, a man with a reputation for integrity, an ardent anticommunist whose writings had become standard fare at military academies, an adviser to the Internal Security Operations Command, and a person closely associated with the palace.[67] Yet Thanin's year in office was not a happy one. Ironically, the very men who had appointed him in October 1976 were to blame him most severely when they overthrew his government a year later.

An evidently inspired statement on the morrow of the 1977 coup explained:

> ... in the beginning the civilian government [whose appointment by the military was "commendable"] received the support of the public and the people were willing to undergo restrictions placed upon them for the sake of national security. However, as time passed by, disillusionment set in as more and more people began to feel that the government was too rigid, was not responsive to public opinion, and repressed the mass media. In the end, large sections of the population, including laborers, became seriously disaffected. ... Meanwhile the domestic and foreign policies of the government also tended to isolate the government from the people, and the country from other Third World countries. ... [It] was felt generally that the communists could take advantage of the situation to mobilise disaffected fractions to set up an effected nucleus for revolution.[68]

65. As General Kriangsak, secretary-general of NARC, put it: "The anticommunist program will be two-pronged. The first prong will be to improve the economy. The second will be to strengthen the armed forces' capability. We will plan to buy more weapons, ships and ammunition." Press conference, reported by Richard Nations, "Bangkok's New Objectives," *Far Eastern Economic Review*, Nov. 19, 1976.

66. Others approached had evidently declined. They included a former deputy prime minister in the Sanya administration, Prakob Hutasingh, privy councillor Prapas Oueychai, and former commerce minister Chao na Sylvana: Norman Peagam, *Far Eastern Economic Review*, Nov. 5, 1976.

67. Thanin was reportedly "a political adviser to Queen Sirikit, who is believed to share his forceful views": ibid. As a signal mark of royal approval, Thanin was appointed by the king to membership of the privy council two months after he had been ousted by the October 1977 coup.

68. "Comment," *Bangkok Post*, Oct. 21, 1977. In an excellent analysis of the situation under Thanin, Montri Chenvidyakan points out: "His government grew increasingly inflexible, excessive and incapable of coping with the seriousness of the national problems." As a result of stringent press censorship, more than 20 news-

As Admiral Sangad, spokesman for the military coup leaders, emphasized: "There was disunity, divisiveness and lack of cooperation. Government officials felt insecure in doing their work. The economy of the country has been going bad.... [Thanin's 12- to 16-year] democracy development program ... was too long and was not according to the wishes of the people."[69] A damning indictment indeed!

The failure of the Thanin government—for which the military bore more responsibility than it cared to acknowledge—had three main causes: (1) Thanin's obsessive anticommunism and its implications, (2) the government's ineffective policies, and (3) the growing divergence between top military leaders—themselves in an unstable position—and Thanin's overly ambitious interior minister, Samak.[70] Ironically, the latter, too, had formerly benefited from military support.

Thanin's anticommunist zeal resulted in rigorous indoctrination of civil servants, regressive educational controls, pressure on labor unions (under martial law they were forbidden to strike), severe press censorship, and rigid isolation from countries like China, Cambodia, and Vietnam. The extremely narrow basis of Thanin's government, which was composed of personal friends of the prime minister, officials and retired officials, and right-wing ideologues, was not conducive to carrying through the vigorous policies required, and expressed, by the ministers. The highly publicized anticorruption and antinarcotics drives, for example, foundered be-

---

papers and weeklies were closed: the press "retaliated by carrying more rumors, innuendoes and sensational crime stories—all of which greatly undermined the creditability of the government." Thanin acted repressively toward the labor movement, claiming that it was infiltrated by communists. And although the government made a start with land reform, this was undermined by the severe drought which hit the country in 1977. Montri, "One Year of Civilian Authoritarian Rule in Thailand: The Rise and Fall of the Thanin Government," in Montri, ed., *Social Science Review*, 1978.

69. Admiral Sangad's announcement of the seizure of power, Oct. 20, 1977.

70. The unstable position of top military leaders was revealed most conspicuously by General Chalard's attempted coup in March 1977. Chalard, a protege of Pramarn, had lost out in October 1976. His was therefore an "outsider's" coup, and no such attempt has yet succeeded, though not for want of trying. Chalard, after failing, was executed a month later. There are a number of obscurities about this event. For a blow-by-blow account, see *Siam Rath*, Mar. 26, 1977. For a recapitulation of available evidence, see *Thai Nikorn*, Mar. 24, 1978.

cause of vested interests deeply entrenched in the system. Military leaders like Kriangsak, secretary-general of the postcoup National Administrative Reform Council and by October 1977 supreme commander of the armed forces, increasingly distanced themselves from an unpopular and largely discredited administration. The last straw for many of the military was the demogogy and ambitions of Samak, which became both embarrassing and a potential threat. The armed forces' leaders insisted on the dismissal of Samak, which Thanin obstinately refused, and the long-anticipated coup took place.

It is clearly an exaggeration to characterize the dismissal of Thanin's government, as the communist party does, as the result of conflict between the "warlords" and the "feudalists." (The "feudalists," according to the communists and socialists, represent royalty and its patronage network; the king himself is referred to as the "big feudalist.")[71] The coup was the result more of a clash of personalities than of established interests. But policies were involved, in the sense that Kriangsak's more relaxed, pragmatic stance (and the able people he attracted to his cabinet) were at least an alternative to the abrasive, yet ineffectual methods of his predecessor.

Essentially, however, the Kriangsak regime was a reversion to the bureaucratic polity. Diverse military interests, though by no means reconciled, were well served. The defense budget has shown a remarkable 25 per cent increase each year since 1976. (The army gets the lion's share, more than the navy and air force combined). Altogether, defense and internal security, which is largely the responsibility of the police, amounted to more than one quarter of the 1978 budget.[72]

Kriangsak's aim was to build on the currently favorable military situation by developing a longer-term governmental structure. In

71. The Communist Party of Thailand's radio station, "Voice of the People of Thailand," Jan. 6, 1978.

72. Figures in the *Bangkok Bank Monthly Review*, September 1977. Defense was also the largest single item in the 1979 budget (19 billion *baht*) followed by education and economic services (each nearly 18 billion *baht*): *Far Eastern Economic Review*, Sept. 1, 1978. In addition, U.S. military sales credits to Thailand amounted to $29.5 million in 1978 and $30 million in 1979. Altogether the Thai government was expected to increase its foreign military purchases from $100 million in fiscal year 1979 to $400 million in 1980: *Far Eastern Economic Review*, Feb. 2, 1979.

doing so, he attempted to maintain a careful balance of forces, particularly within the army, neutralizing adversaries and advancing friends, and to broaden his political support (against rivals to the Right) by making some overtures to the Center and Left.

After the "cold war" of the Thanin period, the time was ripe for detente. Kriangsak moved to reduce tensions with communist neighbors abroad (see Chapter 6); and to relax tensions within Thailand, which had been aggravated by Thanin's rigidity and obsessive anticommunism.[73] The most dramatic example was Kriangsak's granting amnesty in September 1978 to the "Bangkok 18," arrested in October 1976 along with some 3,000 others (most of whom were later released) on charges of communist subversion and lèse majesté. The trial of the 18 before a military tribunal had been widely protested; and the proceedings were in fact turning into a popular triumph for the students, not the prosecutors.[74]

Kriangsak, again in contrast with Thanin, began by easing the censorship of the press, although the amendments to the anticommunist act drafted in November 1978 once more severely curbed freedom of expression, according to the Thai Press Association.[75] Kriangsak also extended his patronage of moderate leaders of labor unions, especially in the state enterprises, which had been under threat of deregistration under Thanin. But by April 1978 he was warning workers: "I will not tolerate anything endangering our country's peace and order. It is time for unity among the people to develop our economy."[76] The reason for his concern was made

73. Students, for example, were allowed to elect their unions or "associations" (*samoson*) in which the Left was well represented. Unions have acted cautiously, emphasizing social rather than directly political issues. In August 1979 they surveyed the needs of poor people in Bangkok and urged the government to control prices of necessities such as bus fares, electricity, and water rates.

74. Leaflets calling for the release of the 18 from trial by the military court, although denounced by the authorities as "the work of communists," could well be regarded as an appeal for justice instead: *Porithat*, Sept. 30, 1977.

75. Amendments to the anticommunist law empower the authorities to close newspapers whenever it is considered appropriate. Somboon Worapong, president of the Thai Press Association, and a leading member of the Thai Lawyer's Association both criticized these sweeping provisions. (Thai Information Center [Sydney], Nov. 15, 1978.) Censorship of foreign news reports and radio/TV features was announced by the government spokesman, the extreme rightist Colonel Uthan Sanitwong, in August 1979. Moreover NARC order no. 42, rigorously controlling the press, was retained. *Nation* (Bangkok), Aug. 23, 1979; *Bangkok Post*, Aug. 24, 1979.

76. *Asiaweek*, Apr. 14, 1978.

clear a few months later, when he pointed out that workers who observed law and order and did not strike "created more confidence among foreign investors."[77] The minimum daily wage was increased in 1978 from 28 to 35 *baht* ($1.40 to $1.75) for Bangkok and the surrounding area; as a result of further increase in the cost of living, in October 1979 the prime minister had to accept the 45 *baht* ($2.25) long demanded by moderate unionists. However, the solidarity of the labor movement has been severely weakened by government manipulation, union disputes, and personal rivalries.[78] Moreover, "security officials . . . continue to view the labor movement as potentially subversive and destructive; they will not hesitate to intervene whenever there is labor unrest . . . for the sake of national security."[79]

Government policy toward the countryside was no less contradictory. The prime minister rhetorically proclaimed 1979 to be the "Year of the Farmer." But land reform, never too evident in performance (as opposed to promise), languished under Kriangsak even more than under Thanin.[80] What is worse, the farmers have

77. *Bangkok Post*, Dec. 27, 1978. And note this recent report: "Director General of the Labor Department Vichit Saengthong said yesterday he still considers necessary the imposition of the law banning strikes by workers and shutdown by employers. . . . Thailand's economy is already in bad condition and any more labor troubles would only ruin the investment atmosphere, Vichit said . . . ": *Nation*, Feb. 26, 1980.

78. "Union leaders themselves are the main instrument of conflict," according to a recent commentary. Paisan Thawatchainan, president of the National Labor Council, is accused of being "Kriangsak's man." The rival Council of Labor Unions of Thailand under Thanong Laovanich is accused of being a tool of ISOC. A third leader is said to be not a genuine worker at all, but merely seeking money and prestige through foreign connections. Finally, the head of the railway workers' union is alleged to be closely associated with a former communist leader (Prasert Sabsunthorn) now working for various military groups. Suntorn Kunwathanaworaphong, "1 May Labor Day," *Prachamit*, Apr. 17–24, 1979.

79. Khien Theeravit, "Thailand: An Overview of Politics and Foreign Policy,": *Southeast Asian Affairs 1979*, pp. 302–303.

80. "While . . . the farm sector participates in the increased funding [for the 1979 budget] there is no major drive to improve rural infrastructure and incomes—despite pledges by the government": Peter Fish, "Kriangsak Spends More on Arms," *Far Eastern Economic Review*, Sept. 1, 1978. With a total cultivated area in Thailand of more than 100 million *rai*, the target for land redistribution under the 1977–81 economic plan is 10 million *rai* (6 million under private ownership and 4 million in state lands) to go to 400,000 farmers: Agricultural Land Reform Office, reported in *Bangkok Post*, Nov. 15, 1976. The target for the first year was 1 million *rai* (about one-third in private hands), but only one-third of that was actually dis-

no organization of their own to defend their interests, but depend on officials who, for the most part, are only remotely concerned with villagers' problems. "Once, the students served as a link between farmers and the government; they frequently voiced the farmers' grievances . . . [but] since the October 6 coup, any contact between students and farmers has been viewed as conspiratorial."[81]

To further strengthen the means of "suppression," the amended anticommunist law was approved by the appointed National Assembly in February 1979. Under the new rules, a suspected communist can be detained for a maximum of 480 days without trial. Directors of communist suppression operations, commissioned military and police officers and grade 3 (mid-level) civil servants are empowered to arrest or conduct searches, without requiring a warrant, for persons or objects connected with communist activities at any place and at any time.[82] Yet the provisions of the previous law were already excessive, as a member of the Seni cabinet had pointed out: "The way it stands now there are vast opportunities for officials to arrest any person they like on a communist charge."[83]

Kriangsak's main objective was to link the bureaucracy, including key supporters in the armed forces, with an assembly effectively under the control of government-appointed members and sym-

tributed. Another 1 million *rai* was the 1978 target, but only one-third seemed likely to be distributed: Special Report on Land Reform, *Siam Rath weekly review* June 5, 1978. See also Kriarkiat Pipatseritham, "Land Reform Program, 1977–1981: An Analysis," *Social Science Review*, 1978. In 1980, a senior official of the Agricultural Land Reform Office (ALRO) pointed out that the land reform program was in limbo, as the government seemed to have lost interest in it. He said ALRO had bought about 120,000 *rai* for distribution to tenants, which was far lower than the target of 2.2 million *rai*: "Land expropriation in our country under the circumstances is a lost cause": quoted in *Bangkok Post*, Apr. 12, 1980. The magnitude of the problem can be gauged from the fact that only about five percent of the land outside the Center has been adequately surveyed: "The Land Squeeze," *Investor*, August 1975. Further, only about one-fifth of the total cultivated area is held under full title deeds, chiefly in the Center. Almost another one-fifth is farmed under either a temporary license or a permanent title with limited transferability and use as collateral. The remaining three-fifths is farmed without any legal title whatsoever, merely by customary usage: *Investor*, August 1975; Toru Yano, "Land Tenure in Thailand," *Asian Survey*, October 1968.

81. Khien, "Thailand: An Overview," pp. 303–304.
82. *Bangkok Post*, Feb. 2, 1979.
83. Deputy Interior Minister Khunthong, reported in *Bangkok Post*, July 15, 1976.

pathizers. With this aim in mind, the appointed National Assembly of the Thanin era was transformed in April 1979 into an appointed Senate and an elected House of Representatives. This was under a constitution (approved in December 1978) that was masterfully manipulated by Kriangsak to assure his continuance as head of government on an established basis rather than as leader of a successful coup.

Under the 1978 constitution there is an appointed upper house of 225 members, and an elected lower house of 301. (Of those actually appointed, all but 31 are from the armed services, particularly the army, whether serving officers or retired. In the 1975 Senate, by contrast, no active service officers were represented.) The upper house votes with the lower in joint session on matters of national security, the throne, national economy, budget, and no-confidence votes. The prime minister and 44 cabinet members do not need to be elected.[84] Under the election bill (January 1979) Thais with alien fathers (i.e., mostly Chinese) were not allowed to vote: this effectively excluded nearly one-quarter of the previously eligible voters in Bangkok.

With his stronghold in the Senate and support from independents (traditionally susceptible to official persuasion) and from parties formed on his behalf, Kriangsak could not "lose" the 1979 election. But the results, nevertheless, were surprising.[85] The major opposition parties—Kukrit's Social Action, with its rural-technocratic base, Samak's Thai Citizens sweeping the Bangkok

---

84. The obstacles to amendment of the illiberal features of the Constitution are formidable: see John McBeth, "Searching for Democracy," *Far Eastern Economic Review*, Aug. 29, 1980.

85. The voting turnout for all of Thailand was less than 44 per cent. Bangkok had the lowest proportion—less than 20 per cent—a fitting commentary on the importance of the exercise. The gains of the Social Action Party, winning 88 seats, reflect Kukrit's performance as prime minister in 1975 and the party pledge to restore the *tambon* grants program. Samak's Thai Citizen Party won 29 of 32 Bangkok seats, humiliating the Democrats, whose lone successful candidate turned out to be none other than former foreign minister Thanat Khoman. (The Democrats with 115 seats in 1976 were reduced to 35 in 1979.) Samak's vigorous demagogic personality, with his ability to mobilize the village scouts and other "patriotic" groups, paid off handsomely. Thai Nation won 47 seats; the pro-Kriangsak *Seritham*, 26 seats; *Chart Prachachon*, 10; the liberal New Force, 8; various minor parties, 16; and independents, 39. Narong Kittikachorn, exiled with Thanom and Praphat after October 1973, failed to win in Petehaburi. None of the Social Democrats were elected.

polls, the Democrats still influential in the South, and the conservative interests behind Thai Nation—claim considerable popular support. And if they come to be allied with one military faction or another, they may well have more than a nuisance value.

Kriangsak's three cabinets corresponded to successive phases in policy. The first was the successful "reconciliation" phase, which was particularly welcome after the rigidity and repressiveness of Thanin. The second cabinet, formed after the April 1979 elections, disappointed the expectations aroused in the previous phase. And the third cabinet, reflecting bureaucratic contempt for elected politicians and the urban public (hard hit by drastic price increases imposed in February 1980), collapsed. Kriangsak's resignation followed soon afterward.

Yet not many months before, a wide spectrum of Thai opinion, concerned at the danger from Vietnam, had rallied around the prime minister in an expression of solidarity against the enemy. In the latter half of 1979, however, the external crisis was overtaken by internal events—especially the soaring cost of living—while the Vietnamese threat receded. National solidarity faded in a wave of domestic criticism of an arrogant and unresponsive regime. Kriangsak's initial support thus eroded in four major areas. In ascending order of importance (to the regime) these are: the urban public, the political parties, the banking community, and the military.

Protests over the harsh effects of inflation caused by the OPEC price increases and compounded by government mismanagement and corruption were vigorously expressed by the parliamentary opposition—the four major parties combining to form a majority of the elected members[86]—by labor unions, notably among workers in state enterprises,[87] and by student representatives. Further, while the Kriangsak government alienated much of the urban population, it had also failed to satisfy the farmers, owing to bureaucratic obstruction of reforms,[88] in addition to long-standing official policies favoring the supply of cheap rice for the towns.

86. One hundred fifty-five members voted to censure Kriangsak in his concurrent post of minister of agriculture in July 1979; 188 (out of 301) elected members voted on a motion of no confidence in October 1979.

87. Unions were demanding the right to strike, representation on government-appointed bodies dealing with labor issues, and increased cost-of-living allowances.

88. See Richard Nations, John McBeth, and Kamolwan Sonsomsook, "A Democratic Trial of Strength," *Far Eastern Economic Review,* Oct. 26, 1979.

The influential banking community, too, was dissatisfied with the government's muddled economic strategy, which was an uneasy blend of welfare paternalism and technocratic ideas.[89] Finally, Kriangsak's vital support among the military[90] was being eroded from two directions: first by the growing independence of the army commander-in-chief and defense minister, General Prem, revealed in the September 1979 promotions list[91] and, second, by the shifting attitudes of reformist and progressive younger officers, notably the "Young Turks," who were well represented in the appointed Senate.[92] The Young Turks had been instrumental in Kriangsak's overthrow of Thanin, later backed Kriangsak against Sangad, and were now moving toward Prem.

The accumulation of grievances against Kriangsak came to a head in February 1980 with the prime minister's rapid-fire decision, without prior public announcement or parliamentary consultation, to drastically increase oil, gas, and electricity prices,[93] followed by the complete overhaul of his cabinet.[94] There was no

89. Ibid.

90. Kriangsak had hitherto stayed on top through an adroit application of checks and balances. With the backing of the Young Turks, Kriangsak had outmaneuvered Admiral Sangad, coleader of the coup against Thanin. In August 1978 Kriangsak won the support of General Yot (Praphat's faction) with the post of deputy defense minister and balanced him with one of his own men, Admiral Amorn. Kriangsak and General Lek then switched positions, Kriangsak taking Defense and Lek the Interior. In the September 1978 promotions, Army Commander-in-Chief Serm was pushed up to the largely ceremonial post of supreme commander of the armed forces, and General Prem, who was close to Kriangsak, was appointed commander-in-chief instead. General Saiyud of ISOC became chief of staff, supreme command. In Kriangsak's second cabinet, formed in May 1979, Prem took charge of Defense, Serm became deputy prime minister, and Lek continued with Interior.

91. Prem's men headed the list. General San Chitpatima was appointed deputy army commander-in-chief; Lt. Gen. Pin Thammasri replaced Lt. Gen. Thep Kranlert as commander of the First Army region. See *Siam Rath weekly review,* Oct. 7 and 14, 1979.

92. Some 25 middle-ranking officers in the Senate felt that Kriangsak had betrayed his promise of reform made on taking power in October 1977: Richard Nations et al., "Democratic Trial of Strength." For an analysis of the ideas of the Young Turks and democratically inclined officers from major to colonel rank, see "Military Dictators '79," *Athit,* Nov. 14, 1978. Among the leaders of the Young Turks are Colonels Chamlong Srimuang, Manoon Rupachorn, and Prachak Swangchit. Chamlong was appointed secretary-general of the Prime Minister's Office in the Prem cabinet.

93. Prices of all oil products went up from between 24 to 60 percent, cooking gas about 33 percent, according to the Feb. 9, 1980 decision. Oil prices had already been twice increased in 1979.

94. Foreign Minister Upadit, a survivor of the Thanin regime, was replaced by

attempt to explain the price rises, to show how the government intended to cope with the problem, or to compensate poor people for the higher costs of living. This extraordinary example of arrogance and contempt, followed by the formation of a cabinet of bureaucrats virtually without elected members, stung the politicians into fury and provoked workers, labor leaders, and students into mounting massive protest demonstrations.[95] When it was evident that Kriangsak faced widespread defections from among his appointed members, and that General Prem ostentatiously remained aloof, the prime minister's position became untenable. Without effective military support Kriangsak could neither hold out against the parliamentary opposition nor, in the traditional style, stage a coup. Kriangsak resigned, and Prem was elected in his place by a large majority from both houses. In March 1980 Prem formed a cabinet, bringing in leaders of the three major opposition parties (but not Samak), in an attempt to solve both the crisis of legitimacy and the economic crisis.[96]

The events of February to March 1980 are something of a

---

Air Chief Marshal Sithi Sawetsila, concurrently secretary-general of the National Security Council (who retained both posts in the Prem cabinet). General Lek was appointed deputy prime minister, but was replaced at Interior by a senior official from the ministry, Pratuang Kiratibut (who continued under Prem); many other ministers were replaced, chiefly by officials. For lists of ministers in the "Kriangsak 1" and "Kriangsak 2" cabinets, see *Thai Rath*, Feb. 13, 1980.

95. For example, some 5,000 rallied at the Thammasat University campus at a meeting organized by 18 student unions, to which politicians, labor unionists, and student representatives were invited to discuss the price increases. The opposition parties also concerted their attacks on Kriangsak: "Crime is rising, the economy is deteriorating, corruption is rife," as one of them put it: *Bangkok Post*, Feb. 20, 1980.

96. Prem, prime minister and minister of defense, on February 12, 1980, appointed four deputy prime ministers: Serm, the supreme commander; Democrat party leader, Thanat Khoman; *Chat Thai* leader, Pramarn; and Social Action's deputy leader, Boonchu Rojanasathien, then president of the Bangkok Bank. Air Chief Marshal Dawee and Generals Yot and Thep, members of Kriangsak's cabinet, were dropped; Sithi and Pratuang were retained in their posts. Kukrit, while approving the cabinet, remained outside it. An experienced commentator emphasized the dominance of the "military-industrial-banking establishment" and urged the government not to forget the interests of labor and the less privileged in town and countryside. He questioned whether Prem would get the sincere cooperation of the wealthy members of the cabinet when it came to issues of social justice and reforms such as an inheritance tax: Theh Chongkhadikij, *Bangkok Post*, Mar. 13, 1980. On the interests at stake, see also Sunissa Hancock, *Bangkok Post*, Mar. 17, 1980. As if to counterbalance the industrialists and technocrats, Prem set up a "brains trust" advising on economic, political, and social affairs, headed by his army deputy, General San, which included prominent academics from NIDA, Chulalongkorn, and

"mini–October 1973": divisions within the army combined with popular protests bring about the fall of a military prime minister; the political parties voicing popular demands are then brought into the system. But, as was the case during the previous democratic period, the resulting parliamentary coalition of divergent personalities and interests is precarious. And, in the present case, Prem, although at present strongly backed by the military, is inexperienced in politics. The acclaimed priorities of his government are to reduce inflation, control the prices of essential goods, aid drought-stricken farmers, suppress crime, and resolve the refugee problem. But questions remain. Can Deputy Prime Minister Boonchu and his team of technocrats cope with the short-term economic crisis, using one set of measures, and at the same time carry through the long-term restructuring of the economy, using a different set?

Among the short-term problems are the rising cost of oil imports, which is likely to double from $1.5 billion in 1979 to an estimated $2.6 billion in 1980, and which could redouble in 1981, creating a formidable trade deficit; inflation running at about 15 percent in 1979 and somewhat more in 1980; the drought threatening rice, fruit, and irrigation supplies in 17 provinces of the Center, North, and Northeast, which could lead to a massive migration of farmers looking for sustenance and work in the towns; and the spectacular increase in crime, fostered by unemployment, inflation, and availability of weapons. The longer-term question is whether the technocratic belief in private enterprise and market forces will pay off in increased production "filtering down" to the underprivileged majority in town and countryside, or will widen the gap between rich and poor, causing social conflict instead.[97]

As for the political prospects, what will be the attitude of the military if the government stumbles? Above all, will the present

---

Thammasat Universities. Professor Somsakdi Xuto, minister attached to the Prime Minister's Office and government spokesman, is chairman of the political and foreign affairs section; members include Drs. Chaianan, Thinapan, Kramol, Saneh, and Khien: for a list of names, see *Bangkok Post,* Mar. 17, 1980.

97. Boonchu's ideas, especially on promoting the private sector, have been forcefully presented in a number of interviews: for example, in the *Bangkok Post,* Apr. 20 and June 9, 1980; and in the report by Ho Kwon Ping, "Thailand Inc.: An Open Door for the World's Multinationals," *Far Eastern Economic Review,* May 23, 1980.

parliamentary experiment, in view of the experience of 1975–76, be given *time* to establish a viable coalition between conservative politicians and moderate bureaucrats, given the contending pressures from the powerful unreconciled Right (suspicious of policies of the center and fearful of subversion) and the demands for thoroughgoing social and economic reforms which can be mobilized by the Left?

In the short term, a military-technocratic alliance, indicated by the division of labor in Prem's own cabinet, is most likely to emerge.[98] The advance of the technocrats is evident in the bureaucracy, banking and business, and the political parties. And the technocrats are quite compatible with military "professionals." Neither technocrats nor military need liberal democracy in order to carry out their objectives; to the contrary, technocrats can work under, and often prefer, the discipline and "order" imposed by authoritarian regimes.

This military-technocratic alliance may well coexist with a conservatively oriented and subordinate parliament. However, if the latter were to prove difficult, assertive, and "obstructive," the military may again resort to repression. Yet military coups are no longer (unlike in the old days) accepted by those outside the bureaucracy as natural or inevitable; they are subject to the law of diminishing returns. Under these conditions, the prospects for Thai society, even if they do not indicate an imminent popular upsurge, are that confrontation will increasingly replace consensus.

## Appendix | Military factions, since the ousting of Marshals Thanom and Praphat in 1973

1. General Krit, army commander-in chief from 1973–75, was the leading military patron and political power broker until his death in April 1976. Associated with him were General Serm na

___

98. The cabinet approval in September 1980 of the extension of Prem's tenure as army commander-in-chief for a further five years (until 1985) is clearly designed to consolidate the military-technocratic alliance. Prem would otherwise have retired from the army in October 1980 (at the age of 60), leaving a contested choice of successor. For General San, the front runner, was opposed by many of the Young Turks and by the ambitious first division commander, Maj. Gen. Arthit Kamlang-

Nakorn, army commander-in-chief 1976–78, then supreme commander of the armed forces and deputy prime minister, 1979 and 1980; and the previous commander-in-chief, General Bunchai Bamrungphong, who became deputy prime minister in the Thanin government and the first Kriangsak government.

2. General Kriangsak Chomanan, a staff man trained in the United States and long associated with the U.S. military, became supreme commander of the armed forces in October 1977, led the coup against Thanin, and formed his own government in November 1977. He outmaneuvered his rival, Admiral Sangad Chaloryu, in 1978, balancing off other factional chiefs, and staged elections in 1979; he resigned as prime minister in 1980. In the key position under Kriangsak was the independent-minded General Prem Tinsulanon, commander-in-chief in 1978, concurrently defense minister, 1979, who replaced Kriangsak as prime minister in 1980; General Lek Naewmali was former head of the National Security Council, a deputy minister under Thanin, defense minister in 1978, and interior minister in 1978 and 1979.

3. Members of the Praphat faction, reinforced by the return of their patron from exile in January 1977, include General Yot Thephasdin, first army commander before and during the October 1976 coup, who became assistant commander-in-chief, then, under Kriangsak, deputy defense minister. Yot's successor as head of the first army, General Amnart Damrikarn, a Serm man, was replaced in 1978 by General Thep Kranlert, who is related to Yot and Praphat. (In 1980 Thep moved to Defense.)

4. General Chalard Hiranyasiri, former commander of Thai forces in Vietnam, leader of the abortive March 1977 coup attempt, had been promoted to deputy commander-in-chief in March 1976 by the then defense minister, General Pramarn, but this was revoked by Krit supporters. Chalard was executed in April 1977.

5. Chalard and General Vitoon Yasavat were the chief losers, among the military, in the October 1976 coup. Vitoon, a former

---

ek. The king, worried about the effect of instability within the military, reportedly played an important role in persuading the political parties of Prem's coalition to back the extension of Prem's army tenure beyond the official retiring age (the relevant act is to be amended). See John McBeth, *Far Eastern Economic Review*, Sept. 12, 1980.

Krit man and opponent of Praphat, had been leader of the Thai "volunteers" in Laos and was linked with the Democrat Party in 1976.

6. Each commander of the three military regions outside Bangkok—the North, Northeast, and South—is important in his own right.

7. Other key bodies are the Internal Security Operations Command, the Special Forces Unit at Lopburi, and the Ministry of the Interior's paramilitary Border Patrol Police, organizations which derived their influence from close association with U.S. military advisers and the CIA in intelligence and counterinsurgency operations. The king is also considered to be a patron of the Border Patrol Police.

8. Finally, there are the "Young Turks," activists among the regimental and battalion commanders, who are discontented with the immobility of the old order but have no concrete proposals to put in its place. The Young Turks backed Kriangsak against Thanin and later against Sangad, but in 1980 abandoned Kriangsak in favor of Prem.

# 6 | External Involvement

Thailand's foreign policy since the end of the Second World War has been shaped by the aims and interests of the Thai military-bureaucratic system in an international environment of super-power rivalry. Thai leaders, during the cold war period, played an important part in the American strategy of containment of communism. Thailand has especially been affected by the fateful struggle for control of Indochina.

Because the army in Thailand was so long and so firmly entrenched in power (right up to the early 1970s) it tended to take an extremely conservative, even reactionary, stance toward other elements of society. The army also reflected the prevailing international currents. Thus before the Second World War the army leadership was authoritarian, nationalistic, and pro-Japanese. It admired Japan as a modernizing, expansionist, militarist Asian power. After the War, following the brief civilian interlude ended by the 1947 coup, the army leadership was authoritarian, nationalistic, and pro-American. It shared the same fear and suspicion of "international communism" and the drives for world domination of Moscow and Peking, aided by Hanoi, as did the United States. The anti-communism of Thai regimes and of successive U.S. administrations coincided: both saw it as in their mutual interest to suppress communism internally (through economic aid intended to prevent discontented elements from turning to communism or, if this failed, through counterinsurgency) and to halt communist expansion externally. Hence the partnership between Thai and American governments, in which Thailand became a forward base or unsinkable aircraft carrier, as an integral part of U.S. strategy to "save" Vietnam, Laos, and (after 1970) Cambodia from communism.

*The U.S. Alliance*

For almost two decades, the security interests of successive U.S. and Thai governments coincided. Thailand became an important ally of, and provided essential services to, the United States in an area considered "vital" to America's security. In return, military-dominated Thai governments, bolstered by U.S. military and economic aid, were assisted in suppressing internal "subversion," which was liberally interpreted to mean any serious domestic challenge to the established order. At the same time they were protected against the threat of external aggression by U.S. intervention against communist-led "national liberation movements."

In the 1950s and 1960s Washington's policy toward Thailand went through four overlapping phases: the United States viewed Thailand as a "free world bastion," a domino, a case for counterinsurgency, and the backup for the Indochina war. Indeed the bastion and domino attitudes persisted throughout the fifties and sixties and well into the 1970s, while counterinsurgency and the Indochina role began with the Kennedy administration in the 1960s.

These attitudes toward Thailand must be seen in the context of America's Asian policy. As early as June 1949, the U.S. National Security Council had warned that "the extension of communist authority in China represents a grievous political defeat for us; if Southeast Asia also is swept by communism we shall have suffered a major political rout the repercussions of which will be felt throughout the rest of the world."[1]

Thailand's strategic importance to the United States thus became evident. A conference of all American ambassadors in the Far East was held only a few months later in Bangkok to assess the implications of the complete communist victory in China.[2] At the same time Washington decided that "all practical measures be taken to prevent further communist expansion in Southeast Asia," and especially in Indochina, which "is under immediate threat"; if Indochina came under communist domination, Thailand and Burma could be expected to fall.[3] Shortly afterward, President Truman

1. NSC 48/1 of June 1949: extracts quoted in *The Pentagon Papers: The Defense Department History of United States Decisionmaking on Vietnam*, The Senator Gravel Edition (Boston: Beacon Press, 1971), vol. 1, p. 37.

2. J. Alexander Caldwell, *American Economic Aid to Thailand* (Lexington, Mass.: Lexington Books, 1974), p. 4.

3. NSC 64, dated Feb. 27, 1950: text in *Pentagon Papers*, vol. 1, pp. 361–362.

granted $10 million in military aid to Thailand. In June 1950 came the outbreak of the Korean war, when Phibun dispatched 400 troops to the U.N. side. The first U.S.-Thai military assistance agreement followed in October.[4]

From the Thai standpoint, "by 1950 Phibun and other government leaders were convinced that Communist China was a menace to all the countries of Southeast Asia . . . but he was not prepared to join an anticommunist alliance until he was sure that it would have the full support of the United States."[5] A year later, Phibun, Phao, and Sarit staged the 1951 coup, abrogating the constitution, dissolving and banning political parties, "because of the present world situation and because of communist aggression and widespread corruption."[6] Such sentiments neatly coincided with those of the next U.S. Secretary of State, John Foster Dulles, who in his first foreign policy statement in January 1953 inveighed against the "deadly serious threat" of communist "encirclement." In 1954 the United States, facing "a determined effort by Communist China to extend its influence southward," moved to fill the "power vacuum" in Southeast Asia: the Southeast Asia Treaty Organisation (SEATO) was established, with its headquarters in Bangkok.[7] Thus Thailand "succeeded in fashioning itself as the bastion of Western defense in Southeast Asia."[8]

Overlapping with the free-world-bastion view of Thailand was the phase of the domino theory. This too, as we have seen, began with the Truman administration. In a statement that was to have major consequences, the National Security Council (NSC) decided in June 1952 that:

Communist domination, by whatever means, of all Southeast Asia would seriously endanger in the short term, and critically endanger in the longer

---

4. Frank C. Darling, *Thailand and the United States* (Washington, D.C.: Public Affairs Press, 1965), pp. 69, 78, 80.

5. Donald E. Nuechterlein, *Thailand and the Struggle for Southeast Asia* (Ithaca: Cornell University Press, 1965), pp. 103–104. Phibun went on to recognize the French-backed Bao Dai government in Vietnam, against strong opposition from the foreign minister (Pote Sarasin), because he "desperately wanted American protection of Thailand, and he believed that he could expect large amounts of aid from the United States in return for his pro-Western policy": ibid., p. 106.

6. Darling, *Thailand and the United States*, p. 92.

7. Nuechterlein, *Thailand and the Struggle for Southeast Asia*, p. 114.

8. George Modelski, ed., *SEATO: Six Studies* (Melbourne: 1962), pp. 87–88, quoted by Nuechterlein, p. 115.

term, United States security interests. The loss of any of the countries of Southeast Asia to communist aggression as a consequence of overt or covert Chinese Communist aggression would have critical psychological, political and economic consequences. In the absence of effective and timely counteraction, the loss of *any single country* would probably lead to relatively swift submission to or an alignment with communism by the remaining countries of this group.[9]

According to the NSC "Statement of Policy," "the danger of an overt military attack against Southeast Asia is inherent in the existence of a hostile and aggressive Communist China"; although "domination through subversion" is more likely. In either event, alignment with communism by India and, in the longer term, the Middle East "would in all probability progressively follow," thus endangering the security of Europe. "The loss of Southeast Asia" would also make it "extremely difficult to prevent Japan's eventual accommodation to communism."

The NSC therefore proposed various "courses of action" to prevent these fatal developments: strengthening "covert operations" to help the United States achieve its objectives; continuing operations to encourage overseas Chinese "to organize and activate anti-communist groups"; and taking "measures to promote the coordinated defense of the area."[10] Such proposed "courses of action" were typical of U.S. policy throughout the Eisenhower, Kennedy, Johnson, and Nixon administrations.[11] And, in one form or another, they were duly carried out by these administrations.

The third phase in U.S. relations with Thailand was one of "ef-

9. NSC 124/2, "Statement of Policy," June 25, 1952: text in *Pentagon Papers,* vol. 1, pp. 384–390. Italics added.

10. Ibid., pp. 386–87. The final course of action was: "Make clear to the American people the importance of Southeast Asia to the security of the United States so that they may be prepared for any of the courses of action proposed herein."

11. See, for example, NSC 5405 of Jan. 16, 1954, repeating almost word for word the 1952 assessment (ibid., p. 436); the Rusk-McNamara report of Nov. 11, 1961, to President Kennedy; Defense Secretary McNamara's memorandum of Mar. 16, 1964, to President Johnson: "Unless we can achieve this objective [security] in South Vietnam, almost all of Southeast Asia will probably fall under communist dominance." (These statements can also be found in *The Pentagon Papers, New York Times* ed. [New York: Bantam Books, 1971], pp. 150, 278). Nixon, too, as late as February 1974 was insisting that if the United States did not prove to others that it was a "dependable" ally by resisting communist aggression, then those countries would lose confidence and be engulfed by "the tide of aggression": Department of State *Bulletin,* Mar. 25, 1974.

fective and timely counteraction" by the United States, recommended in the 1952 policy statement and intended to prevent the dominoes from falling. Vietnam emerged as the "test case" of U.S. determination to help its allies defeat communist wars of liberation, according to McNamara's March 1964 memorandum to President Johnson; the implications for Thailand were obvious. American countermeasures began with programs for "nation-building," which increasingly, especially under Kennedy, became identified with countersubversion and counterinsurgency. Nation-building, besides assisting economic development, naturally included strengthening the Thai armed forces. The latter, for their part, were not reluctant to fall into line with this policy.

Altogether, from 1950 to 1975, the United States provided some $650 million for its economic development program in Thailand.[12] The level of aid was directly determined by the U.S. assessment of the seriousness of the communist threat to Thailand and Southeast Asia. And the kinds of projects undertaken—notably major road construction and other public works—were also largely influenced by defense or counterinsurgency considerations. By 1969, according to the U.S. Agency for International Development (AID), "except for a modest amount of technical assistance projects, most of which we are gradually phasing out, our assistance to Thailand is concentrated on counterinsurgency activities, approximately 75 percent of our total effort in this field."[13]

12. "The Impact of U.S. Aid," *Investor*, May 1977; also *Business in Thailand*, September 1975. However, in the mid-1970s the U.S. aid program diminished to between $10 million and $17 million a year. (It was to be increased in fiscal year 1980 to $15.5 million, and further increases were expected.)

13. Robert H. Nooter, acting assistant administrator for East Asia, AID, testifying before the U.S. Senate Foreign Relations Committee, June 16, 1969: quoted by Eric R. Wolf and Joseph G. Jorgensen, "Anthropology on the Warpath in Thailand," *New York Review of Books*, Nov. 19, 1970. (The title of the article refers to academic research, undertaken for purposes of counterinsurgency, funded by AID, the Defense Department, and other U.S. agencies. See John L. S. Girling, *America and the Third World: Revolution and Intervention* [London and Boston: Routledge & Kegan Paul, 1980] esp. chapter 8.) "GNP," *Bangkok Magazine*, Feb. 7, 1971, makes the point: "All American resources in Thailand, except for the Peace Corps, are said to be directed toward this end of 'political development.' . . . [But] when these Americans make reference to the Thai government in their discussions, they almost invariably mean the power held by one or two men. . . . Almost everything leads to Praphat." See also Caldwell, *American Economic Aid*, pp. 50–62, on the 1965–1970 period.

The total U.S. "regular military assistance" to the Thai armed forces from 1951 to 1971 amounted to $935.9 million. This was the equivalent of 59 percent of the total Thai military budget for the same period ($1,366.7 million).[14] In addition, the United States provided a further $760 million in "operating costs," for acquisition of military equipment, and in payment for the Thai division in Vietnam ($200 million over four years). U.S. base construction—notably the B-52 base at Utapao, half a dozen other airfields, and the Sattahip navy facilities—amounted to a further $205 million. Finally, expenditure by U.S. military personnel in Thailand (around 50,000 at their peak in 1968-69) for rest and recreation, and other items, added a further $850 million or so.[15]

This substantial military and economic aid program was justified on three counts. First, Thailand was a willing partner in the anticommunist cause. Indeed from the very beginning, as a U.S. economic survey mission to Southeast Asia in 1950 had pointed out, "there is hardly any important economic urgency [in Thailand]. There is a political urgency." As a country that has "come out solidly" for the West, "Thailand needs prompt evidence that its partnership is valued."[16] Second, Thailand was a domino, exposed both to external threats from China and Vietnam and to internal subversion and insurgency: this made it a suitable case for treatment. Finally, in the fourth phase of U.S.-Thai relations, Thailand became the springboard for American military involvement in Indochina.

It is in this context that a noted counterinsurgency expert, Maj. Gen. Edward Lansdale, had reported in 1961 to President Kennedy's military adviser on the available "resources for unconventional warfare" in Southeast Asia. These included refugees from

14. Ibid., pp. 171–172, table.
15. Ibid., pp. 171–173. See also *Business in Thailand,* September 1975, for further details of U.S. military expenditures. For example, more than 14,000 Thai military personnel were trained under the U.S. Military Assistance Program. At the peak period of base construction, the United States employed, either directly or through Thai contractors, 44,000 Thais—while the livelihood of another 50,000 or more (shopowners, taxi drivers, bar girls, and hired wives) depended on the U.S. presence.
16. Mission report in Samuel P. Hayes, *The Beginning of American Aid to Southeast Asia* (Lexington: D. C. Heath, 1971), p. 258, quoted in Caldwell, *American Economic Aid,* p. 39.

North Vietnam and hill tribes operating covertly in North Vietnam and Laos; a Thai ranger battalion, and the Border Patrol Police, whose missions would be to undertake guerrilla warfare in the event of a communist invasion of Thailand; and the Thai "Police Aerial Resupply Unit," supported by the CIA, "introduced covertly to assist the Meos [anticommunist guerrillas] in operations in Laos."[17]

During the early 1960s the situation in South Vietnam greatly deteriorated, and the Johnson administration prepared for the air war in Laos and North Vietnam that was intended to force Hanoi to "desist" from aiding the insurgency. By November 1964 there were reports of Thai pilots involved in "harassing activities" against the left-wing Pathet Lao in Laos.[18] That same month the U.S. Joint Chiefs of Staff recommended intensive air attacks on Laos and North Vietnam and discussions to be held "with the Thais in securing authority for unlimited use of Thai bases."[19] These proposals were not implemented at the time by President Johnson, although Thai bases had been prepared by early 1964.[20] But in February 1965, when "the situation in [South] Vietnam is now likely to come apart more rapidly than we had anticipated in November,"[21] Johnson launched the long-prepared air war, followed in April by the decision to commit U.S. ground forces in massive strength. America's war in Indochina had begun—it was to spread to Cambodia with the overthrow of Prince Sihanouk in 1970—and Thailand's fate was ineluctably bound up with its outcome.

The creation of a "war infrastructure" in Thailand—airfields, logistical camps, communications systems, intelligence operations

17. Lansdale to General Maxwell Taylor, July 1961: excerpts in *Pentagon Papers, New York Times* ed., pp. 131–139.

18. State Department report, "Immediate Action in the Period Prior to Decision," Nov. 7, 1964; *Pentagon Papers, New York Times* ed., p. 305.

19. JCS proposal to Defense Secretary McNamara: ibid., p. 321.

20. "In early 1964 the United States helped expand and build new Thai air bases which could be used if necessary by American aircraft operating over Vietnam": George K. Tanham, *Trial in Thailand* (New York: Crane, Russak, 1974), p. 21. Tanham was the special assistant for counterinsurgency at the U.S. Embassy, Bangkok, from 1968 to 1970. By August 1965 there were some 10,000 U.S. air force personnel at three air bases in Thailand; by 1968, 45,000 at six bases: Astri Suhrke, "Thailand: Trapped in the Bamboo Image," *Australian Outlook*, December 1968.

21. Assistant Secretary of State for Far Eastern Affairs William Bundy, to Secretary Rusk, Jan. 6, 1965: *Pentagon Papers, New York Times* ed., pp. 340–341.

—became the first priority of the U.S. mission in Bangkok.[22] "The basic policy of the United States in Thailand," according to the official "Strategy Statement" of the U.S. mission in 1966, "is to maintain that nation as an independent, economically viable nation, firmly allied to the United States." (The list of U.S. objectives in Thailand, by "major categories," was deleted before publication.)[23] Besides providing these facilities for the United States, Thailand itself became a testing ground for new weapons and counter-insurgency devices to be used in Vietnam,[24] provided a U.S.-subsidized division in Vietnam, and became a source of recruits for the "secret war" in Laos.[25]

As a result of the earlier Laos crisis in 1962, the United States had already stipulated in the Rusk-Thanat agreement its unilateral obligation to defend Thailand under the provisions of SEATO, regardless of the attitude of other SEATO members. This agreement was supplemented by a "military contingency plan" drawn up in 1965 between the U.S. military commander in Thailand, General Stilwell, and the Thai military. This plan, whose existence was not revealed until four years later, was almost certainly a quid pro quo for American use of Thai bases, which exposed Thailand to the risk of retaliation by the North Vietnamese.

Thus a relationship that had initially been of considerable advantage to the Thai regime, by conferring international legitimacy to the military coup group and by holding off potential enemies,

22. Ambassador Leonard Unger spoke of "meeting the requirement for a large range of facilities and privileges and so on of one sort or another in Thailand related to the war in Vietnam and activities in Laos": hearings before the Senate Foreign Relations subcommittee on security agreements, November 1969, quoted by Thomas Lobe, *United States National Security Policy and Aid to the Thailand Police* (Denver, Colo.: University of Denver, Monograph Series in World Affairs, 1977), p. 46.

23. "Country Assistance Strategy Statement on Thailand," prepared by U.S. Mission, 1966: *United States Security Agreements and Commitments Abroad, Kingdom of Thailand,* hearings before subcommittee on U.S. security agreements, Senate Foreign Relations Committee, 91st Congress, first session, pt. 3, November 1969, p. 751.

24. Details in Michael Klare, *War Without End* (New York: Knopf, 1972), pp. 136, 139, 168, 177, 209, 215, 218, 226–228, 230, 236–238; and Girling, *America and the Third World,* pp. 179–183.

25. From 1970 to 1972 the CIA had financed and organized a 25-battalion force of Thai "volunteers" at an estimated yearly cost of $100 million: Senate Foreign Relations Committee staff report (heavily censored): quoted in *International Herald Tribune,* May 9, 1972.

gradually changed. As the United States became more and more involved in the "quagmire" of Vietnam, the Thais were drawn into serving U.S. interests and policies; and these increasingly diverged from those of Thailand. Thus when the United States reversed its course on Vietnam in 1968 and started the slow process of military withdrawal from Southeast Asia, the Thais were left stranded with a militant anti-communist commitment, but deprived of the backing to fulfill it.

To put it bluntly, the United States went into Southeast Asia, in the 1950s, for its own purposes—which suited the Thai authorities at the time. And it went out again, in the 1970s, for its own purposes: which did *not*. Ironically, it is to none other than Thanat Khoman, foreign minister from 1958 to 1971, and one of the most hawkish advocates of American intervention in Indochina, that we owe confirmation of this judgment:

> The large body of American troops did not come to Thailand to protect it against internal or external aggression but plainly to fight the Vietnam war from the Thai soil. Instead of defending it against an eventual enemy, they, in fact, could help make it become a prominent target for retaliatory attacks by the other side to avenge the bombing raids carried out from there. . . .
>
> While it is obvious that the continued and even increased American military presence [in 1972] represents a definite advantage for the United States as a leverage to be used against the North Vietnamese, what benefits will accrue to Thailand, the host country? . . . It has also been said that foreign military personnel bring with them a sizeable financial boon . . . [which] is indeed impressive but . . . great care [is taken] not to enter into details as to where the money goes, who gets it and for what . . . It is apparent that even if there may be minor advantages accruing to a small number of people, private or official . . . the disadvantages overwhelmingly outweigh benefits. . . .
>
> Above all, the presence of foreign forces encourages and fosters what may be called "military democracy," an authoritarian regime which deprives or curtails the freedom and civil liberties of the citizens.[26]

26. Thanat Khoman, "Thailand in the Midst of Changes," in *Trends in Thailand*, ed. M. Rajaretnam and Lim So Jean (Singapore: Institute of Southeast Asian Studies, 1973), pp. 110-114. However, one need not feel too sorry for Thanat. As foreign minister of successive "authoritarian regimes" he agreed to the "foreign military presence" that he objected to in 1973. (He switched round again, in 1975–76, arguing that Thailand should maintain the American bases "as a bargaining

Thanat's last assertion is crucial. American political assistance and material support, however well intentioned, became an essential prop of an authoritarian regime. How this came about was explained in a newspaper article during the democratic period. Before 1973, the article argued, the generals were faced with three problems. The first was how to protect Thailand against potentially hostile neighbors. The answer was the U.S. alliance. "The second problem they faced was how to line their pockets and those of their friends elsewhere in the military and bureaucracy. Here again, the foreign connection was crucial." As the article put it:

The close link-up with the free-enterprise West induced considerable foreign investment, of which government leaders took their percentage either off the top, or as open partners using funds borrowed by relying on their official positions. More covertly they took in enormous sums as a result of U.S. military spending and economic assistance through such schemes as the ETO [Express Transport Organization, one of the numerous "state enterprises"] truck monopoly and numerous base concessions run by or on behalf of important officials.

The third problem was how to stay in power. The traditional solution was to prevent other contenders from replacing them by use of military repression, proclamation of martial law, and closing down the parliamentary political process. "Frequent American statements of support to the generals made it plain to potential opponents that the generals had limitless backing."[27]

---

point with the communists.") In January 1967, for example, Thanat praised the "courageous move" of the United States in coming to the rescue of South Vietnam from aggression: "If we give in to them [communists] in South Vietnam, we shall have to give in to them in Laos, in Cambodia and perhaps in the whole of Southeast Asia": *Collected Statements of Foreign Minister Thanat Khoman,* vol. 3, November 1966–October 1967 (Bangkok: Ministry of Foreign Affairs, 1967).

27. "How U.S. Aid Fostered Exploitation," *Bangkok Post,* Nov. 6, 1975. Symptomatic of Washington's attitude, which was conditioned by the cosy relationship with the Thai military in times past, was Kissinger's reaction in 1975 to Thai official complaints that their sovereignty had been violated by U.S. forces during the Mayaguez affair. Kissinger told reporters they should not pay attention to Thai politicians, but rather to the Thai military. The military were happy enough for the United States to use Utapao, and that was what mattered, Kissinger said privately: William Shawcross, "Making the Most of Mayaguez," *Far Eastern Economic Review,* May 30, 1975.

*From Military to Political Options*

For more than two decades, as we have seen, the security interests of successive Thai and U.S. administrations largely coincided. The first check to this convenient mutual-aid arrangement was the Kennedy administration's support in 1961–62 for a neutral Laos, but this was offset by the Rusk-Thanat agreement and was soon overtaken by the massive U.S. military engagement from 1965 in Indochina. The second check was President Johnson's decision in 1968 to negotiate rather than continue to escalate the war in Vietnam, followed by the Nixon-Kissinger aim to "Vietnamese" the war and by the 1972 Nixon visit to Peking. The third and decisive check was the inability of the U.S. administration to prevent the collapse of its allies, the Thieu, Lon Nol, and Souvanna Phouma regimes in South Vietnam, Cambodia, and Laos.

The events of 1975 were the writing on the wall for the old policy of military commitment to the United States in an anticommunist front. It was time for the civilian Thai governments to recognize both the global realities—the retraction of U.S. power in mainland Southeast Asia, resulting in an East Asian tripolar balance among America, China, and Russia—and the regional realities—the triumphant communist liberation movements in Indochina, whose impact on the area was to some extent offset by a gradual increase in cooperation among members of ASEAN (the Association of Southeast Asian Nations—Thailand, Malaysia, the Philippines, Singapore, and Indonesia).

Since 1975, Thai governments have been faced with four main options: to revive the American alliance; to build up regional solidarity; to work for a balance of power; or to pursue nonalignment. Three of four Thai governments (two civilian and two backed by the military), according to the dispositions of their leaders and the nature of the external environment, chose one of these alternatives. (The exception, the Thanin government, tried two).

The Kukrit coalition, made forcibly aware in 1975 that the U.S. commitment (involving Thai facilities directed against Vietnam) was more a liability than an asset, opted essentially for a balance-of-power strategy. The way ahead had already been cleared by the Sino-American rapprochement, which for all but a few diehards had eliminated the bogey of "Chinese aggression," the leitmotif of

the 1950s and 1960s. Peking could henceforth be seen as a constructive force both in the new global balance of power among the
United States, China, and the Soviet Union and in the regional
balance in Southeast Asia between ASEAN and Indochina. The
Kukrit government's pragmatic realignment, based on what Foreign Minister Chartchai Chunhawan called "equidistance" from the
great powers and on reliance on diplomacy and de facto neutrality,
followed. This realignment involved recognition of Peking, withdrawal of all American troops from Thailand by July 1976, and
friendly relations with the Marxist government in Cambodia, in
spite of nationalist feelings affecting both sides and the frequency
of border clashes. Kukrit also sought to resolve tensions with Laos
by diplomatic means, although the legacy of close wartime cooperation between former Thai regimes and rightists in Vientiane was
now aggravated by a stream of refugees from Laos, and on the
Thai side by military-backed clandestine operations against the
Pathet Lao, and, from time to time, economic blockades. As for
relations with Vietnam, attitudes on both sides were clouded by
uncertainty. On the Thai side there was widespread suspicion of
"Vietnamese expansionism" and communist aid to Thai insurgents,
while the Vietnamese could hardly forget Thailand's role in the
Vietnam war or the extensive links that had been forged between
the Thai military and their U.S. counterparts.

    The Seni government, in turn, after some initial wavering, ap-
proved Kukrit's decision for a complete withdrawal of U.S. combat
forces from Thai soil and the abandonment of intelligence facilities
(notably the secret electronic complex at Ramasun, run by the U.S.
National Security Agency, near Udorn).[28] Seni's foreign minister,
Pichai Rattakun, carried the process of nonalignment still further
by his conciliatory attitude toward the Pathet Lao government in
Vientiane and the decision to establish diplomatic relations with

    28. Ramasun was used to monitor low-frequency radio communications in In-
dochina. Unlike other Thai bases, it had no Thai base commander. During Kukrit's
negotiations with American officials, the Thais had insisted on three principles: no
future U.S. interference in the internal affairs of Thailand's neighbors, Thai control
of all U.S. facilities and personnel, and a two-year limit on all future military
agreements with the United States. For details, see Norman Peagam, "Extended
Duty for the 'Advisers,'" *Far Eastern Economic Review,* Feb. 27, 1976. Since
Washington was unable to accept these conditions, all U.S. troops, apart from 270
advisers, were withdrawn by July 20, 1976.

Vietnam. The latter agreement was signed on August 6, 1976—just two months before the military coup.[29]

The Thanin government, appointed by the coup leaders, went into reverse. Thanin, whose anticommunist fervor rivaled that of Dulles twenty years before, straddled the first foreign policy option—reviving the American alliance—and the second—building up regional solidarity. Like the more primitive of his military backers, he yearned for the old-cold war certainties and for the security afforded by the United States.[30] Convinced that Thailand had been in imminent danger of a communist takeover on October 6, 1976,[31] aided by the Vietnamese, Thanin adopted the most uncompromising stance. But, unlike in the old days, the Thai government could no longer count on U.S. military support. "The United States will definitely not return to Thailand in a military role," stated a Washington report, quoted by *Siam Rath*, on October 30, 1976. Although both Kissinger and Defense Secretary Schlesinger had revealed considerable ambiguity over the U.S. role in 1975—and the Defense Department had indicated the need for 10,000 American personnel to remain in Thailand—by 1976 Washington had evidently fallen back on a "Pacific Rim" strategy. This strategy required air and naval forces, operating from bases in Australia, the Philippines, the Pacific Islands, and Japan, instead of U.S. ground forces in mainland Southeast Asia.[32] Thanin rather

29. According to the joint communique, signed in Hanoi, the Vietnamese "highly appreciated" the Thai government's "independent foreign policy," which stated that it would not allow foreign forces and bases in Thailand. The two delegations agreed on four principles: respect for each other's independence and noninterference in each other's internal affairs; prohibition of foreign bases; settlement of disputes through negotiation; and cooperation for "genuine independence, peace and neutrality" in Southeast Asia.

30. The concepts of the cold war—containment, confrontation, monolithic communism, and so forth—are still much in evidence in the thinking of Thai military leaders. Accordingly, the need for American power to deter communism was openly expressed by the army commander-in-chief, General Bunchai, during the democratic period. He believed that the Thai military would be helpless without American support. Similarly the Thai National Security Council continued to express apprehension over the "true" intentions of communist countries, including China, toward Thailand: Sarasin Viraphol, *Directions in Thai Foreign Policy* (Singapore: Institute of Southeast Asian Studies, occasional paper no. 40, 1976), pp. 31, 51.

31. Thanin's news conference, reported in *Bangkok Post*, Nov. 19, 1976.

32. The Defense Department's views reported in the *International Herald Tribune*, May 3-4, 1975. See also J. L. S. Girling, "Southeast Asia and the Great Powers," *Pacific Community*, January 1978.

naively hoped that ASEAN solidarity would deter the threat of communist expansion instead. As his foreign minister appealed in Indonesia, "we must safeguard our country from elements that try to impose their ideology upon us, and I hope that other ASEAN members will come to help if we are attacked from outside."[33]

General Kriangsak, secretary-general of the National Administrative Reform Council, attempted to moderate Thanin's intransigent line. "We cannot forget old friends," he said, referring to the United States, "but we do not anticipate the return of American troops." As for relations with Hanoi, the general claimed that "we combat communists in our country. We are not fighting communism in Vietnam." And he argued, contrary to Thanin's line, that Thai policy toward China had not changed.[34]

Thanin's rigidity in foreign affairs, "isolating" Thailand from other Third World countries, was one of the reasons given for military dissatisfaction with his government, culminating in the October 20, 1977, coup.[35] Kriangsak as prime minister at once moved to improve relations with Cambodia (where border clashes had been frequent), Laos, and Vietnam, and in March 1978 arrived in Peking—the first visit by any ASEAN leader in the past two years.[36] Kriangsak's more sophisticated approach suggested a return to the balance-of-power strategy. In 1978 his foreign policy could be summed up as acknowledging the reluctance of the United States to become militarily involved in Southeast Asia,[37] while sharing

33. Press conference in Jakarta, reported by Bangkok radio, June 20, 1977. However, the Indonesians have stated their preference for "national resilience" (self-reliance) in ASEAN member countries, backed up by multilateral military arrangements, but not a collective military pact: David Jenkins, "The Non-Alliance Pact," *Far Eastern Economic Review*, Mar. 18, 1977. See also "The New Phase," below.

34. Reported in *Bangkok Post*, Oct. 26, 1976.

35. See the obviously inspired "comment," *Bangkok Post*, Oct. 21, 1977.

36. Kriangsak's visit showed the "unmistakable warmth in the air," according to his Chinese hosts; Kriangsak spoke of strengthening friendship and cooperation: *Peking Review*, Apr. 7, 1978. Chinese Communist Party Chairman Hua Kuofeng accepted an invitation to visit Thailand.

37. Admiral Moorer, former chairman of the U.S. Joint Chiefs of Staff, pointed out in the *Strategic Institute Review:* "The task will be to devise more subtle means of projecting military power to substitute for the dwindling nuclear deterrent and for direct military footholds on the Asian mainland. These trends will place a premium on strategic mobility and flexibility": quoted by Stephen Barber, "The New Balance of Power," *Far Eastern Economic Review*, July 2, 1976. The ASEAN foreign ministers agreed that the "United States would no longer be involved physically in any local conflict in Southeast Asia" and that the future role and extent of U.S. political and

China's interest in a stable Southeast Asia. The Chinese leaders have praised ASEAN cooperation as an obstacle to superpower "hegemony," meaning, in practice, Soviet expansionism. The ASEAN leaders in turn consider that "the present foreign policy stance of China and her relations with the United States are factors that may help maintain stability in East Asia and the Pacific."[38]

In pursuit of détente with Indochina, Kriangsak lifted the Thai blockade on imports in Laos and agreed to normalize relations with Vietnam; ambassadors were exchanged with Vietnam and Cambodia. In his 1978 New Year's message, the Thai prime minister pledged that "the government will adhere to a friendly policy toward neighboring countries and will not allow anyone to use Thailand's territory to harm our neighbors." In return the Vietnamese deputy foreign minister, visiting ASEAN countries, declared that the insurgencies in Malaysia and Thailand were internal problems.[39] Although Thai leaders have been "wary about the increasing intelligence and subversive activities" of the Russians, especially in the democratic period, and were concerned about the Soviet presence in Laos and Vietnam,[40] Kriangsak maintained "correct" relations with Moscow.

Kriangsak, like other Thai leaders before him, sought to improve the trade balance with Japan,[41] but had only modest expectations of progress in ASEAN.[42]

---

economic commitments were unclear: secret report by ASEAN foreign ministers to the heads of government at the August 1977 Kuala Lumpur summit, quoted by Michael Richardson, "How the Five See Indochina," *Far Eastern Economic Review,* Dec. 30, 1977. However, there has been a reassertion of U.S. "concern" for the region in recent months.

38. Secret report by ASEAN foreign ministers, quoted by Richardson, "How the Five See Indochina."

39. According to the Vietnamese envoy, "We shall not interfere because it is not our problem, but it is the internal affair of those countries. . . . We do not export our revolution and we hope that others will not export counter-revolution to us": Reuters report from Jakarta, Jan. 1, 1978.

40. Sarasin, *Directions in Thai Foreign Policy,* pp. 25–29. However, Southeast Asia, unlike South Asia, is not an area of priority for the Soviet Union.

41. On Thai-Japanese relations, see ibid., pp. 35–37; Weinstein, "Multinational Corporations and the Third World: The Case of Japan and Southeast Asia," *International Organization,* Summer 1976. On the "Fukuda doctrine," see Girling, "Southeast Asia and the Great Powers."

42. For Thai views on ASEAN, see Sarasin Viraphol, Amphon Namatra, and Masahide Shibusawa, eds., "The ASEAN: Problems and Prospects in a Changing

*The New Phase*

The Vietnamese invasion of Kampuchea in January 1979 followed by China's massive assault on Vietnam a month later have created a new situation in mainland Southeast Asia, with grave implications for Thailand. In the first place, even if the Soviet Union was not drawn into armed retaliation against China, its commitment to Vietnam, emphasized by the November 1978 "treaty of friendship and cooperation," has intensified Sino-Soviet rivalry throughout the region. Second, the struggle between the Vietnamese-supported Heng Samrin administration and the Pol Pot forces in Kampuchea threatens to spill over into Thailand. China itself has taken a much more assertive "big power" stance, shown by its readiness to use force to "punish" Vietnam. If this may seem reassuring to the Thai government, it also has its dangers.[43] For one of the motives behind China's attack on Vietnam was to demonstrate Peking's concern for the overseas Chinese, and this "protective" concern may extend beyond Vietnam to other countries with substantial ethnic Chinese communities—notably Thailand, Malaysia, Singapore, and Indonesia.[44]

In this new situation, Thailand, in spite of its desire to remain neutral, is inescapably caught up in regional and international conflicts. The effect on Thailand of the upheaval in Indochina, com-

---

World," Chulalongkorn University, December 1975, including reports by Somsakdi Xuto, rector of the National Institute of Development Administration, Bangkok, and by Prateep Sondysuwan and Vijit Supinit, assistant directors, Research Department, Bank of Thailand. Also see Somsakdi, *Regional Cooperation in Southeast Asia* (Chulalongkorn University, Institute of Asian Studies, 1973). For developments following the outbreak of the Indochina crises, see "The New Phase" below, esp. n. 51.

43. China's Vice-Premier Deng Xiaoping, said China would help Thailand "in every way" if it is invaded by Vietnam, according to the Thai deputy prime minister, Air Chief Marshal Dawee Chunlasap, who recently visited Peking. "Any threat to Thailand is a threat to China," Deng stated on June 20: Reuter report from Bangkok, June 26, 1979. A month before, China's assistant foreign minister, Song Zhiguang, pointed out: "In the event of Vietnamese aggression against Thailand, we will support [the Thais]. As to by what means, it will be necessary to see how things go"; reported in *Far Eastern Economic Review*, May 18, 1979. Kriangsak diplomatically replied that Thailand would not accept military aid from China in the event of Vietnamese aggression: *Bangkok Post*, May 10, 1979.

44. For a useful and balanced discussion, see Leo Suryadinata, *Overseas Chinese in Southeast Asia and China's Foreign Policy* (Singapore: Institute of Southeast Asian Studies, research paper no. 11, 1978).

pounded by the hostility between China and Vietnam, does, however, require an analysis of the causes of the conflicts. These causes range from explosive "local conditions" to the impact of global strategy. The Vietnamese, for example, attribute the breakdown in Cambodian-Vietnamese relations to the intractability of the "Pol Pot-Ieng Sary clique" and its antagonism toward Vietnam. This is correct, but Hanoi neglects to add that such intractability stems from historic Cambodian fears, shared by Cambodian communists, of being swallowed up by Vietnam.[45]

China, on the other hand, accuses Vietnam of acting as an instrument of Soviet power, as "the Cuba of Asia." Peking considers Vietnam's invasion of Kampuchea to be an integral part of a Soviet grand design, revealed by aggressive actions around the world, from Angola to South Yemen, and Ethiopia to Afghanistan.[46] According to Peking, because the "weaker" superpower (the United States) proved itself unable to stand up to the stronger (the Soviet Union), China itself must provide the necessary example and demonstrate its resolve to counter aggression.[47] China's attack on

45. See Stephen Heder, "Origins of the Conflict," *Southeast Asia Chronicle*, no. 64, September–October 1978. Cambodian fears center on Vietnam's supposed objective of creating an "Indochina Federation" under its domination. Peking claims that Hanoi goes beyond this, by seeking to establish a "Southeast Asia Federation." (See note 46.)

46. According to the Chinese ambassador to Thailand: "Supported by the Soviet Union, Vietnam is dreaming of dominating the whole of the Southeast Asian region. Vietnam's aggression and expansion in Southeast Asia is a component part of the global strategy of the Soviet Union to dominate the world": *Bangkok Post*, Apr. 1, 1979. Vice-Premier Deng, visiting Thailand in November 1978, denounced Vietnam as "the Cuba of the East": *Bangkok Post*, Nov. 9, 1978. For official Thai perceptions of the Vietnamese threat and of Chinese interests, see M. Ladd Thomas, "The Perceived Impact of Communist Indochina on Thailand's Security," in Clark D. Neher, ed. *Modern Thai Politics: From Village to Nation*, rev. ed. (Cambridge, Mass.: Schenkman, 1979).

47. Peking's interpretation holds for the U.S. role in Southeast Asia, at least. Referring to the ASEAN-Indochina crisis, one Carter aide explained: "Given our earlier involvement, in which we were not successful, our capacity to influence the situation is minimal. We will encourage ASEAN, speak to all parties involved and seek to apply international pressures": reported by Simon Barber from Washington, *Far Eastern Economic Review*, June 22, 1979. President Carter did, however, tell Kriangsak on his visit to the United States that the United States is "deeply committed" to Thailand's integrity and the inviolability of its borders: *International Herald Tribune*, Feb. 8, 1979. Washington also increased military sales credits to Thailand ($30 million for 1979): *Asiaweek*, Feb. 2, 1979. U.S. Assistant Secretary of State Richard Holbrooke declared on October 25, 1979, that "the importance of Thailand is obvious. The U.S. is committed to supporting ASEAN and in ASEAN Thailand is

Vietnam is therefore seen as one element in the global struggle against Soviet "hegemony."[48]

The consequences for Thailand depend very much on which of these interpretations, the local or the global perspective, is correct. If, as I believe is more realistic, the Vietnamese were motivated by *specific* considerations—namely, the impossibility of peaceful coexistence with Pol Pot—then occupation of Kampuchea, for this reason, does not *necessarily* imply further expansion.[49] If, as the Chinese allege, however, the Vietnamese are acting as agents of the Soviet plan for world domination, then no amount of "appeasement" of Vietnam (as the Americans used to argue in an earlier context) will stop the process of expansion. The Chinese world view, in its assumption of Soviet hostility, is undoubtedly correct: but not, I believe, the corollary that Vietnam is a tool of Soviet designs.[50] Nevertheless, China's global standpoint leads it to support the U.S. strategic presence in East and Southeast Asia, as a counterweight to the Soviet; to bolster ASEAN as a bloc of third world countries struggling against Soviet or Vietnamese "hegemony";[51] and to downplay (but not eliminate) assistance to revolutionary movements in Southeast Asia.

---

a frontline state." He added that Vietnamese statements that they had no intention of attacking Thailand were of "great importance." Reportedly the U.S. administration is reassigning military personnel to Thailand under contingency plans to cope with a possible Vietnamese incursion into Thai territory; among the arrivals are specialists preparing command-control systems for B-52 bombers: Robert Whymant, "U.S. Military Returning to Thailand," *Guardian Weekly*, Dec. 2, 1979.

48. See J. L. S. Girling, "Indochina," in Mohammed Ayoob, ed., *Conflict and Intervention in the Third World* (London: Croom Helm, 1980).

49. In fact, Prime Minister Pham Van Dong reaffirmed in January 1979 that Vietnam would respect Thai territorial integrity, refrain from using force against Thailand, and give no support to local subversive movements. This was in a personal message to Kriangsak: *Bangkok Post*, Jan. 16, 1979. The danger of conflict, however, stems not so much from a deliberate policy move, as from "unintended consequences" arising from the situation in Kampuchea. By a process of action and reaction these may escalate out of control. A further possibility is that, in the event of an *internal* crisis in Thailand, Vietnam may also be drawn into the conflict.

50. However, Kriangsak visited the Soviet Union from March 20–28, 1979, and came back reportedly reassured that Vietnam would not pose a threat to Thailand: *TIC News* report. See also Kriangsak's interview with *Newsweek*, Aug. 6, 1979.

51. The ASEAN foreign ministers, meeting at Bali in July 1979, strongly condemned "interference by Vietnam and other foreign forces" in the internal affairs of Kampuchea. They declared that "any further escalation of the fighting in Kampuchea or any incursion of any foreign forces into Thailand would directly affect the security of the ASEAN member states." They also announced that ASEAN

The ominous factor, as far as Thailand is concerned, is that what originated as a local conflict between Vietnam and Pol Pot's Kampuchea has become increasingly global. Thus China is determined, as part of a total strategy, to help the Pol Pot forces—and even right-wing Cambodian elements—to maintain resistance to the Vietnamese.[52] This, according to the Chinese, means that supplies of arms are being transferred via Thailand to the Pol Pot guerrillas. The Thai government denies these reports, but faced with the predicament of offending either China or Vietnam, prefers to keep China on its side.

The Vietnamese, on the other hand, embroiled in a protracted war in Kampuchea, facing the possibility of renewed Chinese assaults, and confronted with serious economic problems, are, however reluctantly, becoming more and more dependent on the Soviet Union. This situation gives the Soviet Union increasing opportunities to counter China (and the United States), even though Southeast Asia as such is not an area of high priority for Moscow.[53]

---

would continue to strengthen cooperation "in all fields." Such cooperation, according to one report, refers to "an array of bilateral deals to curb the Vietnamese threat [which] were negotiated outside ASEAN's formal ranks.... Nevertheless, experts say the group's intentions are clear. 'Thailand, Malaysia, Singapore, Indonesia and the Philippines are building a network of links that is having the effect of a military security pact while taking great care to avoid labelling it that,' said one Western diplomat": *Newsweek*, June 25, 1979. Even so, such moves will take time to be effective, and it is unlikely that an "ASEAN force" currently will prove much of a deterrent. As Thanat Khoman puts it: "I don't know what a military alliance could do. I don't think all the five ASEAN nations combined would be a match for Vietnam. There is also the factor of individual egotisms to consider. The ASEAN members are willing to shout in unison, but action is something else": interview with John Jesser in Bangkok, *Canberra Times*, July 5, 1979. See also the interesting assessment of the differences in attitudes among ASEAN members with regard to China and Vietnam by Masashi Nishihara, "A Mosaic Perspective on the Sino-Vietnamese Conflict," reprinted in *Japan Echo*, no. 3, 1979: For a good analysis of Thailand's security relations, see Pranee Saipiroon, "ASEAN Governments' Attitudes Towards Regional Security, 1975–1979," M.A. Thesis, Australian National University, 1980.

52. Nayan Chanda, reporting from Peking: *Far Eastern Economic Review*, Apr. 27, 1979. On Ieng Sary's pledge to cooperate with rightists, see *International Herald Tribune*, June 2–3, 1979. Michael Richardson's interview with Li Xiannian in Peking appeared in *Age*, Nov. 11, 1979. Pol Pot was replaced as prime minister by the more acceptable Khieu Samphan toward the end of December 1979, but was named military commander-in-chief instead.

53. However, Communist sources in Laos suggest that Moscow is "unhappy about the inability of Vietnam to stabilize the situation in Kampuchea quickly," as this renders Soviet relations with the rest of Southeast Asia more difficult: Nayan Chanda, "Hanoi Ponders its Strategy," *Far Eastern Economic Review*, Dec. 7, 1979.

For Thailand, however, the intensification of Sino-Soviet rivalry, the shock waves of conflict between China and Vietnam, and the massive influx of refugees from Indochina[54] are highly destabilizing. Thai attempts to repatriate refugees, including Pol Pot troops, in June 1980 sparked off a Vietnamese incursion into Thailand. This action was roundly condemned by the ASEAN foreign ministers meeting in Kuala Lumpur that month. The Vietnamese incursion has focused attention on the dangers of the opposed Thai and Vietnamese postures over Kampuchea.[55]

Thus the Thai government, as a "partner" in Peking's balance-of-power strategy, and its adversary, the Communist Party of Thailand, pursuing a Maoist policy of rural struggle, are caught in the middle of twin circles of hostility.[56] As far as the Thai government is concerned, the more it defers to the Chinese for the sake of protection, the more it antagonizes the Vietnamese.[57] And the Vietnamese are not short of grievances stemming from Thailand's role in America's Indochina war or of opportunities to put their aims into effect.[58]

54. By the end of May 1979 there were more than a quarter of a million refugees in Thailand, including nearly 138,000 Lao and hill-tribe refugees: John McBeth, *Far Eastern Economic Review,* June 15, 1979. The total number of refugees reported in June 1979 was nearly 150,000 (including 135,000 from Laos, 13,000 from Kampuchea, and 1,400 from Vietnam); 42,000 from Kampuchea were awaiting repatriation as "displaced persons"; 5,000 Vietnamese boat people were also to be removed: AP report from Bangkok quoting officials of the Thai Supreme Command, July 6, 1979. However, in October 1979 there was a dramatic reversal of policy when the Thai government offered sanctuary to Kampuchean refugees evidently to preserve as many Khmers as possible as a potential buffer against the Vietnamese. By the end of 1979 there were some half a million Kampuchean refugees in Thai camps along the border.

55. See John L. S. Girling, "Crisis over Kampuchea: Regional and Global Implications," *Third World Quarterly* (London), October 1980.

56. See the following chapter.

57. Vietnam's minister of state for foreign affairs, Nguyen Co Thach, declared: "The Thais are playing with fire. They are supporting Pol Pot. They are transporting arms from Chinese ships. . . . They say they are neutral, but how can this be?": interview, *Asiaweek,* June 15, 1979. In the view of the Thai military, Vietnam cannot consolidate its power in Kampuchea so long as resistance continues; therefore it is in Thai interests to support the Pol Pot forces, which form the most organized groups, as well as Khmer Serei and others. In time this will create conditions for Khmer nationalism to arise, which will eventually oblige the Vietnamese to withdraw.

58. Opportunities would lie chiefly in support for dissident movements (not necessarily the CPT) in Thailand. Admittedly Peking's pledge to support Thailand may deter Vietnam from direct action; but China in turn may be deterred by the prospect of Soviet retaliation . . . if only to demonstrate its "credibility."

The Communist Party of Thailand, too, is torn between ideological adherence to Peking and the disillusioning experience of seeing China make up to its former enemies—to "U.S. imperialism" no less than to the Thai "feudal, bureaucrat-capitalist" regime. The party, seriously affected in terms of sanctuary, training, and arms supply by the drastic changes occurring in Kampuchea and to a lesser extent in Laos, has (like the Thai government itself) tried not to take sides. But both are being swept up by forces beyond their control.

The Thais alone cannot escape this predicament. The dangers inherent in the China-Vietnam and Vietnam-Kampuchea conflicts can be resolved only by constructive efforts from outside. These could take the form of a "package deal" agreement, with U.S. recognition of Vietnam and massive reconstruction aid from the West, in return for "moderation" of Vietnam's internal and external policies: that is, acceptance that ethnic Chinese in Vietnam have a legitimate role to play, and agreement to a genuinely neutral Kampuchea. But unless and until such neutrality can be achieved, it would be folly to insist on the withdrawal of Vietnamese troops; under the circumstances this could mean only the return of Pol Pot and his colleagues and their atrocious regime. In other words concessions by Vietnam must be balanced by inducements, which only the West (including Japan) can provide. If such an overall agreement is not reached (and there is little sign that either the U.S. administration or Congress is capable of doing much positive work in this area) then the only alternative is further polarization in Southeast Asia, greater diversion of scarce resources from peaceful to military purposes, and a continuing destructive struggle between China and Vietnam.

# 7 | Revolutionary Alternative

Communism in Thailand got off to a poor and difficult start. It has been characterized by regional insurgency, and only since the 1970s has there been a possibility of communism developing into a truly national movement.

Why did the Communist Party of Thailand (CPT) make such slow and laborious headway, so that almost four decades after its foundation in 1942 its origins, leadership, and organization remained obscure?[1]

The explanation is to be found in the condition of Thai society and the environment in which the party has to operate. Before

1. Patrice de Beer, *Le Monde* correspondent in Bangkok from 1974–77, wrote at the end of 1977: "To conclude, I must repeat that we do not know very much about the internal life of the CPT, its leadership, its location.... Are the different [insurgent] areas (North, Northeast, Center and West, mid-South and South) working independently, autonomously? What kind of organisational links exist between the zones and the central leadership and between the different zones?" (de Beer, "History and Policy of the Communist Party of Thailand," in Fast, Turton and Caldwell, *Thailand: Roots of Conflict,* p. 156). It was estimated in 1978 that communist groups operating in the North, Northeast, and South were largely independent of one another, but "there remain many unanswered questions on its [the CPT's] leadership and the functioning of the organisation." As for the location of the party central committee, there was "no consensus of opinion"; most estimates vary from Northeast Thailand, Laos, and, less likely, China: "Thailand's Defense," *Investor* (Bangkok), June 1978. George K. Tanham, special assistant for counterinsurgency to the U.S. ambassador in Bangkok from 1968 to 1970, asks why the communists launched their armed struggle (in the Northeast) in 1965, when conditions were hardly ripe for revolution and if China's was the "directing hand." He answers, "No one really knows": *Trial in Thailand* (New York: Crane, Russak, 1974), p. 64. Although Tanham considers that Bangkok is "probably" the site of party headquarters, another U.S. specialist puts it in Sayabouri province in Laos: Robert F. Zimmerman, "Insurgency in Thailand," *Problems of Communism* (Washington, D.C.: U.S. Information Agency), May–June 1976, pp. 18–39. Zimmerman was on the research staff of the U.S. aid mission (USOM) in Bangkok in the early to mid-1970s. Such uncertainty, or lack of knowledge, even among the experts, is revealing.

World War II, the communist organization in Thailand was an offshoot of the Chinese Communist Party, carrying out educational work, agitation, and recruitment among workers, teachers, and other members of the Chinese community in Thailand, as in other countries of Southeast Asia. Communist interest and activity in Thailand had actually begun in the 1920s, but work was limited chiefly to the Chinese and Vietnamese immigrant communities. Ho Chi Minh himself, as a Comintern agent, stayed for a year in Northeast Thailand in the late 1920s. In 1930 the Chinese party committee in Thailand prepared a document for a meeting of communist representatives in the "South Seas" [Southeast Asia].[2] But, as the communists later acknowledged, "lacking experience, the party could not exert much influence upon the society and its political role was limited."[3]

The communist movement in Thailand differs remarkably from the movements in all other Southeast Asian countries except, significantly, Cambodia before the fall of Sihanouk in 1970. Elsewhere communism was a substantial force, usually with nationalist credentials: for example in Burma, Indonesia (the PKI was the strongest popular movement from the 1950s to 1965), the Philippines (the Huks came near to success in the late 1940s and early 1950s), Malaya (among the Chinese during the communist uprising known as the Emergency), Laos (with tribal support), and, above all, Vietnam. In Cambodia communism was as unimportant as in Thailand right up to the 1970s when war, exposing the fatal flaws of the Lon Nol regime, created conditions for revolutionary success.

In Thailand, the communist party was a minority movement. The party's ethnic origins were reflected in the Sino-Thai leader-

2. Chai-Anan, draft chapter, "Communist Party of Thailand," in David Morell and Chai-Anan Samudavanija, *Reform, Reaction, Revolution: Political Conflict in Thailand* (Cambridge, Mass.: Oelgeschlager, Gunn and Hain, forthcoming). This document, captured by the Thai government, is reproduced in Benjamin A. Batson, *Siam's Political Future: Documents from the End of Absolute Monarchy* (Ithaca: Cornell University Southeast Asia Program, Data Paper no. 96, 1974), pp. 60–71. See also the brief historical account by Smarn Woothiporn, "The Communist Party and the People's War in Thailand," *Samakki Surob* [Militant Unity], ed. Thirayut et al., bulletin of the exiled Socialist Party of Thailand, no. 2, 1977.

3. CPT thirty-fifty anniversary statement, December 1977: printed in Andrew Turton, Jonathan Fast, and Malcolm Caldwell, eds., *Thailand: Roots of Conflict* (Nottingham, U.K.: Spokesman, 1978), app. 1.

ship of the central committee, long after it separated from the mainland Chinese communist movement in 1949. During the 1950s the bulk of party members was still largely ethnic Chinese.[4]

Party activities depended on the vagaries of Thai politics. In the early postwar period, under Pridi and his followers, the 1933 ban on communism was lifted, in return for Soviet acquiescence to Thailand's membership in the United Nations. The party for a short time operated legally, electing one member of parliament, as well as clandestinely.[5] The party was driven underground again by the 1947 military coup, which was directed against Pridi, but also had anticommunist undertones.[6] Phibun's adherence to the "free

4. Chinese communists in the 1950s were estimated to number about 4,000, Thai communists about 200: Frank Darling, *Thailand and the United States* (Washington, D.C.: Public Affairs Press, 1965), p. 85. Zimmerman, writing in 1976, asserts that "the backbone of the Communist Party of Thailand still consists predominantly of the same 55 Sino-Thai leading cadres who formed the Central Committee in 1952," but he does not reveal the source of this information (presumably U.S. or Thai intelligence), nor does he indicate their names: "Insurgency in Thailand," p. 19.

5. Prasert Sabsunthorn, at the time reportedly party secretary-general, was the member. By the 1952 second party congress he had been replaced by Prasong Vongivat. Prasert was purged from the party in 1964 (1959, according to other reports) and denounced in 1968 as a "revisionist" renegade. "He strongly opposed our party's policy of armed violence and our preparation for a struggle in rural areas. He also suggested that the party follow a peaceful line [through parliamentary means]": party declaration, August 1968, quoted by Donald E. Weatherbee, *The United Front in Thailand: A Documentary Analysis* (Columbia, S.C.: University of South Carolina, 1970), pp. 77–78. Prasert became an adviser to the Thai government's Communist Suppression Operations Command (CSOC), directed by General Saiyud Kerdphon. See "Who is Prasert Sabsunthorn, where does he come from?," *Thai Nikorn,* Apr. 21, 1978; this describes his early years in Surat Thani, his leadership of the Thai Communist Party, and his exile in China from 1947 to 1958, where he expressed disagreement with the party line of seizing power by armed force. On his return to Thailand he was arrested, along with many others, but after approving Sarit's "patriotism" was released. He became an adviser on communism to the chief of the police "special branch," *Santiban,* and to CSOC, and a lecturer at the national defense college. The CPT launched a further campaign against revisionism (over the question of appealing to the masses, including the "backward" elements, or relying only on the progressive groups) in its debates with Phin Bua-on, a leading party theorist who had been captured in 1967. See Chaianan Samudavanija, *Prachathipatai sangkom niyom khomunit kab kan muang thai* (Bangkok-Phikhaner, 1975), pp. 292–293. On the related debate over armed or peaceful struggle, see ibid., pp. 225–229.

6. For example, Seni Pramot, former prime minister and a leader of the Democrats, welcomed the coup, declaring: "We could never get over the suspicion that Pridi was a communist." Incredibly, Pridi's use of the Free Thai movement appeared to Seni to be the first step in "establishing a communist state": Seni's political memoirs, in Jayanta Kumar Ray, *Portraits of Thai Politics* (New Delhi: Orient Longman, 1972), pp. 171–172.

world" resulted in a sharp increase in government harassment of communists or suspected communists, especially in the Chinese community after the communist victory in China. An interlude of relaxation in the mid-1950s was followed by severe repression under Sarit. Hundreds of suspected communists, among students and professionals in Bangkok, as well as socialist politicians and militant farmers in the Northeast, were arrested.

From the 1950s, the party began to forge links with existing opposition groups in the Northeast which, though not originally communist, had been labeled subversive by the Thai government and forced underground. In his valuable account, Keyes shows how depressed economic conditions in the Northeast led to extensive migration by farmers seeking work as unskilled laborers to Bangkok and elsewhere. They returned resentful over what they felt to be both class and ethnic discrimination. Meanwhile a number of deputies from the Northeast had been associated with the Free Thai Movement and were arrested after the 1947 military coup and charged with plotting a separatist state. In the 1950s all the deputies from the Northeast demanded better agricultural and educational conditions in their region; again, many of these deputies were arrested or exiled following Sarit's 1958 coup. The Thai government increasingly feared the possibility of subversion of the Northeast from Laos, particularly after Kong Le's 1960 coup, and tended to view all northeastern political dissent as part of a larger communist-led conspiracy.[7]

As a result of Sarit's communist-suppression campaign, the party organization, hitherto located in Bangkok, oriented toward Chinese workers and intellectuals, and largely concerned with urban affairs, was driven out of the capital to seek refuge in remote forested and mountainous areas. Out of the sheer need to survive, the party switched from urban to rural operations, and from the attempt to combine legal with illegal activities to the emphasis on armed struggle.

The party at first moved circumspectly, convertly promoting in 1964 a "Thai Independence Movement," which was perhaps intended to rally members of the Left-opposition to the struggle

7. Charles F. Keyes, *Isan: Regionalism in Northeastern Thailand* (Ithaca, N.Y.: Cornell University Southeast Asia Program, Data paper no. 65, 1967), pp. 37–39, 41–43, 51–53.

against the "Sarit-Thanom dictatorial clique." A major charge against the latter, according to the movement's 1964 manifesto, was that it had allowed Thai territory to be used "as a base for [U.S.] military aggression against neighboring countries."[8] The next step was the formation of a "Thai Patriotic Front" in January 1965, followed in August by the first armed clash between northeastern guerrillas and Thai security forces. But it was not until December 1966 that the Communist Party of Thailand, in its twenty-fourth anniversary message, formally took responsibility for launching the "people's war."[9] Two years later, in January 1969, the formation of the "Thai People's Liberation Armed Forces"—*kong taharn plod aek prachachon thai*—was announced, under the leadership of the CPT.[10]

8. Manifesto of Nov. 1, 1964: text in Weatherbee, *The United Front in Thailand*, pp. 30–34.

9. Weatherbee, *The United Front in Thailand*, pp. 62–64. For a discussion of the Chinese model, followed by the CPT, see J. L. S. Girling, *People's War: Conditions and Consequences in China and Southeast Asia* (London: Allen & Unwin, 1969). For an analysis of "revolutionary conditions," see John L. S. Girling, *America and the Third World: Revolution and Intervention* (London and Boston: Routledge & Kegan Paul, 1980), pt. 1. For an analysis of the CPT's Maoist party policy, based on the "four classes—workers, peasants, petty bourgeoisie or "small capitalists" (*nai thun noi*), and national capitalists (*nai thun chat*)—see Chaianan, *Prachathipatai sangkom niyom khomunit*, pp. 261–267.

10. Regional party leaders in the early 1970s were said to be: Song Nopakun, a Sino-Thai former teacher and supervisor of Thai trainees in Hanoi, responsible for party operations in the North; Charoen Wanngam, ethnic Thai, who studied five years at Marxist-Leninist Institutes in China, in charge of the Northeast; Udom Srisuwan, trader and journalist, active in the North and Northeast, who studied both in China and the Soviet Union; Wirat Angkhathawan, party theorist, from Trang in the mid-South; Prasit Tiensiri, also from the mid-South; and in the far South, Chin Peng, veteran Malayan Communist Party leader: "A Correspondent," *Far Eastern Economic Review*, May 13, 1972. After October 6, 1976 the party announced the real names of its leaders, some of whom were well-known Thai politicians, not Chinese or Vietnamese, as government propaganda tried to make out. Among them were Mitr Samanan, alias Song Nopakun, first secretary; Udom Srisuwan, secretary for the Northeast; Pleung Wanasri, former member of Parliament from Surin, in the Northeast; Lt.-Col. Payom Chulanont, former member of Parliament for Petchaburi, southwest of Bangkok; Taeng-on Chandawong, widow of Krong, former member of Parliament from Sakon Nakorn in the Northeast, executed in 1961 by order of Sarit: Somchai Rakwijit, "Problems of Thai Internal Security," *Southeast Asian Affairs 1978* (Singapore: Heinemann for Institute of Southeast Asian Studies, 1978), p. 292. See also Chaianan, *Prachathipatai sangkom niyom khomunit*, p. 269, who includes in his list Asani Phonlachan, a notable poet, especially popular among students. (Asani has reportedly been purged.)

*Regional Insurgency*

Even since the 1965 clash, said to mark the beginning of the "people's war," the armed struggle in Thailand still has the character of an insurgency rather than a revolution. It is an insurgency in terms of protracted, still fairly small-scale, guerrilla-type operations: "armed propaganda" in villages, attacks on police posts, blowing up bridges, ambushes of military convoys, and so on.

Compared with the "revolutionary situation" in South Vietnam, evident as early as 1960, the struggle in Thailand even now results in nothing like the heavy casualties suffered nearly twenty years ago by both sides in Vietnam.[11] Nor are there yet in Thailand battles between regimental-sized units, nor effective control of the countryside by the revolutionaries, nor demoralization of government forces, such as occurred in South Vietnam.

As for the current assessment of communist military strength in Thailand, it stands at something like 12,000 to 14,000 armed guerrillas in all regions. Around 5,000 of these operate in the Northeast, 5,000 to 6,000 in the South, and the rest in the North (2,000 to 3,000) with small numbers in three West-Central provinces.[12] They

11. The government of South Vietnam stated that in 1960 about 1,400 local officials and civilians were assassinated by the "Vietcong." In Thailand, 112 villagers and 24 officials were killed by the communists in the sixteen months after the formation of Communist Suppression Operations Command in December 1965. As for the armed forces, it was estimated that Saigon forces lost 6,500 killed, wounded, and captured in 1960 and the Viet Cong almost as many. The Thai figures for "officials killed in clashes," presumably soldiers and police, in the 16 months was 63, with 105 wounded: J. L. S. Girling, "Northeast Thailand: Tomorrow's Vietnam?" *Foreign Affairs*, January 1968. However, communist casualties in Thailand doubled from 1970 to 1971 to 201, with government losses at 361; in 1972, casualties were 369 and 592, respectively; in 1973, 255 and 358: Chaianan, "Communist Party of Thailand," quoting figures from the Internal Security Operations Command, successor of SCOC. The grim toll of 4,406 deaths among members of government forces, from 1969 to March 1977, was reported in *Ban Muang*, Mar. 24, 1977. In 1977, 582 military and civilian officials were killed and in 1978, 646: *Bangkok Post*, Mar. 29, 1979. In 1979, 544 officials were killed: *Bangkok Post*, Apr. 17, 1980.

12. *Far Eastern Economic Review*, July 27, 1979; also *Bangkok Post*, Mar. 25 and 26, 1979. However, General Prem stated in 1978 that there were altogether only 8,000 to 10,000 armed insurgents: *Bangkok Post*, May 30, 1978. Some caution should be observed. According to Tanham, qualitative factors in an insurgency—people's motivation and behavior—are more important than quantitative (numbers of weapons and equipment, etc.). He criticizes the tendency to rely on "body count" or number of "incidents" in attempting to evaluate the progress of counterinsurgency.

face around 140,000 soldiers in the Thai army and 20,000 in the paramilitary Border Patrol Police.[13]

The conflict in Thailand can be considered an insurgency rather than a revolution also because of the sectional, rather than national, composition and character of those taking up arms. From the Lao-speaking peasants of the Northeast, to the tribal fighters in the North, and Malay-Muslims and Chinese in the far South, the struggle is based on ethnic more than class solidarity. And the goals of some of the most militarily successful of these disparate forces— the hill tribes and the Malays, both operating from rugged terrain—have been defensive and even conservative rather than revolutionary. Both seek to defend their autonomy and restore their traditional way of life against the encroachments of the Thai majority. The latter include migrating farmers in the North and Buddhist officials in the South, and, in general, the centralizing, "modernizing" impulse of government.

Regional autonomy remains both the strength and the weakness of the insurgency in Thailand. It is strong, regardless of the overall party outlook, because it is rooted in local conditions: it unites people of a particular locality (tribal areas, parts of the Northeast, Muslim settlements in the South) in protest against the neglect, abuses, or arrogance of the "center" and in defense of their own identity. But for most of its existence the insurgency has been limited by its particularist appeals to these very regions and has not become a nationwide force. Because of the strength of particularity, it is important to consider these areas—the Northeast, North, and South—in some detail.

### Northeast

In the Northeast the "basic causes of insurgency," according to one specialist, "revolve primarily around poor economic and social conditions—i.e. low wages, land alienation, high land rentals, ad-

---

He concludes: "After many years of counter-insurgency activities, an accurate and accepted assessment capability is one of the greatest weaknesses": *Trial in Thailand*, p. 95.

13. John McBeth, *Far Eastern Economic Review*, July 13, 1979, with details of the armed forces and equipment; Amporn Tantuvanich, "Guardians of the Thai Frontier," *Bangkok Post*, Jan. 29, 1979. There are also reported to be more than 170,000 "village self-defense volunteers" in the Northeast: *Bangkok Post*, May 30, 1978.

ministrative inefficiency and corruption, and inadequate educational services."[14] For this is a region where the average per capita income is only half the national average, and where, according to some reports, nearly three-quarters of the rural families are subsisting below the poverty line.[15] Conscious of being Thai citizens and yet keenly aware of the psychological and economic discrimination they believe the people of *Isan* [the Northeast] are subject to, the Northeasterners are at the same time proud of their Lao culture and speech, akin to that of the lowland inhabitants of Laos across the river Mekong. It is from such mixed feelings of injured pride, resentment of Bangkok's indifference and neglect, and the desperate struggle to survive in a harsh and arid environment, that the roots of insurgency are to be found.

The "forest fighters," as the guerrillas call themselves, are not ideologically committed, but they have been persuaded by the few who are—the communist cadres who have been working among the villagers for years—that under present conditions they face only hardship and suffering. They hear that the government is corrupt, oppresses the people, and is interested only in Bangkok. Communist agents tell the villagers that they themselves must take the initiative to change the situation, and that if they join the forest army, they will get money, training for a good job, land and tractors, schools and hospitals—all that they now lack.[16]

As a concerned Thai specialist reports:

The insurgency continues to pose with extreme clarity the fundamental political problems facing Thailand. . . . The villagers are poor; though not starving, they are increasingly conscious of inequity, exploitation and injustice, as the development process gradually impoverishes them in relative if not absolute terms. More critical than their economic situation, however, is the villagers' relationship to the political system and the social structure which it reflects. In their personal contacts with government officials—civilian, police and military—the villagers are constantly treated

14. Zimmerman, "Insurgency in Thailand," p. 25. Poor and arid soils are actually more of a problem than land tenure.

15. Methee Krongkaew and Chintana Cheonsiri, "Determination of the Poverty Band in Thailand," originally published in *Warasarn Thammasat* (Thammasat University Journal) June–September 1975, trans. in *Social Science Review,* no. 2, 1976: see especially p. 70, table.

16. Girling, "Northeast Thailand."

badly—with disdain, exploitation and discourtesy. Corruption is rampant at all levels of the government, and any villager exposed to it can only reach the conclusion that each official is only interested in lining his own pockets, at the expense of his countrymen and his country itself. [The villager on his own can do little about this. But there is a profound change when the communist village organizer arrives on the scene.] Working with the particular set of grievances in that individual village, he offers them a sense of unity and organisational focus for acting upon their anger and sense of injustice. "Join with me," he says, "and we will replace this corrupt, unfair government with one of our own, from the people themselves."[17]

The communist party itself has been most active in areas near the Mekong River, forming the border with Laos, where sanctuary is available; along the uplands of the Phuphan range, with forests extending from near Ubon to beyond Udorn; in the rugged "tri-province" area, also bordering Laos, where the northern region joins the Northeast; in remote areas of other northeastern provinces, where villagers have long been isolated because of poor communications, which become almost nonexistent in the rainy season; and, especially since the 1970s, along the Dangrek mountain range separating Thailand from Kampuchea.[18] (See the map on page 261.)

Armed violence is sporadic, if also endemic, in the Northeast. One of the reasons for the relative restraint, compared with Vietnam, shown by the Thai communists is that they are anxious not to alienate the mass of villagers by indiscriminate or widespread terrorism. Another is that they seek to avoid provoking intensified government reprisals. Finally, they are thinking more in political than in military terms. Given the absence of good defensive terrain

17. Chaianan, "Communist Party of Thailand." He concludes that there is but one way to prevent the insurgency from developing: "corruption must be eliminated; mistreatment of villagers by officials must cease; officials must be induced (or compelled) to act as servants of the people, not as their masters. . . . Only with such a revolutionary change in the relationship between the Thai government and its citizens can the nation hope to cope successfully with the insurgents' challenge."

18. The Thai countersubversion specialist, Somchai Rakwijit, reports that communist battalion-sized units are already operating in certain provinces of the Northeast, such as Nakorn Phanom, Sakon Nakorn, Udorn, Loei, Kalasin, Burirum, and Ubon: interview with the author in Bangkok, Nov. 3, 1978. "'The CPT's military operations are directed at destroying the government's power structure by every means at its disposal, blocking the government's rural development programmes, as well as destroying the people's confidence in the Government,' the commander of the Second Region Police command said": *Nation*, Oct. 29, 1978.

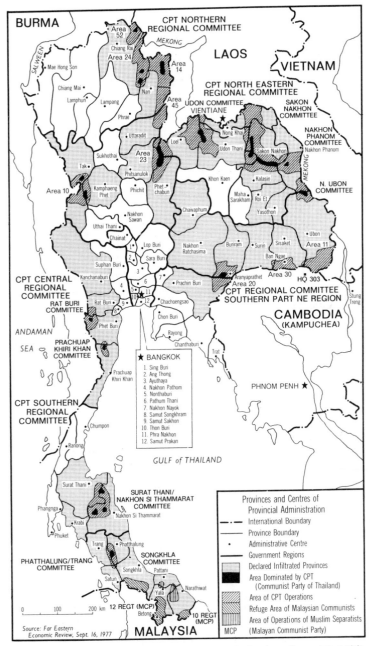

Thai insurgency, from *Far Eastern Economic Review*, Sept. 16, 1977.

(in this respect Northeast Thailand is very different from Laos and much of Vietnam) the Thai communists' best chance of success lies in building up a powerful political organization in the villages.

In their organizational drive, the communists divide the population into three categories: the enterprising, the middle group, and the backward. Their aim is to make leaders out of the first, raise the level of the second, and persuade the backward. Like the Chinese communists, they work by numbers: the "four goods," "five togethers," and "seven opportunities [changwa]." The "four goods" are the qualities required of a communist: good knowledge, good work, good friendship, and good cadres. The "five togethers" are: to eat, live, work, think, and acquire knowledge together with the masses. The "seven opportunities" are: to analyze the situation of villagers, officials, and the locality; define the propaganda slogan (kham khwan), arousing hatred of the authorities, etc.; develop organization among the villagers; select progressive villagers for education and training to become cadres; to lead the masses so that they cooperate economically and politically, and resist [the authorities]; consolidate mass organizations; and to expand to other areas. By spreading party influence in this way, the aim is to "transform" villages in four stages: (1) "establishing" the party organization, (2) "struggle" [su rob], (3) "liberated village," and (4) "village under state power" [muban amnat rat], when members of the provincial party executive exercise control.[19]

In a growing number of localities, the party has established an "elaborate organization" at the village level, typically with members of the village party committee in charge of subcommittees for youth, military affairs, political propaganda, labor and trade, women's affairs, and so on.[20] These village cadres are able to mobilize sufficient popular support in insurgent areas to generate the re-

19. Gen. Saiyud Kerdphon and Somchai Rakwijit, Anakhot khong thai [Future of Thailand] (Bangkok: Krung Sayam, 1975), pp. 130–148, 163–167.
20. According to Thai government assessments, as of January 1975, communists in the Northeast have "some" or "growing" influence in about 2,700 villages, with a population of more than 1.5 million; they "contend" with the government in 400 villages, with nearly a quarter of a million people; and they have strong influence or control in 176 villages, with 130,000 people. (Assessments for the North show that nearly half a million villagers are affected; in the Center nearly a quarter of a million); and in the South, more than one and a quarter million): survey published in the *Investor*, October 1975, table, "Communist-Terrorist Influence in Thai Villages." But on these statistics note Tanham's qualification, note 12 above.

sources required in manpower, food, shelter, and finances (partly through local taxation) and to form an effective intelligence network.[21] For the party agents and organizers are of the same stock, and they have shared the same experiences, as the peasants with whom they live, eat, and work. As one Thai researcher has pointed out, almost 60 per cent of communist party recruiting cadres, who carry out political work among lowland Thais, are friends, relatives, or neighbors of the people they aim to contact.[22] It is not surprising that many young villagers, in spite of government propaganda, believe that "the communists are Northeastern villagers like themselves." According to this officially sponsored survey of rural opinion, villagers considered the communists to be "enemies of the RTG [Royal Thai Government] and the U.S. but not of the people."[23]

### North

The situation in North Thailand is rather different. Although farms are very small, with a high incidence of tenancy and considerable migration due to rapid population growth, it is the hill tribes rather than lowland Thai villagers who are most disaffected. General Saiyud Kerdphon, for many years director of operations of the Internal Security Operations Command (ISOC), has attributed this to "internal colonialism" in an illuminating analogy to the position of the Thai monarchy in the nineteenth century. To face up to the external colonial challenge, he explains, the monarchy needed to obtain a firm grip on the countryside to use its resources in support of the capital. But "avoiding colonisation by Europe meant simply that we colonised our own people. This internal colonialism has led to obvious difficulties when applied to ethnic Thais themselves. . . . When applied to non-Thai areas, such as those occupied by the

21. Zimmerman, "Insurgency in Thailand," pp. 25, 27. He quotes from a study by Somchai "Rakjiwit" [Rakwijit], *The Jungle Leads the Village*, trans. Chumsri Race, ed. Zimmerman (USOM Bangkok, 1974). Tanham also notes that "the guerrillas' intelligence operations work well," giving them the initiative in hit and run attacks: *Trial in Thailand,* p. 98.

22. Somchai Rakwijit, "Security Situation in Thailand," *Trends in Thailand II* (Singapore: Institute of Southeast Asian Studies, 1976), p. 47.

23. Tanham's paraphrase of a research study primarily of Ubon province between late 1967 and March 1969, sponsored by the joint Thai-U.S. Military Research and Development Center: *Trial in Thailand,* pp. 106–107.

hill-tribes in the North, the policy has led to a disastrous tribal revolt."[24]

While there are some quarter of a million hill-tribe people inhabiting the forested and mountainous northern and western frontier regions of Thailand, it is among the 50,000-odd Hmong (known to others as Meo) in particular that the rebellion has been kindled. It is ironic that in Laos many of the Meo, after being aided and recruited by the CIA, had the reputation as the mainstay of the anticommunist cause in that country, for in Thailand they have become the communists' most effective partisans. This situation is the result, first, of the increasing competition between land-hungry Thai lowlanders and Meo tribespeople (fleeing from disturbed conditions in China, Vietnam, and Laos) to clear and cultivate forested areas in Thailand. Second, many Thai military and civilian officials have shown contempt or indifference for the Meo "savages." Finally, there are two distinct cultures and ways of life—the Meo growing opium, using "slash-and-burn" agriculture, and moving on; the Thais cultivating rice and settling down in villages.[25]

The burning of a Meo village in 1967, following Meo resistance to a "series of extortion attempts" by local government officials, first sparked off the armed conflict.[26] The Thai military used heavy-handed and even ruthless methods to crush the revolt. Heavy artillery, napalm strikes, air bombardment, and massive troop assaults were employed. The guerrillas usually escaped, but villages were destroyed, and a flood of embittered refugees were forcibly resettled.[27] But the Thai armed forces were no match for

24. Interview, *Bangkok Post,* Jan. 4, 1975, quoted by Zimmerman, "Insurgency in Thailand."

25. Traffic in opium, especially from the "golden triangle" (where the borders of Thailand, Burma, and Laos meet), is one of the murkiest problems in Thai politics. Thai military and political leaders in the past profited greatly by conniving at or "protecting" the opium trade and were often closely involved with the middlemen, including remnants of the Kuomintang active in Burma and formerly in Laos. In recent years the security aspect has become more prominent. The Thai government is understood to have tacitly encouraged the opium "warlords" as an anticommunist force capable of countering tribal "dissidents."

26. Jeffrey Race, "The War in Northern Thailand," *Modern Asian Studies,* January 1974.

27. Ibid., and Thomas A. Marks, "The Meo Hill-Tribe Problem in North Thailand," *Asian Survey,* October 1973. An interview with soldiers of a CPT base in North Thailand, discussing the work of village committees, education, and agriculture, is in the Japan-Asia quarterly *Ampo,* no. 1, 1979.

guerrillas operating in their own favored terrain. The Meo, according to Jeffrey Race, were "almost always successful and inflicted heavy casualties on the government" at practically no cost to themselves. The guerrillas, reportedly advised by Sino-Thai and Thai party cadres even before the outbreak of fighting, had been moving down into the northern valleys, penetrating the Karens (the largest tribe) in the West, and seeking to win over the lowland Thais.[28]

### South

By far the most complex, even chaotic, situation is in southern Thailand. Here the economy consists mainly of Chinese smallholder rubber planters and important tin-mining concerns directed by both foreign and Chinese enterprises. In the four southernmost provinces, a deprived, Malay-speaking Muslim peasantry, very much attached to traditional ways, surrounds urban enclaves of Thai Buddhists. The whole region is administered, taxed, and regulated by Thai officials responsible to Bangkok.[29] This mixed ethnic, cultural, occupational, and religious environment is further complicated by the existence along the jungle frontier of units of the largely Chinese "Malayan Communist Party," which had been driven out of Malaya in the 1950s.[30]

Such are the different elements in the insurgency: Malay-Muslim separatists, looking back to the former independent Malay sulta-

28. Tanham, *Trial in Thailand,* pp. 57–62. Another American researcher, formerly with USOM, points out that by 1971 only 40 percent of Northern guerrillas were tribal (chiefly Meo), the majority being Sino-Thai: J. Alexander Caldwell, *American Economic Aid to Thailand* (Lexington, Mass.: Lexington Books, 1974), p. 130. Somchai Rakwijit observes that communists in the North are devoting more effort to political work among lowland Thais: interview with the author in Bangkok, Nov. 3, 1978.

29. Eighty-five per cent of *tambon* and village heads in Yala, Pattani, and Narathiwat provinces cannot read or write Thai and know only the local (Malay) dialect, according to a senator originally from Pattani: *Bangkok Post,* Nov. 14, 1975. See also "Southern Focus," *Business in Thailand,* September 1975; D. J. W. Berkoff, "Land and Development in South Thailand," *Southeast Asian Spectrum,* January–March 1976.

30. They are led by the redoubtable Chin Peng, organizer of the communist insurrection in Malaya (the "Emergency") which started in 1948. Chin Peng was at one time reported killed by a rival communist faction, but Malaysian security officials believe he had been in China for some years and only recently returned to the jungle: report from Kuala Lumpur in the *Nation,* Jan. 21, 1977. Chin Peng is now reported to be back in Peking: K. Das, *Far Eastern Economic Review,* June 8, 1979. Two rival factions are the MCP (Marxist-Leninist) active around Betong, and the "revolutionary faction" in Sadao.

nates; Chinese and Malay bandits, the product of unsettled and unruly frontier conditions, exacerbated by the fluctuating fortunes of the tin and rubber economy; hardened Chinese communists, biding their time in jungle camps, recruiting and organizing among local Chinese, but with their attention fixed not so much on Thailand as on their goal of renewed revolution in Malaysia;[31] and finally, the Thai government officials. As one scholar put it, "the predominance of Thai Buddhist government officials in the South, most of whom do not speak Malay, is a crucial factor in creating an adversary relationship between the local people and the administration. This ranges from complaints by the Muslims of petty harassment and corruption to more serious accusations of persecution and imprisonment of Muslims based on tenuous allegations of banditry or subversion.[32]

The "Malay nationalists" are divided between the older, conservative element and the younger generation of activists, a number of whom go to the Middle East for their education.[33] But they are poorly organized, lacking in leadership, and continually quarreling among themselves. Consequently, they still lack credibility as an effective opposition movement and attract little external support. The alarm expressed by the Thai government about "separatism" is exaggerated.[34]

31. As a result, according to a Malaysian correspondent, for a decade Thai government efforts were "little more than shadowboxing with the communists." It was only after the October 1976 coup that the Thanin government agreed with the Malaysians to "wage all-out war" against the Malayan Communist Party, and joint operations began in 1977. K. Das, *Far Eastern Economic Review*, Feb. 4, 1977.

32. Astri Suhrke, "Loyalists and Separatists: The Muslims in Southern Thailand," *Asian Survey*, March 1977. For further informative studies, see: M. Ladd Thomas, *Political Violence in the Muslim Provinces of Southern Thailand* (Singapore: Institute of Southeast Asian Studies, occasional paper no. 28, 1975); Astri Suhrke, "Irredentism Contained: The Thai-Muslim Case," *Comparative Politics*, January 1975; Ruth McVey, "Southern Thailand," Australian National University seminar, Feb. 18, 1976. Symptomatic of the depth of Muslim distrust was the protest by more than 1,000 Muslim villagers and students over the alleged killing by Thai troops of five villagers in Pattani province in November 1975: Paisal Sricharatchanya, "Muslims have reason to be bitter," *Bangkok Post*, Dec. 13, 1975. For a further assessment, especially of the problem of the educated unemployed, see Astri Suhrke, "The Muslims in Southern Thailand: An Analysis of Political Developments 1968–78," unpublished paper, American University, December 1978. See also articles on the economy of South Thailand in the *Nation*, beginning on June 24, 1980.

33. Surin Pitsuwan, "Thai Politics from a Southern Perspective," paper at annual meeting of the Association for Asian Studies, Los Angeles, Mar. 31, 1979.

34. Astri Suhrke, "South Thailand: Ethnic Problems, International Implica-

The veteran Malayan Communist Party (MCP), on the other hand, is "probably the best organised and led communist group in Thailand," according to Tanham. It collects taxes and administers justice, actively recruits for its armed bands, which include two regiments of Chinese and one of Muslims, and makes great use of mass organizations. The latter include the Malayan Communist Youth League, with several thousand members recruited from Chinese communities in towns and countryside.[35] MCP armed strength in 1976 was estimated at some 2,000 guerrillas, more than one-third of whom are Malaysian Chinese, about one-third Thai-Chinese, and the rest Thai Muslim.[36]

The mainly ethnic-Thai southern wing of the Communist Party of Thailand operates chiefly in the mid-South provinces of Trang, Phathalung, and Surat Thani, extending to Satun (Muslim but Thai-speaking) and Songkhla. Cooperation between the CPT and MCP resulted in joint training of cadres since 1969;[37] in August 1977, under CPT leadership, the "Liberation Armed Forces of the Muslim Thai People" were set up.[38] Altogether, communists in the South number around 6,000,[39] and they fight effectively from rugged terrain.[40]

### Indigenous Support

Yet the convenient belief that the insurgencies in Thailand are either instigated by communists from outside or mainly the work of

tions," Australian National University seminar, Aug. 9, 1978. However, the *potential* strength of Malay nationalism should not be underrated.

35. Tanham, *Trial in Thailand*, pp. 65–66. Thai and Malaysian authorities usually refer to the Malayan Communist Party as the "Communist Terrorist Organization."

36. Derived from the *Straits Times*, Aug. 14, 1976, quoted by Daniel Chew, "The Insurgency Situation in Peninsular Malaysia," Australian National University, 1978.

37. Somchai Rakwijit, interview with the author, Nov. 3, 1978.

38. Announced by the Voice of the People of Thailand, Feb. 28, 1978.

39. *Bangkok Post*, Mar. 25, 1979. They are active in eight provinces: Nakorn Sri Thammarat, Surat Thani, Phathalung, Trang, Satun, Songkla, Yala, and Narathiwat. See also articles by John McBeth and K. Das, *Far Eastern Economic Review*, June 29, 1980.

40. Ambushes of government troops and officials are frequent. Police General Monchai, for example, reported a "deteriorating situation" after an inspection tour: *Bangkok Post*, June 6, 1978. The governor of Phathalung pointed out in February 1979 that communists based in the Ban That mountain range spanning several provinces were seeking to extend their influence to the lowlands. The insurgents in the South are reportedly led by Prasit Thiensiri: *Bangkok Post*, Mar. 23, 1979. However, one of the CPT province chiefs, Wichit Chongchit, gave himself up in March 1979.

"alien" minorities—Vietnamese in the Northeast,[41] Chinese in the South, hill tribes in the North—still persists in the outlook of Thai officials, especially the military, despite the weight of evidence against it.[42] As an American counterinsurgency expert has pointed out, the "overwhelming majority" of insurgents in the Northeast are Thai; communist cadres in the North are Thai or Sino-Thai; and if guerrillas in the far South are mainly Chinese or Thai-Muslim, those in the West-Center and mid-South are Thai.[43]

The activities of the insurgent movements in Thailand arise almost entirely out of local needs and resources.[44] External support was at no time very great and in recent years has dwindled considerably. Tanham and Zimmerman both report a figure of more than 2,500 Thais trained in China, Vietnam, and Laos since the 1950s.[45] But taking arrests and casualties into account over two decades, this would not represent a large proportion of the present

41. There are some 40,000 Vietnamese, mostly settled in the Northeast. Originally refugees from the French war in Indochina, many were sympathetic to or supporters of the Vietminh; and they are still regarded with deep distrust by many Thai people and officials. But there is no reliable evidence that the Vietnamese community as such, apart from the activities of a few individuals, has participated in the *Thai* insurgency. This, as Flood points out, has not stopped Thai authorities from denouncing the Vietnamese as "spies," "terrorists," and "communists" over the years; the campaign was stepped up after the collapse of right-wing governments in Indochina in 1975. One example was the U.S. army study, "External Support to the Thai Insurgency: the 35 PL/NVA [Pathet Lao/North Vietnamese Army] Combined Command," circulated among Thai officials, and purported to be a Vietnamese master plan to bring the Thai provinces along the western bank of the Mekong under Hanoi's political and economic control. The riots instigated against the Vietnamese in December 1975 and in mid-1976 were another example. E. Thadeus Flood, "The Vietnamese Refugees in Thailand: Minority Manipulation in Counterinsurgency," *Bulletin of Concerned Asian Scholars*, July–September 1977, pp. 38–40. Negotiations with Vietnam to repatriate the Vietnamese resumed under Kriangsak, but became bogged down (no doubt because of the wider international crisis) toward the end of 1978.

42. The cold war mentality of the Thai military, notably in the National Security Council, is amply attested to: see Sarasin Viraphol, *Directions in Thai Foreign Policy* (Singapore: Institute of Southeast Asian Studies, occasional paper no. 40, 1976), pp. 12, 23, 50–51. This attitude is reflected in the government "white paper" on communism, issued by Prime Minister Seni in June 1976. The paper details support by China, Vietnam, Laos, and Cambodia in terms of education, training, propaganda, weapons, and infiltration: *Samutpokkhaw prachachon khwanru* (Bangkok 1976) esp. pp. 20–43.

43. Tanham, *Trial in Thailand*, p. 89.

44. Caldwell, *American Economic Aid to Thailand*, p. 129.

45. Tanham, *Trial in Thailand*, p. 95; Zimmerman, "Insurgency in Thailand," p. 28. U.S. government estimates in late 1969 were that 700 or more cadres had been trained in China, 600 in North Vietnam, and 100 in Laos: Caldwell, *American Eco-*

total of up to 14,000 armed guerrillas in all regions. Tanham does note a large increase in supply of Chinese arms to hill-tribe guerrillas in the North from 1971 to 1973, but otherwise, and apart from radio propaganda,[46] Chinese efforts are "small and low key."[47] Although Zimmerman argues somewhat dubiously that Chinese and Vietnamese aid is "vital" to the CPT,[48] his own assessment of conditions in the affected regions and the motivation of party members and supporters implies substantial popular support. In any case, even if there were a massive external supply operation, whether or not these arms could be used effectively would still depend not on the supplier, but on the "absorptive capacity" of the local insurgents.[49]

According to analysts in Bangkok, "Peking's active support for the Thai insurgency was dramatically reduced early in the decade [1970s]."[50] This trend is likely to persist while China seeks support from ASEAN governments against Soviet and Vietnamese "expansionism." At the same time, owing to "bad relations" between Hanoi and the pro-Chinese leadership of the CPT, the relatively small provision of arms and training by Vietnam was suspended in 1976.[51] This situation would appear to give some substance to Pham Van Dong's pledge, in September 1978, that Vietnam would

*nomic Aid to Thailand*, p. 129. Somchai Rakwijit refers to a three- to six-month training course in Laos, compared to two- to five-year course for high-level cadres in China. The provincial party committee members of the CPT go through the party school in China: interview with the author, Nov. 3, 1978.

46. The CPT radio, *Siang prachachon haeng prathet thai* [Voice of the people of Thailand, or VOPT], is believed to be based in Southwest China.

47. Tanham, *Trial in Thailand*, p. 48. Chinese support was further reduced, as friendly relations with the Thai government were promoted, in the later 1970s.

48. Zimmerman, "Insurgency in Thailand," p. 28.

49. Sir Robert Thompson, *Defeating Communist Insurgency* (London: Chatto & Windus, 1966).

50. Richard Nations, *Far Eastern Economic Review*, July 28, 1978.

51. Somchai Rakwijit, interview with the author, Nov. 3, 1978; Huynh Kim Khanh suggests that the Vietnamese leadership withdrew its support from the CPT because it realized it could not compete with the Peking-oriented and ethnically Chinese communist parties in mainland Southeast Asia: interview with the author, Singapore, Nov. 13, 1978. U.S. State Department and Pentagon sources reported in April 1977 that Vietnam had refused to supply guerrillas in Thailand and Malaysia, or elsewhere in the region, with arms: *New York Times*, May 1, 1977, quoted by Robert C. Horn, "Soviet-Vietnamese Relations and the Future of Southeast Asia," *Pacific Affairs*, Winter 1978-79. See also Carlyle Thayer, who reports apparently "minimal material support" by Vietnam to the CPT: "Vietnam's External Relations," *Pacific Community*, January 1978.

not support, directly or indirectly, subversion or insurgency in Thailand.[52]

## National Prospects

External support may supplement, but cannot be a substitute for, self-reliance: this revolutionary maxim has been well learned. At no time in the last three decades has the revolutionary movement in Thailand depended for survival on aid from China or Vietnam. Yet if the party struggle is rooted in local conditions, only in the last few years has it been able to break out of these limitations. Only in the 1970s did the possibility of development on a national scale arise. This national development was made possible by the new social forces that emerged following the collapse of the autocracy. These forces were responsible for the ferment of radical ideas, especially among the youth; the formation of militant working class organizations; and the beginnings of a peasant movement, particularly among tenant farmers and the landless. Radical students, who had been the catalyst for constitutional change, played a major role in stimulating and assisting all these activities. For by such means, it was believed, the mass of the people would no longer feel themselves to be isolated, powerless individuals in a society impervious to change.

In providing a penetrating intellectual content to such beliefs, the life and works of Chit Phumisak, especially *Chom na sakdina thai* [The face of Thai feudalism], had an enormous impact on the radical student generation. *Chom na sakdina thai* was first published in 1957, in the relatively relaxed period between the shift to "democracy" by Phibun and Sarit's coup in 1958. In that year Chit Phumisak was arrested and imprisoned. He was released only after the death of Sarit, but found it impossible to work freely, went underground, and was killed in 1966 by government forces. Like Che Guevara, Chit Phumisak, poet, scholar and "fighter of the new generation,"[53] became a cult-hero of the Left in the exciting and turbulent years of democracy after October 1973.

---

52. He made this pledge on September 10, 1978, at the end of a five-day visit to Thailand, when he signed a joint communique with Kriangsak. The impact of more recent developments on the CPT, notably the Vietnamese-led occupation of Kampuchea and the Chinese attack on Vietnam, is discussed in the last section of this chapter.

53. Subtitle of *Chit Phumisak: nakrob khong khon run mai* (Bangkok: Phikanet, 1974), proceedings of a seminar and articles by poets, professors, and political

The message of *Chom na sakdina thai* is the protest of the Thai people against imperialism, compradore capitalism and "aristocrat-capitalism," and feudalism (*sakdina*). The Thai people, according to Chit Phumisak, see clearly who the enemy is who plunders them and exploits them economically; they know the life of misery and poverty they lead, whether as peasants or workers. The people understand how the government oppresses them politically by unjust laws and exploits them by heavy taxation. And the people experience the decline of morality under the influence of Western culture. Therefore "the fundamental enemy they must urgently eradicate is imperialism from outside and *sakdina* from within."[54]

Chit Phumisak's work is not only a brilliant, if controversial, analysis of Thai history according to the classic Marxist stages—primitive communism, slave society, feudalism, capitalism, and socialism—but it also seeks to bring home to the Thai people the way in which the few dominate and exploit the many. According to this perspective, peasants or workers will become aware that they are suffering, not because of their individual "fate," but because of the way in which society is organized. Peasants, workers, and others will then become conscious that they are members of an oppressed *class,* and not isolated individuals, and act accordingly. Collective consciousness leads to collective action ("class struggle"), which, in the final stage, whether the path is rough or smooth, brings about a new, classless, and therefore just society. Such is the analysis, the "formula," and the vision of Marxists.[55]

---

workers, including accounts of his life and work by two of Chit Phumisak's friends: Supha Sirimanon, review editor and reporter, and Thongbai Thongpao, a fellow prison inmate (after 1976, defense lawyer for the "Thammasat 18"). A fascinating record of Chit's experiences at Chulalongkorn and his views (his love of reading, his respect for Buddhist philosophy: one "should not simply believe, without reason") is provided by the court transcript of his evidence at the trial in 1959: reprinted in *Athit,* May 16, 1978.

54. *Chom na sakdina thai* (Bangkok, 1974), pp. 1–10, 18. However, the bulk of the work is a detailed analysis of Thai society in the slave-owning and feudal period. The book was published incomplete and does not examine, after the end of absolute monarchy in 1932, the contemporary period of "semifeudal, semicolonial" Thai society.

55. Despite Chit Phumisak's mastery of his subject, and his clear and methodical approach, his work raises a number of problems. Chief among them is whether or not the classic Marxist schema, derived from western European history, is applicable to the very different situation of historical Siam and even of modern Thailand. This

However penetrating the analysis or profound the vision, the majority of popular struggles in Thailand in the mid-1970s were inspired less by Marxist ideology than by immediate, practical demands. Most of the workers taking part in strikes were not organized in unions; those who were acted for the most part as moderates. The militant Farmers' Federation of Thailand, prior to the murder in July 1975 of its leader, Intha Sribunruang, did not use Marxist slogans or advocate violence to achieve its ends.[56] Even the crowds of students who noisily demonstrated against "American imperialism," "bureaucratic capitalism," and "feudalism" were nationalists, democrats, or populists rather than Marxists—though many of the leaders were Marxists. What the struggle movement was intended to do, and to a certain extent achieved, was to "raise the consciousness" of those taking part. As one of the student leaders explained:

Some of the people misunderstood that after October 1973 we already had complete freedom. But this was not so. Dictatorial elements are still deeply rooted in Thai society. The bureaucrats, for example, are still masters of

---

point is brought out by Charnvit Kasetsiri, "Chit Phumisak's Interpretation of Thai History" (in Thai), in Charnvit and Suchat Sawatsri, eds., *Prawatsat lae nakprawatsat thai* [History and Thai historians] (Bangkok: Phikhanet, 1976), pp. 378–379; also printed in *Chit Phumisak*. See also Kajorn Sukpanich, "The Free Man Status: The Free Man-Patron Relationship in Siam with Economic and Cultural Implications, from 1341 to 1905," trans. in *Social Science Review*, no. 1 (1976). Moreover, Chit was not aware of Marx's major modification of his thesis in his writings on the "Asiatic mode of production" since these particular works were not available in Thailand at that time: Chaianan Samudavanija, *Sakdina kab phatanakan khong sangkom thai* (Bangkok: Nam Aksorn Press, 1976) p. 94. Marx had stressed that as a result of "climate and territorial conditions" in Asia, extensive irrigation networks had become basic to agriculture over the centuries, and they required a powerful centralizing state to control them—quite unlike the feudal system in western Europe. Had he known of this distinction, Chit Phumisak would no doubt have given greater prominence to the historic role of the bureaucratic state. A final problem is the "ownership" or control of the means of production in the *sakdina* era, which is now seen as control of manpower rather than of land. The question of land ownership and the origin of slavery in Thailand are matters of historical controversy. Yet the character of economic power in *contemporary* Thailand creates no fewer problems for Marxists. (See Chapter 2.)

56. It was *after* the death of Intha that the Federation's journal, *Chaona thai*, declared (July 20, 1975): "The murder of our leaders by capitalists and landlord gangsters teaches us another lesson of our struggle: that in our fight violence is inevitable": quoted by Chai-Anan, draft chapter, "Farmers and Modern Thai Politics," in Morell and Chai-Anan, *Reform, Reaction, Revolution*.

the people. In the last [1975] elections most of the candidates elected were rich, rather than true representatives of the farmers and the poor. When they are in the parliament they naturally protect the interests of the capitalists.

The political pendulum has now swung from the military to the economic elite. . . . [But] the military themselves are trying to win their power back by using the bureaucracy as their instrument to create the proper circumstances in which to sabotage this capitalist government.[57]

This was indeed a plausible analysis of Thai conditions, which, in the course of events, might have been expected to broaden its appeal among more and more workers, peasants, and even middle class elements. But the way ahead through legal organization, direct action, and open discussion, pioneered by the students, was not to be. Instead of the "peaceful transition to socialism" envisioned by the more optimistic or naive among Thai Marxists, all were faced by the brutal alternative, in October 1976, of submission or armed struggle.

For the Marxist or Marxist-influenced Left, the 1976 military coup was of the utmost significance. Such a shattering blow to the democratic experiment demonstrated the futility of relying on peaceful evolution to bring about the improvement of Thai society. This ideological "lesson" was reinforced by the violence of the right-wing assault against both moderates and the Left, which compelled hundreds of people—mainly students, but also politicians, teachers, union leaders, peasant activists, journalists, and others—to flee for safety to communist-controlled areas in the forests and jungles, especially in the Northeast and South. Thus for the first time in its history the party received a major influx of supporters from the urban educated Left—precisely the "nationalist and progressive" component it had hitherto lacked.

57. Pichian Amnatworaprasert, NSCT deputy secretary-general for economic and political affairs, interviewed by *Prachachat Weekly*, Oct. 23, 1975, quoted by Chai-Anan, draft chapter, "The Student Movement," in Morell and Chai-Anan. On "consciousness raising," see Chaianan, *Prachathipatai sangkom niyom khomunit*, pp. 273–278. Many leftists were not members of the CPT, but shared a common viewpoint. The CPT, however, believed that student activists were too rash and "unwary" in staging strikes and demonstrations, especially in the capital, as these were likely to provoke a rightist reaction. This would result in a purge of leftist movements which the party hoped to use as a front: *Prachathipatai sangkom niyom khomunit*, pp. 310–311.

According to Somchai Rakwijit, about 1,500 students and other young intellectuals fled and joined the CPT in the six months following the October 1976 coup. As he puts it, this was a major victory for the CPT, because it had never before won over such a large number of better-educated citizens, who would be able to provide a higher quality of leadership.[58]

Toward a Common Front

A fortnight after the October 1976 coup, Khaisaeng Suksai, deputy leader of the Socialist Party of Thailand, a well-known political figure from the Northeast, along with other party members broadcast over the CPT radio's *Siang prachachon haeng prathet thai* [Voice of the people of Thailand] an appeal for unity of the people against the destroyers of democracy. Seven from the dedicated and brilliant group of student leaders of the early 1970s, including Thirayut and Seksan, broadcast a few days later.

The youth and students of Thailand have always fought for independence, democracy, and the basic needs of the poorest in society in a peaceful way, within the letter of the law and the constitution. . . . Our peaceful struggle has only been met with bombs and bullets. . . . The hard lesson learned with so much blood and paid for with so many lives is that independence and democracy for our people can never be obtained by reforms within an unjust and corrupt society. We, the people, have no other choice but to unite forces to defeat the power of the reactionary state and establish a new popular and revolutionary state.[59]

Members of the Socialist Party, in a further statement in April 1977, urged the formation of a "broad national democratic front" and announced its readiness to "cooperate with the struggle of the people's armed forces in the rural areas."[60] Meanwhile the CPT

58. "Problems of Thai Internal Security," *Southeast Asian Affairs 1978,* p. 291.
59. Statement of Oct. 14, 1976, broadcast over VOPT, Oct. 31, 1976. Transcripts of these and other broadcasts are published daily, in English, by the U.S. government's Foreign Broadcast Information Service, Asia and the Pacific, and the British (BBC) Summary of World Broadcasts, the Far East.
60. Broadcast over VOPT, May 7, 1977. The Socialist Party leader, Col. Somkid Srisangkom, however, remained in Bangkok. He resumed political activities in 1979 as leader of the (unsuccessful) Socialist Democracy Party.

spokesman, Udom Srisuwan, had already pledged communist "cooperation with all political parties, organisations, patriotic and democratic people in fighting against the common enemies... The time has come for all people's groups to unite into the broad revolutionary front."[61] The result, announced in September 1977, was the formation of a "Committee to Coordinate Democratic and Patriotic Groups," headed by Udom, with Thirayut as secretary-general, and socialist, labor, and peasant representatives.[62]

Thus students, socialists, and radicals, on the one hand, and veteran communist revolutionaries, on the other, came together in the struggle against the common enemy. To a certain extent, they shared a common Marxist ideology, which is reinforced in the case of the new allies by the bitter experience of the 1976 coup.[63] But the question remains, despite the agreement to cooperate and the eventual formation of the coordinating committee, whether these two very different forces can be meshed together

61. Speech by Udom Srisuwan, CPT representative, on February 28, 1977, to commemorate the first anniversary of the death of Dr. Boonsanong Boonyothayan, the first secretary-general of the Socialist Party of Thailand. (Dr. Boonsanong, a Cornell-educated sociologist, was assassinated during the 1977 election campaign; his murderers were never discovered): report in *Samakki Surob*, no. 2, 1977. The bulletin is edited by Thirayut Boonmee, Saman Luadwonghat, Prasarn Maruekhaphitak, Wisa Kantap, and Prayong Moolsarn for the Socialist party.

62. Among the adherents are: Sri Intrapanti, a former government spokesman and reporter; Therdphum Jaidee, president of the banned Hotel Workers Federation; Prasit Chaiyo, president of the banned Textile Workers Union; Sithon Yotkantha, deputy chairman of the Farmers Federation of Thailand (the FFT chairman and other leading members had been assassinated during 1974–75); and many members of the Socialist Party and of the National Student Center of Thailand. Chaianan provides details of forty-six of the most prominent figures, who announced their collaboration with the CPT from October 1976 to March 1977: Chai-Anan, "Communist Party of Thailand." See also biographical details in "Sounds from the Jungle," *Asiaweek*, July 14, 1978. The committee later broke up.

63. See "A Note from the Jungle to the City" by Chontira Sattayawatana, a former lecturer at Chulalongkorn, who was doing research on Chit Phumisak. She points out that a good number of the students who fled after October 1976 have enrolled in the CPT's "School of Political and Military Affairs" where they learn from the party's experience, its "general line theory of people's war, base building, army building, mass line and mass work." She concludes: "The study gears us toward a correct understanding of the nature of the Thai revolution, its significance and its future." Reprinted by "Sixth October Thai United Front for Democracy," May 1978. See also the interview with a former student leader, emphasizing the need to create a new and just society and the importance of a "correct line" in winning state power: *Thai Nikorn*, Mar. 24, 1978.

effectively in a unified organization with a common working strategy.[64]

The students' experience has been one of direct action—protest meetings, demonstrations, and strikes—in an open, largely urban, environment. Energetic and strongly motivated, a number of them expect quick results, perhaps in the form of more or less spontaneous revolutionary insurrection. In this respect at least, these activists may be closer to the Leninist model of the Bolshevik revolution than to the protracted rural guerrilla warfare of the Chinese leader Mao Tse-tung, whom they so fervently admire.

The Communist party, on the other hand, consists of veteran "professionals," habituated to underground activities and hardened by decades of struggle, which are only gradually changing the balance of forces. Can these experienced and doctrinaire party leaders adapt themselves sufficiently to the new radical influx of youth, students, and intellectuals? Can they concede genuine participation in policy decisions and strategic organization to their turbulent and untested allies; or will they try to limit their role to the important, but lesser, tasks of recruitment and publicity? A division of labor at the latter level might well suit the needs of party discipline, organization, and cohesion. But only active participation at all levels, however gradually this may come about, will enable the party to transcend the regional, "minority," and class limitations which, at present, place the party at a disadvantage in confronting the existing regime.

### Problems of Integration and Policy

Evidently the rallying of urban radicals and intellectuals to the party has strengthened its verbal commitments to moderate, immediate social goals, rather than drastic collectivization; to attempts

64. One experienced reporter commented, before the October 1976 coup, on the "talk of fierce dissension in the Party between the mainly Chinese or Sino-Thai veterans and newcomers, and over 'leftist deviationist' and 'revisionist' tendencies advocated by some members. In particular, these debates are said to have focused on such questions as whether the Party should blindly follow a Maoist line, imitating almost all aspects of Maoist doctrine, or whether it should base its policy and tactics on a more rigorous analysis of local conditions. Another question is whether it should concentrate less on organisation . . . or make greater efforts in the ideological political consciousness of members. Again, what should be the Party's targets in the towns and its relationship to the political struggle [then going on] in Bangkok and

to create a broad united front, including democrats, "patriots," and the national bourgeoisie, rather than directly waging class struggle; and to tactical flexibility rather than rigid adherence to dogma. But the more open, popular, and creative approach introduced by the newcomers fits uneasily with the secretive and conspiratorial background of the old party leaders, their sectarian origins, the importance they attach to discipline, and their narrowly "professional" outlook.

For the problem of integration goes far beyond matters of organization and technique. It concerns vital issues of policy. Among them are the perennial question of armed or "legal" struggle (again conceivable during the more relaxed period after the downfall of Thanin); "rural encirclement of the cities" or urban revolt; peasants or workers as the leading force; and class struggle or united front. Advocacy of the united front, for example, however expedient in the present situation, cannot but detract from the class basis of party support: that is, its reliance on peasants and workers as the "motive force" of struggle. The problem, as other communist parties have found, comes down to this: the more widespread the appeal, the less intensive the revolutionary commitment.

The party has been able to straddle these dichotomies in theory—formulating the two-stage revolution, from "national democracy" to socialism—and, to a certain extent, in practice. The (Maoist) concept of "national democratic" revolution represents the first stage of struggle, which is intended to unite both dispossessed and possessors—up to a certain level—against the "three enemies" they have in common: i.e., "U. S. imperialism, feudalism, and bureaucratic capitalism," according to the introduction to the "immediate policy" of the CPT, announced in January 1979.[65] The goals at this stage are therefore "national," because they seek to eliminate *foreign* monopoly power, which exploits the "national bourgeoisie" and at the same time sustains the domestic elite; and they are also "democratic," since the overthrow of the authoritarian military, political, and economic structure will open the way (in

---

other urban centers?" While such dissension is plausible, the correspondent went on, "there is almost total lack of reliable information to substantiate it": Norman Peagam, *Far Eastern Economic Review,* July 9, 1976.

65. VOPT, Jan. 4, 1979.

theory) to political democracy and economic and social reform. It is under conditions of democracy, according to the formula, that the majority of the people—peasants and workers—will be able to reassert their interests, under the leadership of the party, and thus bring about the second stage of "socialist" revolution. The problem that *in practice* faces the party, however, is first to convince the middle strata of "democrats, patriots and national bourgeoisie" that the "three enemies" *are* the most immediate and pressing danger, and, second, to convince both the middle and the lower strata that their differing interests are best served by and through the party.

How to create a united front, linking rural and urban struggle, has long been a preoccupation of the party leadership. As early as the 1950s, the party urged the coordination of armed struggle in the rural areas with other forms of struggles in towns. "Without this coordination, the revolutionary bases in the rural areas will be isolated."[66] Moreover, party cadres were specifically urged in December 1973 to "develop the national democratic front extensively both in the towns and in the countryside."[67] And although "peaceful struggle was still impossible" for the CPT even during the 1973–76 period, the party "supported various student and popular movements," demanding the withdrawal of U.S. troops, and working for social justice and better conditions for the peasants.[68] Finally, speaking on behalf of the united front, Thirayut himself explained in September 1978 that the front "exists everywhere, taking various shapes and forms," using armed struggle and without weapons, "legal, semi-legal, even illegal; covert and overt; formal and formless. . . ." The front's task, he added, was that of all Thai patriots, in accordance with their ability and their circumstances, whether they lived in urban or rural areas or abroad.[69]

66. Smarn Woothiporn, "The Communist Party and the People's War in Thailand," *Samakki Surob,* no. 2, 1977.

67. CPT thirty-first anniversary statement, Dec. 1, 1973, quoted by Somchai Rakwijit in *Trends in Thailand II* (Singapore University Press for Institute of Southeast Asian Studies, 1976).

68. Smarn, "The Communist Party and the People's War." But see note 57, above.

69. Thirayut Boonmee, secretary of the Committee for Coordinating Patriotic and Democratic Forces, on its first anniversary, Sept. 28, 1978: reported by Thai Information Center (Sydney), TIC News, Nov. 15, 1978. And see Thirayut on the national democratic front, *Far Eastern Economic Review*, Sept. 19, 1980.

The Thai authorities, for their part, fear the revival of communist influence particularly among students and workers in and around Bangkok,[70] and they are alarmed at the possibility of a shift to urban guerrilla warfare.[71] A well-informed reporter notes: "a proliferation of CPT cells in Bangkok's key utilities and in the factories stretching along its major roads. One Thai intelligence source estimates the number of CPT cadres in Bangkok at 2,000 and says that the majority of student and labor leaders are in constant touch with communist front organisations. If these reports are not grossly exaggerated, the CPT would appear already well-positioned to direct the next wave of urban unrest to creating the classic Leninist 'disposing conditions' for paralysing the government."[72]

Indeed it was widely believed, both before and after October 1976, that urban insurgency was imminent. This belief reflected the "turbulence" of political demonstrations, workers' strikes, and student protests during the democratic period and the Thai authorities' fear that radical students would retaliate after the October coup by launching sabotage and terrorist operations in Bangkok. (A similar view of the critical importance of urban insurrection was held both by revolutionaries and counter-revolutionaries in Latin America in the 1960s and early 1970s). But it would be a very high-risk strategy, resulting in either complete success (seizing the citadel of power) or total destruction because

70. "There is much evidence to suggest strong organisational links between the urban Left and the CPT in their jungle bases": Somchai Rakwijit, "Problems of Thai Internal Security," p. 287. He claims that although the "hardcore Left activists" in Bangkok were reduced by government arrests from 3,000 to about 1,000 in early 1977, they soon rebuilt their organization and made it stronger and more disciplined than before. Former independent radicals and even Moscow-oriented Marxists, as a result of the October 1976 coup, could survive only under the protection of the CPT. There are now reportedly 2,500 CPT cadres in Bangkok. According to Somchai, radical labor groups publicly cooperate with the authorities, but carry out clandestine propaganda among the workers: they stress the impact of martial law as well as the "unscrupulous and opportunistic acts of some employers" (Somchai's description): *ibid.*, pp. 289–291.

71. See interview with general Thuanthong Suwannathat, deputy chief of staff, Supreme Command headquarters, on the possible formation of a pro-Vietnamese or pro-Soviet communist party. This would be dangerous, he said, because it would shift from the strategy of "countryside surrounding towns" to one of urban violence: *Siam Nikorn*, May 14, 1979.

72. Richard Nations, *Far Eastern Economic Review*, July 28, 1978.

the capital is so heavily defended. A Thai student document in early 1977 appears to recognize this: "Though the urban open front proved significant, the political terror, and later the October coup d'etat have shown the limits of the urban struggle. Because the state functionaries and the military represent the Bangkok ruling class, it is impossible to struggle only by peaceful and democratic means. [We] must find another arena...the rural area...maintained through the last 30 years by the less well-known Communist Party of Thailand."[73]

The *rural* strategy is the key to the CPT's future.[74] In 1974, the party reiterated the Maoist strategy of "using the countryside to encircle the cities" and urged that the struggle for "national independence and people's democracy" be integrated with the "struggle for liberation of the peasants" and the minority nationalities.[75] In December 1976, following the October coup, the party issued an "adjusted" ten-point policy statement intended to embrace both agrarian and united front tactics. The party appealed not only to workers and farmers, but also to "small capitalists and national

73. Statement by the "National Anti-Fascism Front of Thailand" reported in *Asian Student News* (Hong Kong), January–February 1977. On the possibility of violence resulting from the uncontrolled growth of the urban population, it is often argued that "marginals"—including migrants from the countryside, casual workers, underemployed, and criminals—are a potentially destabilizing or even revolutionary element. Against this argument, there are two things to note. First, the evidence is that many migrants *prefer* urban squalor to rural poverty and hopelessness. Second, if marginals are a potentially volatile element, they tend to act spontaneously—through riots, gang warfare, or other criminal or near-criminal activities (like the Red Gaurs). They need to be organized if they are to become a political force. Even then, depending on leadership and motivation, they are as likely to become an instrument of the extreme Right (as Ben Anderson suggests in "Withdrawal Symptoms: Social and Cultural Aspects of the October 6 Coup," *Bulletin of Concerned Asian Scholars,* July–September 1977) as of the extreme Left.

74. The CPT's ten-point policy was announced in 1968, evidently inspired by Mao Tse-Tung's "new democracy." Among these points were: formation of a people's government; confiscation of the land and property of the "Thanom-Praphat clique," counterrevolutionaries, and "tyrannical landlords," for the benefit of the people and nation; abolition of feudal exploitation "step by step," reducing rents and abolishing "unjust debts"; carrying out the agrarian revolution "according to the conditions of various places"; giving the peasants "land to earn a livelihood"; and, significantly in view of the insurgency movements developing in North and South, giving "the various nationalities the right of autonomy within the big family of Thailand": Weatherbee, *The United Front,* provides the text, pp. 67–69.

75. The party's thirty-second-anniversary statement: text in *Journal of Contemporary Asia* 5, no. 2 (1975).

capitalists of all nationalities" as well as "all patriotic and democracy-loving political parties, organisations and people" to "expand people's war, get rid of U.S. imperialist influence, overthrow the reactionary, fascist and nation-selling government." The objective was to "set up a government of the people composed of representatives of all revolutionary forces." Confiscation of property of reactionaries; freedom of speech, writing, and demonstrations; and autonomous administrations in minority areas were reaffirmed. Land to the tillers and guaranteed employment, wages, and welfare for workers and office employees were also emphasized. Women's rights received special notice, along with development of state enterprises and protection of the industry and commerce of national capitalists.[76] In its "introduction" to the December 1976 statement, the party emphasized in 1979 that it would confiscate the land of landowners and rich farmers and distribute it to those with insufficient land or without land. "Land resolution" would be carried out "step by step" according to the "character of each locality". It was "not true" that the CPT would confiscate all land and treat it as communal property. The land of farmers depending on their own labor to make a living would not be touched; small plots rented out by those unable to till—such as old people, teachers, and the sick—also would not be touched.[77]

Nevertheless, the rural struggle will almost certainly be combined with what is predominantly political struggle, whether legal or illegal, in the cities. The crucial test of party policy will be in the Central region, where the countryside is more closely linked with the cities, and where conditions of tenancy and landlessness are creating unrest. But economic discontent has not yet been organized politically or transformed into effective struggle.

### International Repercussions

If the party has benefited from internal changes in Thailand, which have broadened its support as well as the scope of its policies and activities, *external* events have had the opposite effect. Changes in China's international line, the conflict between China and

76. VOPT, Dec. 1, 1976.
77. VOPT, Feb. 1 and 8, 1979.

Vietnam, and the Vietnamese-backed invasion of Kampuchea have thrown the Communist Party of Thailand into confusion.[78]

The most immediate, practical effect has been the loss of bases for training, recruitment, and operations provided by Pol Pot's Kampuchea to an important segment of the CPT active in the southern part of the Northeast.[79] An even more far-reaching ideological blow, however, has been caused by the growing tension, culminating in outright hostility, between neighboring states under communist rule.[80] In addition, the flow of refugees into Thailand fleeing from the hardship and insecurity of life in Laos, compounded by the plight of all who suffered from the atrocious conditions of Pol Pot's regime, have certainly made an impression on the Thai people.[81] This is all the more significant because it has

78. Commenting on the decline in communist attacks in the Northeast after the fall of Pol Pot, an officer of the Thai second army region noted that because more CPT members were pro-Peking than pro-Moscow [or Hanoi], they were uncertain which side to link up with once pro-Vietnamese forces controlled Kampuchea: report in *Bangkok World*, Jan. 24, 1979. A correspondent in an otherwise sympathetic article notes the impact of the Indochina conflict on the Left in general. He considers that the CPT, already confused by the Sino-Soviet dispute, has become more demoralized by the Vietnamese invasion of Kampuchea and by China's invasion of Vietnam. "Some groups on the Left are dissatisfied with the CPT; people lose faith in it": "Left Going, Right Coming," *Tawan mai*, May 11, 1979. A perceptive internationalist assessment appears in the radical Japan-Asia quarterly *Ampo*: "And if the liberated areas are not liberated? . . . A call to debate," no. 1, 1979.

79. "Vietnam's strike into Kampuchea dealt a serious blow to CPT ambitions in the provinces along the Kampuchean border. Counter-insurgency experts describe it as the 'hottest place in the country' between December 1976 and December 19-78 . . . accounting [in 1978] for 42 percent of nation-wide guerrilla-initiated military incidents." Some 1,500 guerrillas were operating out of four or five base camps up to 15 miles inside Kampuchea: John McBeth, "A Battle for Loyalty in the Jungles," *Far Eastern Economic Review*, June 8, 1979. See also the report by the police second region commander on the operations of the "Siem Organization" in Southern Isan, led by Sor Boonma. (Northern Isan is under the direction of the prominent CPT leader, Udom Srisuwan.) *Nation Review*, Oct. 29, 1978. See also detailed reports by Richard Nations, *Far Eastern Economic Review*, June 9 and July 14 and 28, 1978, and Feb. 2, 1979. Also Roger Kershaw, "'Unlimited Sovereignty' in Cambodia: The View from Bangkok," *The World Today*, March 1979.

80. See J. L. S. Girling, "Indochina," in Mohammed Ayoob, ed., *Conflict and Intervention in the Third World* (London: Croom Helm, 1980).

81. General Prem, army commander-in-chief and former second region commander, spoke of the effect on communist morale of the flight of people from Laos and Kampuchea, who declared how happy they were to be in Northeast Thailand: interview, *Motichon*, May 8, 1978. Kukrit makes much the same point in an interview with Theh Chongkhadikij: *Bangkok Post*, May 6, 1979.

affected particularly those living in the Northeast, who otherwise have been most receptive to the appeals of communism.

The CPT, like the Thai government itself, sought to avoid being dragged into the dangerous conflict between the far more powerful China and Vietnam. Unlike the communist revolutionaries in Burma and Malaysia, who openly denounced Vietnamese "aggression" against Kampuchea and supported the Peking line, the CPT at first refrained from comment.[82]

In spite of its caution, the CPT has been increasingly buffeted by these contradictory trends. Party leaders and followers, staunchly Maoist in ideology, are disillusioned by the extraordinary changes emanating from Peking. Not only has China made its spectacular opening to the West, demonstrated by the "four modernizations" program and its diplomatic relations with the United States, but the Chinese leaders have outspokenly given priority to good relations with Third World regimes, of whatever stripe, before support for struggling revolutionary movements. This was brought home to the CPT by the welcome offered Deng Xiaoping by the Thai government in November 1978; and by Deng's attendance, at his own wish, at the ordination ceremony of the crown prince. Indeed one analyst attributes the "temporary suspension" of VOPT broadcasts from July 1979 to Chinese pressure on the "outlawed communist guerrilla movement in Thailand to join the army-backed government in Bangkok in a de facto united front against Vietnam," while

---

82. For example, on December 14, 1978, the Burmese communist party and the Malayan communist party radio (both broadcasting from China) denounced Vietnamese aggression against Kampuchea and Hanoi's "expansionist" designs, while the VOPT refrained from comment: *Far Eastern Economic Review*, Jan. 12, 1979. Some months later, however, the VOPT began indirectly to criticize Vietnam. For instance, the CPT left it to Sri Inthapanti, representing the "patriotic and peaceloving forces," to take a strongly nationalistic line against the Vietnamese threat. "The Thai people," he declared, "are aware of the changes in the situation. [There is a] conflict between two sides: one side, which is the owner of the country, wants to be independent; and the other side . . . wants to be master." He went on: "The truth is that Vietnam has sent its troops near the Thai border and is ready to invade Thailand at any moment. Attempts have been made to set up a puppet united front and puppet army." However, "our nation will never be defeated or destroyed, although the ruling class might be crushed . . .": VOPT, June 7, 1979. But the VOPT announced it would "temporarily suspend" broadcasting, from July 11, 1979.

another believes that the CPT leadership decided to go off the air until the party could resolve its internal differences.[83]

The party's last broadcast is susceptible to either interpretation. It strongly emphasized "people's patriotism" and the "unity" of the Thai people in the face of a "greedy and arrogant aggressor" (not named, but obviously Vietnam). However, the patriotic struggle was being undermined by the "fascist laws" and self-interest of "groups within the ruling class." For this reason, the patriotic struggle must be *combined* with the struggle for democratic rights and the people's welfare.[84] The obvious question is: if the message is so clear and urgent, why cease broadcasting? One answer is the importance of *domestic* "obstacles" for the CPT, which have been a major target of revolutionary struggle for the past three decades. The party cannot easily be expected to make a total change of direction: from concentrating the attack on the "three enemies" of the people—the imperialists, feudalists, and bureaucrat-capitalists—to supporting them, or even uniting with them, against Vietnamese (and Soviet) hegemony. Thus the crucial question for the CPT and its allies is whether the Vietnamese are the major threat to Thai independence or whether domestic problems are still the main area of concern.[85]

In a related development, the established CPT leadership, partly Chinese in ethnic origin and ideologically oriented toward Peking,

83. Michael Richardson, reporting from Singapore (Melbourne) *Age*, July 14, 1979, and John McBeth, "Communists at the Crossroads," *Far Eastern Economic Review*, July 27, 1979, respectively.

84. VOPT, July 9 and 10, 1979, followed by announcement of temporary suspension from July 11.

85. In 1980 this question still seems unresolved. One analyst points out that despite Peking's pressure on the CPT to join the Thai government in opposing "Vietnamese hegemony"—openly advocated at an interview in Bangkok by Chinese Vice-Premier Ji Pengfei—CPT manifestos issued after the closing of the VOPT radio maintain a strong antigovernment line, also emphasizing self-reliance, and military activity against government forces continues unabated: Martha Winacker, "Two Views of the Thai Guerrilla Movement," *Southeast Asia Chronicle*, January–February 1980. There is some evidence that the Thai government itself asked Peking to close down VOPT in return for Thai compliance with China's policy over Kampuchea and Vietnam. Despite the CPT's "sacrifice" in this regard, party leaders believe they can restore communist influence and expand their power under the prevailing conditions of tension, and possibly conflict, between Thailand and Vietnam. In the longer term, too, they count on the worsening economic position of the Thai people to create preconditions for a successful revolutionary struggle: private information, February 1980.

has been rebuffed by the Vietnamese. While Prime Minister Pham Van Dong could truthfully declare on his visit to Thailand in September 1978 that Vietnam was not aiding the Thai insurgents—and pledged that it would not do so in future, which is more problematic—Hanoi has put pressure on Laos to the same effect.[86] According to Thai government sources in December 1978 the Lao government requested the CPT to withdraw from its various bases in Laos to Thai territory because of "differences in the political line."[87] Reportedly the Lao party central committee justified the move, in an official communication to Udom Srisuwan, by accusing Thai communist cadres of privately criticizing the Vietnamese invasion of Kampuchea and Hanoi's role in Lao internal affairs.[88] In a further development, Prime Minister Kriangsak and his Lao counterpart, Kaysone Phomvihan, agreed in January 1979 that each country would prohibit the use of its territory, directly or indirectly, for purposes of subversion or aggression against the other.[89]

Caught in the crossfire between Peking and Hanoi, the Thai communist movement has split into three factions: the old-style pro-Peking leadership; those who are prepared to go along with the Vietnamese; and the "nationalists," represented especially by

86. The possibility of Vietnamese intervention in Thailand would appear to result not so much from a deliberately expansionist policy by Vietnam as from an unintended consequence of the Kampuchean conflict, dragging in Vietnam and Thailand on opposing sides. Obviously the greater the instability in Kampuchea, the more chance that this may happen. A further possibility, of course, is that in the event of an *internal* crisis in Thailand, the Vietnamese may also be drawn in.

87. Thai Information Center report, Apr. 15, 1979.

88. McBeth, "Battle for Loyalty." He adds that Bangkok-based intelligence sources are still not clear on whether Laos—and Vietnam—intend going through with the expulsion of the CPT or "are trying to extort some sort of cooperation."

89. The joint communique was signed in Vientiane on Jan. 6, 1979. It was followed up by Kaysone's visit to Bangkok Apr. 1-4, 1979, when the two leaders reaffirmed the "five principles" of the January declaration of friendship and cooperation. (The *Bangkok Post* editorial of Jan. 8, 1979, commenting on the agreement, pointed out that Laos had been known to provide a major training area for communist insurgent leaders from Thailand. Camps in Sayabouri province were said to be under the control and supervision of Vietnamese in Laos.) Another Thai delegation, led by the minister of the interior, visited Vientiane in August 1979 and further strengthened the January and April agreements. Lao Prime Minister Kaysone told the delegation that Laos would continue to crush the remnants of the pro-Peking CPT, according to the Thai deputy foreign minister: *Bangkok Post*, Aug. 18, 1979.

the socialists and democrats from the younger generation, who insist on an independent course. The nationalists are equally repelled by the authoritarian methods of the party and by the international communist conflicts.[90] Still others, believing that the Thai people are losing faith in the communist movement, have given themselves up,[91] or returned quietly to their homes.[92] The return of leaders like Seksan in October 1980 may well lead to a *renewal* of the urban Left on an autonomous, nonsectarian, nationalist basis. Thus at a time when the party might have expected to realize its greatest triumph, with the rallying of the young-radical generation, it is facing its severest test.

Perhaps as a result the party is fated to bring about what it does *not* want—evolution of Thai society through reforms—but which *without* its militancy and endurance would not have arisen, for there would otherwise have been insufficient pressure on the ruling sys-

---

90. Private information (May 1979). See also McBeth's report of serious discussions taking place within the party Central Committee and the twelve-man Politburo over the effects of the China-Vietnam conflict. He considers the party split to be chiefly at lower levels, while "the top men are united on a pro-China line": "Battle for Loyalty." The core of the CPT leadership reportedly returned to base areas in Nan province (in the North) after a year's stay in Peking: John McBeth, *Far Eastern Economic Review*, July 27, 1979. The two main dissidents prepared to cooperate with the Vietnamese are said to be former Socialist deputy Bunyen Wotong and labor union leader Therdphum Jaidee: *Siam Rath weekly review*, Sept. 30 and Oct. 7, 1979.

91. A notable example is Wichit Chongchit, who surrendered in March 1979 after fourteen years in the jungle. A farmer, he had fled in 1965 to escape arrest as a suspected communist terrorist, which he denied. At the Kung Sing base in Nakorn Sri Thammarat province he studied Marxism-Leninism, joined the communist party, and in 1971 was selected to be a member of the province party committee. Interviewed after his surrender, he said he decided to quit for a number of reasons. He wanted to be an ordinary citizen, living in peace, and he had heard that the government would take care of those who left the forest. Also, he felt that party policy went too far in trying to set up the communist system—it led to the bloodshed of ordinary folk—and he was "fed up with the killing of Thai people." Transcript of official interrogation, *Matuphum*, Apr. 25, 1979.

92. One of the most important figures to return is Boonsong Chalethorn, a former deputy secretary-general of the National Student Center of Thailand, who recently reappeared in Bangkok after two and a half years in the jungle. (He was able to return under Kriangsak's amnesty offer to those who fled to the jungle after October 1976.) He said he defected after a violent ideological disagreement in late 1978, when he was at a base camp in northern Thailand. "I didn't agree with the party point of view. Revolution can only be accomplished successfully through an approach that is both consistent and independent": McBeth, "Battle for Loyalty." The well-known northeastern writer, Khamsing Srinawk, is also reported to have left the jungle for Sweden at about the same time, apparently because he disagreed with the party insistence on armed struggle. (Therdphum returned in October 1980.)

tem to produce peaceful change. Or perhaps, in a region of instability, external factors will instead play the incalculable but determining role.

*Conclusion*

Underlying all the issues facing the party—the problem of urban
or rural struggle; reliance on workers or peasants; coalition with
the national bourgeoisie or class struggle; alignment with China or
Vietnam or independence—are two fundamental questions. The
first is not so much whether the united front policy, and all that
follows from it, makes sense or not—it clearly does—but whether
the party itself, given its historical experience and organizational
structure, is capable of acting in the open-minded and "creative"
way that a united front requires. The second, even more crucial,
question is whether conditions in Thailand are such as to bring
about the success of a revolutionary united front. That is, has the
polarization of Thai society—the gap between urban and rural
dwellers, between rich and poor—developed to the extent that the
great majority of the Thai people can be mobilized (and by whom?)
for effective struggle (by armed or peaceful means?) against a
small, if broadening, elite minority? Is the elite *structurally* incapable of change or are there genuinely reformist possibilities?

Evidently the coup of October 1976 has speeded up the process
of polarization in Thailand, even though some of its effects have
been limited by Kriangsak's and Prem's "moderation" or reversed
by international events. In contrast to the more volatile and more
repressive character of elitism in a number of other developing
countries, the "assets" of the Thai ruling system, which are so important for its continuity, are formidable. But they are also being
eroded. The monarchy, hitherto the symbol of national pride and
respect, has become intimately involved in conservative and even
reactionary politics. The Buddhist ethos is pervasive, but it is being
undermined by secular values. The economy is productive, but the
distribution of material benefits is highly unequal. Patriotism and
the desire for independence are deeply felt, but there is no
monopoly of these by any one group. The military leaders, whatever the professional qualities of the present commander, are fac-
tionalized, disunited, and unable to act constructively. The administration is immobilized. Although liberal-minded officials have
emerged, they feel isolated and inhibited from carrying out the

changes they know are required. The merging of Chinese and Thai businesspersons into a national bourgeoisie is under way, but this does not necessarily indicate progress toward democracy. The modernizing intellectual-professional element, in spite of its stake in stability, is alienated by the suppression or (currently) restriction of democracy—a system which more effectively represents its interests. Socially aware students, while presently reserved in their attitude toward politics, cannot forget the example of the heroes of 1973. Finally, industrial workers and the poor peasants, tenants and the landless, on whose "apathy" the ruling system so long depended for its ability to override challenges, have been made aware in recent years of their potential strength, although they are at present deprived of effective leadership.

These "assets" of the ruling system remain powerful. Although the trend is toward decline, it has not yet reached the stage when assets become "liabilities"—as was so conspicuously the case with countries like Nationalist China and South Vietnam. The strength of the Thai elite is its ability to keep going from day to day, to "muddle through." It is flexible, not rigid; pragmatic, not doctrinaire. Its weakness is the obverse of its strength: its inability to look ahead, to discern the larger issues, and to cope in time with the deteriorating trend. Undoubtedly the most serious problem is the worsening condition of millions of people in the countryside—proportionately twice as many as those who have benefited in recent years. The bureaucracy, linked with the affluent few, shows no sign of being willing or able to deal with this situation.

The fundamental *political* problem (in the broad sense) is whether the regime is capable of creating new conditions for rebuilding consensus—by achieving military cohesion, instilling a sense of purpose in the administration, and thus gaining a grudging acceptance by the currently excluded and alienated groups. If the regime will not or cannot do so, its only alternative is to continue to rule by repression. The fundamental *social* problem is whether even political consensus is sufficient to carry out, through the existing machinery of government, those rural reforms (notably land redistribution, tenancy laws, availability of credit, and so on), combined with the administrative reforms (putting an end to "feudal" attitudes and abuses, subjection to "influence," and bias in favor of the rural and urban elite) that the situation demands.

# Suggested Readings

## History

Akin Rabibhadana. *The Organization of Thai Society in the Early Bangkok Period 1782-1873*. Ithaca, N.Y.: Cornell University Southeast Asia Program, data paper no. 74, 1969. A classic study. Fascinating interpretation of the *sakdina* system and evolving patronage networks.

Batson, Benjamin A. *Siam's Political Future: Documents from the End of the Absolute Monarchy*. Ithaca, N.Y.: Cornell University Southeast Asia Program, data paper no. 96, 1974.

Charnvit Kasetsiri. *The Rise of Ayudhya: A History of Siam in the Fourteenth and Fifteenth Centuries*. New York: Oxford University Press, 1976. By far the best coverage of this formative era of Thai history.

Hall, D. G. E. *A History of South-East Asia*. London: Macmillan, 1955. 2d ed., 1964. 3d ed., 1968. Informative and widely used.

Steinberg, David J., David K. Wyatt, et al. *In Search of Southeast Asia: A Modern History*. London: Pall Mall, 1971. Highly recommended. Wyatt wrote the sections on Thailand.

Tej Bunnag. *The Provincial Administration of Siam, 1892-1915*. London: Oxford University Press, 1976.

Thompson, Virginia. *Thailand: The New Siam*. New York: Macmillan, 1941. Still useful for the prewar period.

Vella, Walter F. *Chaiyo!: King Vajiravudh and the Development of Thai Nationalism*. Assisted by Dorothy B. Vella. Honolulu: University of Hawaii Press, 1978.

Vella, Walter F. *The Impact of the West on Government in Thailand*. Berkeley: University of California Press, 1955. Clear and concise; a useful introduction to the modern period.

Vella, Walter F. *Siam under Rama III, 1824-1851*. New York: J. J. Augustin, 1957. Still the best coverage of this period.

Wyatt, David K. *The Politics of Reform in Thailand: Education in the Reign of King Chulalongkorn*. New Haven: Yale University Press, 1969. Valuable study of changing educational policies and their political context during the reign of Rama V.

Society

Ayal, Eliezer B., ed. *The Study of Thailand.* Athens, Ohio: Ohio University Center for International Studies, Southeast Asia Series, no. 54, 1978. Valuable bibliographic surveys and analyses. See Charles F. Keyes, "Ethnography and Anthropological Interpretations in the Study of Thailand," on Thai world-view, moral action, and reformed Buddhism; David Feeny, "Economic Studies of Thailand," including many recent Thai studies; Constance M. Wilson, "Thai and Western Approaches to the Study of Thai History," on chronological, topical and interdisciplinary, regional, and comparative approaches; and Benedict R. O'G. Anderson, "Studies of the Thai State: The State of Thai Studies," a splendid critique that is provocative and stimulating.

Hanks, Lucien M. *Rice and Man: Agricultural Ecology in Southeast Asia.* Chicago: Aldine Atherton, 1972.

Ichimura, Shinichi, ed. *Southeast Asia: Nature, Society, and Development.* Honolulu: University Press of Hawaii, for Center for Southeast Asian Studies, Kyoto University, 1977. See Koichi Mizuno, "Thai Pattern of Social Organization"; Toru Yano, "The Political Elite Cycle..."; Takeshi Motooka, on agricultural development.

Ishii, Yoneo. "Church and State in Thailand." *Asian Survey* 8, no. 10 (1968): 864–71.

Keyes, Charles F. *The Golden Peninsula: Culture and Adaptation in Mainland Southeast Asia.* New York: Macmillan, 1977. Chapter 3, "Rural Life in Theravada Buddhist Societies," is valuable for insights into social structure and economic and political aspects of rural Thai society.

Keyes, Charles F. *Isan: Regionalism in Northeastern Thailand.* Ithaca, N.Y.: Cornell University Southeast Asia Program, data paper no. 65, 1967. Informative, persuasive; pioneering work on an important region.

Keyes, Charles F. "Buddhism and National Integration in Thailand." *Journal of Asian Studies* 30, no. 3 (1971): 551–67.

Keyes, Charles F. "Political Crisis and Militant Buddhism in Contemporary Thailand." In *Religion and Legitimation of Power in Thailand, Burma, and Laos,* edited by Bordwell Smith. Chambersburg, Pa.: Wilson, 1978. Incisive study of right-wing Buddhist extremism in contemporary Thailand.

Kunstadter, Peter, ed. *Southeast Asian Tribes, Minorities and Nations,* 2 vols. Princeton: Princeton University Press, 1967. In volume 1, pages 369 to 674 deal with Thailand.

Landon, Kenneth P. *Siam in Transition: A Brief Survey of Cultural Trends in the 5 Years Since the Revolution of 1932.* Chicago: Distributed by the University of Chicago Press, Shanghai, Kelly and Walsh, Ltd., 1939. Still probably the most valuable coverage for the immediate postrevolution period.

Mabry, Bevars D. *The Development of Labor Institutions in Thailand.* Ithaca,

N.Y.: Cornell University Southeast Asia Program, data paper no. 112, 1979.

Mulder, Niels. *Everyday Life in Thailand: An Interpretation.* Bangkok: D. K. Books, 1979. Imaginative interpretation of Thai perceptions and personal behavior.

Potter, Jack. *Thai Peasant Social Structure.* Chicago: University of Chicago Press, 1976. Controversial, but clear and useful description and classification.

Sharp, Lauriston, and Lucien M. Hanks. *Bang Chan: Social History of a Rural Community in Thailand.* Ithaca, N.Y.: Cornell University Press, 1978.

Skinner, G. William. *Chinese Society in Thailand: An Analytical History.* Ithaca, N.Y.: Cornell University Press, 1957. A classic study.

Skinner, G. William. *Leadership and Power in the Chinese Community of Thailand.* Ithaca, N.Y.: Cornell University Press, 1958. Fascinating investigation of the interlocking network of business power and military-bureaucratic power, carried out at just the right time. There is still nothing to compare with this study.

Skinner, G. William, and A. Thomas Kirsch, eds. *Change and Persistence in Thai Society: Essays in Honor of Lauriston Sharp.* Ithaca: N.Y.: Cornell University Press, 1975. See the excellent summary by Akin Rabibhadana of his data paper 74; Steven Piker's thought-provoking piece on post-peasant society; and Herbert P. Phillips on Thai intellectuals, pre-1970s variety.

Somboon Suksamran. *Political Buddhism in Southeast Asia.* New York: St. Martin's, 1976. Valuable material on the internal politics of the Thai Sangha.

Tambiah, S. J. *Buddhism and the Spirit Cults in North-East Thailand.* Cambridge: Cambridge University Press, 1970. Imaginative interpretation of rituals; illuminating discussion of magico-animism, Buddhism, and Brahminism.

Tambiah, S. J. *World Conqueror and World Renouncer: A Study of Buddhism and Polity in Thailand.* Cambridge: Cambridge University Press, 1976. Long and uneven, but the sections on traditional cosmology and contemporary Buddhism are well worth reading.

Turton, Andrew, Jonathan Fast, and Malcolm Caldwell, eds. *Thailand: Roots of Conflict.* Nottingham, U.K.: Spokesman, 1978. Turton's "The Current Situation in the Thai Countryside" is particularly good: he shows sympathy for plight of peasants, but handles the evidence fairly and objectively. See also Patrice de Beer on the Communist Party of Thailand.

Yano, Toru. "Land Tenure in Thailand." *Asian Survey* 8, no. 10 (1968): 853-63.

## Economics

Caldwell, J. Alexander. *American Economic Aid to Thailand.* Lexington, Mass.: Lexington Books, 1974.

Ingram, James C. *Economic Change in Thailand, 1850–1970.* Stanford, Calif.: Stanford University Press, 1971. Pioneering study of economic development.

Morell, David L. "Legislative Intervention in Thailand's Development Process: A Case Study." *Asian Survey* 12, no. 8 (1972): 627–46.

Motooka, Takeshi. *Agricultural Development in Thailand.* Kyoto: Kyoto University Center for Southeast Asian Studies, 1971. Useful early study of Siam's growing agrarian problems.

Prateep Sondysuwan, ed. *Finance, Trade and Economic Development in Thailand.* Bangkok: Sompong, 1975. See especially Ammar Siamwalla's "Stability, Growth and Distribution" and Udom Kerdpibule's "Distribution of Wealth and Income."

Puey Ungphakorn. *Glancing Back, Looking Forward.* Melbourne: Shepparton Press, 1977. The author is a distinguished economist, technocrat, and reformer. Includes articles on the economy, society, morality, and the October 1976 coup.

Sein Lin and Bruce Esposito. "Agrarian Reform in Thailand: Problems and Prospects." *Pacific Affairs* 49, no. 3 (1976): 425–42.

Silcock, T. H., ed. *Thailand: Social and Economic Studies in Development.* Canberra: Australian National University Press, 1967. See especially Silcock's overview, his chapter on banking and politics, and his chapter (with Hans-Dieter Evers) on "Elites and Selection."

## Politics

Anderson, Ben. "Withdrawal Symptoms: Social and Cultural Aspects of the October 6 Coup." *Bulletin of Concerned Asian Scholars* 9, no. 3 (1977): 13–30.

Coast, John. *Some Aspects of Siamese Politics.* New York: Institute of Pacific Relations, 1953.

Darling, Frank C. "Student Protest and Political Change in Thailand." *Pacific Affairs* 47, no. 1 (1974): 5–19.

Flood, E. Thadeus. "The Thai Left Wing in Historical Context." *Bulletin of Concerned Asian Scholars,* April–June 1975, pp. 56–67.

Flood, E. Thadeus. "The Vietnamese Refugees in Thailand: Minority Manipulation in Counterinsurgency." *Bulletin of Concerned Asian Scholars* 9, no. 3 (1977), pp. 31–47. The best discussion of the political fate of the Vietnamese minority in modern times.

Jacobs, Norman. *Modernization without Development: Thailand as an Asian Case Study.* New York: Praeger, 1971. Illuminating use of the Weberian concept of patrimonial bureaucracy, but many opaque passages dull the thrust of argument.

Likhit Dhiravegin. *The Bureaucratic Elite of Thailand.* Bangkok: Thai Khadi Research Institute, Thammasat University, 1978. Detailed survey of officials in the top "Special Grade" and "First Grade" shows that the largest number of officials still come from "official" families, but that business is increasingly important. There is some indication of social mobility, but it is restricted largely to the Central region. Likhit also discusses educational attainment and careerism.

Likhit Dhiravegin. *Political Attitudes of the Bureaucratic Elite and Modernization in Thailand.* Bangkok: Thai Watana, 1973. Thammasat political scientist argues that higher (especially Western) education influences younger generation of bureaucrats toward liberalism. But, as the military are not yet persuaded, Likhit falls back on tutelary democracy.

Lobe, Thomas. *United States National Security Policy and Aid to the Thailand Police.* Colorado: University of Denver, Monograph Series in World Affairs, 1977. A masterly study. An account of U.S. counterinsurgency activities with some revelations of bureaucratic infighting.

Morell, David, and Chai-Anan Samudavanija. *Reform, Reaction, Revolution: Political Conflict in Thailand.* Cambridge, Mass.: Oelgeschlager, Gunn & Hain, forthcoming. Excellent study, perceptive and persuasive. Particularly good on personalities and events during the 1973–76 democratic period. See chapters on students, labor groups, and peasants and on parliamentary activities.

Mosel, James N. "Communications Patterns and Political Socialization in Transitional Thailand." In *Communications and Political Development,* edited by Lucian Pye. Princeton: Princeton University Press, 1963, pp. 144–228.

Nakata, Thinapan. "Political Legitimacy in Thailand: Problems and Prospects." *Journal of Social Science Review* (Bangkok) 1, no. 1 (1976): 42–121.

Neher, Clark D. "Constitutionalism and Elections in Thailand." *Pacific Affairs* 43, no. 2 (1970): 240–57.

Neher, Clark D., ed. *Modern Thai Politics: From Village to Nation.* Cambridge, Mass.: Schenkman, 1976. Rev. ed. 1979. Collection of articles mostly from 1950s and 1960s. See chapters by Prince Dhani Nivat, Lucien Hanks ("Merit and Power"), David Wyatt, Fred Riggs, William Siffin, Steven Piker, James Scott, and Herbert Phillips. The 1979 edition includes three new articles: one on the 1976 elections, one on Thai official perceptions of China and Vietnam, and a much-needed critique by Neher of research on Thai politics.

Prudhisan Jumbala. "The Democratic Experiment in Thailand, 1973–1976." *Dyason House Papers* (Melbourne) 3, no. 3 (1977): 1–6.

Race, Jeffrey. "The War in Northern Thailand." *Modern Asian Studies* 8, no. 1 (1974): 85–112.

Riggs, Fred W. *Thailand: The Modernization of a Bureaucratic Polity*. Honolulu: East-West Center Press, 1966. Classic study of factional rivalry and political-economic networks. Riggs suggests the need for a force to countervail the bureaucracy, but largely fails to consider the changing social context in which the bureaucracy operates and to distinguish between the military and civilian components of the bureaucracy.

Saneh Chammarik. "Thai Politics and the October Revolution." *Journal of Social Science Review* (Bangkok) 1, no. 1 (1976): 1–41.

Siffin, William J. *The Thai Bureaucracy: Institutional Change and Development*. Honolulu: East-West Center Press, 1966. Well-organized account of the bureaucracy and bureaucratic values.

Srinawk, Khamsing. *The Politician and Other Stories*. Kuala Lumpur: Oxford University Press, 1973. Well-translated collection of satirical stories by one of Thailand's best-known writers. "The Politician" shows deep insight into Thai political realities at the local level.

Suhrke, Astri. "Loyalists and Separatists: The Muslims in Southern Thailand." *Asian Survey* 17, no. 3 (1977): 237–50.

Tanham, George K. *Trial in Thailand*. New York: Crane, Russak, 1974. Tanham was special assistant on counterinsurgency to the U.S. ambassador to Thailand from 1968 to 1970. A useful and informative account. The author is aware of the strengths and weaknesses of the government and its adversary in the rural areas.

Thak Chaloemtiarana. *Thailand: The Politics of Despotic Paternalism*. Bangkok: Social Science Association of Thailand and Thai Khadi Institute, Thammasat University, 1979. Excellent study of the Sarit regime and its implications.

Thak Chaloemtiarana, ed. *Thai Politics: Extracts and Documents, 1932–1957*. Bangkok: Social Science Association of Thailand, 1978.

Thomas, M. Ladd. *Political Violence in the Muslim Provinces of Southern Thailand*. Singapore: Institute of Southeast Asian Studies, occasional paper no. 28, 1975.

Von der Mehden, Fred R. "The Military and Development in Thailand." *Journal of Comparative Administration* 2, no. 3 (1970), pp. 323–40.

Wilson, David A. *Politics in Thailand*. Ithaca, N.Y.: Cornell University Press, 1962. Pioneering study of Thai politics, breaking away from the legal-institutional or narrative forms. Good on clique politics in a consensus society.

Wilson, David A. "Thailand and Marxism." In *Marxism in Southeast Asia*, edited by Frank N. Trager. Stanford, Calif.: Stanford University Press, 1960, pp. 58–101.

Zimmerman, Robert. *Reflections on the Collapse of Democracy in Thailand*. Singapore: Institute of Southeast Asian Studies, occasional paper no. 50, 1978. Interesting account of patronage networks in the first half; rather shallow interpretation of collapse of democracy in the second.

*Foreign Policy*

Darling, Frank C. *Thailand and the United States*. Washington, D.C.: Public Affairs Press, 1965. Critical review of U.S. relations with dictatorial regimes.

Direk Jayanama. *Siam and World War II*, trans. Jane Godfrey Keyes. Bangkok: Social Science Association of Thailand Press, 1978. A significant study, incorporating a substantial body of documents, of the country's foreign relations from 1940 to 1948 by one of its leading diplomats.

Sarasin Viraphol. *Directions in Thai Foreign Policy*. Singapore: Institute of Southeast Asian Studies, occasional paper no. 40, 1976. Admirable, well-informed, and persuasive study.

# Index

*Library of Congress Cataloging in Publication Data*

Girling, J L S
  Thailand, society and politics.

  (Politics and international relations of Southeast Asia)
  Bibliography: p.
  Includes index.
  1. Thailand—Politics and government. I. Title. II. Series.
DS586.G57     959.3′044     80-69822
ISBN 0-8014-1130-0          AACR1